UNIVERSE OF THE MIND

UNIVERSE OF THE MIND

A Semiotic Theory of Culture

Yuri M. Lotman

Translated by
Ann Shukman

Introduction by
Umberto Eco

INDIANA UNIVERSITY PRESS
Bloomington and Indianapolis

First published in the U.S.A. in hardcover 1990
First U.S. paperback printing 2000

First United Kingdom publication in 1990 by I.B.Tauris & Co Ltd

Printed in Great Britain

Library of Congress Cataloging-in-Publication Data

Lotman, IU. M. (Iurii Mikhailovich). 1922–
Universe of the mind: a semiotic theory of culture / Yuri Lotman;
translated by Ann Shukman.
p. cm.
Translated from the Russian.
Includes bibliographical references and index.
ISBN 0–253–33608–2 (cloth)   ISBN 0–253–21405–X (paper)
1. Semiotics. 2. Culture. I. Title
P99.L68   1990
302.2—dc20

2 3 4 5 6 04 03 02 00

Contents

PART THREE
CULTURAL MEMORY, HISTORY AND SEMIOTICS

Introduction

UMBERTO ECO

In the course of his intellectual career, Yuri M. Lotman has applied his mind to a wide range of disciplines: aesthetics, poetics, semiotic theory, the history of culture, mythology, and cinema, in addition to the principle themes of the history of Russian literature of which he is Professor at the University of Tartu in Estonia. His works range from the analysis of cultural phenomena such as blue jeans, and observations on demonology, through readings of poetic texts and consideration of the problems of interpretation, to references to mathematics and biology. However, even readers unfamiliar with the entire range of Lotman's work will be able to identify in this book the broader theoretical approach on which Lotman's work is built. It may be useful, however, to outline here certain aspects of Lotman's work which contribute to a fuller understanding of the themes and methods at work in this book.

During the Sixties, two disturbing words erupted into the calm waters of the European academic world: semiotics (or semiology) and structuralism. The centre of this research paradigm was Paris, although the phenomenon spread steadily throughout Europe and to many North and Latin American universities. The devastating effect created in Britain by these new approaches to language (and, as a result, to the study of the languages of art) is recorded by David Lodge's novel *Small World*, (clear proof that literary works can often be much more informative about the world and our society than many scientific treatises).

Small World was published in 1984, at a time when the series of English translations of Russian and Soviet semiotic texts produced by L.M.O'Toole and Ann Shukman, *Russian Poetics in Translation*, had already been in in progress for several years. However, during the Sixties and Seventies, Lotman's works were more widely known on the Continent than in Britain. Interest in structural studies of language had led (particularly through the influence of Roman Jakobson) to an interest in the works of the Prague School, and at the same time to the re-discovery of the Russian Formalists of the Twenties. Up until this time, the Formalists had been known only at second hand through the seminal text *Russian Formalism* by Victor Erlich.[1] In 1965, Tzvetan Todorov translated many of the Russian Formalist texts into French,[2] and little by little, in steady progression, the most important works of Shklovsky, Tomashevsky and Tynyanov were translated into the European languages (especially into Italian).

Alongside this growth of interest in Russian Formalism, during the early Sixties scholars in Italy and France were beginning to discover the semioticians at work during this period in Russia – principally in Moscow and Tartu. These were such figures as Ivanov, Revzin, Uspensky, Zolkovsky, Sceglov, Segal, Toporov and Egorov, as well as two names from the earlier generation, the linguist Saumijan and the mathematician Kolmogorov. However, at the centre of this new field of research, as both link and fulcrum (through the series *Trudy po znakovym sistemam [Works on Sign Systems]*, produced in Tartu) stood the figure of Yuri Lotman.

According to the teachings of the Formalists, a work of art was a semiotic *device* which could be analyzed as a set of rules and inventions, of pre-fixed effects and conscious modifications of socialized codes. The new Russian and Estonian semioticians took up the notion of 'device' and 'de-familiarization' and took one step further the techniques involved in the creation of a work of art as an individual re-construction of the store of procedures which go to make up the social fabric in which communication works.

Unfortunately, in their attempts to explain the artistic 'mystery' in terms of an analyzable device, the Formalists had become entangled in a series of contradictions. They had been unable, for example, to free themselves completely from the aesthetics of the image as an ineffable event. In addition, as may be seen in the work of Lévi-Strauss and Propp in particular,[3] they were not able to achieve the passage from formal analysis to full structural awareness. They had not fully understood that the putting into form of a work of art has also to involve the organization of content; they had therefore been working on signifying systems without taking into consideration those semantic systems which the new Russian semioticians were able to re-discover at the level of religious systems and world views. A final difficulty may be evidenced by Tomashevsky's or Shlovsky's theories on the structure of the novel. Here it becomes clear that the Formalists had at most brought to light individual devices or systems of rules which were valid only within the confines of one specific genre.

In this sense, then, the neo-semioticians went a step further. The advent of Information Theory, of Game Theory and of structural analysis in Linguistics and Cultural Anthropology allowed them to distinguish and postulate a universal field of communication phenomena. It is not possible to distinguish the rule system appropriate to a given communicative phenomenon without at the same time postulating a structural homology with the rule systems which apply to all other communicative phenomena. The new Russian semioticians developed a universal semiotic theory (and method) whereby the rules governing each communicative sector were to be seen as variations of more general codes.

In order to understand the interest aroused by these critics, who had been up until now unknown in the West except to a few Soviet Studies experts, it must be remembered that semiotics and structuralism form a highly complex pair of terms. Semiotics aims to study the entire range of sign systems (of which verbal language is the most important) and the various processes of communication to which these systems give rise. Such a study also involves the demonstration of the existence of sign systems even where least immediately apparent or expected. Structuralism is a method which has been shown to be extremely useful in the explanation of linguistic systems, in the work of Saussure and, later, of Hjelmslev and Jakobson. In the Sixties, especially in France, this method was also used to explain other systems, one of which was (and the work of Lévi-Strauss is pre-eminent here) the system of cultural phenomena. However, not all semioticians used the structuralist method. Charles Sanders Peirce and Charles Morris, for example, propounded a semiotic theory which was by no means structuralist. This is a point which bears emphasis, for Lotman, in my view, is a critic who started from a structuralist approach to the phenomena of signification and communication, and indeed retains much of this method, but who does not remain bound by it. This may be seen clearly in this book. For example, the first theoretical problem which the structuralists of the Sixties found most difficult to deal with was the fact that certain systems, through communication processes (which are historical processes, that is processes which take place in time) changed. The second problem was that given that a semiotic system was seen as a code, or rather as a system of rules, how could there be communication processes in which it was difficult to identify codes or where there seemed to be a conflict between different codes? It is these problems which hold the key to an understanding of the evolution of Lotman's thought.

In the Sixties, Lotman stressed the usefulness of the structural approach and the application of exact methods to the study of literature. That is, he remained faithful to Saussure's opposition of *langue* and *parole*, and to that proposed by Jakobson and Information Theory of code and message. In 1967, Lotman wrote an article on 'Exact Methods in Russian Literary Science' for the Italian journal *Strumenti critici*. This article repeated the positions already taken in his other writings and expounded some of the main principles of his research methods. These are outlined briefly below:

1. The opposition of exact sciences and humanistic sciences must be eliminated.
2. The study of literature, if carried out in a purely historical way, blends into the history of social thought.
3. The Russian Formalists of the Twenties had initiated the study of the 'techniques' of literary phenomena but it was now time to introduce into the study of literary texts the methods of linguistic structuralism, semiotics (and he was thinking here of Peirce too), of Information Theory, cybernetics and mathematical-statistical analysis.
4. Semiotic systems are *models* which explain the world in which we live (obviously, in explaining the world, they also construct it, and in this sense, even at this early stage, Lotman saw semiotics as a cognitive science). Among all these systems, language is the *primary modelling system* and we apprehend the world by means of the model which language offers. Myth, cultural rules, religion, the language of art and of science are *secondary modelling systems*. We must therefore also study these semiotic systems which, since they lead us to understand the world in a certain way, allow us to speak about it.
5. If texts represent models of the world, the set of texts which is the culture of a period is a secondary modelling system. It is thus necessary to attempt to define a *typology of cultures*, in order both to discover universal aspects common to all cultures and to identify the specific systems which represent the 'language' of Medieval culture or the 'language' of Renaissance culture.
6. When a culture is analyzed as a code or system (as also happens with natural languages), the processes of use are richer and less predictable that the semiotic model which explains them. Reconstructing the code of a culture does not mean explaining all the phenomena of that culture, but rather allows us to explain *why* that culture has produced those phenomena.

Lotman realized, however, that seeing a text as a message elaborated on the basis of a linguistic code is by no means the same as seeing a text (or a culture as a set of texts) as a code. For Lotman was and is aware of the fact that no historical period has a sole cultural code (even if the construction of a model-code can be a useful abstraction) and that in any culture there exist simultaneously various codes. It seems to me that in attempting to deal with this problem, Lotman is moving beyond structuralist dogmatism and offering a more complex and articulated approach. Faced with the rigidity of the structuralist opposition between code and message, Lotman introduces, even within the same culture, a difference between grammatical learning and textual learning.

Cultures can be governed by a *system* of rules or by a *repertoire* of texts imposing models of behaviour. In the former category, texts are generated by combinations of discrete units and are judged correct or incorrect according to their conformity to the combinational rules. In the latter category, society directly generates texts, which constitute macro-units from which rules can eventually be inferred, but which initially and most importantly propose models to be followed and imitated.

A grammar-oriented culture depends on 'Handbooks', while a text-oriented culture depends on 'The Book'. A handbook is a code which permits further messages and texts, whereas a book is a text, generated by an as-yet-unknown rule which, once analyzed and reduced to a handbook-like form, can suggest new ways of producing further texts.

Lotman recalls the customary twofold experience of language learning. Adult learners are usually introduced to an unknown language by means of rules. They receive a set of units along with their combinational laws and they learn how to combine these units in order to speak. On the other hand, a child, when first learning to speak, is trained through exposure to a continuous textual performance of pre-fixed strings of language and s/he is expected to absorb competence even though not completely conscious of the underlying rules.

The difference between grammatical learning and textual learning had led Lotman to look at the various texts which are current in a culture in order to see that culture as a set of texts and a *non-hereditary collective memory*.[4]

On this basis, Lotman has effected subtle analyses of cultures, some interesting examples of which are included in this book. A particularly rich example of this kind of analysis is offered by 'The Notion of Boundary'. In this way, Lotman has managed to fuse the structural method (which takes a synchronic approach, that is, the description of a culture system at a given moment in time) with his vocation as historian, a historian interested in explaining how a culture is formed and how different culture systems, distant from one another in time, can be compared.

Even when different cultures seem to be using the same terms, they fit into a different system. Lotman gives us a brilliant example of typology of cultures with his comparison between the cultural language of the Middle Ages and that of the Enlightenment. On the one hand, we have a culture in which everything (not merely words but also things) signifies a higher reality and where objects themselves are important not for their physical nature or their function, but rather in so much as they signify something else. On the other, we have a cultural system where the world of objects is real, while words and signs in general are conventional constructions and vehicles of falsehood, and where only the 'noble savage', who is not aware of the constructions of culture, can understand reality.[5] Another example is given in the analysis of the concepts of 'honour' and 'glory' in medieval Russia. Whereas we may think that the terms are more or less synonymous, in medieval Russian culture 'honour' represents a recognition and a favour granted to an inferior by a superior and 'glory' pertains rather to those at the highest levels of the social order.[6]

In these studies of the typology of cultures, the analytical method is structural in the sense that honour and glory are opposed in just the same way that two phonemes are opposed and are reciprocally given their appropriate value within a phonological system. However, in the course of his research Lotman realized that a code identified in a culture is much more complex than that which can be identified in a language and his analyses became increasingly subtle and took on a rich, complex historical awareness.

Even in the Sixties, Lotman understood clearly that the multiplicity of codes in a given culture gives rise to contrasts and hybrids, or 'creolizations'. In his later works, and particularly in what he has written during the last decade, he has worked out the concept of the *semiosphere*, in analogy with the concept of the biosphere.

The present work sets out clearly what Lotman intends by the semiosphere, and here I would like to draw attention to a crucial definition:

> . . . imagine a museum hall where exhibits from different periods are on display, along with inscriptions in known and unknown languages, and instructions for decoding them; there are also the explanations composed by the museum staff, plans for tours and rules for the behaviour of the visitors. Imagine also in this hall tour-leaders and visitors and imagine all this as a single mechanism (which *in a certain sense it is*). This is an image of the semiosphere. Then we have to remember that all elements of the semiosphere are in dynamic, not static, correlations whose terms are constantly changing. We notice this specially at traditional moments which have come down to us from the past.

Thirty years ago, Lotman was already considering the concept of the text as a unity. This concept forms the basis of his *Lessons on Poetic Structure* of 1964 which was then re-issued as *The Structure of the Poetic Text* in 1970. However, in more recent work, this interest has been extended to cover the entire semiosphere. In his 'O semiosfere' (*Trudy*, 17: 1984), Lotman states that the whole semiosphere (culture as semiosphere) must be considered as a single mechanism and it is only in this way that we will be able to understand its various aspects. He concludes by saying that 'if we put together lots of veal cutlets, we do not obtain a calf. But if we cut up a calf, we obtain lots of veal cutlets.'

In case· this metaphor disturbs the squeamish reader unwilling to consider art and culture in terms of calves and raw meat, I can attempt to translate it with a more 'noble' equivalent (though by doing so, the basic concept which Lotman has so forcefully expressed remains the same). If we put together many branches and great quantity of leaves, we still cannot understand the forest. But if we know how to walk through the forest of culture with our eyes open, confidently following the numerous paths which criss-cross it, not only shall we be able to understand better the vastness and complexity of the forest, but we shall also be able to discover the nature of the leaves and branches of every single tree.

This book gives an indication of both the vastness and the allure of the forest and helps us to understand the form and the colour of the leaves and branches through which the forest lives.

UMBERTO ECO

NOTES

1. Victor Erlich, *Russian Formalism* (New Haven, Yale University Press, 1954)
2. *Théorie de la littérature – Textes des formalistes russes* (Paris, Seuil, 1965).
3. 'La structure et la forme. Reflexions sur un ouvrage de Vladimir Propp'. *Cahiers de l'Institut de Science Economique et Appliquée* 99, 1960.
4. 'O semioticestom mechanizme kul'tury', *Trudy*, 5 (1971), pp.144-76.
5. 'K probleme tipologii kul'tury', *Trudy* 3 (1967), pp.30-8.
6. 'Oh oppociii 'cest'-'slava' v svetskich tekstach kievskogo perioda', *Trudy* 3 (1967), pp.100-112.

Preface

INTRODUCTORY REMARKS

Ein grosser Vorsatz scheint im Anfang toll;
Doch wollen wir des Zufalle künftig lachen,
Und so ein Hirn, das trefflich denken soll,
Wird künftig auch ein Denker machen.

Goethe, *Faust*, part two

[A mighty project may at first seem mad
But now we laugh, the ways of chance foreseeing:
A thinker then, in mind's deep wonder clad,
May give at last a thinking brain its being.[1]]

The project of creating a thinking brain adumbrated by Goethe is still relevant today: indeed with each new advance in science it has been raised anew, though in different terms. But a very real barrier stands in our way, namely that we cannot satisfactorily explain what is the thinking brain we are trying to create artificially. I am reminded of an anecdote in the memoirs of the Russian writer, Andrei Bely. His father, N. V. Bugaev, who was Professor of Mathematics and President of the Moscow Mathematical Society, was once chairing a meeting where a paper was read on the intelligence of animals:

> My father who was presiding interrupted the lecturer to ask whether he knew what intelligence was; the lecturer didn't. Then my father began asking the people sitting in the front row: 'Do you know?' 'Do you?' No one knew. Then my father declared: 'Since no one knows what intelligence is we cannot discuss the intelligence of animals. I declare the meeting closed.'[2]

1

This incident took place early this century, but the situation has hardly changed. Evidently the reason is that intellectual activity is usually regarded as a quality unique to man, though something that is taken in isolation and not compared with anything else cannot be the object of science. Our task is thus to find a *series* of 'thinking objects', to compare them, and to deduce the invariant feature of intelligence. The concept 'intelligence' has many aspects and I do not feel competent to make an exhaustive definition of it. However, the task becomes manageable if we restrict ourselves to its semiotic aspect.

If we define intelligence from this point of view then we can reduce it to the following functions:

1. the transmission of available information (that is, of texts);
2. the creation of new information, that is, of texts which are not simply deducible according to set algorithms from already existing information, but which are to some degree unpredictable;
3. memory, that is, the capacity to preserve and reproduce information (texts).

The study of the semiotic systems created by humanity over the course of its cultural history has led to the unexpected finding that these functions are also characteristic of semiotic objects. In texts intended to communicate the first function predominates, while in artistic texts it is the capacity to generate new information. It has been established that a minimally functioning semiotic structure consists of not one artificially isolated language or text in that language, but of a parallel pair of mutually untranslatable languages which are, however, connected by a 'pulley', which is translation. A dual structure like this is the minimal nucleus for generating new messages and it is also the minimal unit of a semiotic object such as culture. Thus culture is (as a minimum) a binary semiotic structure, and one which at the same time functions as an indissoluble unit. Thinking along these lines has led us to the concept of the semiosphere and convinced us of the importance of studying the semiotics of culture.

Moreover we can now define semiotic objects of this kind as 'thinking structures' since they fulfil the functions of intelligence formulated above. The fact that in order to work they require an intelligent interlocutor and an 'input' text need not concern us. For even an absolutely normal human intelligence, if it is completely isolated from birth from external texts and from any dialogue, still remains a normal machine, though one which has not yet been set in motion. It cannot switch itself on by itself. For an intelligence to function there must be another intelligence. Vygotsky was the first to stress: 'Every higher function is divided between two people, is a mutual psychological process.'[3] Intelligence is always an interlocutor.

To our surprise, observations about the bipolar asymmetry of semiotic mechanisms has been paralleled by research into the functional asymmetry of the large hemispheres of the brain. The discovery of mechanisms in the individual thinking apparatus which are functionally isomorphous to the semiotic mechanism of culture has opened up a wide field for future scientific study. The question of the overlap between the semiotics of the humanities and neurophysiology has surprised some people, but was enthusiastically supported by the linguist Roman Jakobson who called those hostile to this approach the proponents of 'brainless linguistics'. In the Soviet Union these problems have been actively pursued in the neurophysiological laboratory of the late L. Ya Balonov (and his colleagues V. L. Deglin, T. V. Chernigovskaya, N. N. Nikolaenko and others), and from the semiotic aspect by V. V. Ivanov.

This question has, however, led to the even more general scientific problem, that of the relationship of symmetry to asymmetry, a question which in its time concerned Louis Pasteur.

The idea that 'thinking' semiotic structures need an initial impulse from another thinking structure and that text-generating mechanisms need a text from outside to set them going reminds us on the one hand of so-called autocatalytic reactions, that is those reactions where, in order to obtain the final product (or to hasten a chemical process), the final result has to be already present in some quantity at the beginning of the reaction. And, on the other hand, this question finds a parallel in the as yet unsolved problem of the 'beginning' of culture and the 'beginning' of life. The biologist V. I. Vernadsky refused to respond to such questions, finding it more productive to study the interrelationship of structures that are binary, asymmetrical, and at the same time, unitary. This is the approach we shall be adopting.

In accordance with the three functions of semiotic objects outlined above, this study is divided into three parts. Part One considers the mechanism of meaning-generation as a result of the mutual tension between such mutually untranslatable and at the same time mutually interprojected languages as the conventional (discrete, verbal) and the iconic (continuous, spatial). This corresponds to the minimal act of elaborating a new message. Part Two is devoted to the semiosphere, that synchronic semiotic space which fills the borders of culture, without which separate semiotic systems cannot function or come into being. The central concept of Part One is the *text*, and of Part Two is *culture*. Part Three is devoted to questions of memory, diachronic depth, and history as a mechanism of intellectual activity: it centres on the *semiotics of history*.

Taken together these three parts are intended to demonstrate the working of the semiotic space or intellectual world in which humanity and human society are enfolded and which is in constant interaction with the individual intellectual world of human beings.

AFTER SAUSSURE

Over the last few decades semiotics and structuralism in the Soviet Union as in the West have lived through testing times. Of course the experiences have been different. In the Soviet Union these disciplines had to endure a period of persecutions and ideological attacks, and this was followed by a conspiracy of silence or embarrassed semi-recognition on the part of official science. In the West these disciplines endured the test of fashion. They became a craze which took them far outside the bounds of science. Yet neither persecution nor fashion, both of which seem so crucial in the eyes of the watching public, have a determining effect on the fate of scientific ideas. The decisive factor is rather the profundity of the actual ideas themselves. For the profundity and significance of scientific ideas are determined first, by their capacity to explain and marshal facts which had previously been scattered and unexplained, that is by their capacity to combine with other scientific ideas; and second, by their capacity to reveal problems needing solutions, especially in areas where earlier opinion had seen no problems. This second feature is an indication of their capacity to combine with *future* scientific ideas. In consequence the ideas that have a long scientific life are those which are capable, while preserving their initial premises, of going through a dynamic transformation and evolving together with the world that surrounds them.

When we speak of semiotics today, at the end of the twentieth century, we should bear in mind its three different aspects. In the first place semiotics is the *scientific discipline* adumbrated by Ferdinand de Saussure. This is the domain of knowledge whose object is the sphere of semiotic communication: 'It is therefore possible to conceive of a science which studies the role of signs as part of social life. It would form part of social psychology, and hence of general psychology. We shall call it semiology.'[4] The notion of language as one of the semiotic systems would, said Saussure, lie at the base of all the social sciences: 'In this way, light will be thrown not only upon the linguistic problem. By considering rites, customs, etc. as signs, it will be possible, we believe, to see them in a new perspective. The need will be felt to consider them as semiological phenomena and to explain them in terms of the laws of semiology.'[5]

In its second aspect, semiotics is a *method* of the humanities, which is relevant to various disciplines and which is defined not by the nature of its object but by the means of analysing it. From this point of view one and the same scientific object may be studied from a semiotic and a non-semiotic point of view. Linguistics itself provides numerous examples.

Finally, the third aspect of semiotics can best be defined as a special feature of the scientific psychology of the researcher, the way his cognitive consciousness is made up. Just as a film director will look at the world around him/her through his/her fingers which are placed to form a frame and to 'cut' separate pieces from the totality of the view, so the semiotic researcher has the habit of transforming the world around him/her so as to show up the semiotic structures. Everything that King Midas touched with his golden hand turned to gold. In the same way, everything which the semiotic researcher turns his/her attention to becomes semioticized in his hands. This is the problem of the effect of the describer on the object being described which we shall be discussing below.

Together, these three aspects make up the domain of semiotics.

If we look back over the course of semiotics since that time in the late fifties when, largely thanks to the efforts of Roman Jakobson and also to a general trend in scientific thought, semiotics began to attract widespread scientific attention, we can summarize its main trends by the words: continuing and overcoming. These words refer both to the legacy of Russian formalism and to the works of Bakhtin and Propp. But above all they relate to the legacy of Saussure whose works, even after Jakobson had criticized them and contrasted them with the ideas of C. S. Peirce, remain in force as the foundation stones of semiotics.

In the aspect which we are considering the following ideas of Saussure's are significant:

- the opposition language [*langue*] and speech [*parole*] (or code and text).
- the opposition: synchrony and diachrony.

For Saussure both these oppositions were fundamental. Language for him is

> a grammatical system existing potentially in every brain, or more exactly in the brains of a group of individuals; for the language is never complete in any single individual, but exists perfectly only in the collectivity.
>
> By distinguishing between the language itself and speech, we distinguish at the same time: 1) what is social from what is individual, and 2) what is essential from what is ancillary and more or less accidental.[6]

Starting from these premises Saussure formulated his main proposition about language both in the speech act and in the science of linguistics:

1) Amid the disparate mass of facts involved in language, it stands out as a well defined entity. It is the social part of language, external to the individual who by himself is powerless either to create it or to modify it. It exists only in virtue of a kind of contract agreed between the members of a community.

2) A language system, as distinct from speech, is an object that may be studied independently. Dead languages are no longer spoken, but we can

Preface

perfectly well acquaint ourselves with their linguistic structure. A science
which studies linguistic structure is not only able to dispense with other
elements of language [here: speech! Yu. M. L.], but is possible only if
those other elements are kept separate.[7]

No less fundamental was the second of the oppositions mentioned
above. For synchrony is what he saw as having a structural character, and
it is synchrony that is the bearer of the relationships which make up the
essence of language. Synchrony is homeostatic while diachrony is made
up of a series of external and accidental infringements of it, in reacting
against which synchrony re-establishes its integrity: 'Language is a
system, all parts of which may and should be studied in their synchronic
mutuality.'

Changes never take place in the whole system but only in one or other
of its elements, they can be studied only outside the system. 'In the
diachronic perspective one is dealing with phenomena which have no
connection with linguistic systems, even though the systems are affected
by them.'[8] Language is opposed to all that is accidental, unstable, extra-
systematic: 'Languages are mechanisms which go on functioning, in spite
of the damage caused to them.'[9]

These ideas cannot be rejected by modern semiotics. To reject them
would mean pulling out its cornerstones. But from this we can see how
deep are the transformations that even the fundamental propositions and
the whole cast of semiotics have undergone in the second half of the
twentieth century.

*   *   *

My work on this book was greatly helped by the scholarly atmosphere
created by my colleagues at Tartu University, by my students and friends
and especially Z. G. Mints and L. N. Kiseleva. To them all I express my
warm thanks.

NOTES TO PREFACE

1. J. W. von Goethe, *Faust*, Part Two, translated by Philip Wayne, Penguin Classics, Harmondsworth, 1987, p. 101.
2. Andrei Bely, *Na rubezhe dvukh stoletii* [Bridging Two Centuries], 2nd edition, M/L, 1931, pp. 71–2.
3. L. S. Vygotsky, *Sobranie sochinenii v 6 tomakh*, [*Collected Works in Six Volumes*], vol. 1, Moscow, 1982, p. 115.
4. Ferdinand de Saussure, *Course in General Linguistics*, translated and annotated by Roy Harris, London, 1983, p. 15.
5. Ibid., p. 17.
6. Ibid., pp. 13–14.
7. Ibid., p. 14.
8. Ibid., p. 85.
9. Ibid., p. 86.

PART ONE

The Text as a Meaning-generating Mechanism

1

Three functions of the text

In the Saussurean system of thought, which has long determined the course of semiotic thinking, there is a clear preference for the study of language rather than speech, and of the code rather than the text. Speech and its delimited articulated hypostasis, the text, is of interest to the linguist merely as raw material, as a manifestation of the linguistic structure. Everything that is relevant in speech (or text) is given in language (or code). Elements occurring in a text without any correspondence in the code cannot be bearers of meaning. This is what Saussure means when he says: 'The linguist must take the study of linguistic structure as his primary concern, and relate all other manifestations of language to it'.[1] To take linguistic structure as the norm means making it the scientific reference-point for the definition of what is essential and what is inessential in language activity. Naturally, whatever has no correspondence in the language (code) when the message is decoded is 'removed'. After which just as the metal of the language structure is sifted out from the ore of speech there remains only the dross. This is what Saussure had in mind when he said, 'the science of language can do without the analysis of speech'.

Behind this scientific position, however, stands a whole complex of assumed, almost non-scientific ideas about the function of language. While the theoretical linguist is interested in the linguistic structure extracted from the text, the everyday receiver of information is concerned with the content of the message. In both cases the text is treated as something that is valuable, not in itself, but merely as a kind of packaging from which the topic of interest is extracted.

For the receiver of a message the following sequence seems logical:

thought (content of the message)   thought (content of the message)

the encoding mechanism of language   the decoding mechanism of language

the text

We should, of course, heed Benveniste's warning. He pointed out that because we are unaware of the linguistic operations we carry out and because 'we can say whatever we want', there is a widely held belief that

> the process of thinking and speaking are two totally different activities which are combined only for the practical purposes of communication, but each of them has its own field and its own independent possibilities; and besides language offers the mind the means for what we usually call the expression of our thoughts.

Moreover:

> Of course language when it is manifest in speech is used to convey 'what we want to say'. However the phenomenon which we call 'what we want to say' or 'what we've got on our mind', or 'our idea', or whatever, this phenomenon is the content of thought; it is very difficult to define it as an independent essence without using terms such as 'intention' or 'psychological structure', etc. This content acquires form only when it is uttered, and only in this way. It is formulated by language and in language.[2]

We can, however, imagine a meaning that remains invariant however much the text is transformed. We can imagine this meaning as a pre-textual message realized in the text. This is the premise on which the 'meaning-text' model is based (see below). From this point of view it is assumed that in the ideal case the informational content does not change either qualitatively or quantitatively: the receiver decodes the text and receives the initial message. Once again the text is regarded as a 'technical packaging' for the message which is what the receiver is interested in.

Behind this view of the functioning of a semiotic mechanism lies the belief that the function of the mechanism is to transfer the message adequately. The system works 'well' if the message received by the addressee is wholly identical to the one despatched by the addresser, and it works 'badly' if there are differences between the texts. These differences are classed as 'errors' and there are special mechanisms in the structure (for instance, redundancy) to prevent them.

There are good grounds for this approach: it points to a uniquely essential function of semiotic structures. But we must admit that if we take this function to be the only function, or even the basic one, then we are faced with a whole number of paradoxes.

If we take the adequacy of the transfer of the message as the basic criterion in the evaluation of the efficiency of semiotic systems, then we have to admit that all naturally occurring linguistic structures are rather badly constructed. For a fairly complex message to be received with absolute identity, conditions are required which in naturally occurring situations are practically unobtainable: addressee and addresser have to have wholly identical codes, i.e. to be in fact semiotically speaking a bifurcation of one and the same personality; for a code includes not only a certain binary set of rules for encoding and decoding a message, but also a multi-dimensional hierarchy. Even the fact that both participants in the communication use one and the same natural language (English, Russian, Estonian, etc.) does not ensure the identity of code; for there has to be also a common linguistic experience, and an identical dimension of memory. And to this must be added the common understanding of norm, linguistic reference and of pragmatics. If one then takes into account cultural traditions (the semiotic memory of culture) and the inevitable factor of the individual way with which this tradition is revealed to a particular member of a collective, then it will be obvious that the coincidence of codes between transmitter and transmittee is in reality possible only to a very relative extent. It follows then inevitably that the identity of the transmitted and received texts is relative. From this point of view it might indeed seem that natural language fulfils its function badly. And poetic language even worse.

It is obvious, therefore, that for a total guarantee of adequacy between the transmitted and received message there has to be an artificial (simplified) language and artificially simplified communicators: these will have a strictly limited memory capacity and all cultural baggage will be removed from the semiotic personality. The mechanisms created in this way will be able to serve only a limited amount of semiotic functions; the universalism inherent to natural language is in principle alien to it.

Should we then think that this artificial model is a model of what language should be, an ideal, from which it is distinguished only by imperfections which are the natural result of the 'irrational' workings of Nature? Artificial languages model not language as such but one of its functions – the ability to transmit a message adequately; because semiotic structures when they achieve this function to perfection lose the capacity of serving other functions which are inherent to them in the natural state.

So what are these functions?

First of all, the creative function. Every system which fulfils the entire range of semiotic possibilities not only transmits ready made messages but also serves as a generator of new ones.

But what is it we are terming 'new messages'? Let us agree first of all on what we are so terming. We are not terming 'new messages' those messages received from inputs as a result of simple transformations, i.e. messages which are the fruit of symmetrical transformations of the input (an input text obtained by a reverse transformation). If the translation of text T_1 from language L_1 to language L_2 leads to the appearance of text T_2 in such a way that the operation of a reverse translation results in the input text T_1, then we do not consider text T_2 to be new in relation to text T_1. So from this point of view the correct solution of mathematical problems does not create new texts. We might recall Wittgenstein's remark that within logic you cannot say anything new.

The polar opposite of artificial languages are those semiotic systems in which the creative function is strongest: it is obvious that if the most hackneyed of poems is translated into another language (i.e. into the language of another poetic system) then the operation of reverse translation will not produce the input text. The very fact that one and the same poem can be translated by different translators in many ways testifies to the fact that in place of a precise correspondence to text T_1 in this case there is a certain space. Any one of the texts t_1, t_2, t_3 ... t_n which fill this space may be a possible interpretation of the input text. Instead of a precise correspondence there is one of the possible interpretations, instead of a symmetrical transformation there is an asymmetrical one, instead of identity between the elements which compose T_1 and T_2 there is a conventional equivalence between them. In the translation of French poetry into Russian the rendering of the French twelve-syllable syllabic line by the Russian six-foot syllabo-tonic iambics is a convention, the result of an accepted tradition. Yet in principle it is possible to translate French syllabic verse into Russian syllabic verse. The translator is forced to *make a choice*. There is even greater indeterminacy when, for instance, a novel is transformed into a film.

The text that is produced in these instances we shall term a new one and the act of translation that creates it a creative act.

We can represent the adequate transmission of a text using artificial language by the following diagram:

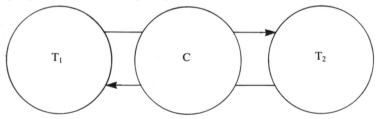

In this case the transmitter and the receiver share the same code, C.

The diagram representing artistic translation shows that transmitter and receiver use different codes C_1 and C_2 which overlap but are not identical. A reverse translation will result not in the input text but in a third text, T_3. Even closer to the actual process of the circulation of messages is the case when the transmitter is faced with not one code but a plural space of codes c_1, c_2, c_3 ... c_n, and each of them is a complex hierarchical construction capable of generating a set of texts in equal degree corresponding to it. The asymmetrical relationship, the constant need for choice, make translation in this case an act of generating new information and exemplify the creative function both of language and of the text.

Particularly indicative is the situation where it is not simply difference which exists between codes, but mutual untranslatability (for instance, in the translation of a verbal text into an iconic one). The translation is done with the help of the conventional system of equivalences accepted in that particular culture. So, for example, when transmitting a verbal text by a pictorial one (for instance, a picture on a Gospel theme), the space of the theme will overlap in the codes, while the space of the language and style will be merely conventionally correlated within the bounds of the particular tradition. The combination of translatability–untranslatability (each to different degrees) is what determines the creative function.

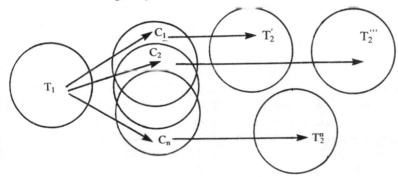

Since in this case the meaning is not only an invariant remnant which is preserved under all manner of transformational operations, but is also what is altered, we can claim that there is an accretion of meaning in the process of such transformations.

And there is another point. When we use artificial languages (or natural and poetic languages as artificial languages, for instance if we transmit a novel by Tolstoy by a brief annotation of the plot), we are isolating meaning from language. Under the complex operations of meaning-generation language is inseparable from the content it expresses. In this last instance we are concerned not merely with a message in a language, but also a message about language, a message in which the interest is shifted on to its language. This is the 'set to the code' which Roman Jakobson saw as being the fundamental feature of the literary text.

In this case many phenomena are paradoxically transposed. So, for example, when we stress the constancy of the message the fact that language precedes the message written in it and is available to both participants in the act of communication seems so natural that it is not specially remarked upon; even in complex cases the receiver first finds out some indications as to which of the codes he knows the message is encoded in, and then proceeds to the 'reading'. When the heroes of Jules Verne's novel *The Children of Captain Grant* extracted the three

fragments of a document from the bottle they first ascertained that one
fragment was written in English, one in German and one in French, and
only then did they set to work reconstructing the sense of the torn
document. In another case the order may be the opposite: first the
document is acquired and only then is its language reconstructed. This
order is quite normal when we get hold of a fragment from a culture that
is remote from our own. This happens not only with verbal texts in
unknown languages, but also with relics of art and material culture
detached from their contexts, whose functions and meaning the
archaeologist has to reconstruct. In the history of art this is especially
common, since every innovatory work of art is *sui generis* a work in a
language that is unknown to the audience and which has to be
reconstructed and mastered by its addressees. An addressee is capable of
this kind of 'self-tutoring' because in the first place in any individualized
language, however extreme, not everything is individual: inevitably there
are levels which are common to both participants in the act of
communication and which serve as a basis for the reconstruction. In the
second place even what is 'individual' and new inevitably derives from
some tradition, the memory of which is actualized in the text. And finally,
in the third place, the language of art is inevitably heterogeneous and
even though it is far removed from the pole of metalanguage and artificial
languages it must, paradoxically, include elements of self-reflexivity, i.e.
metalingual structures. The experience of the European avant-garde
provides convincing proof that the more individualistic the artistic
language, the greater place is given over to authorial reflection on the
language and the structure included in it. The text deliberately turns into
a language lesson.

So the spectrum of texts which fill the space of culture can be
represented as if they are disposed along an axis, one pole of which is
formed by the artificial languages and the other by artistic ones. Other
languages are disposed at points along the axis closer to one or other
pole. We should bear in mind, however, that the poles of this axis are an
abstraction unrealizable in actual languages: just as artificial languages
are impossible without some rudimentary synonymity and other 'poetic'
elements, so languages with an observable tendency towards 'pure'
poetism must have metalingual tendencies.

We should also bear in mind that the place of the text on the above-
mentioned axis is a moveable one: the reader may assess the 'poetic' and
'informational' correlation of the text differently from the author. When
Aseev wrote:

> *Ya zapretil by 'prodazhu ovsa i sena'* . . .
> *Ved' eto pakhnet ubiistvom ottsa i syna*
> [I would forbid 'oats and hay for sale' . . .
> You see it smells of the murder of father and son]

and when in Pilnyak the peasant comes to town and reads: '*kommutatory, ukkumulyatory*' [commutators, accumulators] as '*komu tatory, a komu lyatory*' [some get tators, some get lators], then it is obvious that the text, which in both cases is an advertisement, is being read in the first example as if it were a poetic text, and in the second as if it were a proverb: in Aseev's lines the phonetic aspect is wrongly being highlighted and in Pilnyak's the syntagmatics are being decoded according to the laws of proverb-construction.

The possibility of choosing either one of two positions to be the point of reference in one's approach to language has important consequences. From the one position the informational point of view (using 'informational' in the narrow sense) represents language as a machine for transmitting invariant messages, and poetic language is then regarded as a small and, generally speaking, abnormal corner of this system. According to this approach poetic language is seen merely as natural language with an overlay of supplementary restrictions and hence a significantly reduced informational capacity.

The other position is, however, also possible and has been frequently demonstrated in linguistics: according to this view the creative function is a universal quality of language and poetic language is regarded as the most typical manifestation of language as such. From this point of view it is precisely the opposite semiotic models which then are regarded as a small corner of the linguistic space.

The story of the 'debate' between those two linguists of genius, Saussure and Jakobson, is of particular interest in this respect. Saussure clearly saw the first function as the main principle of language. Hence the precision of his oppositions, his emphasis on the universal significance of the principle of arbitrariness in the relation of signified to signifier, and so on. Behind Saussure we can sense the culture of the nineteenth century with its faith in positivistic science, its conviction that knowledge is good and ignorance an absolute evil, its aims at universal literacy, the novels of Zola and the Goncourts. Jakobson was always a man of avant-garde culture, and his first work, *The Latest Russian Poetry. First Sketch* (1921) was as it were the brilliant prologue to his whole scholarly career. The language of Khlebnikov, the language of the Russian Futurists, was for Jakobson not an anomaly, but the most consistent realization of the structure of language, and one of the most important stimuli to his later phonological researches. From his experience of studying poetic language came his sensitivity to the aesthetic side of semiotic systems. This explains the intensity of his criticism of Saussure when he attacked Saussure's central proposition, the principle of the arbitrariness of the connection between signifier and signified in the sign. (See Roman Jakobson, *Quest for the Essence of Language*.) Indeed, the language of the artistic text acquires secondary features of iconism, which sheds light on the problem of the 'untranslatability' of poetic language. In the article referred to, Jakobson makes an exceedingly subtle analysis of the features of iconism inherent in the language of everyday usage, i.e. the presence of artistic potential in language as such. In the early sixties, Academician Kolmogorov proved that you cannot write poetry in artificial languages, and Roman Jakobson convincingly proved the potential iconism and hence the artistic aspect of natural languages, thereby confirming Potebnya's idea that the entire sphere of language belongs to art.

The third function of language is the function of memory. The text is not only the generator of new meanings, but also a condenser of cultural memory. A text has the capacity to preserve the memory of its previous contexts. Without this function, there could be no science of history, since the culture of preceding ages (and more broadly speaking, its picture of life) inevitably comes down to us in fragments. If a text stayed in the consciousness of the perceiver only as itself, then the past would be represented to us as a mosaic of disconnected fragments. But for the perceiver a text is always a metonymy of a reconstructed integral meaning, a discrete sign of a non-discrete essence. The sum of the contexts in which a given text acquires interpretation and which are in a way incorporated in it may be termed the text's memory. This meaning-space created by the text around itself enters into relationship with the cultural memory (tradition) already formed in the consciousness of the audience. As a result the text acquires semiotic life.

Any culture is constantly bombarded by chance isolated texts which fall on it like a shower of meteorites. What we have in mind are not the texts which are included in a continuing tradition which has an influence on the culture, but isolated and disruptive invasions. These may be the remnants of other civilizations unearthed by chance from the ground, texts brought in by chance from cultures far off in time or space. Unless texts had their own memory and were capable of creating a particular semantic aura around themselves, these invasions would all remain museum pieces set apart from the main cultural process. But in fact they are important factors in the stimulus of cultural dynamics. For a text, like a grain of wheat which contains within itself the programme of its future development, is not something given once and for all and never changing. The inner and as yet unfinalized determinacy of its structure provides a reservoir of dynamism when influenced by contacts with new contexts.

There is another side to this question. One might expect a text as it lives through the centuries to become faded and to lose the information contained in it. Yet texts that preserve their cultural activity reveal a capacity to accumulate information, i.e. a capacity for memory. Nowadays *Hamlet* is not just a play by Shakespeare, but it is also the memory of all its interpretations, and what is more, it is also the memory of all those historical events which occurred outside the text but with which Shakespeare's text can evoke associations. We may have forgotten what Shakespeare and his spectators knew, but we cannot forget what we have learnt since their time. And this is what gives the text new meanings.

2

Autocommunication: 'I' and 'Other' as addressees

One of the premises of modern culturology is that there is an organic link between culture and communication. A consequence of this is that models and terms taken from communication theory are being transferred to culture. By applying Roman Jakobson's basic model we have found it possible to establish a link between the theory of communication systems, and a wide range of problems in the study of language, art and more broadly culture. Jakobson's well-known model looks like this:[3]

context

message

addresser . . . . addressee

contact

code

This single model for communication situations has made a significant contribution to the semiotic sciences and much research work has been done in response to it. However, the automatic application of preconceived notions to the field of culture gives rise to number of difficulties. Foremost among them is the following: in the cultural mechanism, communication is carried on by at least two differently constructed channels.

Later in this study we shall be considering how, in a single cultural mechanism, there must be present both the pictorial and the verbal channels, which we may treat as two differently constructed channels for the transmission of information. However, both these channels can be described using Jakobson's model, and in this respect they are the same. But if we set ourselves the task of constructing a culture-model on a more abstract level then we can identify two types of communication channel, only one of which can be described by the classic model we have been talking of. To do this we must first identify two possible directions in the transmission of a message. The most typical situation is the 'I s/he' direction in which the 'I' is the subject of the communication, the possessor of the information, while the 's/he' is the object, the addressee. In this instance it is assumed that before the act of communication there was a message known to 'me' and not known to 'him/her'.

The predominance of communications of this type in the culture we are used to overshadows the other direction in the transmission of information, a direction which we can schematically describe as the 'I–I' direction. The case of a subject transmitting a message to him/herself, i.e. to a person who knows it already, appears paradoxical. Yet it occurs quite frequently and has an important part to play in the general system of culture.

When we speak of communicating a message by the 'I–I' system we are *not* thinking primarily of those cases where the text fulfils a mnemonic function. When that happens the perceiving, second, 'I' is functionally equivalent to a third party. The difference comes down to the fact that while in the 'I–s/he' system information is transferred in space, in the 'I–I' system it is transferred in time.[4]

What we are interested in is the case when the transfer of information from 'I' to 'I' is not associated with a time-shift but fulfils not a mnemonic but some other cultural function. Communication to oneself of already known information takes place in all cases when the rank of the message is raised. When, for instance, a young poet reads his poem in print the message remains textually the same as it was in his manuscript text. Yet being translated into a new system of graphic signs which have another degree of authority in the given culture it acquires supplementary value. Analogous cases are when the truth or falsehood of a message are made dependent on the fact whether the message is spoken out loud or only implied, whether it is spoken or written, handwritten or printed, etc.

But 'I–I' communication takes place in a whole host of other instances. These include cases when a person addresses him/herself, for instance in diary jottings which are made not in order to remember certain things but to elucidate the writer's inner state, something which would not be possible without the jottings. Addressing oneself in texts, speeches, ruminations – this is a fact not only of psychology, but also of the history of culture.

In what follows we shall try to demonstrate that the place of autocommunication in the system of culture is far more significant than is commonly supposed.

But how does this odd situation come about whereby a message transmitted through the 'I–I' system is not wholly redundant and even acquires some new supplementary information?

In the 'I–s/he' system the framing elements of the model are variables (addresser could be replaced by addressee), while code and message are invariables. The message and the information contained in it are constants, while the bearer of the information may alter.

In the 'I–I' system the bearer of the information remains the same but the message is reformulated and acquires new meaning during the communication process. This is the result of introducing a supplementary, second, code; the original message is recoded into elements of its structure and thereby acquires features of a *new* message.

The diagram for this type of communcation is as follows:

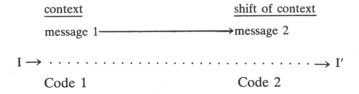

The 'I–s/he' system allows one merely to transmit a constant quantity of information, whereas the 'I–I' system qualitatively transforms the information, and this leads to a restructuring of the actual 'I' itself. In the first system the addresser transmits a message to another person, the addressee, but remains the same in the course of the act. In the second system, while communicating with him/herself, the addresser inwardly reconstructs his/her essence, since the essence of a personality may be thought of as an individual set of socially significant codes, and this set changes during the act of communication.

The transmission of a message along the 'I–I' channel is not a self-contained process since it is caused by the intrusion of supplementary codes from outside, and by external stimuli which alter the contextual situation.

A typical example of this is the effect of measured sounds (the drumming of wheels or of rhythmic music) on a person's inner monologue. There are numerous literary texts which ascribe a wild and vivid fantasy to the measured rhythm of a horse's paces (Goethe's 'The Forest King', several poems in Heine's 'Lyrical Intermezzo') or to the rocking of a boat (Tyutchev's 'Dream at Sea') or to the rhythms of the railway (Glinka's 'Journey Song' set to words by Kukol'nik).

Let us analyse Tyutchev's 'Dream at Sea' in this respect.

DREAM AT SEA

1. Both the sea and the storm rocked our boat;
2. Drowsy I gave myself over entirely to the whim of the waves.
3. There were two infinities in me,

4. And they began wilfully to play with me.
5. Around me the rocks sounded like cymbals,
6. The winds answered and waves sang.
7. Deafened I lay in the chaos of sounds,
8. But my dream rose up over the chaos of sounds.
9. Painfully bright, magically dumb,
10. It wafted lightly over the sounding dark.
11. In the rays of sheet lightning it unfolded its world
12. The earth grew green, and air grew bright,
13. Labyrinth-gardens, palaces, columns,
14. And the multitudes of the silent crowd swarmed.
15. I recognized many faces I had not known.
16. I saw marvellous beasts, mysterious birds,
17. Like God, I trod over the heights of creation,
18. And the world immobile under my feet was radiant.
19. But through all my dreams, like the howl of a wizard,
20. I heard the thunder of the sea's whirlpool,
21. And into the silent domain of visions and dreams
22. Burst in the foam of the roaring waves.[5]

We are not at the moment concerned with the ideas, which were important for Tyutchev, about the juxtaposition or contrast between a person's inner life on the one hand, and the sea on the other ('Thought after thought, wave after wave', 'There is music in the sea's waves').

The text is evidently based on a real experience, the memory of a storm which lasted for four days in September 1833 when Tyutchev was travelling through the Adriatic. Our interest in the poem concerns the evidence it provides of the author's psychological self-observation (surely no one will deny the legitimacy of this approach, among others, to a text).

The text distinguishes two components in the author's inner state of mind: the soundless dream and the measured roar of the storm. The latter component is marked by the unexpected intrusion of anapaestic lines into the amphibrachic text (lines 4, 5, 7, 18).

4. Ĭ mnói svŏĕvól'nŏ ĭgrálĭ ŏné,
5. Vkrŭg mĕnýa kăk kĭmválў, zvŭchálĭ skălý,
7. Yă v kháŏsĕ zvúkŏv lĕzhál ŏglŭshén,
18. Ĭ mír pŏdŏ mnóyŭ nĕdvízhnўi sĭyál,

The lines dealing with the noise of the storm, and the two symmetrical lines beginning with 'but' which depict the intrusion of the dream into the noise of the storm, or the noise of the storm into the dream, are anapaestic. The line dealing with the philosophical theme of the 'dual

abyss' (the 'two infinities'), a theme which is to be found in other
Tyutchev poems, is marked out as the only dactylic line in the poem (line
2).

The noise of the storm against the background of the soundless world
of the dream ('magically dumb', the 'silent' crowds) is just as clearly
emphasized by an abundance of phonetic features. But it is precisely
these *measured* and deafening sounds which make the rhythmic
background which serves to liberate the poet's soaring and vivid thoughts.

To take another example (from chapter 8 of *Eugene Onegin*):

XXXVI

1. What happened? Though his eyes were reading,
2. his thoughts were on a distant goal:
3. desires and dreams and griefs were breeding
4. and swarming in his inmost soul.
5. Between the lines of text as printed,
6. his mind's eye focused on the hinted
7. purport of other lines; intense
8. was his absorption in their sense.
9. Legends, and mystical traditions,
10. drawn from a dim, warm-hearted past,
11. dreams of inconsequential cast,
12. rumours and threats and premonitions,
13. long, lively tales from wonderland,
14. or letters in a young girl's hand.

XXXVII

1. Then gradually upon sensation,
2. and thought, a sleepy numbness steals;
3. before his eyes, imagination
4. brings out its faro pack, and deals.

XXXVIII

9. Who could have looked the poet better,
10. as in the nook he'd sit alone
11. by blazing fireplace, and intone
12. *Idol mio* or *Benedetta*,
13. and on the flames let fall unseen
14. a slipper, or a magazine?[6]

In this example there are three external, rhythm-forming codes: the
printed text, the measured flickering of the fire, and the 'intoned' tune.
Very typically the book Onegin is reading is not supplying a message: the

hero reads it but without noticing the content (XXXVI, lines 1–2); the book serves to stimulate the flow of his thoughts. And it does this not by its content, but by the mechanical automatism of the reading. Onegin 'reads without reading', just as he watches the fire without seeing it, and hums without being aware of what he is doing. None of these three rhythmical series, which are perceived through different sense-organs, bears any direct semantic relationship to his thoughts, to the 'fairo pack' of his imagination. But he needs these rhythms so that with 'his mind's eye' he can read 'other lines'. The intrusion of the external rhythm organizes and stimulates the internal monologue.

A third example is the Japanese Buddhist monk contemplating a 'stone park'.[7] This park is a relatively small gravel area on which stones have been placed in accordance with an elaborate mathematical rhythm. The contemplation of the elaborate pattern of the stones and gravel is intended to evoke a mood conducive to introspection.

* * *

These various rhythmical series, ranging from musical repetitions to repeated ornamentation, are constructed according to clearly expressed syntagmatic principles but have no semantic meaning of their own; we can treat them as external codes whose effect is to restructure verbal communication.[8] However, for the system to work there has to be a confrontation and interaction between two different principles: a message in some semantic language and the intrusion of a purely syntagmatic, supplementary code. Only when these principles are combined can there be the communicative system which we term an 'I–I' language.

We have therefore established the existence of this special channel of self-communication. And by the way, this question has already been researched. Vygotsky pointed out the existence of a special language, intended for the autocommunicative function, which he described as 'internal speech'. He pointed out its structural features:

The essential difference between inner speech and external speech is the absence of vocalization.

Inner speech is dumb, soundless speech. This is its main distinguishing feature. But the evolution of egocentric speech tends in this direction towards the gradual increase of this feature. . . . The fact that this feature develops gradually, that egocentric speech can be distinguished by its function and structure before vocalization, demonstrates only what we have made the basis of our hypothesis about inner speech, namely that inner speech develops not by the outer weakening of its phonic aspect, passing from speech to whisper and from whisper to silent speech, but by its functional and structural demarcation from external speech; for it moves from external speech to egocentric speech, and from egocentric speech to inner speech.[9]

Let us attempt to describe some of the features of the autocommunicative system.

The first feature which distinguishes it from the 'I–s/he' system is the reduction of the words in this language: they tend to become signs of words, indices of signs. In Kyukhelbeker's prison notebook there is a remarkable entry on this topic:

> I have noticed something odd which psychologists and physiologists would find curious: for some time now I have been dreaming not of objects, or events, but of some kind of strange abbreviations which relate to them like hieroglyphs to a picture, or like the contents page of a book to the book itself. I wonder if this is the result of having so few objects around me and so few events happening to me?[10]

The tendency of words in an 'I–I' language to become reduced is to be seen in the abbreviations we use in notes to ourselves. In the final analysis the words in these notes become indices which can be deciphered only if one knows what has been written. Compare Academician Krachkovsky's description of the early written tradition of the Koran: '*Scripto defectiv*. The absence not only of short vowels, but also of long ones, and of diacritical marks. Can be read only when the text is known by heart.'[11] A vivid example of this type of communication is to be found in the famous scene in *Anna Karenina* when Levin declares his love for Kitty; the scene is all the more interesting in that it reproduces Tolstoy's proposal to his fiancée Sofya Andreevna Bers:

> 'Here', he said, and wrote down the initial letters, w, y, t, m, i, c, n, b – d,t,m,n,o,t? These letters stood for, "When you told me *it could not be* – did that mean never, or then?" . . .
> 'I know what it is,' she said, flushing a little.
> 'What is this word?' he asked, pointing to the *n* which stood for *never*.
> 'That means never,' she said.[12]

In all these examples we are concerned with cases where the reader understands the text only because he knows it beforehand. (In Tolstoy's novel Kitty and Levin are emotionally already *one* being; the fusion of addresser and addressee takes place before our very eyes.)

The index-words which are formed as a result of this reduction have a tendency to iso-rhythmicality. It is a feature of the syntax of this type of speech that it does not form completed sentences, but tends to be an unfinalized chain of rhythmical repetitions.

Most of the examples we have presented here are not pure examples of 'I–I' communication, but are compromises which have come about as a result of the deformation of a normal linguistic text under the influence of the laws of this type of communication. At this point we should distinguish two kinds of autocommunication: those with a mnemonic function and those without.

An example of the first type is Pushkin's well-known note written under the manuscript text of the poem 'Under the blue sky of your native land':

Usl. o sm, 25
U o s. R.P.M.K.B: 24[13]

This has been deciphered as: '*Uslyshal o smerti Riznich 25 iyulya 1826 g.*' '*Uslyshal o smerti Ryleeva, Pestelya, Murav'eva, Kakhovskogo, Bestuzheva 24 iyulya 1826 g.*' ['Learnt of Riznich's death 25 July 1826.' 'Learnt of the death of Ryleev, Pestel', Murav'ev, Kakhovskoi, Bestuzhev 24 July 1826'].

This note clearly had a mnemonic function, although we should not forget another factor: in view of the unusual connection between signified and signifier in the 'I–I' system, it lends itself to cryptography since it is constructed according to the formula: 'Let those who understand, understand.' When a text is enciphered it is as a rule translated from the 'I–s/he' to an 'I–I' system (members of a group who use a cipher are in this instance regarded as a single 'I', and in relation to them, the people from whom the text must be concealed form a composite third person). In Pushkin's text it is true there is an action, obviously an unconscious one, which is not to be explained either by the mnemonic function or by the secret nature of the note: in the first line the words are abbreviated to groups of several letters, while in the second line the words are abbreviated to a single letter. Indices tend towards equality in length and towards rhythm. In the first line since the preposition ['*o*' – about] tends to elide with the noun, two groups are formed ['*usl*' and '*osm*'], and these groups, given the phonological parallelism between 'u' and 'o' on the one hand, and between 'l' and 'm' on the other, reveal not only a rhythmical, but also a phonological organization. In the second line, the conspiratorial need to abbreviate the surnames to one letter only produces another internal rhythm, and all the other words were reduced to the same degree. It would be bizarre and monstrous to assume that Pushkin deliberately constructed this tragic note with the intention of giving it a rhythmic and phonological organization – that is not the point at all: the immanent and unconscious activating laws of autocommunication reveal structural features which we usually observe in poetic texts.

These features become even clearer in the next example which has neither a mnemonic nor a conspiratorial function and which is an example of self-communication in its purest form. We have in mind the

unconscious jottings which Pushkin did while in the process of thinking
and which probably he did not even notice.

On 9 May 1928 Pushkin wrote a poem 'Alas! The tongue of garrulous
love', which he dedicated to Anna Alekseevna Olenina whom he was
hoping to marry. There we find the following jotting:[14]

> *ettenna eninelo*
> *eninelo ettenna*

And next to it the note: 'Olenina
                                   Annette'

Above 'Annette' Pushkin wrote 'Pouchkine'. It is not difficult to re-
establish Pushkin's train of thought: Pushkin was thinking of Annette
Olenina as his bride and wife (the note 'Pouchkine'). The text is an
anagram (read from right to left) of the name and surname of Annette
whom he was thinking of in French.

The mechanism of this note is interesting. First the name, read
backwards, turns into a conventional index, then the repetition establishes
a rhythm, while the transposition is a rhythmical destruction of the
rhythm. The verse-like nature of this construction is obvious.

*   *   *

The mechanism for transmitting information along the 'I–I' channel can
be envisaged as follows: a message in a natural language is introduced,
followed by a supplementary code, of purely formal organization; this
supplementary code has a syntagmatic construction and is either totally
without semantic value or tending to be without it. Tension arises
between the original message and the secondary code, and the effect of
this tension is the tendency to interpret the semantic elements of the text
as if they were included in the supplementary syntagmatic construction
and have thereby acquired new, relationary meanings from this
interaction. However although the secondary code aims to liberate the
primary signifying elements from their normal semantic values, this does
not happen. The normal semantic values remain but secondary meanings
are imposed on them which are the result of the effect of the various
rhythmical series on the signifying elements. But this is not the only thing
that transforms the text's meaning. The growth of the syntagmatic
connections within the message stifles the primary semantic connections
and, at a certain level of perception, the text may behave like a complex
a-semantic message. But a-semantic texts, with a high degree of
syntagmatic organization, tend to become organizers of our associations.
Associative meanings are imputed to them. If, for instance, we stare at
the pattern on the wallpaper or listen to abstract music, we ascribe
meanings to the elements of these texts. The more the syntagmatic
organization is stressed the freer and more associative will be our
semantic connections. So the 'I–I' text has a tendency to build up

individual meanings and to take on the function of organizing the disordered associations which accumulate in the individual consciousness. It reorganizes the personality who engages in autocommunication.

So the text bears a three-fold semantic value: the primary general linguistic semantic value; the secondary semantic value, which arises from the syntagmatic reorganization of the text and from juxtaposition with the primary values; and thirdly, values that arise from the introduction into the message of extra-textual associations, ranging from the most general to the extremely personal.

It must be obvious that the mechanism we have been describing serves also to describe the processes which lie at the heart of poetic creation.

But the poetic principle is one thing and actual poetic texts another. To identify the latter with 'I–I' messages would be an oversimplification. An actual poetic text is transmitted through two channels simultaneously (exceptions are: experimental texts, glossolalia, children's nonsense songs, *zaum*', as well as texts in languages which the audience do not understand). A poetic text oscillates between the meanings transmitted along the 'I–s/he' channel and those formed in the process of autocommunication. And the text is perceived as 'verse' or 'prose' according to its proximity to either end of the axis or to the type of transmission.

Of course, a text's orientation towards a primary linguistic message or towards the complex reconstruction of meanings and build-up of information does not by itself signify that it will function as poetry or prose; it depends also on how it relates to the cultural models of these concepts at any given period.

Our conclusion is that human communication can be constructed along two models. In the first instance we are dealing with already given information which is transmitted from one person to another with a code which remains constant for the duration of the act of communication. In the second instance we are dealing with an increase in information, its transformation, reformulation and with the introduction not of new messages but of new codes, and in this case the addresser and addressee are contained in the same person. In the process of this autocommunication the actual person is reformed and this process is connected with a very wide range of cultural functions, ranging from the sense of individual existence which in some types of culture is essential, to self-discovery and auto-psychotherapy.

Different kinds of formal structures can function as such codes. The more their organization is a-semantic the better they fulfil their role. Structures of this kind include spatial objects such as patterns or architectural ensembles which are meant to be looked at, or temporal ones such as music.

The question of verbal texts is more complicated. Since the autocommunicative function may be masked and seem like other kinds of communication (for example, a prayer may be thought of as a message to an external powerful force rather than as a message to oneself; a second reading of a familiar text may be thought of as communication with the author, etc.) the addressee who receives a verbal text has to decide whether the text is code or message. This will depend largely on the addressee's inclination since one and the same text may play the role of text and code, or by oscillating between these poles, of both at the same time.

We must distinguish two aspects to this question: the features of the text which allow it to be interpreted as a code, and the way the text functions so that it is correctly used.

The signal that we have to treat a text not as an ordinary message but as a code model are rhythmical series, repetitions, supplementary text-organizations, all of which are quite superfluous from the point of view of 'I–s/he' communication. Rhythm is not a structural level in natural languages. Note that while the poetic functions of phonology, grammar and syntax have analogies in the corresponding non-literary levels of the text, there is no such analogy for metrics.

Rhythmical-metrical systems take their origin not in the 'I–s/he' system but in that of the 'I–I' system. The widely used principle of repetition on the phonological and other levels of natural language is an invasion by autocommunication into a language sphere that is alien to it.

Functionally speaking, a text is used as code and not message when it does not add to the information we already have, but when it transforms the self-understanding of the person who has engendered the text and when it transfers already existing messages into a new system of meanings. If reader N receives the message that a certain woman called Anna Karenina has as a result of an unhappy love affair thrown herself under a train, and if that reader instead of adding this information to what she already has in her memory, comes to the conclusion: 'Anna Karenina is me' and starts changing her understanding of herself, her relationships with people and perhaps even her behaviour, then obviously she is using the novel not as a message like any other, but as a kind of code in her own process of self-communication.

Pushkin's Tatyana read novels in just such a way:

X

1. Seeing herself as a creation –
2. Clarissa, Julie, or Delphine –
3. by writers of her admiration,
4. Tatyana, lonely heroine,
5. roamed the still forest like a ranger,

6. sought in her book, that text of danger,
7. and found her dreams, her secret fire,
8. the full fruit of her heart's desire;
9. she sighed, and in a trance co-opted
10. another's joy, another's breast,
11. whispered by heart a note addressed
12. to the hero that she'd adopted.
13. But ours, whatever he might be,
14. ours was no Grandison – not he.[15]

The text of the novel Tatyana was reading turns into a model for reinterpreting reality. Tatyana has no doubt that Onegin was a romantic character; the only thing she did not know was which role to give him:

> *Kto ty, moi angel li khranitel',*
> *Ili kovarnyi iskusitel'?*

> . . . But who are you:
> the guardian angel of tradition,
> or some vile agent of perdition
> sent to seduce?[16]

It is very characteristic that Tatyana's letter to Onegin falls into two parts: in the frame (the first two and the last verse) where Tatyana writes like a lovesick young lady to a neighbouring landowner, she naturally addresses him by the formal '*vy*', but in the central part where she is modelling both herself and him on romantic schemes she uses the intimate '*ty*'. Since, as Pushkin warns us, the original of the letter was written in French which would use '*vous*' in both these cases, the form of address in the central part of the letter is just a sign of the bookish, unreal, code-like nature of this text.

It is interesting that the Romantic Lensky also explains people (including himself) to himself by identifying them with texts. Pushkin here demonstratively uses the same clichés: *spasitel'/khranitel'* [saviour/guardian] – *rasvratitel'/iskusitel'* [debaucher/tempter]:

> *on myslit: 'budu ei spasitel'.*
> *Ne poterplyu, chtob razvratitel'*

> [he murmurs: 'Olga's mine for saving;
> I'll stop that tempter from depraving.'][17]

In all these instances the texts are obviously functioning not as messages in a particular language (neither for Pushkin, nor for Tatyana and

Lensky), but as codes which concentrate information about the actual type of language.

Our examples are taken from literature, but it would be wrong to conclude that poetry is 'I–I' communication in its purest form. The same principle can be seen in a more consistent form, not in art, but in moralistic and religious texts such as parables, in myths and in proverbs. Repetitions found their way into proverbs at a time when they were not yet perceived aesthetically but had a much more important mnemonic or moralizing function.

The repetition of certain architectural elements in the interior of a church makes one perceive the structure not as something bound up with the technical demands of construction, but, let us say, as a model of the universe or of the human personality. Just because the interior of a church is a code and not merely a text, we perceive it not only aesthetically (only a text, not the rules for its construction, can be perceived aesthetically), but also in a religious, philosophical, theological, or other non-artistic way.

Art is born not from the 'I–s/he' system or the 'I–I' system. It uses both systems and oscillates in the field of structural tension between them. The aesthetic effect arises when the code is taken for the message and the message as a code, i.e. when a text is switched from one system of communication to another while the audience keeps awareness of both.

The nature of artistic texts as a phenomenon that oscillates between two types of communication does not preclude the fact that certain genres are angled so as to be perceived more or less like messages or codes. A lyric poem and an essay are obviously not to be correlated with one or other system of communication in the same way. But besides the genre orientation, at given moments, because of historical, social or other factors of the period, a literature as a whole (and more broadly speaking, art as a whole) may be characterized by its orientation towards autocommunication. A good working criterion for diagnosing the general orientation of literature towards the message is a negative attitude towards the standard text. But literature which is oriented towards autocommunication will not only not avoid standard texts, but will manifest a tendency to turn texts into standard ones and to identify what is 'elevated', 'good' and 'true' with what is 'stable', 'eternal', i.e. with the set standard.

Yet to distance oneself from one pole (and even to carry on conscious polemics with it) does not mean leaving its structural influence. However much a work of literature imitates a newspaper report it preserves a typical feature of the autocommunicative text – its quality of being re-readable many times. We more naturally re-read *War and Peace* than the historical sources that Tolstoy used. At the same time, however much a verbal artistic text strives, for reasons of polemic or experimentation, to cease to be a message, it never can, as the entire history of art proves.

Poetic texts are evidently formed from a peculiar 'swing' of structures: texts created in the 'I–s/he' system function as autocommunication, and vice versa; texts become codes and codes messages. By following the laws of autocommunication – the division of the text into rhythmic segments, the reduction of words to indices, the weakening of the semantic connections and the emphasis on syntagmatic ones – the poetic text is in conflict with the laws of natural language. And yet we perceive it as a text in a natural language, otherwise it could not exist or fulfil its communicative function. But on the other hand, if the view that poetry is merely message in a natural language gets the upper hand we lose a sense of its specificity. The high modelling capacity of poetry is associated with its transformation from message to code. The poetic text is a kind of pendulum that oscillates between the 'I–s/he' system and the 'I–I' system. Rhythm is raised to the level of meaning, and meanings are formed in rhythm.

The laws of construction of the artistic text are very largely the laws of the construction of culture as a whole. Hence culture itself can be treated both as the sum of the messages circulated by various addressers (for each of them the addressee is 'another', 's/he'), and as one message transmitted by the collective 'I' of humanity to itself. From this point of view human culture is a vast example of autocommunication.

*   *   *

Simultaneous transmission along two communication channels is not only a property of artistic texts, it is also a feature of culture if we take culture as a single message. We can therefore divide cultures into those where the message transmitted along the general linguistic 'I–s/he' channel is predominant, and those oriented towards autocommunication.

Since 'message 1' may consist of broad layers of information which in fact make up the specificity of the personality, the restructuring of these layers will result in the alteration of the structure of the personality. We should remember that if the 'I–s/he' schema implies the *transmission* of information with no change of volume, the 'I–I' schema is geared towards *increasing* the information ('message 2' does not destroy 'message 1').

Modern European culture is consciously oriented towards 'I–s/he' communication. The cultural consumer is in the position of an ideal addressee, he or she receives information from all sides. Peter the Great formulated this position very clearly when he said: 'I am a pupil and demand to be taught.' *The True Mirror of Youth* advises young people to see education as the *acquisition* of knowledge, 'desirous of learning from everyone, and not being haughty'.[18] We must emphasize that we are talking of an orientation, since on the level of textual reality, every culture consists of both kinds of communication. Besides which, this marked feature is not specific to modern culture – it can be found in different forms at different periods. We had to pick out European culture of the eighteenth and nineteenth centuries because this culture has conditioned our normal scientific ideas and especially our identification of the act of information with acquisition and exchange. Yet by no means all cases known to the history of culture can be explained from these positions.

Consider the paradoxical situation we find ourselves in with regard to the study of folklore. We know that folklore has provided the firmest evidence for structural parallels with natural languages and that linguistic methods have been applied to folklore with the greatest success. In fact the researcher will find in this field a defined number of elements in the system and comparatively easy rules for their combination. But here we must point out also a profound difference: language provides a formal system of expression, but the field of content remains, from the point of view of language as such, extremely free. Folklore, and especially such forms of it as the magic tale, make both spheres extremely automatized. But this is a paradox. If the text were in fact constructed in this way it would be wholly redundant. And the same could be said of other forms of art oriented on canonic forms, on the fulfilment and not the violation of norms and rules.

The answer evidently lies in the fact that if texts of this type at the moment of their inception had a certain semantic value (the semantics of the magic tale evidently was a function of its relationship to ritual), these values were subsequently lost and the texts began to acquire features of purely syntagmatic organizations. While on the level of natural language they obviously have semantic value, on the level of culture, they tend towards pure syntagmatics, i.e. from being texts they become 'codes 2'. When Lévi-Strauss spoke of the musical nature of myth he had in mind this tendency of myths to become purely syntagmatic, a-semantic texts, not records of particular events, but schemas for organizing messages.

For culture to exist as a mechanism organizing the collective personality with a common memory and a collective consciousness, there must be present a pair of semiotic systems with the consequent possibility of text translation.

The 'I–s/he' and 'I–I' communicative systems form just such a pair (by the way we should mention that a seemingly universal law for human cultures is that one of the members of any culture-forming semiotic pair must be natural language, or include natural language).

Actual cultures, like artistic texts, are constructed on the principle of pendulum-like swings between these systems. But there will be a predominant tendency for the culture to be oriented either towards autocommunication or towards the acquisition of truth from without in the form of messages. This tendency will show up particularly clearly in the mythologized image which each culture creates as its own ideal self-portrait. This self-model has an influence on the culture's texts but cannot be identified with them, being sometimes a generalization of structural principles concealed behind the textual contradictions, and sometimes the direct opposite of them. (In the field of culture typology there is the known fact of grammars which are in principle inapplicable to the texts in the language they are claiming to describe.)

Cultures, oriented to the message, are more mobile and dynamic. They have a tendency to increase the number of texts *ad infinitum* and they encourage a rapid increase in knowledge. European culture of the nineteenth century is a classic example of this. The reverse side of this type of culture is the sharp division of society into transmitters and receivers, the rise of a psychological tendency to acquire truth in the form of pre-packaged information about other people's mental efforts, an increase in the social passivity of those who find themselves in the position of receivers of information. Obviously a reader of a modern European novel is more passive than a hearer of a fairy tale who has to transform the standard story s/he is acquiring into texts of his/her own consciousness; a theatre-goer is more passive than a participant in a carnival. The trend towards mental consumerism is a dangerous aspect of the culture which is lopsidedly oriented towards the acquisition of information from outside.

Cultures oriented towards autocommunication are capable of great activity, but are often much less dynamic than human society requires.

Historical experience has shown that the most viable cultures are those systems where the struggle between these structures has not resulted in an all-out victory for one of them.

But we are still a long way from being able to make any well-grounded prognosis of the optimal structures of culture. Until that time we must understand and describe their mechanism, at least in its most typical manifestations.

3

Rhetoric as a mechanism for meaning-generation

Human consciousness is heterogeneous. A minimal thinking apparatus must include at least two differently constructed systems to exchange the information they each have worked out. Studies carried out on the specific functioning of the large hemispheres of the human brain have revealed a profound analogy between it and the organization of culture as a collective intellect. In both cases we find there are at least two essentially different ways of reflecting the world and working out new information, and that in both cases there are complex mechanisms for exchanging texts between these systems. In both cases we observe a generally analogous structure: within one consciousness there are as it were two consciousnesses. The one operates as a discrete system of coding and forms texts which come together like linear chains of linked segments. In this system the basic bearer of meaning is the segment (= the sign), while the chain of segments (= the text) is secondary, its meaning being derived from the meaning of the signs. In the second system the text is primary, being the bearer of the basic meaning. This text is not discrete but continuous. Its meaning is organized neither in a linear nor in a temporal sequence, but is 'washed over' the n-dimension semantic space of the given text (the canvas of a picture, the space of a stage, of a screen, a ritual, of social behaviour or of a dream). In texts of this type the text is the bearer of the meaning. We may have difficulty in isolating its component signs, and this task smacks of artificiality.

Thus both the individual, and the collective consciousness, contain two types of text-generator: one is founded on discreteness, the other is continuous. In spite of the fact that each of these mechanisms has a self-contained structure, there is a constant exchange of texts and messages between them. This exchange takes the form of a semantic translation. But an accurate translation presupposes that mutually equivalent relationships have already been established between the units of the two

36

systems, as a result of which one system can be represented in the other. This is what makes it possible for the text of one language to be adequately expressed in another one. However, when we are dealing with discrete and non-discrete texts, translation is in principle impossible. The equivalent to the discrete and precisely demarcated semantic unit of one text is, in the other, a kind of semantic blur with indistinct boundaries and gradual shadings into other meanings. If in these other texts we do find segmentation of a sort, it is not comparable with the type of discrete boundaries of the first ones. Given these factors, we are faced with a situation where translation is impossible; yet it is precisely in these situations that efforts to translate are most determined and the results most valuable. For the results are not precise translations, but approximate equivalences determined by the cultural-psychological and semiotic context common to both systems. This kind of 'illegitimate', imprecise, but approximate translation is one of the most important features of any creative thinking. For these 'illegitimate' associations provoke new semantic connections and give rise to texts that are in principle new ones.

A pair of mutually non-juxtaposable signifying elements, between which, thanks to the context they share, a relationship of adequacy is established, form a semantic trope. Tropes are not, therefore, external ornaments, something applied to a thought from the outside – they constitute the essence of creative thinking, and their function extends beyond art. They are inherent in all creativity. For example, all attempts to create visual analogues for abstract ideas, to depict continuous processes in discrete formulae with the help of broken lines [*ottochie*], to construct spatial physical models of elementary particles, and so on, are rhetorical figures (tropes). And just as in poetry, so in science, an 'illegitimate' juxtaposition often provokes the formulation of a new law.

Over the centuries, the theory of tropes has accumulated an extensive literature on defining the main types: metaphors, metonymies and synecdoches. This literature is still growing. But whatever attempts are made to give tropes a logical definition, it is obvious that one term of the trope has a verbal aspect and the other a visual one, however masked the latter aspect may be. Even in logical models of metaphor drawn up for teaching demonstrations, a non-discrete image (visual or acoustic) is presupposed as the mediating link between the two discrete verbal components. However, the deeper the abyss of untranslatability between two languages, the more acute is the need for a common metalanguage to bridge the gap between them by creating equivalences. So the hypertrophy of metastructural formulae found in 'the rhetoric of figures' was the result of such linguistic incompatibility. The dogmatism on the level of metadescription compensated for an inevitable indeterminacy on the level of the tropic text. Such compensation is particularly significant since rhetorical texts are distinguished from general language texts by one special feature: namely, while language texts are produced by the speaker of that language spontaneously, the explicit rules being apparent only to the researcher who constructs logical models of unconscious processes, in rhetoric the process of producing texts is 'learned' and deliberate; the rules are actively included in the actual text, not only at the metalevel but also on the level of the immediate text structure. Herein lies the specificity of tropes: for they are in part both irrational (because they make elements that are known to be non-equivalent and totally disparate, equivalent), and hyper-rational (because they include a conscious construct directly into the rhetorical figure). We see this most clearly when a metaphor is not verbal but, for instance, cinematic.

A striking montage of two visual images would, supposedly, avoid the confrontation of discrete with non-discrete, or any other situation of untranslatability. But on closer inspection we shall see that the metastructure of the cinematic metaphor is built up by relating the shot to natural language discourse, and so the mechanism of discreteness is brought right into the structure of the cinema-metaphor. What is more, while one term of the cinema-metaphor is as a rule predicted in the flow of the verbal text (and is consciously related to it), the other term more often than not is independent of it. For example, the film *The Anthill* by the Hungarian director Zoltan Fabry centres on an exceptionally complex and multi-layered drama taking place in a Hungarian convent at the beginning of this century. The events are in complex metaphorical relationships with the close-up shots of the details of the Baroque façade of the church. Among these architectural details is a relief of a sower. This term of the metaphor can be understood by a direct translation into the verbal text of the Gospel parable of the Sower (Matthew 13.2–3; Luke 8.5–11; Mark 4.1–2). The other term of the metaphor, the events that take place, are not verbally narrated but are interpreted by reference to the first term (and to others like it).

The 'rhetoric of figures' belongs to the level of secondary modelling and metamodels; and this distinguishes it from the level of primary signs and symbols. For example, an aggressive gesture by an animal, which serves as a substitute for an actual aggressive act, is an element of symbolic behaviour; in this case the symbol is used in its primary sense. In another example, a symbolic sexual gesture is used in the animal group to indicate submission to the dominant partner and so loses its sexual content; in this instance we can talk of the gesture's metaphorical value and of gestural rhetoric. The latter example shows that the opposition 'discrete–continuous' is merely one possible form, an extreme one, of producing tropes of semantic untranslatability. Other juxtapositions between less distant semantic spheres are possible, and these create contrasts which we might term 'rhetoricogeneous'.

Rhetorical Figures (tropes)   In traditional rhetoric, 'devices for changing the basic meaning of a word are termed tropes' (Tomashevsky). In the neo-rhetoric of recent decades there have been numerous attempts to define the significance of tropes in general, and of particular kinds of them (metaphor, metonymy, synecdoche, irony), in the light of linguistic and semiotic ideas. Roman Jakobson started the trend.[19] Jakobson distinguished two basic types of trope: metaphor and metonymy, and associated them with the two axes of language: the paradigmatic and the syntactic. According to Jakobson a metaphor is a substitution of a concept along the paradigmatic axis, involving: a selection .from the paradigmatic series, a substitution *in absentia*, and the establishment of a semantic link by similarity. A metonymy is disposed along the syntactic axis and is not a selection, but a combination *in praesentia* involving the establishment of a connection by contiguity. As regards the cultural function of rhetorical figures, Jakobson, on the one hand, broadens it, seeing there the basis for meaning-formation in any semiotic system. So he applies the terms 'metaphor' and 'metonymy' to cinema, painting, psychoanalysis, and so on. On the other hand, he narrows it relegating metaphor to the domain of semiotic structures = poetry, and metonymy to the sphere of the text = prose. 'Thus for poetry, metaphor, and for prose, metonymy, is the line of least resistance'.[20] So the question of the demarcation between poetry and prose was put on an objective basis, has ceased to be merely a question of literary categories, and has become a semiotic universal. Jakobson's conception has been developed and clarified in numerous works. Umberto Eco, for instance, studying the linguistic bases of rhetoric, considers metonymy to be the primary figure. At its basis he sees the presence of chains of associative contiguities: 1. in the structure of the code; 2. in the structure of the context; 3. in the structure of the referent. The connection between linguistic codes and cultural ones make it possible to construct metaphoric figures on the basis of metonymy. Tzvetan Todorov thinks along the same lines: he connects metaphor with a doubling of synecdoche. Incidentally, his position is quite close to that of the groupe μ (the Liège group). In 1970 the groupe μ (J. Dubois, F. Edeline, J.-M. Klinkenberg, P. Minguet) worked out a detailed taxometric classification of tropes based on the analysis of semes and semantic-lexical components. They treat synecdoche as the primary figure. Metaphor and metonymy are derivative figures, resulting from the elaboration of the basic types of synecdoche. Their classification has been criticized by Nicholas Ruwet from the point of view of linguistics, and by P. Schofer and D. Rice from the literary point of view.[21] Ruwet puts forward a convincing argument:

> In the question of rhetoric in general, and of tropes in particular, the main task of a predictive theory is to attempt to answer the question: in what

circumstances does the given linguistic expression acquire a figurative sense.[22]

A summary definition of a trope arrived at in neo-rhetoric goes like this:

> A trope is a semantic transposition from a sign *in praesentia* to a sign *in absentia*, 1) based on the perception of a connection between one or more semantic features of the signified; 2) marked by the semantic incompatibility of the micro- and macro-contexts; 3) conditioned by a referential connection by similarity, or causality, or inclusiveness, or opposition.[23]

Classical rhetoric elaborated an extended classification of figures. The term 'figure' (σχῆμα) was first used by Anaximenes of Lampsacus (4th century BC). The topic was thoroughly studied by Aristotle, whose pupils (especially Demetrius of Phaleron) introduced the distinction between 'figures of speech' and 'figures of thought'. Later, the system of figures was reworked and elaborated by classical and medieval authors, by writers of the age of Classicism. Neo-rhetoric operates basically with three concepts: metaphor – the semantic substitution of a 'seme' according to the principle of similarity or likeness; metonymy – a substitution according to the principle of contiguity, association, causality (different authors emphasize different types of connection); synecdoche, which some authors regard as the primary figure and others as a particular example of metonymy – a substitution on the basis of participation, inclusiveness, partiality or the substitution of plurality by singleness. Schofer and Rice have attempted to re-include irony in the number of figures.

The Typological and Functional Nature of Figures   Study of the logical foundations of trope-classification should not overshadow the question of their typological and functional teleology; the question, 'what are tropes?' does not exclude questions such as, 'how do they function in the text?' and 'what is the point of them in the semantic mechanism of the text?' Of the neo-rhetoricians, Jakobson and Eco come closest to considering these questions, the former by pointing out the connection between this problem and the poetry/prose opposition, and the latter by introducing his notion of associative chains into the discussion.

There are cultural epochs, we should remember, which are wholly or largely oriented towards tropes and in which tropes are the obligatory markers of all artistic discourse, and indeed even of all discourse. On the other hand, there are whole epochs when the *rejection* of rhetorical figures is artistically significant, and when, for speech to be perceived as *artistic*, it has to reproduce the norms of *non-artistic* speech. Examples of epochs oriented towards tropes are the mytho-poetic period, the Middle Ages, the Baroque Age, Romanticism, symbolism and the avant-garde. If we could find the semantic principles common to all these different text-forming structures we might be able to establish a typology of tropes. In all the periods mentioned above, the substitution of some semantic units by others is widely practised. But we must emphasize that in every instance the substitute and what it replaces are not equivalent according to any essential semantic or cultural parameters, but on the contrary are incommensurable. Substitution is realized on the principle of collage, whereby the painted details of a picture are juxtaposed with natural objects which are glued on to it (the glued-on detail is, in relation to a painted one next to it, a metonymy, and, in relation to the potential painted detail for which it is the substitute, is a metaphor). Painted and glued-on objects belong to different and incompatible domains by virtue of features of: reality/illusion, two-dimensionality/three-dimensionality, semiotic value/absence of semiotic value, and so on. There are numerous traditional cultural contexts where their juxtaposition within the confines of one text would be absolutely forbidden. And precisely because of that, when they are combined, the result is that exceptionally strong semantic effect which is the quality of tropes. The effect of a trope does not derive from the presence of a common 'seme' (the greater the number of common 'semes', the less effective is the trope, while a tautological identity precludes any trope), but from the dispersal of semes in incompatible semantic spaces and from the degree of semantic distance between semes which are incompatible. There are various factors which determine the semantic distance between substitute and substituted. Such factors may be relationships of single-/multi-dimensionality, discreteness/continuousness, materiality/non-materiality, earthly/heavenly, and so on. Both on the level of the referent, and as regards the juxtaposition of the semantic spaces involved, the boundaries of substitute and substituted are so incommensurable that the task of establishing a correspondence between them verges on the irrational. It becomes a matter of conventions, approximations, suppositions, a work involving creating not a simple semantic shift, but a semantic situation that is in principle new and paradoxical. Not surprisingly, cultures which tend towards tropes are those which base their picture of the world on the principle of antinomy and irrational contradiction.

All this may be obvious with regard to metaphor, but not with regard to metonymy where, since the substitution is made from within a single semiotic series, both substitute and substituted would supposedly be homogeneous. But in fact, metaphor and metonymy are in this respect iso-functional: their purpose is not to employ a particular semantic shift to express what could be expressed without it, but to express a content, transmit information, which could not be transmitted any other way. In both cases (metaphor and metonymy) there is no mutually equivalent correspondence between the direct and the figurative meanings, all that one can establish is an approximate equivalence. When, because of constant usage or for some other reason, a mutually equivalent correspondence is established instead of a semantic oscillation, then the trope becomes a worn-out one and is classed as a rhetorical figure merely on account of its origins, though it still functions as a phrase in its fixed, dictionary meaning. This then must be the response to Ruwet's point. Let us take some examples. If an icon, understood in the semiotic significance it acquired in Byzantium and the whole Eastern Church, is a metaphor, a holy relic is a metonymy. A relic is part of the saint's body, or an object which was in direct contact with him. In this sense the material, embodied, bodily aspect of the saint is replaced by a bodily part of him or by a material object connected with him. An icon, on the other hand, as Origen first remarked and Gregory of Nyssa and the Pseudo-Dionysius confirmed, is a material and expressed sign of the non-material and inexpressible divine essence. What is painted on an icon is a depiction in the primary and direct sense. Clement of Alexandria likened the visible directly to the verbal: writing of how Christ incarnate took on an 'unprepossessing' form, without physical beauty, he remarked: 'For we must always understand not the words, but what they mean'.[24] So between metaphoric expression and metaphoric content complex semantic relationships of non-equivalence and polysemy are established, which preclude the rational operation of mutual substitution in either direction. We recognize an icon's rhetorical character particularly by the fact that the first term of this metaphor can only be a depiction which has been painted in accordance with the fixed canon of icon-painting, which determines the rhetoric of the composition, colour spectrum and other artistic features. Moreover, the icon is a metaphor which arises from the conjunction of two differently directed energies: the energy of the divine Logos which seeks to reveal itself to humanity (this is why the creation of an icon is an active act on the part of the icon; an icon is a worthy artist, and is not just painted by one), and the energy of humanity which is directed upwards in search of higher knowledge; so an icon is part of a ritualistic-rhetorical context which involves not only the process whereby the icon-painter creates the icon, but the entire spiritual make-up of the icon-painter's life, presupposing a strict and righteous life on his part, prayer, fasting and spiritual exaltation. It is interesting that when Gogol set demands like these for artists and the writers (the second version of 'The Portrait', his article 'The Historical Painter Ivanov' in the second part of *Selected Passages from Correspondence with Friends*) it seemed to him that all his creative work had taken on the character of a grandiose metaphor.

Against the background of this approach to the icon, the relic might seem to be a simple semantic phenomenon. But this is a superficial view of things. The material relic, of course, relates to the body of the saint on one level. But the very phrase 'body of a saint' conceals within it a metaphor of the incarnation and a complex and irrational relationship between expression and content.

The metaphorism of the Age of the Baroque is founded on quite different ideological and cultural premises. But here too we find that tropes (and the boundaries which separate one kind of trope from another are, in Baroque texts, exceptionally fluid) are not an external substitution of some elements in the expression level by others, but a means of forming a special ordering of consciousness. Once more we find a typical conjunction of mutually untranslatable spheres of verbal and iconic, discrete and non-discrete signs. Lope de Vega, for instance, called Marino 'a great painter for the ears', and Rubens 'a great poet for the eyes' [*Marino, grand pintor de los oidos, y Rubens, grand poeta de los ojos*]. Tezauro called architecture 'metaphor in stone'. In 'Aristotle's Spyglass' [*Il Cannochiale Aristotelico*] Tezauro elaborated his theory of Metaphor as the universal principle of the human and of the divine consciousness. It is based on wit – thinking that brings together the dissimilar and unites what is not unitable. The metaphoric consciousness is equated with the creative consciousness, and even the act of divine creation is thought of by Tezauro as a supreme Witticism which, through metaphor, analogies and conceits, creates the world. Tezauro objects to those who regard rhetorical figures as external ornament; for him they are rather the very foundation of the mechanism of thought, of that supreme Genius which gives life both to mankind and to the universe.

Turning to the epoch of Romanticism, we find a similar picture: although metaphor and metonymy have a tendency to merge,[25] the general orientation towards tropes as the basis of style-formation is quite obvious. On the one hand, the idea of organic synthesis, of the fusion of aspects of life which are irrevocably set apart, and on the other hand, the idea that the essence of life cannot be expressed by any one language (natural language or any language of art taken in isolation), stimulated the metaphoric and metonymic recoding of signs of different semiotic systems. Wackenroder in *Herzensergiessungen eines kunstliebenden Klosterbruders* [*Outpourings from the Heart of an Art-Loving Monk*] identifies the language of symbols, emblems and metaphors with art as such:

The language of Art is quite different from the language of Nature; but Art has the capacity by unknown and obscure ways profoundly to affect the heart of man. It expresses itself through human images and speaks as it were in hieroglyphs, which we understand only through their outer features. But this language is so touching and so marvellously blends the spiritual and suprasensual with external depictions that, in its turn, it moves our whole being.[26]

Finally, the principle of juxtaposition lies at the basis of various branches of the avant-garde. The figures formed in this way can as a rule be read as metaphors or as metonymies. What is important is that the meaning-generating principle of the text as a whole lies in the juxtaposition of segments that are in principle not juxtaposable. Their mutual recoding creates a language capable of many readings, a fact which opens up unexpected reserves of meaning.

A trope, therefore, is not an embellishment merely on the level of expression, a decoration on an invariant content, but is a mechanism for constructing a content which could not be constructed by one language alone. A trope is a figure born at the point of contact between two languages, and its structure is therefore identical to that of the creative consciousness itself. This is why all logical definitions of rhetorical figures and the models associated with them, which ignore their bilingual nature, are a part of the metalanguage of theoretical description, but can never be generative mechanisms for producing tropes. Moreover, if we ignore the fact that the trope is a mechanism for producing semantic diversity, a mechanism which brings into the semiotic structure of culture a necessary degree of indeterminacy, we shall never arrive at an adequate description of this phenomenon.

The function of the trope as a mechanism of semantic indeterminacy explains why it appears openly on the surface of culture in systems which hold that truth is complex, polysemic or inexpressible. Yet 'rhetoricism' does not belong exclusively to any cultural epochs: like the opposition 'poetry/prose', the opposition 'rhetoricism/anti-rhetoricism' is one of the universals of human culture. The terms of this opposition are mutually connected, and the semiotic activity of one of them presupposes the actualization of the other. In a culture where the tradition of rhetoric has accumulated, becoming part of the inertia of reader-expectation, the trope becomes part of the neutral store of the language and ceases to be perceived as a rhetorically active unit. Against such a background the 'anti-rhetorical' text, consisting of elements of direct, non-figurative semantics, comes to be perceived as a *meta-trope*, a rhetorical figure which has undergone a secondary simplification, with the second language being reduced to zero. This 'minus-rhetoric', which is subjectively perceived as resembling reality and simplicity, is a mirror-image of rhetoric and includes its aesthetic opponent in its own cultural-semiotic code. For instance, the artlessness of a neo-realist film in fact contains a latent rhetoric, activated against the background of the worn-out rhetoric of pretentious pseudo-historical epics and high society comedies, a rhetoric which has ceased to 'work'. In its turn the cinematographic baroque of Fellini's films rehabilitates rhetoric as the basis for constructing meanings of great complexity.

Meta-rhetoric and the Typology of Cultures Metaphor and metonymy are ways of thinking analogously. In this respect they are organically connected with creative consciousness as such. So, to repeat, it would be a mistake to contrast rhetorical thinking with scientific thinking on the grounds that rhetorical thinking is specifically artistic. Rhetoric is just as much part of the scientific consciousness as it is of the artistic one. We can distinguish two spheres in the area of scientific consciousness. The first one is the rhetorical sphere of conjunctions, analogies and modelling. From this domain emerge new ideas, new postulates and hypotheses which previously were thought to be absurd. The second sphere is that of logic. It is concerned with testing the new ideas, drawing conclusions from them, removing internal contradictions in proofs and reasoning. The first, 'Faustian', sphere of scientific thinking is an essential component in research and, since it belongs to science, can be scientifically described. But the apparatus for such a description must itself be specially constructed, forming a language of meta-rhetoric. For example, we could regard as meta-metaphors all instances of isomorphism, homomorphism and homeomorphism (including epio-, endo-, mono- and automorphism). These meta-metaphors taken together serve as an apparatus for describing a wide range of analogies and equivalences, making it possible to co-join and even to an extent to identify phenomena and objects which seem far apart. An example of a meta-metonymy is Cantor's theory, according to which if any set contains in itself aleph number of dots (i.e. is an infinite set), then any part of this set will contains the same number aleph of dots and in this sense any of its parts will be equal to the whole. Operations such as transfinite induction may be regarded as meta-metonymies. Creative thinking both in science and in art is based on analogy and follows the principle of co-joining objects and concepts which could not be brought together without a rhetorical situation. It follows that the creation of meta-rhetoric is a task facing the whole of science, and meta-rhetoric could be defined as the theory of creative thinking.

Rhetorical texts, then, are always a realization of a certain rhetorical situation which is posited by types of analogies and by the parameters which establish them. The parameters, which establish analogies and equivalences within a group of texts or communicative situations, are determined by the type of culture. Similarity or dissimilarity, equivalence and non-equivalence, commensurability and incommensurability, the perception of any two objects as not juxtaposable or as identical – all this depends on the type of cultural context. One and the same text may be perceived as 'correct' or 'incorrect' (it cannot be perceived as a non-text), 'correct and trivial' or 'correct, but unexpected, violating norms, yet remaining within the bounds of comprehensibility', and so on: it depends on whether we classify it as an artistic or a non-artistic text, and what rules we ascribe to the one or the other, i.e. it depends on the cultural context in which we place it. For instance, if texts of esoteric cultures are taken out of their general context and isolated from the special codes of that culture (which are as a rule available only to the initiate), they cease to be comprehensible or are understood merely from the point of view of their external semantics, while the hidden meanings are kept to a narrow circle of the initiate. Skaldic texts, Sufi texts, Masonic texts and many others are constructed in this way. The question whether a text is understood in a direct or in a figurative (rhetorical) sense also depends on how we apply more general cultural codes to it. Since a culture's own orientation, expressed in the way it regards itself, is an important factor, a text may, in the system of self-descriptions which form the meta-cultural level, appear semantically 'normal' from one point of view and 'anomalous', semantically dislocated, from another. The relationship of the text to the different meta-cultural structures sets up a semantic game, which is a condition for the rhetorical organization of the text. For example, a secondary semantic encipherment of a semantically simple text may result in a secret esoteric language, but is not a trope and does not relate to the sphere of rhetoric. On the other hand, at a time when verbal games intensified, when the metaphorism of the Baroque had become a tradition and a predictable norm not only of the literary language, but also of the affected speech of society salons and of the *précieux*, discourse that was purged of secondary meanings and reduced to direct and precise semantics, came to have literary significance.

In this situation the most active rhetorical figures came to be rejections of rhetorical figures. The text, liberated from metaphors and metonymies, started a game, on the one hand with the reader's expectations (i.e. with the cultural norm of the Baroque period), and on the other with what was the new, as yet unestablished norm of Classicism. The Baroque metaphor was in this context perceived as a sign of triviality and did not serve any rhetorical function, while the absence of metaphor, now playing an active role, turned out to be aesthetically significant.

Just as in science, the tendency, which is connected with 'scientific rhetoric' and 'scientific wit', to create all-embracing hypotheses which establish correspondences between what seem to be distant fields of experience, alternates with positivistic stress on the expansion of empirical fields of knowledge, so in art 'rhetorical modelling' periodically alternates with empirical modelling. The aesthetics of realism, for instance, at its early stage was characterized mostly by a negative feature of anti-romanticism and was perceived against a projection of romantic norms, so creating a 'rhetoric of the rejection of rhetoric' – rhetoric of a second level. Subsequently, however, as positivistic tendencies developed in science realism acquired its independent structure, which in its turn, formed the semiotic background to the neo-romanticism and avant-garde trends of the twentieth century.

The Rhetoric of the Text   Once we turn to the text, i.e. to an isolated, self-contained semiotic formation, with its integral indivisible meaning and its integral indivisible function, then the relationship of its elements to the problem of rhetoric radically alters. If the whole text is encoded in the culture-system as a rhetorical one, then any of its elements will become rhetorical, irrespective of whether that element, taken in isolation, has a direct or a figurative sense. For example, since any artistic text features in our consciousness *a priori* as rhetorically organized, any title of a work of literature will function in our consciousness as a trope or a minus-trope, i.e. as rhetorically marked. Since the textual nature of the utterance forces one to interpret it in this way, the elements of the text, which signal to us that it is indeed a text we have before our eyes, take on a special rhetorical load. For instance, the categories 'beginning' and 'end' are highly marked rhetorically and the significance of them greatly increases. The diversity of the structural connections within a text makes the individual units which enter it much less independent, and raises the coefficient of the text's bondedness. The text aims to become one 'great word' with one single meaning. This secondary 'word' is always, when we are speaking of literary texts, a trope: in relation to ordinary non-literary speech, the literary text as it were switches over into a semiotic space with a greater number of dimensions. To grasp what we are talking about let us imagine a transformation of the following type: scenario (or verbal literary narrative) → film, or libretto → opera. With this type of transformation a text with a certain quantity of semantic space coordinates turns into a text with a greatly increased dimensionality in its semiotic space. An analogous procedure occurs also when a verbal (non-literary) text is turned into a literary one. Therefore there is no simple relationship either between the elements or the integral wholes of artistic and non-artistic texts, and consequently there cannot be a two-way equivalent translation. All that is possible are conventional equivalences and various types of analogy. And this precisely is the essence of rhetorical relationships. But in cultures oriented towards a rhetorical organization, each step in the increasing hierarchy of semiotic organization produces an increase in the dimensions of space of the semantic structure. In early Russian and Byzantine culture, for instance, the hierarchy: world of everyday life and non-literary speech → the world of secular art → the world of ecclesiastical art → the divine liturgy → the transcendental divine light, makes up a chain of continuous, irrational complexity: first the transition from the non-semiotic world of things to the system of signs and social languages; then a unification of the signs of the different languages, a unification which cannot be translated into any one of the languages taken by itself (the unification of word and melody, singing, wall-painting, natural and artificial light, the aroma of incense; the unification in architecture of the building and the setting, and so on); and finally the unification of art with the transcendental divine Truth. No stage of the hierarchy can be expressed by the means of the preceding stage, which is merely an image (i.e. an incomplete representation) of it. The principle of rhetorical organization lies at the base of this culture as such, transforming each new stage into a semiotic mystery for those below it. The principle of rhetorical organization of a culture can be found also in the purely secular world: for Paul I, for example, the military parade was just as much a metaphor of Order and Power as the battle for Napoleon was a metonymy of Glory.

Rhetoric, therefore (like logic, from another point of view), reflects a universal principle both of the individual consciousness and of the collective consciousness (culture).

In contemporary rhetoric, attention has been focused on the range of problems associated with text-grammar. This is a field where the traditional problems concerning the rhetorical construction of text-segments encounters modern linguistics. We must emphasize that the traditional rhetorical figures involving the introduction into the text of supplementary features of symmetry and orderliness, are, in certain respects, analogous to the construction of the poetic text. However, while the poetic text presupposes a necessary ordering of the lower levels (according to which what is not ordered, or optionally ordered, in the system of the given language is raised to the rank of obligatory and relevant ordering, and the lexico-semantic level acquires supra-linguistic ordering as a result of the primary organization), in the rhetorical text the reverse applies: the lexico-semantic and syntactic levels must be ordered, while the rhythmic and phonetic ordering is something optional and derivative. Our point is that the effect is the same: in both instances what, in natural language, is a chain of independent signs is transformed into a semantic whole with its semantic content 'washed over' the entire space, i.e. there is a tendency for the text to be transformed into a single sign which bears the meaning. While a text in natural language is organized linearly and is discrete, the rhetorical text is semantically integrated. On entering the rhetorical whole words not only are 'jolted' semantically (every word in a literary text is a trope in ideal form), but they merge, their meanings becoming integrated. We get the effect which Tynyanov, speaking of the poetic text, called 'the density of the poetic line'.

In the science of recent decades, however, the question of the poetic coherence of the text was been treated both as a literary and as a linguistic problem: the rapid development of that branch of linguistics known as 'text-grammar' which is concerned with the structural unity of speech communication at the level above the sentence, has made the traditional problems of rhetoric a crucial linguistic concern. Since the mechanism of supra-phrase coherence has been approached either in terms of lexical repetitions or their substitutes, or in terms of the logical and intonational bonds,[27] the traditional forms of the rhetorical structure of paragraph or of text as a whole have evidently acquired significance for linguistics. This approach has been criticized by B. M. Gasparov[28] who pointed out the inadequacies of this procedure for describing supra-phrase text coherence and the loss of linguistic content. Instead, Gasparov proposed a model of obligatory grammatical links bonding the speech segments at the supra-phrase level: according to him, the immanent grammatical structure of the sentence imposes already defined grammatical restrictions on any sentence which can be joined to it in the given language. The structure of these bonds is what forms the linguistic unity of the text.

So we may summarize the two approaches: according to one, the rhetorical structure automatically emerges from the laws of the language and is nothing more than their realization on the level of whole text construction. From the other point of view, there is a difference of principle between the linguistic and the rhetorical coherence of the text; the rhetorical structure does not arise automatically from the language structure, but is a deliberate reinterpretation of the latter (in the system of linguistic bonds it produces displacements by which optional structures are raised to the rank of essential ones, and so on); the rhetorical structure is brought into the verbal text from outside, giving it a supplementary orderedness; such for example are the various devices for introducing supplementary laws of symmetry, which belong to spatial semiotics and are not inherent to the structure of natural language, into the text. We favour this second approach, and would further claim that the rhetorical structure not only objectively involves introducing into the text from outside organizational principles which are alien to it, but is subjectively experienced as something alien to the text's structural principles. For instance, the striking inclusion of a section of non-literary text into a literary one (or of newsreel into a film) can be effective rhetorically speaking only if it is recognized by the audience as something alien and inappropriate for that text. And the striking introduction of a section of art film into a newsreel would have the same effect. Traditional rhetorical prose, which we accept as the domain of rhetoric *par excellence*, may be described as the invasion of poetry into the domain of prose and the translation of poetic structure into the language of prose. Similarly, the invasion of prose-language into poetry creates a rhetorical effect. Moreover, oratorical speech is perceived by the audience as 'dislocated' oral speech, speech into which elements of 'bookishness' have been introduced. In oratory we perceive both the syntactic figures of classical rhetoric, and constructions which would appear neutral in a written text if they were not pronounced aloud, as rhetorical elements. In the same way when oral speech is introduced into a written text, which is a feature of twentieth-century prose, or when 'internal' speech changes place with 'external' speech (for instance in 'stream of consciousness' prose), the rhetorical level of the text-structure is activated. Foreign language texts included in another linguistic context have the same effect. The rhetorical function appears particularly clearly when the foreign language text can be read as a pun in one's own language. Pushkin, for instance, put the epigraph 'O rus, O *Rus*' to the second chapter of *Eugene Onegin*, i.e. a homonymic pun based on a quotation from Horace (satire 6, from the second book of *Satires*) and the Russian name for ancient Russia. Compare in Stendhal's *Henri Brulard* the reference to the events of 1799: 'In Grenoble the Russians were expected. The aristocrats, and, it seems, my relatives too said: "*O Rus, quando ego te aspiciam*".' These are extreme examples, but they show the essence of the mechanism of *any* alien intrusion into the text: such an intrusion is not isolated from the general context-structure, but sets up playful relationships with it, by belonging and not belonging to it. We might extend this statement and say that the rhetorical level must have an alien structure. Rhetorical organization is produced in the field of semantic tension between 'organic' and 'foreign' structures, and its elements can thus be doubly interpreted. The 'foreign' element, even when mechanically introduced into a new structural context, ceases to be equivalent to itself and becomes a *sign* or an *imitation of itself*. A real document included in a literary text becomes a literary sign of documentality and an imitation of the real one.

Stylistics and Rhetoric   From the point of view of semiotics, stylistics is constituted by two opposites: by its opposition to semantics and by its opposition to rhetoric.

The opposition stylistics/semantics works as follows: every semiotic system (or language) has a hierarchical structure. Semantically speaking, we can see this hierarchy in the fact that the semantic field of the language is divided into separate, self-contained spaces, between which a relationship of similarity exists. We could liken this system to the registers of a musical instrument, such as an organ. The same tune can be played on the instrument in the different registers, and the tune will be the same though the colouring will alter. If we take any single note, it has a meaning which is the same in all registers. A comparison of notes of the same value but in different registers will show up both what they have in common and what the particular register endows them with. The first meaning relates to semantics and the second to stylistics.

We are, therefore, dealing with stylistics when, first, one and the same semantic content can be expressed in at least two different ways, and, second, when each of these ways activates a memory of a self-contained and hierarchically bonded group of signs, that is, of a 'register'. If the two different ways of expressing a semantic content belong to one and the same register, there will be no stylistic effect.

The second fundamental opposition, that between stylistics and rhetoric, follows from this. A rhetorical effect arises when there is a *conflict* of signs relating to *different* registers, and when this conflict leads to a structural renewal of the feeling of a boundary between the self-contained worlds of signs. The stylistic effect is formed *within* a hierarchical subsystem. Stylistic consciousness, therefore, arises from hierarchical boundaries which it constitutes as an absolute, while the rhetorical consciousness arises from hierarchical boundaries which it constitutes as relative. These become its playthings. What we have been saying concerns the non-literary text. In the literary text, with its tendency to regard any structural element as optional and a 'plaything', there can be a rhetorical attitude towards stylistics. What is known as 'poetic stylistics' can be defined as the creation of a special semiotic space, within which a free choice of stylistic register is possible, this register no longer being automatically defined by the communicative situation. As a result style acquires supplementary significance. In non-literary communications, the choice of a style register is determined by the sum of pragmatic relationships inherent to the actual type of communication. In artistic communication the text is primary and its stylistic indicators set the imagined pragmatic situation. This makes it possible within the confines of one text to encounter different, more often than not, contrasting, styles, and this produces a game of pragmatic situations (Hoffmann's romantic irony, the stylistic contrasts in Byron's *Don Juan* and Pushkin's *Eugene Onegin*).

In the historical dynamics of art we can point to periods which are oriented towards rhetorical (inter-register) meta-constructions, and those oriented towards stylistic (intra-register) meta-constructions. In the general cultural context the former are perceived as 'complex', the latter as 'simple'. The aesthetic ideal of 'simplicity' is bound up with a veto on rhetorical constructions and a heightened attention to stylistic ones. But even in this case the literary text is radically different from the non-literary one, although subjectively speaking the latter may serve as an ideal model for the former.

There is a paradox connected with those literary epochs oriented towards a stylistic consciousness. In these periods there is a heightened sense of the significance of the entire system of stylistic registers of the language, although each separate text tends towards stylistic neutrality: when the reader begins to read, or even before beginning, s/he includes him/herself in a particular system of genre-stylistic norms. Thereafter, for the whole extent of the text, there is no possibility of changing the norms, as a result of which the norms themselves become neutral. The rhetorical type of artistic consciousness, however, gives hardly any thought to questions of the general hierarchy of registers. So for example the whole system of genre markers, their 'appropriateness' or 'inappropriateness', their relative value, which was so important to the theoreticians of Classicism, lost all meaning in the eyes of the Romantics. But then, from the point of view of the Classicist, the value and skill of an author in a particular text is manifest in the 'purity of his style', i.e. in the strict fulfilment of the norms in operation in that register and in that area, while, for the Romantic, it is manifest in the 'expressiveness' of the text, i.e. in the switch from one system of norms to another. In the first case the individual text is valued for the neutrality of its style which is associated with 'correctness' and 'purity', while in the second case this 'correctness' will be perceived as 'drabness' and 'lack of expression'; stylistic contrasts within the text will be preferred. When therefore the stylistic consciousness is predominant in art, this will paradoxically lead to a weakening of the structural significance of style categories within a text; and when the rhetorical consciousness is predominant, the significance of style will be heightened.

The evolutionary process of art is complex and dependent on many factors. Yet one evolutionary constant we can point to is the fact that, within a large-scale historical period, 'rhetorical' orientations usually precede the 'stylistic' ones that take their place. D. S. Likhachev pointed out this law. This sequence can be compared with something that is typical in the individual development of many poets: they start their career with a complex style and move towards 'classical' simplicity at the end. Pasternak pointed out that the culmination of a poet's development is, at the end of the road,

> to fall, as into a heresy,
> into unheard of simplicity,

a process which is characteristic of too many poets for it to be accidental. Catch-phrases such as 'The transition from Romanticism to realism', 'the transition from Rococo to Classicism', 'the transition from the avant-garde to Neo-classicism' are applicable to the individual development patterns of an enormous number of poets. All these transitions come down to the formula: 'the transition from a rhetorical organization to a stylistic one'.

This evolutionary path can be understood as a search for an individual language in poetry. At first the poet's language takes shape as a rejection of the already existing poetic dialects. A new linguistic space is outlined, within which linguistic units, which previously had never been united because they were felt to be incompatible, are now combined. These new circumstances naturally produce a heightened feeling of the specificity of each unit and of their incompatibility together. This is how the rhetorical effect comes about. In the case of a great poet, however, he will have the ability to make *this* language seem unified to the reader. Subsequently, the poet continues to create *within* this new, but now already culturally established language, and turns it into a stylistic register. The elements entering this register will seem naturally compatible, even neutral, but on the other hand, the boundary which separates such a poet's style from the general literary context will become more marked. In Pushkin's early work *Ruslan and Lyudmila*, for instance, his contemporaries saw a diversity of styles, a conglomeration of stylistic reminiscences from different literary traditions. Whereas in *Eugene Onegin*, the style of which is marked by exceptional intertextual complexity, and an abundance of hints, quotations and reminiscences, the reader sees only the artlessness of the author's simple speech. But at the same time we are also acutely aware of its incomparable 'Pushkinian' quality.

A literary text cannot, therefore, be exclusively 'rhetorical' or 'stylistic', for it is a complex interweaving of both tendencies, and the complexity is added to by the conflict of these tendencies in the metacultural structures which serve as codes in the processes of social communication.

The correlation of stylistic and rhetorical structural elements can be represented in the following diagram:

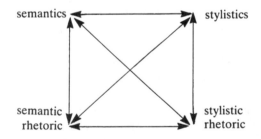

The shifts which may bring any of these elements to dominance account for the variety of combinations we find in the major historico-semiotic categories such as 'Romanticism', 'Classicism', and so on. And we should bear in mind that in actual texts the same tension between textual and meta-textual (encoding) levels is in operation so that the pattern can be duplicated.

4

Iconic rhetoric

The point has often been made in aesthetics that art has to do with the replication of reality. There is a profound significance in the ancient legends which tell how rhyme was born from echo, and drawing from an outlined shadow. But equally, the magic function of objects such as mirrors which create another world similar to the one being reflected yet not the same as it, an 'as if' world, is just as significant for the self-awareness of art as the metaphor of reflection and of the mirror-image. The transformation of the world of objects into the world of signs is founded on the ontological presupposition that it is possible to make replicas: the reflected image of a thing is cut off from its natural practical associations (space, context, intention, and so on), and can therefore be easily included in the modelling associations of the human consciousness. A face in the mirror does not share the natural associations of a real face – it cannot be touched or caressed, but it can easily be included in semiotic associations – it can be abused or used for magic manipulations. In this respect a mirror-image is typologically the same as a cast or an imprint (for example, foot- or fingerprints). Magic performed by sorcerers on human footprints is a practice which ethnographers have remarked on in many different cultures, and it has usually been explained by reference to the archaic consciousness which allegedly cannot distinguish part from whole and which regards the footprint as something that is in principle the same as the person who imprinted it. We suggest another explanation as follows: because the footprint while being the person at the same time obviously is not the person, and because it is cut off from the whole mass of its everyday and practical associations, it can be included in a semiotic situation.

In the elementary fact of making a replica, however, the semiotic situation is hidden as a pure possibility. As a rule it stays unnoticed by the naive consciousness which is not used to perceiving the world semiotically. Things are different when there is a double replication, when a replica is made of a replica. In these cases the object and its representation are so glaringly not equivalent, and the transformation of the representation in the process of replication is so obvious, that attention is naturally drawn to the *mechanism whereby the replica is made*, and the semiotic process becomes a conscious one rather than a spontaneous one. In pictorial texts multiple replication, and the transformation of the represented image in the course of this process, has a special function. In verbal texts the relationship between content and expression is much more obviously a matter of convention. This conventionality is fairly easy to expose and the creation of a poetic text is an effort to overcome it: for poetry fuses content level and expression level in a complex formation of a higher level of organization.

The pictorial arts (and their potential semiotic kernel – a mechanical reflection of an object in the surface of a mirror) create an illusion of identity between object and image. So another link has to be inserted in the process of creating an artistic sign (a text): the semiotic and conventional principle which lies at the heart of every semiotic fact has to be exposed and the text, which is perceived by the naive consciousness without its conventionality, must be recognized for what it is. In practical terms this means that at this stage features inherent to a verbal text are ascribed to the non-verbal text. And only at the next stage does the secondary iconization of the text take place; this corresponds to the moment in poetry when non-verbal (iconic) features are ascribed to the verbal text.

We can illustrate how important a double replication is in this process (especially at the first stage) by considering the function of the mirror at certain moments in the development of pictorial art. It could be said that at such periods a mirror on the canvas played the same typological role as a verbal game in poetry: by demonstrating the conventionality which lies at the heart of the text, it made the language of art the object of the viewers' attention. Double replication as a rule affects not the whole canvas but just a part of it. In that section where the secondary replication occurs, there is a much higher degree of conventionality, and this exposes the semiotic principle of the text as such.

For example, one of the aims of Renaissance art was to establish a 'natural' perspective as the realization of a constant point of view.[29] But in Velasquez' 'The Toilet of Venus' the introduction of the mirror makes it possible, within the generally accepted system of perspective, to show the central figure (Venus) from two points of view at once: the viewer sees her from the back but the mirror shows her face. Point of view is thus identified as an independent structural element which can be detached from the object as seen by the naive viewer and recognized as an independent concept. In Jan van Eyck's 'The Marriage of Giovanni

Arnolfini and Giovanna Cenami' the mirror has the same function: the central figures are seen face on and their backs in the reflection. In this picture, however, the effect is more complicated because, first, the reflection in the mirror is distorted: the convex surface of the mirror transforms the figures, a fact which focuses attention specifically on the reflection. This makes it self-evident that every reflection is at one and same time a dislocation, a deformation which, on the one hand, emphasizes certain aspects of the object, and on the other hand shows up the structural principle of the language into whose space the given object is being projected. The convex and rounded surface of the mirror emphasizes how flat and rectilinear are the figures of the banker and his wife, who have as it were been stuck on to the flat glass of the mirror which is situated in the illusory three-dimensional space of the room (the illusion is built up by the detailed and realistic treatment of the objects). The system of the mirror-image and of the spatial perspective runs at a perpendicular to the surface of the picture and extends beyond the picture's boundaries. An effect is created similar to the one noted by Jan Mukařovsky in cinema when the sound space extends beyond the limits of the screen and with greater dimensionality than the screen. (For example, a carriage is shown on the screen, taken from an angle perpendicular to the screen so that the horses are excluded from the shot, i.e. the carriage is photographed by a camera placed where the horses are; if the sound is then so placed as to reproduce the drumming of the hooves then the axis of the sound-space is as it were placed at a perpendicular to the screen.) In fact it is the mirror and the perspective reflected in it which reveal the contradiction between the flatness of the canvas and the three-dimensionality of the world represented on it, i.e. reveal the very language of art.

In 'Las Meninas'[30] Velasquez combined a mirror with metastructural elements (the artist is depicted on the canvas at the moment when he is painting an image on to a canvas, and what he is painting is visible to the viewer as a reflection in a mirror behind the artist's back) and thus made the very essence of the pictorial language, its relationship to its object, into a topic of visual cognition.

In all these examples, as in many others (compare, for instance the convex mirror which extends the lateral space of the picture 'Banker and his wife' by Massys), the mirror duplicates what the artist had already duplicated, and, at the same time, brings into the canvas things which, because of the specific limitations of the pictorial language being used, should apparently be outside it; and by so doing the mirror as it were separates the means of representation from what is represented. The means of representation becomes an object of representation. The process of self-awareness of the nature of the language which this device brings about has close analogies in the literature of the Baroque Age.

The examples cited illustrate particular points which, taken together, also relate to the problems of text-rhetoric.

Rhetoric, a philological discipline with a long tradition, has recently received a new lease of life. Neo-rhetoric and its extensive literature were born of the attempt to relate the discoveries of linguistics to those of text-poetics. Without going deeply into these problems, we shall single out one aspect which we need for our argument.

The rhetorical utterance in our terminology is not just any simple message with an 'embellishment' imposed from above which can be removed without altering the sense. In other words, a rhetorical utterance cannot be expressed non-rhetorically. The rhetorical structure lies not in the domain of expression but in the domain of content.

We shall define the rhetorical text, as distinct from the non-rhetorical text, as one which can be conceptualized as a structural unity of two (or more) subtexts encoded with the help of several, mutually untranslatable, codes. These subtexts may be conceptualized as local subsystems and the text therefore, in its different parts, must be read with the help of different languages, or alternatively, the text looks like different discourses which have equal rights throughout its course. In the latter case the text can be read on two levels, for instance, realistically and symbolically. Rhetorical texts include all instances of contrapuntal collision of different semiotic languages within a single structure.

Typical of the rhetoric of Baroque texts is the collision within one whole of segments marked by different degrees of semioticity. In the collision of languages, one of them inevitably appears as 'natural' (a non-language), while the artificiality of the other is stressed. In wall paintings of the Baroque churches of Czechoslovakia the motif of little angels in a frame is frequently encountered. The frame is painted to look like a window, and the angel sits on the 'window-sill', as it were dangling one leg over the edge of the frame. This leg which does not fit into the composition of the picture is sculptural. It is added on to the painting as a continuation of it. So the text is a combination of painting and sculpture, besides which the background behind the angel's back imitates the blue sky and is thus a rupture in the space of the fresco. The three-dimensional leg also ruptures this space but by another method and in the opposite direction. The whole text is constructed as a game between real and unreal space and as a collision of art-languages, of which one has the 'natural' quality of the actual object while the other is an artificial imitation of it.

The art of the age of Classicism required the unity of style. The Baroque alternation of local subsystems seemed like barbarism. In Classicism the entire text for its whole extent had to be uniformly organized and uniformly encoded. But this did not entail a rejection of rhetorical structure. The rhetorical effect was achieved by different methods – by the division of the language structure into many layers. The most widely used method was to encode the object of representation first by a theatrical code and then by a poetic (lyric), historical or representational code.

In many cases (and this was especially typical of the historical prose, pastoral poetry and painting in the eighteenth century) the text was a direct reproduction of the corresponding theatrical exposition òr scenic episode. Depending on the genre, this mediating code-text could be a scene from a tragedy, a comedy or a ballet. For example, Charles Coypel's painting 'Psyche Abandoned by Love' reproduces a scene from a ballet with all the conventions appropriate for this sort of spectacle in an eighteenth-century interpretation. The secret behind this sort of borrowing is not to be found in the painter's biography, though he was also active in the theatre, since we find the same phenomenon with other painters of the time, including Watteau.[31]

In speaking of the 'theatralization' of painting at certain periods we should not reduce the problem to a superficial metaphor. For the question has deep roots on the one hand in theatre as such, and on the other hand in 'intermediary encoding' as such.

Let us now turn to some aspects of this dual problem.

Any act of semiotic recognition must involve the separation of significant elements from insignificant ones in surrounding reality. Elements which, from the point of view of that modelling system, are not bearers of meaning, as it were do not exist. The fact of their actual existence recedes to the background in face of their irrelevance in the given modelling system. Though existing, they as it were cease to exist in the system of culture. The first and most important act of any semiotic modelling of a culture is to pick out the layer of culturally relevant phenomena in the surrounding world. To do this there has to be some primary encoding. This primary encoding may be realized by identifying real-life situations with mythological ones, and real people with the people of myth or ritual. At different stages of culture, etiquette or ritual may serve as the mediating link ('only what has an equivalent in ritual has existence'), or historical narrative ('only what is inscribed in the annals of history has real existence'). But the theatre, which combines many aspects of the systems mentioned above, is an especially active primary code.

Portraits where the sitter is dressed in theatrical costume are a frequently found illustration of theatre serving as an intermediary code between a life object and the painter's canvas. There are for instance many eighteenth-century female portraits where the sitter is dressed as a Vestal Virgin, as Diana or Sappho, and male portraits where the sitter is dressed as Titus, Alexander the Great or Mars. Proof that the encoding mechanism is indeed the theatre and not just one of the cultural-mythological ideas in circulation is that the sitters' costumes reproduce those prescribed for that particular character in eighteenth-century theatrical tradition. For a real person to become worthy of the artist's brush, he or she had to be identified with a character particularly valued in that culture and made to look like a well-known stage hero. This was the significance of the costume stylization. This encoding had a reverse effect on the actual behaviour of people in real-life situations. There are numerous examples of this.[32] As regards the topic we are concerned with, we can mention the curious effect on actual fashion of the stylized and conventionalized portrait-costumes. The portraits of Vigée-Lebrun strongly influenced the fashion for classical dress in the Empire style *à la grecque* in St Petersburg. Their effect was stronger than governmental prohibitions and the Empress Mariya Fedorovna appeared at an intimate supper on 11 March 1801 (the last in the life of her husband Paul I!) in a proscribed 'antique' dress.

Another matter was the choice of topics for paintings and notions of the picturesque connected with that choice. The selection of what, from the point of view of the cultural system, was worthy to be painted, the questions of how it should be painted, and what aspect of it was 'picturesque', were influenced by preliminary encoding into the system of another art language, most often that of theatre or literature. When a 'picturesque situation' is identified, the time-flow in which the object in its real existence is situated has to be segmented. The continuous uninterrupted time-flow in which the object of the representation is immersed contrasts with the demarcated, arrested moment of the painting itself. One psychological way to bring this change about is often to imagine life as theatre. While imitating the dynamic continuity of reality, the theatre at the same time parcels it out into small segments or scenes, thereby isolating integral, discrete units within the continuous flow. Each such unit, when taken on its own, can be thought of as self-contained and suspended in time. Terms such as 'scene', 'tableau', 'act', which relate equally to theatre and to painting, are not accidental.

Between the non-discrete flow of life and the demarcated discrete 'arrested' moments which are typical of representational art, the theatre occupies an intermediary position. On the one hand, it is different from a picture and resembles life in its continuity and movement, and on the other, it is different from life and resembles a picture by the fact that it divides the stream of events into segments, each of which at each particular moment tends to have an organized composition within any synchronic section of the action: instead of the continuous flow of non-artistic reality we have as it were a series of separate, immanently organized pictures linked to each other by transitional moments.

Theatre's position as an intermediary between the moving and non-discrete real world and the immobile and discrete world of the representational arts is the reason for the constant switch of codes on the one hand between the theatre and people's actual behaviour, and on the other hand between theatre and the representational arts. The consequence is that life and painting in many cases relate to each other through theatre which serves as a mediating code, a translation-code.

Because the theatre and behaviour mutually interact we find that, alongside the tendency which has been active throughout the history of the theatre to make life on the stage resemble real life, there is another just as constant opposite tendency which is to make real life (or aspects of it) resemble the theatre. The latter tendency is especially obvious in cultures which have elaborated vivid forms of ritualized behaviour. If at its origins theatre comes from ritual, in its subsequent historical development there is often a reverse borrowing: ritual seeps into the norms of the theatre. For instance, the court ceremonial devised by Napoleon for the imperial court was explicitly derived not from the traditions of court etiquette which had been destroyed by the revolution, but from the norms established in eighteenth-century French theatre for representing the court of the Roman Emperors. Talma took a leading part in working out the etiquette. Ballet swept victoriously into the field of military art and the parade. Theatrical spectacle took over even what would seem to be the alien sphere of military practice. Lermontov described the feelings of spectators who watched a military skirmish: 'without blood-thirsty agitation, as if it were a tragic ballet'.

While the epoch of Classicism drew the line sharply betwen the domains of ritualized and of practical behaviour, it was a feature of Romanticism that theatrical norms penetrated into everyday behaviour. On the one hand, the special domain of 'elevated' statesmanlike behaviour was done away with, and on the other the 'middle' area involving the behaviour of friends and lovers, situations such as 'communing with nature', or isolation 'in the midst of the noisy ball', became ritualized.

A 'theatre of everyday behaviour' came into being which altered people's view of themselves. 'Poetic' moments and situations were identified and declared to be the only ones that were important, and even the only ones to be existing. At 'non-poetic' moments a person as it were went off stage and, from the point of view of 'the drama of life' being played on stage, that person as it were ceased to exist until his or her next entry. In the Romantic consciousness of the age of the Napoleonic Wars, for example, military life was significant and possessed genuine reality (i.e. might serve as the content of all kinds of texts) only when it was thought of as a chain of heroic, nobly tragic and touching scenes. This is why Stendhal's and Tolstoy's depiction of war had such an effect on the reader, because these authors shifted the action off-stage declaring that real life was there, while what was happening on stage was illusory and without real existence.

Not only certain situations, but also certain stabilized norms of role play were considered to be 'genuine reality'. In order to exist ('to be more strongly aware of ourselves', as Lavater wrote to Karamzin[33]) a person had to add semiotic existence to his physical existence. By this Lavater meant simple replication ('our eye is not so constituted to be able to see ourselves without a mirror'). In some cultural periods this replication was achieved by the identification of one's own personality with some role that was significant in the given culture.

The choice of role was accompanied by a choice of gesture. A domain of 'significant movements' was established, gestures different from everyday movements which had no significance.[34]

Those who criticized the age of Classicism for being the 'age of posing' did not do away with gesture – they simply moved the domain of the significant: ritualization and the semantic content was shifted into those spheres of behaviour which previously were considered to be quite without semiotic value. Simple clothing, a careless demeanour, a touching impulse, a demonstrative rejection of semioticity, a subjective rejection of gesture – all these things became bearers of special cultural significance, i.e. turned into gesture. In Lermontov's heroine 'all her movements' were at the same time 'full of expression' and 'of charming simplicity'.[35] ('Charming simplicity' is a rejection of gesture; but the animation of these movements, and their significance, makes them into gestures of a new type; we might compare this with the rejection of the system of stage gestures which Karatygin had elaborated in favour of the 'sincere' gestures of Mochalov.[36])

> . . . What a difference
> The eyes of my Olenina!
> How pensive is their genius,
> and how much childlike simplicity,
> and how many languorous expressions,
> and how much voluptuousness and fantasy! . . .
> she closes them with a Lel's smile –
> the modest graces triumph in them;
> She raises them – it is as if a Raphael angel
> contemplates God.[37]

Significant here is that while Pushkin demonstratively affirms 'childlike simplicity' as a supreme good, he introduces a theatrical-pictorial code in order to make *sense* of what, without it, would have mere physical existence; the 'Raphael angel' refers to the Sistine Madonna which Pushkin knew from engravings (and most likely literary descriptions also had a part to play), Lel – the Slavonic god of love (perhaps here simply

Love) – is a reference to a pictorial and theatrical-ballet tradition.

A triangle is created which consists of the person's actual behaviour in the given cultural system, the theatre and the pictorial arts. Within this triangle there is an intense circulation of symbols and expressive means. Theatricality invades life and influences painting, life affects both the one and the other under the slogan of 'naturalness', and finally painting and sculpture have an active influence both on theatre where they determine the system of poses and movements, and on non-artistic reality which they raise to the level of 'being significant'.

What is important is that when a significant structure passes into another sphere it preserves its association with its own natural context. This is how there comes into being 'theatricality' of gesture both in pictures and in life, 'picturesqueness' of theatre or of actual life, 'naturalness' of the stage and canvas. It is this dual correlation to different semiotic systems which creates the rhetorical situation which holds a powerful source for elaborating new meanings.

Rhetoric, the transfer into one semiotic sphere of the structural principles of another, is possible at the confrontation of other arts as well. The totality of semiotic processes found on the boundary 'word/picture' are extremely important in this respect. For example, surrealism in painting, can in a sense be interpreted as the transfer into a purely pictorial sphere of verbal metaphor and purely verbal principles of fantasy. However, precisely because rhetoric has been naturally associated with the verbal principle we thought it would be useful to demonstrate the possibility of rhetorical construction in areas other than discourse.

5

The text as process of movement
Author to Audience, Author to Text

A text and its readership are in a relationship of mutual activation: a text strives to make its readers conform to itself, to force on them its own system of codes, and the readers respond in the same way. The text as it were contains an image of its 'own' ideal readership, and the readership one of its 'own' text. There is a story about the celebrated mathematician P. L. Chebyshev. An unexpected audience consisting of tailors, modistes and fashionable young ladies turned up to one of his lectures on the subject of the mathematical problem of cutting the cloth [*rasskroika tkani*]. But the lecturer's opening words: 'Let's suppose for simplicity's sake that the human body is spherical' put them to flight. Only the mathematicians who found nothing strange in the remark stayed on to hear him. The text 'selected' its own audience, creating it in its own image and likeness.

Communication with another person is only possible if there is some degree of common memory. However, a text addressed 'to everyone', i.e. *to any addressee*, is in principle different from a text which is addressed to one particular person *known personally* to the speaker. In the first instance the memory-capacity of the addressee is presumed to be common to *any* person who speaks the same language and belongs to the same culture. There is nothing individual about it, it is abstract and its contents are minimal. Naturally the poorer the memory the longer and more detailed the message must be, and the less comprehensible will be its ellipses and silences, its rhetoric of hints and complex pragmatic-referential associations. Such a text presupposes an abstract interlocutor endowed with no more than the common memory and without any personal or individual experience. Such a text is addressed to all and sundry.

But when a text is addressed to someone known personally, to someone we refer to by name rather than just by pronoun, it is differently constructed. We have intimate knowledge of its memory-capacity and the contents of it. Now there is no need to burden the text with unnecessary details: it is enough to appeal to the addressee's memory. A hint is enough to activate memory. Elliptical constructions, local semantics tending towards a 'domestic', 'intimate' lexis, will be widely used. This text will be valued not only for the extent to which it is comprehensible to the addressee, but also for the extent to which it is incomprehensible to other people. So orientation towards one or other type of memory will make the addresser use either 'a language for others', or 'a private language', that is, one of the two opposite structural possibilities inherent to natural language. Knowing the set of linguistic and cultural codes we can analyse a text and discover which type of audience it is oriented towards. A text can be defined by the type of memory it needs for it to be understood. By reconstructing the type of 'common memory' which a text and its consumers share, we shall discover the 'readership image' hidden in the text. A text, therefore, contains in embryo a system of all links in the communicative chain, and just as we can derive the authorial position from it, so we can reconstruct its ideal reader. The image of the ideal reader actively affects the actual readers, making them in its likeness. A reader's personality, which is a semiotic unity, is always a variable and capable of being 'tuned to the text'. On its side too, the readership image, since it is not explicit but merely inherent to the text as a potential position, is also subject to variation. As a result between text and readership there is complex game of positions.

The antithesis of the single memory common to all members of a community, to the extremely individualized memory of a particular person, can, in the most general terms, be compared with the antithesis of official speech to intimate speech; and in contemporary culture this antithesis has a parallel in the opposition: written speech/oral speech. This last opposition, however, has many gradations: a written printed text, for instance, obviously has a quite different pragmatic function from that of a handwritten one, like the difference between public speaking and whispering. The final stage in this gradation is inner speech. Mandel'shtam's line:

> *Ya skazhu eto nacherno, shopotom*
> [I'll say it as a draft, in a whisper]

is a striking comparison of an uncorrected, unfinalized rough draft, a note 'to oneself', with a whisper.

Much more complex is a literary text, where the readership image and its attendant pragmatic aspects do not automatically determine the type of text, but become elements of a free artistic game and consequently acquire supplementary significance. An intimate poem about friendship or love would seem because of its title or purport to be addressed to a *single* person, but when such a poem is published in a book or journal its readership changes; the poem, now addressed to any reader, is no longer a private letter, a fact of life, but a fact of art. The change of readership entails a change in the common memory-capacity of the text and its addressees. In a literary text, which is addressed to an actual real-life person, a duality of addressees is created: on the one hand, the text imitates a message directed to a single addressee, and this demands intimacy; and on the other hand, the text is addressed to any reader and this demands an expanded memory-capacity.[38] In a literary text orientation towards a certain type of common memory does not automatically ensue from the communicative function; the memory-orientation becomes a signifying (i.e. free) artistic element which plays with the text.

We shall illustrate these ideas with examples taken from Russian poetry of the eighteenth and early nineteenth centuries.

In the hierarchy of eighteenth-century poetic genres, a criterion determining the value of the poem was the degree of abstraction of the addressee. The text assumes that the person to whom the poem was addressed is representative of the most abstract, cultural, political or national values and memory.[39] Even if the addressee was a real person well known to the poet, the canons demanded that that person should be addressed as a 'stranger', and the emphasis was to be put on those qualities which were 'general knowledge' and kept in an abstract memory. For instance, the poet Vasili Maikov, in verses addressed to the grandee Count Z. G. Chernyshev, recounted facts of the count's biography which were perfectly well known to the count himself. But the poem builds up a 'lofty' image of Chernyshev as an abstract 'statesman' sharing a memory common to all persons of that rank. So the real biographical facts of the actual Chernyshev are not part of the memory of Chernyshev the hero of the poetic text (nor of the memory of the readership either who here represent generalized political memory). And in a poem addressed to Chernyshev the poet describes who Chernyshev is:

> O thou, hero tested by the fates,
> Whom the Russian army looked on as its leader
> And knows the greatness of thy soul
> When thou didst fight against Frederick!
> Then when that monarch became our ally
> He tested for himself thy valour and thy reason.[40]

The poet Voeikov constructed the opening of his epistle to his wife in exactly the same way. Taking away the official address and not listing the qualities and the circumstances of the addressee's life meant transferring the epistle from an elevated genre to an intimate one, i.e. implying that addresser and addressee shared a common memory, exclusive to them alone.

We can compare eighteenth-century official portraiture: even if the client ordered a portrait of him- or herself or family and the picture was intended to be hung in the family home, the sitter had to be shown wearing dress uniform with all medals and regalia; in other words, the viewer was presumed to be a 'stranger'. On the other hand, late in the century Count Sheremetev's serf-artist, I. P. Argunov, painted an outstanding portrait of the count's mistress and later wife, his serf Parasha Zhemchugova-Kovaleva, in her negligé and – an unheard of boldness – pregnant; the viewer had to identify him- or herself with one person only, Parasha's lover and husband, Count Sheremetev.

Pushkin often made use of the convention whereby a text puts its readership in a position of intimacy with the addresser. In such cases the poet consciously omits to mention circumstances which are assumed to be well known, but which the reader of the printed text could not possibly know, or merely hints at them. By deliberately hinting at facts known only to a small circle of his friends, Pushkin seems to invite his readers to feel that they are close friends of the author and to share in the game of hints and omissions. For instance the fragment 'Women'[41] contains the lines:

> In the words of the prophetic poet
> I too am allowed to say:
> Temira, Daphna and Lileta –
> are like a dream which I have long since forgotten.

A modern reader wanting to know who the 'prophetic poet' is turns to a commentary and finds out that it is Del'vig and that the lines refer to his poem 'Fanny':

> Temira, Daphna and Lileta
> long since, like a dream, I have forgotten
> and for the poet's memory of them
> there remains only my successful verse.[42]

However we must remember that Del'vig's poem was published only in 1922. In 1827 it had not been printed and his contemporaries, if by them we understand the great majority of the readers whom Pushkin was addressing in his poem of 1827, could not have known it since Del'vig was ruthless towards his early poetry, published very little and did not circulate what he had rejected.

So Pushkin was referring his readers to a text which they had no way of knowing. What was the sense of that? The fact is that among the potential readers of *Eugene Onegin* there was a small group to whom the reference was crystal clear – these were Pushkin's Lycée friends (Del'vig's poem was written in the 1810s, most likely at the Lycée) and possibly a close group of friends of the post-Lycée period. To them Del'vig's poem was certainly well known.[43]

So Pushkin's text split his readership into two groups: an extremely small group who could understand the text thanks to their detailed familiarity with extra-textual experiences shared with the author; and the great mass of readers who sense that something is being alluded to, but cannot decipher what it is. But the readers grasp that the text is demanding an attitude of close friendship with the poet, and they *imagine* themselves to be in such a relationship with the poem. A secondary effect of the undeciphered allusion is to put *each* reader into the position of intimate friend of the author, one who possesses a special, unique, shared memory which enables him or her to explain the allusions. It is like a person joining a close group of friends who allude to circumstances he or she does not know about and who at first feels alienated and excluded from the group, but once he or she feels accepted as an equal the lack of direct experience is compensated for by indirect experience, and he or she is especially conscious of the trust being shown, and of *being included* in the circle of friends. Pushkin draws the reader into just such a game.

The opposite game is also possible: people who are very close may adopt a position of 'strangers'. An example is to refer to children by their full official names. In Tolstoy's 'Family Happiness' the father addresses his newborn son: '"Ivan Sergeevich" said my husband, chucking him under the chin with a finger.' And the mother who narrates the episode enters into the spirit of the game: 'But I made haste to cover Ivan Sergeevich up again.'[44] Compare how adults and distant acquaintances may use a 'childish' name or nickname to refer to another adult.

In a real speech-act whether a speaker uses official or intimate language depends on his or her non-linguistic relationship to the other person. A literary text can move the reader up or down the scale of this hierarchy in accordance with the author's intentions. For the period of the reading, an author can make a reader as close as he or she wants. At the same time the reader does not stop being a person with a real relationship to the text, and the play between the reader's real pragmatics and that imposed by the author is what constitutes the special experience of the literary work. On the one hand, an author is at liberty to change the dimension of the readership's memory and may force the readership to *remember something they did not know*. On the other hand, a reader cannot forget the real contents of his or her own memory. So the text shapes its readers and at the same time the readers shape their text.

We have already discussed the dichotomy between the two intentions: the intention to produce a maximally accurate transmission of a message, and the intention to create a new message in the course of the transmission. Each of these intentions has its own idea how active the addressee is to be.

A model of perfect transmission is the chain of biochemical impulses which regulate the physiological processes *within* a single organism. In this case the final link in the chain of transforming impulses is the recipient. And in a well-constructed chain this will be a passive checking mechanism, valuable for its 'transparency', for the fact that it adds nothing 'of its own' to the information.

The potential for distortion and errors, and with them the transformation of the content of the information and the appearance of new messages, comes about when the impulses are replaced by signs which by definition relate content to expression asymmetrically. But signs become necessary when the circulation of information *within* an organism is replaced by communication *between* organisms. Though at a certain stage the direct impulses still play an important role even in communication between individuals (parapsychological phenomena may be associated with this), they are increasingly ousted by signs as the contacting units become more complex.

We might deduce from the foregoing that the closer knit a particular group is, the less activity there will be on the part of the recipient of the message. A recipient will be an executor or preserver of information rather than a creator of it. Hence the paradox: the mythological rituals and other performances which at given moments as it were weld archaic collectives together into a single organism, and which provide the members of these collectives with a unity of emotions and a heightened sense of involvement (the experience of the self as a part) are functionally similar to the metalinguistic and metacultural structures of an individualistic society. Both are like the hoops on a barrel, which bind a conglomerate into a single organism. The popularity of frenetic dancing and the music that stimulates it in the twentieth century conform absolutely to this principle. Late twentieth-century culture has heightened the contradiction between a person's experience of him- or herself as a part, and as a whole (an individual). On the one hand, a person experiences the pressure of social relationships which prevent him or her from expressing any individuality and which reduce him or her to a mere recipient of commands. On the other hand, extreme individualization and specialization throughout life has the effect of clamping down all impulse-like, unmediated relationships, of hampering all communication, including semiotic communication, of making people feel that they are alienated, and of disrupting communication. Spontaneous outbursts of passion, frenetic art experiences, destructive rioting are in this sense therapeutic. On the one hand, they jolt a person out of his or her daily routine and place him or her in extremely simplified situations, thereby letting people experience the illusion of emancipation and individual freedom. On the other hand, they intensify unmediated, intuitive and impulse-like relationships with other people. People experience *at one and the same time* opposing psychological states: 'I'm doing what I want' and 'I'm just like everyone else' (as Mayakovsky put it: 'I'm flowing like a drop with the masses').

For a simple message-transmission to become a creative process a condition is that the semiotic structure of the text-receiver be more complex and be a *personality*. But the degree of creative activity may vary greatly between the various elements of the communicative chain. At the one pole is the case when activity is concentrated on the link between author and text and the receiver's activity is correspondingly lessened; and at the other pole is the case when the creative potentialities of the addressee are maximally activated and those along other links in the chain are weakened.

Let us take two examples: (1) An already recorded text is transmitted along a communicative chain: for instance an actor recites a poem or a reader reads a book. (2) A text does not exist until the act of communication and arises in the process of the transmission.

1. The text's first movement is its *actualization*: the text which exists in a state of potentiality (the book on a shelf, the as yet unstaged play, and so on) acquires reality in the consciousness of the addresser. The first semiotic transformation of the text takes place here on the boundary between the collective memory of culture and the individual consciousness. The artistic text is a text 'with set to expression' (in Jakobson's terms). So the actualization of the text always involves emphasis on 'hearing' its structure (no matter whether it is actually read aloud or heard internally). This experience is like a musician 'reading' a score and listening to it with his inner ear. Jakobson, reflecting on the works of C. S. Peirce, pointed out that a certain degree of iconicity is inherent to all linguistic signs. This is particularly so in poetic language. And we might add that a word in oral speech is much more iconic than in written language. Besides the psychological attention fixed on its sounds, the word is accompanied by gesture (intonational, kinetic, facial) and is made visible. For instance the recitation (even soundless) of Derzhavin's lines:

> *Smert' muzha pravedna prekrasna!*
> *Kak umolkayushchii organ.*

> [The death of a righteous man is sublime!
> Like the sound of an organ dying away.][45]

shows up the structural organization of the text, as a photographic developer shows up the picture, and the inevitable reading of the words *umolkayushchii organ* with a lowered voice at the end of the word *umolkayushchii*, a slight raising of the voice on the last word and an almost inevitable dropping of the hand at the same time, creates an iconic sound-image of the notes of the organ dying away and the answering echo, as well as subjective visual associations. The text as it were splits in two: it remains in printed rows of graphically expressed words and at the same time it is realized in some iconic space. The meaning also splits in two, oscillating between these semantic spheres. But linguistic signs and iconic ones belong to spaces which cannot be fully translated into each other. So this is a point where that incomplete determination of correspondences which creates conditions for semantic augmentation comes into being. At this stage an increase of information has already taken place.

So as the text crosses the frontier into the semiotic space of the transmitting personality, it as it were acquires a supplementary semantic dimension. But the text is subjected to further transformations as it travels more deeply into this space. The structure of codes which shape the semiotic personality of the text's author and that of its first interpreter are known to be not identical. Some degree of correspondence is essential for a primary elementary understanding of the text (a minimal condition for understanding it is knowledge of the language it is written in), but the sheer diversity of traditions, contexts, coincidences and non-coincidences at different hierarchical levels of the encoding structure creates not a one-to-one translation from 'your' language to 'mine', but a spectrum of interpretations which is always susceptible to possible new readings.

When we say that one of the mechanisms for recoding is the cultural tradition, we must bear in mind that 'tradition' as a code is different from 'contemporaneity'. 'Contemporaneity' when it encodes (interprets) a text is as a rule realized in the *form of the language*, i.e. by the norms, rules, prohibitions, expectations – i.e. prescriptions, according to which texts which have not yet been created (or those which are 'incorrectly' interpreted from the point of view of 'contemporaneity') are to be created (or interpreted). 'Contemporaneity' is oriented towards the future. 'Tradition' is always a *system of texts* preserved in the memory of the given culture or subculture or personality. It is always realized as a *partial occurrence which is regarded as a precedent, norm or rule*. 'Tradition' therefore can be more broadly interpreted than 'contemporaneity'. A text which is filtered through the code of tradition is a text filtered through other texts which serve as its interpreter. But since a literary text cannot in principle be interpreted in one way only, in the case of literature a certain set of interpretations is filtered through another set, and this results in a new competition of possible interpretations and a new semantic augmentation. Moreover, texts which form part of 'tradition' are not for their part inert ones: when they come into the context of 'contemporaneity' they 'come to life' revealing their previously concealed meaning-potential. So the picture we have before us is that of organic interaction, of a dialogue, in the course of which each of the participants transforms the other and are themselves transformed under the action of the other; the picture is not one of passive transmission, but of the lively generation of new messages.

An analogous process takes place on another semiotic boundary, that where the transmitted text encounters the addressee. The generation of new meanings is the most important of a literary text's tasks in the culture system.

2. When a text is not transformed, but actually created in the process of transmission several things are to be noticed. Since the reader in a certain respect (and *only* in a certain respect, as we shall discuss below) mirrors the path of the text-creator, the generative aspect is important for the understanding of a text. Yet little attention has so far been paid to the question of the generation of the literary text. As far as I am aware the most thorough study of this problem is that by A. K. Zholkovsky and Yu. K. Shcheglov whose works we shall now discuss.

Since 1967 when the authors published a programme for generative poetics[46] and up to the early 1980s the authors have published over sixty works covering extensive and varied material in order to illustrate their model for the generation of the literary text. The books *Mathematics and Art* (Moscow, 1976) and *Poetics of Expressivity* (Vienna, 1980)[47] summarize their ideas.

Zholkovsky and Shcheglov's theory has apparently not yet been properly evaluated, though the very attempt to construct an integrated system for the generation of the literary text and to illustrate it with a wide range of material deserves attention. It is not our intention to analyse the weak and strong points of their model, though we must discuss some of its aspects.

The basic points of the 'theme – expressive devices – text' model are the following:

The content-invariant of the different levels and components of the literary *text* (T) we term its *theme* (θ). The text is the *expressive* embodiment of the theme, and the structure of the text is like a *deduction* of T from θ on the basis of typological transformations – the *devices of expressivity*. Themes are 'expressionless', they function to fix pure content; devices are 'contentless', they heighten expressivity without altering the content.[48]

And further:

The correspondence between the theme and the text is a kind of *deduction of the text from the theme*, a deduction which is carried out on the basis of universal transformations, the devices of expressivity (PV) [205].

. . . the individual text is regarded as a particular turn of an invariant theme, its passage through new material [147].

The theme is intuitively arrived at by the researcher by extracting a meaning-invariant from a number (as large as possible) of texts. The 'theme' which has been thus revealed is worked on by the 'expression devices', as a result of which the literary 'text' is obtained. There is a relationship of symmetry between theme and text and while an author generates a text from a theme, the reader arrives at the theme from the text:

> Generally speaking, the discovery of the theme and of the whole thematic-expressive structure can be thought of as a procedure of 'finding out' the PV from the T in the opposite direction to the procedure of deduction, this procedure being just as strict and explicit as the latter. [58, n.3]

The difference between these procedures lies only in the fact that when moving from theme to text, a non-literary type of utterance becomes a literary one. (In fact, a non-literary *text* turns into a literary one, because the theme, even when taken in its most abstract form, is expressed in words, and therefore must be a *text*; expressions such as 'supreme peace', 'window', 'confession', are of course on the level of natural language, *texts*.) In fact, we are back with the ideas of traditional rhetoric according to which the literary text is treated as 'decorated', something formed from the given theme with the aid of the rhetorical figures.

We have doubts about the authors' main assumptions:

1. That a literary text is obtained from a non-literary one by means of 'ornamentation', i.e. in terms of the 'poetics of expressiveness' model, by 'working on it' with the devices of literary expressivity.
2. That a literary text, translated into the language of 'expression devices' 'acquires heightened expressivity without changing its content', and that, consequently, art is a way of speaking at length about what could be spoken of briefly.
3. The authors warn us:

> We must emphasize categorically that here and elsewhere we have in mind 'derivation' in the sense of 'competence' and not of 'performance',[49] i.e. we have in mind a method for fixing the logic of correspondences between text and the theme available to it, but we are not at all concerned wtih a reconstruction of the history of the creation of the text from the original intention [237].

On these grounds they make no attempt to verify their procedures with records of actual cases of a writer's process from intention to final text (such as we have, for instance, in Pushkin's manuscripts, those of Dostoevsky and the early Pasternak, etc.).

In spite of the authors' warning let us begin precisely with the question of the actual process of literary text-generation. Their conclusion that the logical first step in the creative procedure is the 'theme' as they understand the term, is in no way proven and is arrived at simply by analogy with the 'meaning-text' generative model for the non-literary text. Yet there is plenty of evidence to suggest that the first link in the chain is as a rule a symbol (even when artists and writers speak of a sound or even a scent as the 'kernel' of the future text, they are referring, as we shall be demonstrating below, to a symbolic expression of an individual semiotic process, for instance to a childhood associative symbolization, or a crucial moment in their emotional biography, and so on). In other words, the artistic function is present from the very beginning, even if only as a potentiality. Take for example the evidence of Dostoevsky. Dostoevsky's insistence is striking that the creation of the original theme of a novel was the most artistically significant part of his work, calling it 'poet's work'. The development of the theme he called 'artist's work', using the word artist in the sense of 'craftsman'. See his note in the drafts to the novel *A Raw Youth*:

> In order to write a novel an author has to be provided with *one* or *several* strong impressions which have actually been experienced emotionally. *This is the poet's work.* The theme, the plan, the structured whole, develops from this impression. This is now the work of the artist, though artist and poet help each other at both stages, in both cases.[50]

Dostoevsky returned many times to this topic. He even called this primary 'theme' of a novel a poem to emphasize its poetic nature. On 15/27 May 1869 he wrote to Apollon Maikov:

> in my opinion a poem is like a unique precious stone, a diamond in the poet's heart, something ready made, in all its essence, and this is the first work of the poet as creator and originator, this is the first part of his creative work. If you like, it's not even he who is the creator, but life, the powerful essence of life.

And further: 'Then follows the poet's second work no longer so profound and mysterious, the work merely of the artist, namely, having acquired the diamond to set it and mount it.' And in another letter he wrote: 'Being more of a poet than an artist I'm for ever taking on themes which are beyond my capabilities.'[51] Pushkin had the same thing in mind when he wrote that even the plan of Dante's *Inferno* was a creation of artistic genius (the notion of 'plan' was for Pushkin similar to Zholkovsky and Shcheglov's 'theme'). We can therefore conclude that there is authoritative evidence to show that the chain which generates the literary text begins both psychologically and logically not with a logically expressed, non-literary 'theme' but with a capacious symbol with the potential to develop many images and interpretations, a symbol which is already literary.

Our second substantial objection is connected with the notion of the symmetry of the 'poetics of expressiveness' model. We have already had occasion to state our belief that the generation of new meanings is always connected with asymmetrical structures. While the preservation of information is most reliably ensured by symmetrical structures, the generation of information involves asymmetrical mechanisms. When asymmetrical binarity is discovered in a semiotic object this always presupposes some form of intellectual activity. We cannot envisage the generation of a literary text as an automatic working of a single, set algorithm. The creative process is an irreversible process (see below, Part Three), and hence the passage from one stage to another must involve elements of randomness and unpredictability. Consequently, to adopt Zholkovsky and Shcheglov's terminology, if we 'roll up' the text in the reverse direction we will not arrive at the original theme, just as, if we unroll the theme twice we are no more likely to arrive at the same text than we are to get *War and Peace* if we scatter typeface over the floor.

And this is to leave out of account the fact that different artistic structures (in Zholkovsky and Shcheglov's terms, different expressive devices) cannot express one and the same content and that the theory that 'devices are content-free' is highly dubious.

An examination of the actual creative process when a writer's manuscripts make it possible to document this gives convincing weight to our argument.

A study of the logical aspect of the creative process is not capable of reproducing the strange paths taken in the creation of any actual work, but on the other hand, it should not ignore the typical stages in the generation of actual texts when we are able to follow this process in sufficient detail. Moreover we suggest that the actual process might serve as a criterion for verifying our logical models, and the logical models as a means for interpreting textological realities.

A regular feature which can be deduced from a study of the working manuscripts of many writers is that the stages succeed one another: intention is followed by narration. In this process, stress on symbolic, polyvalent, multi-dimensional text-semantics gives way to a striving for precise expression of a thought. On the boundaries between these stages relationships of asymmetry and untranslatability come into being, and this process entails the generation of new meanings.

We mentioned above that the first stage in the generation of the text is like the emergence of a primary symbol, whose capacity is proportional to the range of potential plots concealed in it. This is why, when headings and epigraphs are defined, these seemingly marginal points can be the signal that the 'theme' (in Zholkovsky and Shcheglov's terminology) has been defined. For instance, because Dostoevsky had to work on several projects at once, because of the richness of his imagination, and the integral connection between his various projects, it is in practice impossible to tell which of the several plots he was working on at the same time a particular manuscript text relates to. The start of work on *The Devils* was surrounded by a veritable cloud of parallel plans, some of which were in part incorporated into *The Devils*: 'Kartuzov', 'The Life of a Great Sinner', the novel about the Prince and the Moneylender. Some of them, for instance, 'Envy', is directly associated with his work on *The Devils*. But it seems that the 'theme' of the novel became fixed at that moment when his impressions from the Nechaev trial, his polemics with Turgenev, his thoughts on the question of 'the men of the forties and the Nihilists', as well as many other impressions from life and literature, became concentrated in the symbol of the epigraph taken from Pushkin's ballad 'The Devils' and fleshed out in the Gospel story of the Gadarene swine.[52] This symbol as it were lit up the rudiments of the plots he already had and pointed the way to their future development. *The various drafts and half-worked projects were sorted out into a story*. Thus the concentration of many things in the one symbol was replaced by a linear development of the one symbol into various episodes.

This changeover, if we continue looking at the history of the writing of *The Devils*, is expressed in Dostoevsky's plans, his summary enumeration of episodes which thread themselves along the syntagmatic axis of the narrative. However, as soon as this tendency to *exposition* or narrative construction can be observed, we are witness also to a growing inner opposition to this tendency. Each serious movement of the plot Dostoevsky immediately smothers with variants and alternative versions. The wealth of Dostoevsky's imagination which allows him to 'play over' a vast quantity of possible story-lines, is truly amazing. The text in fact loses its linearity. It turns into a paradigmatic set of possible lines of development. And the same thing happens at almost every turning point in the plot. The syntagmatic construction is replaced by a multi-dimensional space of plot potentialities. When this happens the text becomes harder to fit into verbal expression: we have only to look at a page of Dostoevsky's manuscripts to see how far the writer is at this stage from writing a 'normal' narrative text. Phrases are tossed on to a page without any temporal sequence being observed in the way he fills up lines and sheets of paper. There is no guarantee that two lines set next to each

other were written one after the other, rather the reverse. Words are
written in different handwriting and in different sizes, at different
angles.[53] A page looks like a wall of a cell on which a prisoner has at
different times scribbled his feverish jottings which for him have some
inner associations, but which for the outside observer seem unconnected.
Many of the jottings are not texts, but mnemonic abbreviations of texts
preserved in the author's mind. Thus Dostoevsky's manuscript pages at
this stage tend to become signs of a vast multi-dimensional whole living in
the author's mind, rather than a logical exposition of a linearly organized
text. Besides, these jottings deal with many levels: here we shall find
versions of plot episodes, asides to himself, theoretical thoughts of a
philosophical nature, and isolated symbol-words which have not yet
found a place but which will be unravelled into future episodes which the
author's ,imagination has not yet created. Dostoevsky uses different
means of emphasis – he underlines, he writes in large letters, in printed
script, for at this stage in the work he is consciously recording the
intonation, as if stressing that his graphics are not a text but just a
projection of one.

The next stage follows when he extracts linear elements out of this
continuum and constructs a narrative text. Linearity takes the place of
multi-dimensionality. The preceding stage was marked by an abundance
of rich symbols which opened the way to the most diverse concretizations
in the narrative web of the future novel. For instance, the word 'slap'
which is a powerful symbol for Dostoevsky, often occurs in the
preliminary materials to *The Devils*. Already in 'Kartuzov', an early
version of *The Devils*, this word occurs in the title and is emphasized in
his handwriting. Later on in the preliminary material for *The Devils* (and
subsequently in that for *A Raw Youth*), the circumstances surrounding
the 'slap', and who gave one to whom, change, but the slap itself remains
as a symbol of utter humiliation. A symbol may determine a cluster of
possible plot developments, but it cannot determine which one of them
will be chosen. In the same way the little red spider which appears in
'Stavrogin's Confession' (not part of the final text of the novel) and which
the hero looks at while his victim is hanging herself, turns up in the
preparatory material to 'A Raw Youth' as a conventional sign for a whole
set of situations which the author's imagination has produced.

This is how the relationship between the preparatory material and the
subsequent narrative text is shaped. This relationship is like a ball of wool
and the thread unwound from it: the ball exists spatially and in a
particular single time, while the thread is unwound from it in a temporal
movement, linearly.

We can represent the process which Dostoevsky follows to create a text
by the following diagram:

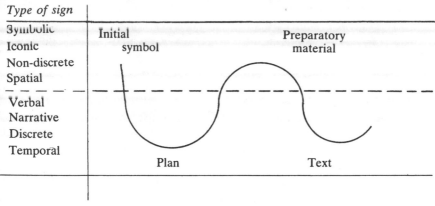

Type of sign	
Symbolic	Initial Preparatory
Iconic	symbol material
Non-discrete	
Spatial	
Verbal	
Narrative	
Discrete	
Temporal	Plan Text

So the 'generation' of a text involves numerous semiotic transformations. On the boundary between different semiotic regimes (at the intersections with the zero line) an act of translation takes place and there is a not wholly predictable reformulation of meanings.

We must stress that we are talking of a logical model and not describing an actual creative process, since it is frequently impossible in practice to isolate the 'initial symbol' moments in the continuous cross-weaving of Dostoevsky's intentions for his novels. In the same way the 'preparatory material' always includes portions of narrative, and the narrative texts tend, in the continuously corrected and reworked drafts, to turn into preparatory material, so that the distinction between them is conventional and logical rather than a matter of fact. Even the boundaries which separate one of Dostoevsky's novels from another are frequently blurred. Tomashevsky wrote that 'Dostoevsky writes novel after novel in the search for one single novel', while the most recent researchers who have studied Dostoevsky's notebooks rightly comment that 'it seems more expedient to talk of a single draft distributed over the sequence of the different stages of his writing'.[54]

Iconic (spatial, non-discrete) texts and verbal (discrete, linear) ones are mutually untranslatable, and cannot in principle express 'one and the same' content. At the points where they confront each other there is an increase in indeterminacy and this creates a reserve for more information. In the process of creating a text, then, a writer is doing several things at once: s/he creates a channel from the huge amount of potential material available (tradition, associations, his/her own previous works, texts from surrounding life, etc.); s/he passes the new texts which arise in his/her creative imagination through this channel, leading them across the transformational thresholds, and increasing their semantic load on account of unexpected combinations, translations, linkages, etc. When as a result of all this a structurally organized dynamic whole takes shape, we can say that the text of the work has appeared.

The reader repeats this process in the opposite direction, passing from the text to the intention. But we must remember that any actual reading in the opposite direction is also inevitably a creative act. A meaning-generating structure is always asymmetrical and this is especially noticeable when we take such essentially symmetrical texts as palindromes. The well-known sinologist, Academician V. M. Alekseev, analysed a Chinese palindrome: he pointed out that a Chinese hieroglyph, taken in isolation, merely gives an idea of a semantic kernel, while its concrete semantic and grammatical characteristics are revealed only when it is set in correlation with a textual chain; and that without taking account of the sequence of the word-signs one cannot identify either their grammatical categories or the actual semantic content which concretizes the very general abstract semantics of the isolated hieroglyph. Alekseev pointed out the amazing grammatical and semantic shifts which occur in a Chinese palindrome depending on which direction it is read in. In a '[Chinese] palindrome (that is, when the words are in the opposite order to that of normal verse) all Chinese syllable-words, while staying in exactly the same place, are called upon to play quite different syntactic and semantic roles.'[55] Alekseev drew an interesting methodological conclusion from this: namely that a palindrome is invaluable material for studying Chinese grammar.

> The conclusions are clear: 1. The palindrome is the best of all possible means for illustrating the interconnection of Chinese syllable words, without having recourse to the artificial though not artful, talentless, crudely classroom exercise of transposition when teaching students Chinese syntax. 2. The palindrome . . . is the best Chinese material for constructing a theory of the Chinese (and perhaps not only Chinese) word and simple sentence.[56]

Reverse reading therefore results in the dismemberment of signs which cannot normally be dismembered into elements which are the bearers of grammatical and semantic meanings.

The Russian palindrome has a different effect. The poet Semen Kirsanov made some extremely interesting self-observations about the psychology of authoring Russian palindromes and made a brief record of them. He writes that 'when still in high school' he 'involuntarily said to himself *tyulen' ne lyut* ['seal not fierce'] and suddenly noticed that this sentence could be read backwards as well [*tyul en' nelyut*]. Since that time I have often caught myself reading words backwards.' 'In time I began to see words "at one go" and self-rhyming words and their combinations would come to mind involuntarily'.[57] So the mechanism of the Russian palindrome consists in *seeing* the word, even if with an inner eye. This makes it possible to read it backwards. Consequently reading a Chinese word backwards turns the indivisible hieroglyph-word, a sign with strong iconic features, into a segmented sequence of morpho grammatical elements; it reveals its hidden structure. In Russian, however, the palindrome requires one to 'see the word at one go', i.e. to perceive it as an integral picture (the eye does not move linearly from letter to letter, but grasps the word as a whole not in the time-flow; and in the same way palindromic phrases consisting of more than one word are grasped at one go). Thus reading backwards changes the semiotic nature of the text to its opposite one.

We may assume that if, on the one hand, reading from right to left activates the mechanisms of the functional asymmetry of the large hemispheres of the brain, then, on the other hand, on the highest levels of culture reverse reading is associated with the opposition between what is revealed and what is secret, between the profane and the sacred and esoteric. It is significant that palindromes are used in incantations, magic formulas, inscriptions on gates and graves, i.e. at boundaries and magically active places of cultural space, places where earthly ('normal') powers confront infernal ('reverse') ones. And these boundaries are also places of intensified semiotic activity.

We might recall at this point that that the poet bishop St Sidonius Apollinaris ascribed the well-known Latin palindromes to the Devil himself:

> *Signa te signa, temere me tangis et angis*
> *Roma tibi subito motibus ibit amor.*

The relationship of writer to reader can in a sense be likened to the two-directional reading of a palindrome. First, their relationship to the text is asymmetrical. From the point of view of a writer a text is never finalized, a writer is always prone to reworking or reshaping it knowing that any detail of a text is only one of the possible realizations of the potential paradigm. Anything could be changed. For the reader the text is a cast-iron structure, where everything is in the only possible place, where everything bears a meaning and nothing can be changed. An author perceives the final text as a last draft, while a reader takes what is a last draft as to be a finalized text. A reader hyper-structuralizes a text and tends to reduce the role of the accidental in the structure to a minimum.

But that is not the only thing. A reader brings his or her own personality, his or her own cultural memory, codes and associations, to bear on the text. And they are never identical to the author's.

Between text and reader (audience) two opposing types of relationships inevitably take shape: a situation of understanding and a situation of not understanding. Understanding is achieved when there is a unity between the coding systems of the author and those of the readership, the most elementary situation being when there is a shared natural language and shared cultural tradition. However the notion of cultural tradition can be treated in a narrow sense and a wide one. To take the widest sense, the presence in all earthly human civilizations of a certain number of universals[58] makes any text of human culture in principle to some degree translatable into the language of another culture, i.e. to some extent comprehensible. However, a degree of comprehension is at the same time a degree of non-comprehension. To take an example: the textual composition of different cultures inevitably includes a certain set of genres, since the fact that a text belongs to a particular genre which is known to the reader, creates a significant economy of codes on account of what Bakhtin called 'genre memory'. If we understand genres to be the most general text-groupings, falling into the categories of sacred or profane, official and public or individual and everyday, scientific (tending towards metalanguages) or literary (tending towards expression in the languages of art), etc., then we shall find we have a relatively uniform set. From this point of view we can, for instance, write a history of science or of religion, of the novel or folktale. But from the point of view of value we get a quite different categories. Every culture inevitably has a dichotomy between texts of higher and lower value. An extreme example of this is the opposition between what leads to salvation and what to perdition. Salvation may be what is expected of religion (and religion can be set in opposition to science, or to art, or to secular politics). The 'one who saves' may be science or art, which can also be set in various oppositional relationships. And what to an author may have seemed pernicious may to the reader seem salvific. When an archaeological find is defined as a toy, the receiver of this information still does not know whether to react with delight or with condescension. The question will be solved by comparing how the world of the child is valued in the transmitting and receiving cultures.

Text and readership as it were seek mutual understanding. They 'adapt' to each other. A text behaves like a partner in dialogue: it re-orders itself (as far as its supply of structural indeterminacy allows) in the image of the readership. And the reader responds likewise, using his or her informational flexibility for the restructuring which will draw him or her closer to the world of the text. At this pole there is a relationship of tolerance on each side.

We should not, however, forget that not only understanding but also misunderstanding is a necessary and useful condition in communication. A text that is absolutely comprehensible is at the same time a text that is absolutely useless. An absolutely understandable and understanding partner would be convenient but unnecessary, since he or she would be a mechanical copy of my 'I' and our converse would provide us with no increase in information: just as there is no increase in money if one passes a purse from one pocket to another. A dialogue situation does not blur the distinctions between the partners, but intensifies them and makes them more significant.

6

The symbol as plot-gene

Karl Bryullov's picture 'The Last Day of Pompei' was exhibited in St Petersburg in 1834. Pushkin, who was deeply affected by it, attempted to sketch some of the details of the picture and then immediately jotted down a verse fragment:

> Vesuvius opened its maw – smoke gushed out in swirls – a flame
> Flared wide, like a military banner.
> The earth shudders – from the reeling columns
> The idols fall! The people driven [by fear],
> Under a rain of stones, [under the burning ash],
> In crowds, old and young, flee away from the city.[59]

If we compare this text of Pushkin's with Bryullov's picture we find that Pushkin's eye moved along the diagonal from the top right corner of the picture to the bottom left. This movement follows the main compositional axis of the picture. Nikolai Tarabukin, the artist and art-theorist, has made a study of diagonal compositions: 'A picture compositionally constructed along this diagonal often has as its subject a demonstration or procession.' And further: 'In this case the viewer is placed as it were among the crowd depicted on the canvas.'[60]

Tarabukin's observation is a shrewd one and a poll among viewers of Bryullov's picture has fully confirmed that the viewers' attention is as a rule focused on the crowd. The reaction of Martynov, the court commander, was typical in this regard. On seeing the picture, he is reported to have said: 'What I like best is old Pompey being carried by the children.'[61] Martynov was, according to Pushkin, a 'dolt' and a 'swine' [XII, 336] and his reaction to the picture, which showed up his ignorance of Roman history, circulated as an anecdote. But for us in our present concern his remark is of interest as a reaction by a naive and unsophisticated viewer, whose attention was riveted on the large figures in the foreground.

If we compare Pushkin's 'The Bronze Horseman' with Bryullov's 'The Last Day of Pompei' we discover something very important about Pushkin's poetics. Boileau's poetics, and that of the German Romantics, as well as the aesthetics of German classical philosophy – all assumed that the artist first verbally formulated a thought and that this was then clothed in an image which served as sensory expression of the thought. Even according to objectively idealist aesthetics which takes the idea to be the supreme, supra-human reality, the artist who unconsciously portrays that reality, is objectively speaking giving a clear new mode of existence to the idea which previously was obscure and unself-aware. So here too the image is treated as a kind of packaging covering its true verbal (i.e. rational) interpretation. The long-standing disputes over, for instance, the significance in 'The Bronze Horseman' of the flood and the interpretation of the image of the monument, are the result of approaching Pushkin's writings from positions like these.

Pushkin's thought-paradigm is formed not by words but by model-images; these model-images have a syncretic verbal-visual existence and their contradictory nature means that it is possible to make different readings, as well as complementary ones (complementary, in Nils Bohr's sense, that is, readings that are equally adequate as interpretations and at the same time mutually exclusive of each other). Furthermore, an interpretation of one of the nodes in Pushkin's structure automatically also determines how the whole series corresponding to that node is concretized. So the argument about how to understand the symbolic significance of particular images in 'The Bronze Horseman' when these are *taken in isolation*, is pointless.

The first member in Pushkin's three-part paradigm for 'The Bronze Horseman' could have been anything in the poet's mind which at a given moment he associated with the catastrophic flood. The second member was distinguished from the first by the distinctive features: 'having been made', 'belonging to the world of civilization'; rather as we differentiate 'what is conscious' from 'what is unconscious'. The third member was distinguished from the first one by the distinctive features: personal vs. impersonal. The other features could be redistributed within the three-member structure in various ways depending on how the structure is actually interpreted in historical and plot terms.

For instance, in the fragment 'The motionless guard slept on the royal threshold', Pushkin writes:

> Long since the peoples of the world
> Have glorified the downfall of the Great Idol.
> [II, 1, 310]

Here the fallen idol is to be understood as the feudal order of 'old Europe'. The image of the elements can be similarly interpreted in a political sense. Compare in the tenth chapter of *Eugene Onegin*:

> The Pyrenees shook menacingly –
> Naples' volcano flared up.
>
> [VI, 523][62]

Pushkin was strikingly consistent in his use of the very same words to clothe the same model-image of the elemental forces. For instance, in versions of 'Vesuvius opened its maw' we find: 'The earth shook/The columns reel', 'The columns reel', 'The earth reels', 'The earth shuddered – the city shuddered'. In 'The motionless guard slept on the royal threshhold' we find 'Austria reeled, Naples rose up'. The fragment entitled 'And the Sovereign himself was amazed at his deed', which was the germ of a poem about Alexander I and Napoleon, was evidently supposed to include the triumph of an 'idol'; the image in this fragment of an iron foot quashing the rebellion points beyond Alexander I to the figure of Falconet's monument of Peter, though the appearance of the ghost of Napoleon probably implied a prophecy of the future triumph of the elements: 'From the gloom of exile/He foretold eternal freedom to the world' [II, 1, 216]. The possibility of splitting the image of the 'idol' into Alexander I (or any other living person who could bear the complex imagery of this member of the structure) and the statue of the Bronze Horseman was hinted at earlier in the mysterious poem 'The Tsar scowling. . .' (which perhaps is not just a joke):[63]

> The Tsar scowling,
> Said: 'Yesterday
> The storm overthrew
> The monument to Peter.'
>
> [II, 1, 430]

But because the members of the paradigm were correlated to each other, the paradigm had semantic flexibility and, as Pushkin's thought developed, he could actualize different semantic facets. For instance, if destructive power was emphasized in the elements, then constructive power would be a function of the opposite member; similarly the irrationalism of the 'senseless and merciless' elements served to accentuate consciousness.[64] At the same time, in a variant dating from the early 1820s, 'idols' were the passive element, and the 'volcano' was the active one. In Pushkin's mind when writing 'The Bronze Horseman' this juxtaposition becomes a conflict between two equally powerful forces. And this involved the activization of the third member – a human personality and his or her fate caught in the struggle between these forces. We must stress once again that even in 'The Bronze Horseman' the conflict between the model images is in no sense an allegory with a single meaning, but is more like a cultural-historical 'equation' which admits of any semantic substitution provided the correlation between the members of the paradigm is maintained. Pushkin studied the possibilities hidden in the tragically contradictory elements which compose his paradigm of history; his aim was not to make us understand 'in images' a finalized idea which he already fully understood and to which he could give *complete and final form*.

We shall better understand how Pushkin understood this crucial historical conflict if we look at all the realizations and complex transformations of the paradigm we have been describing in all of Pushkin's known texts. We shall see then that, for instance, in Pushkin's novel *The Captain's Daughter*, the snowstorm which gets the plot going ('"Well master," shouted the driver, "we're in trouble: it's a blizzard"')[65] is of significance because of the fact that Pugachev emerges out of it and saves Grinev from it.[66] Accordingly, in the novel Pugachev is associated now with the first member of the paradigm (the 'elemental') and now with the third (the 'human') one. The fragmentation of the second member into complementary functions (i.e. functions that are compatible–incompatible) leads in 'The Bronze Horseman' to the extreme complication of the image of Peter: the Peter of the introduction, Peter as antithesis to the flood, Peter as antithesis to Evgenii – these images, which seem to be all quite different from each other and incompatible, have the effect of transforming the whole paradigm. Yet they all occupy one and the same structural position and form micro-paradigms which in this sense are identical.

What is essential, then, is that the triangle consisting of the rebellious elements, the statue and the human being is preserved. Subsequently, when these images are projected onto the world of concepts, different interpretations emerge. One such projection is a mythological one: water (or fire) – chiselled stone – a human being. When, however, the second member is historically interpreted as culture, *ratio*, authority, city or laws of history, then the first member will be transformed into the concept 'nature', 'unconscious element', 'rebellion', 'steppe', 'elemental opposition to the laws of history'. But this can also be interpreted as the opposition of 'wild freedom' to 'dead captivity'. The relationships of the first and second members of the paradigm to the third can be just as complex: the third member can be actualized by what Gogol called the 'poor riches' of a simple human being, whose right to life and happiness is in opposition both to the unbridled elements and to 'boredom, cold and granite', to 'iron will' and inhuman rationality; though the third member may also display the petty egoism which transformed Liza in 'The Queen of Spades' ultimately into a clockwork doll and made her tread the path taken by another. But in Pushkin none of these possibilities is ever the sole one. The paradigm is presented in all its potentiality. And the reason why Pushkin's images are so profound and unfinalized, why they answer the questions both of Pushkin's contemporaries and of later generations, is precisely because the manifestations of the paradigm are incompatible with each other.

Other oppositions which were extremely important for Pushkin were keyed in to the system we have been discussing: living vs. dead, human vs. inhuman, mobile vs. immobile – the permutations are extremely diverse;[67] when we add to all this the author's shifting point of view which brings in axiological criteria, we realize how multiple are the possible interpretations and evaluations. We have only to imagine Pushkin watching the festivities of the Lycée anniversary on 19 October 1828 when the 'clown' Yakovlev showed the Petersburg flood 'very realistically', dressing up as 'a wax person', i.e. a moving statue of Peter,[68] to realize how within the one paradigm comic and tragic find a place.

The dynamism and contrasts of Pushkin's poetics explain not only the vitality of his literary works but also the depth of his thinking: still today we value him both as an artist of genius and as a great thinker.

*   *   *

Pushkin's 'Little Tragedies' are among the peaks of his achievement in the 1830s and have frequently been discussed. It is not our intention to make an exhaustive study of them here. Our task is much more modest: to introduce one more image into the world of Pushkin's realist symbolism. In the mid-1930s Jakobson, in his article 'The statue in Pushkin's symbolics', wrote:

> In the multiform symbolism of a poetic *oeuvre* we find certain constant, organizing, cementing elements which are the vehicle of unity in the multiplicity of the poet's works and which stamp these works with the poet's individuality. These elements introduce the totality of a poet's individual *mythology* into the variegated tangle of often divergent and unrelated poetic motifs. (Jakobson's italics)[69]

A poet's symbolic 'alphabet' is not just an individual matter: a poet may draw symbols from the arsenal of epoch, cultural trend or social circle. A symbol is bound to cultural memory, and an entire series of symbolic images runs vertically through the whole course of human history, or large areas of it. An artist's individuality is manifest not only in the creation of new, unique symbols (i.e. in a symbolic reading of the non-symbolic), but also in the actualization of symbolic images which are sometimes extremely archaic. But it is the *system of relationships* which the poet establishes *between* the fundamental image-symbols which is the crucial thing. Symbols are always polysemic, and only when they form themselves into the crystal grid [*kristallicheskaya reshetka*] of mutual connections do they create that 'poetic world' which marks the individuality of each artist.

In Pushkin's realist writings his symbols form themselves into an exceptionally dynamic, flexible structure which generates an amazing wealth of meanings which – and this is the important point – are almost as capacious and many-layered as life itself. It is not our task to describe the full system of Pushkin's symbolics, because of limitations of space and because of the complexity of the problem. But the 'Little Tragedies' gives us the opportunity to consider some further symbols and how they are connected with the structure we have been describing.

The semantic centre of 'The Stone Guest', 'Mozart and Salieri' and 'The Feast during the Plague' is a motif which we may term 'the fatal feast'.[70] In the plots of all three plays the feast is associated with death: a feast with an invited statue ('The Stone Guest'), a feast where murder is committed ('Mozart and Salieri') and a feast in the city of the plague. And in all these instances the feast is not only dangerous but also unnatural: a blasphemous violation of certain fundamental taboos essential for humanity. The motif of the fatal feast is an archaic one: we have only to recall the feast of Atreus. But in Pushkin this motif is especially significant because it recurs throughout his creative career.

The feast in Pushkin, in its basic meaning, has positive connotations. The theme of the feast is the theme of friendship:

> May God help you, my friends,
> In the cares of life, of royal service,
> And at the feasts of merry friendship,
> And in the sweet mysteries of love!
>
> [III, 1, 80]

> Yesterday, leaving my friends' nocturnal feast
>
> [II, 1, 82]

> And they sat down with the vanquished
> To friendly feasts
>
> [IV, 16]

A feast is the coming together of people into a brotherly circle. The festive table, merry-making and brotherhood are persistently associated with freedom. Merry-making is a mark of liberty, while boredom and frustration are born of slavery. 'Their nightly encampment is merry as liberty'; 'accustomed to merry . . . liberty'; 'Now he is a free inhabitant of the world,/And the sun merrily on him/Shines its midday beauty' [IV, 179, 408, 183]. The triple association of the feast with merriment and freedom makes up the first and basic layer of this symbol:

> I love the evening feast,
> Where Merriment presides,
> And Freedom, my idol,   ˎ
> Is legislator at table.
>   [II, 1, 100]

Hence the supplementary feature of the ring or circle: the circle of friends, of brothers, of comrades. This is why the symbol of the feast is active in Pushkin's lyrics to his friends, and also in his political lyrics: the ideas of struggle, shared opinions, political union are associated with wine, merry-making and friendly disputes. At the same time, we must remember that the feast is communion, the shared taking of the bread and the wine – that ancient symbol of indissoluble unity, the union of sacrifice. Hence the association of the feast and the Eucharist ('Epistle to V. L. Davydov'). But the feast also has Bacchanalian connotations of wildness and overflowing energy.

Among Pushkin's poems his 'Bacchic Song' has an unusual cluster of basic feast-elements; the first line refers to the theme of delight, though the Church Slavonic forms of *veselie* ['merry-making'] and *glas* ['voice'] give the poem a solemn, almost ritual resonance. The solemnity of a major key permeates the poem. Only the first line has a questioning intonation: it refers to the coming moment of silence and contains a word with the semantics of silence and perhaps also sadness: *smolknul* ['he fell silent']. The whole of the rest of the poem contrasts with the first line and is full of an exuberant, joyful lexis. Numerous exclamations are combined with imperative forms of the verbs. Only the verb of the first line is in the indicative: all the other verbs are imperatives. The poem sounds a strong-willed note. The main symbolic meaning of the poem is the victory of light over darkness. This refers first to the extra-textual situation, the moment when the song is sung: 'Bacchic Song' is a ritual hymn to the sun, sung at the end of a night-long feast, at the moment when the sun rises.

The theme reveals the symbolism of the image of the feast step by step:

- the Bacchanalian merriment
- love
- wine, the double image of the ring (the precious rings thrown into the round glasses, and the circle of the friends' assembled goblets)[71]
- the muses and reason
- the sun.

The comparison of the sun with reason ('the immortal sun of the mind'), the contrasting of the sun with the lamp 'of fake wisdom' and the epithet 'holy' applied to the sun, all give the image of the sun an extremely generalized sense, not just an astronomical one (the significance of the circle as a most ancient sign of the sun is found here too).

The complexity of the feast-symbol is apparent also in the fact that the feast as a manifestation of friendship does not exclude other combinations: 'the noise of feasts and of rowdy arguments', and admiration for Reason and even the ritual worship of it do not preclude the 'mad jollity of the feasts'. Neither Reason nor Poetry is hostile to the madness of festive merry-making.

> Pray both to Bacchus and to love
> And scorn the jealous murmurings of the rabble;
> It does not know that one can live in friendship
> With Cythera, with portico, with book, and wineglass;
> That a lofty mind can be concealed
> Under the light covering of madcap pranks
> > [II, 1, 27]

> I took my spirited Muse
> To the noise of feasts and rowdy arguments,
> To the threats of midnight patrols[72]
> And she brought her gifts
> To them at the mad feasts
> > [VI, 166]

Another sense of feast is associated with abundance: 'feast of the imagination', 'feast of young escapades'.

A third sense goes back to the folklore association of battle and feast, although this association has a long literary tradition before Pushkin. This is why feast in this sense is to be found in many of Pushkin's early Lyceum verses.[73]

In the poem 'Andre Chenier' there is a unique usage: 'In the morning the execution, the customary feast for the people' [II, 1, 397]. Here the feast seems to be a premonition of the semantics of the fatal feasts which is our immediate concern. In a recent article on 'The Feast during the Plague', which, though containing many interesting ideas, is highly subjective, Pankratova and Khalizev[74] start out with the notion of the 'sinful' young Pushkin and the mature Pushkin whose dominant feeling was that of repentance, and so they relate Pushkin's feast poetry to the sins of his youth. They summarize Pushkin's development in the following words: 'In 1835 the words of "The Wanderer" rang out: "I see the light"', words which, in the opinion of these scholars, summed up 'Pushkin's moral evolution'.[75] If we adopt this approach, then we have also to assume that the lines 'The earth is motionless. The vaults of heaven/ Creator, are upheld by thee' express Pushkin's own cosmogonic ideas.

A thorough analysis of the texts,[76] and not one that is selectively subjective, leads to a different conclusion: the image of the feast in the direct meaning of the symbol is to be found all through Pushkin's poetry as something positive (see 'The Feast of Peter the Great', a poem with which Pushkin opened the first issue of *The Contemporary*, thereby emphasizing the programmatic significance he gave to this text). The terrifying images of the unnatural feast are powerful *precisely against this background*: they are felt to be strange and anomalous. The repentance, which Pankratova and Khalizev think they see in Pushkin's attitude to the ideal of the feast as such, totally distorts the semantic development of this symbol.

The feast is an image which symbolically expresses alliance, unification, a merry gathering of brothers. But can there be unification and merging between life and death? In the 'Little Tragedies' these are the forces that play the major parts, true, though, in such a generalized form that the conflict between them observable deep below the surface. Closer to the plot surface the life and death conflict is played out between our familiar triad of symbols (the elements, law, humanity). Finally, on the actual surface of the plot these forces are embodied in concrete historical and cultural images of the period. A preceding level does not automatically and completely 'impress itself' into the next one, but plays with it, only partially expressing itself in the language of the next level which is by definition a different one.

In the 'Little Tragedies' the main symbols of Pushkin's artistic world in the 1830s are interpreted in a new way: things, ideas and people conflict with each other. And these conflicts are not just unusual ones, but run their course in monstrous and unnatural forms. The world of the 'Little Tragedies' is a dislocated and broken one (as Gukovsky perceptively noticed, though we cannot agree with all aspects of his analysis); it is a world where each phenomenon acquires uncharacteristic features: what is immobile moves, love triumphs among the tombs, refined aesthetic sensibility logically leads to murder, and feasts turn out to be feasts of death. But this rupturing of the norm is what builds up the image of the truly essential but unrealized norm.

The need for harmony, and the belief that harmony is both possible and natural, this is the semantic ground of these tragic stories which leave the reader with a sense of profound artistic well-being, in spite of the pictures they draw of sickness and perversion.

In 'The Miserly Knight' things take over from people. The unnatural feast which the Baron shares with his trunks of gold, as if they were his brothers, is complemented by the hostility between father and son and their mutual readiness to murder each other. The money becomes animate and is referred to as 'servants', 'friends' and 'gentlemen'. But above all, the coins are gods.[77] And it is in the company of these god-like friends that the Baron decides 'Today shall be a feast-day'.[78] Gukovsky detected features of knightly psychology in the son Albert's words about Count Delorges:

> Still, his armour's whole;
> His new Venetian breastplate wasn't damaged;
> As for his breast, no loss to him on that –
> He'll not be put to purchasing another.[79]

But something else strikes us in these words: under the power of money, the living and the non-living have changed places. What is dead, artificially made and exchangable is valued, but what is living, natural and inalienable appears devalued. In earlier times Simeon Polotsky had referred to a similarly unnatural world when he wrote: 'the artist's work is preserved with honour, while the person himself is not treated honourably'.[80] All human relationships are broken, and objects – gold, trunks, keys – have taken over from people.

In 'The Miserly Knight' the Baron had his feast, and the other feast to which Albert wanted to despatch his father is merely hinted at. But that other feast takes place in 'Mozart and Salieri' and thus a 'situation rhyme' links these two plays, which in all other respects are so different, into a single 'montage phrase'.

Gukovsky pointed out that the conflict of 'Mozart and Salieri' does not lie in the envy of an ungifted person for a great talent. Salieri is a great composer, devoted to art and felt himself to be the equal of Mozart. Gukovsky, true to his conception of realism as the portrayal of human socio-historical determinism, sees the meaning of Pushkin's play in the triumph of historically progressive forms of art over those forms that are receding into the past, and he consequently describes Salieri as a musician of the eighteenth century and Mozart as a Romantic:

Mozart came to take over from the cultural and aesthetic complex which shackled Salieri. If we are not to risk constricting the meaning and significance of Pushkin's conception we could conventionally designate the system embodied in the image of Salieri as Classicism, and the system embodied in the image of Mozart as Romanticism as Pushkin understood it.[81]

Gukovsky is vulnerable as regards his facts: what Pushkin knew about Salieri could not have led him to create the image of a Classical musician. Against Gukovsky we can point, for instance, to the mention of

Beaumarchais (a name which Pushkin associated with the beginning of the revolution) and the reference to *Tarare*, a Romantic revolutionary opera which was most popular in the 1790s, in which spirits, genies and the ghosts of heroes appeared on the stage to glorify tyrranocide (Karamzin called the work 'strange').

But this is not the only point. A change of cultural epochs might explain envy. But Salieri is not just envious: he kills.

Pushkin portrays the psychology of envy, and with extraordinary mastery also demonstrates the mechanics for the birth of murder. To believe that Classicism at the moment of its historical apogee could engender a mind set on murder is just as bizarre as ascribing such ideas to Pushkin.

Let us look at Salieri's path to murder.

Salieri is a born musician ('I was born with a love of art'). From early childhood he has dedicated himself to music. His attitude to his art was one of self-denying dedication. Salieri's words are frequently quoted:

> . . . killing sound, dissecting
> Music as if it were a corpse, I checked
> My harmony by algebra.[82]

We have become so accustomed to thinking of these words as a declaration of arid rationalism in art, that their true meaning in the context of the whole monologue has been overlooked. Yet immediately after these words come these:

> . . . At last,
> Having achieved a mastery of theory,
> I ventured *on the rapture of creation*. (my italics)[83]

Salieri is not at all opposed to inspired creation, not an enemy of 'creative fantasy'. With his stern self-discipline he simply believes that the right to inspired creation has to be won by a prolonged novitiate and a commitment which give right of entry into the circle of dedicated creators. This view reminds one rather of an order of knighthood than an academy of mathematicians. Neither the idea of commitment to art, nor that of a harsh novitiate as the time to master skills, was alien to the theory of Romanticism. Wackenroder, for instance, who took Dürer to be his ideal, wrote that Dürer, 'combining spirit with perfection of mechanics',[84] took to 'painting with incomparably more seriousness, solemnity and dignity than the refined artists of our days'.[85] We could easily imagine these word coming from Pushkin's Salieri.

Salieri adhered to a medieval, priestly attitude towards art, which involved not only commitment and duty and self-denial but also a special kind of grace which descends upon those worthy of it. And just as grace comes to the priest from on high, so art comes to the artist from above. None of these remarks would have shocked the Romantic who wrote: 'Glory to art, but not to the artist: he is its weak instrument.'[86]

This is the point from which Salieri begins his fateful path to crime. Pushkin takes the most noble of abstract ideas, one which is essentially humanistic, the idea of art, and shows that, when this idea is valued more highly than a human being and turned into a self-directed abstraction, it can become the instrument of murder. By valuing human art more than humanity, it was easy for Salieri to take the next step, once he had convinced himself that a man and his life might be sacrificed to this fetish.

A thought detached from its human content turns into a chain of sophisms. Pushkin wrote of Angelo in Shakespeare's *Measure for Measure*: 'He justifies his cruelty with the thoughtful arguments of a statesman; he seduces innocence with irresistibly beguiling sophisms.'[87] The thought grows cold, puts on the armour of false truths, hardens to stone, in fact becomes dead. The stone rises up against the person, the abstraction threatens life.

The first step on the road to murder is taken when the murderer asserts that he is merely an instrument of a higher will and bears no personal responsibility. Salieri says: 'For I am chosen', 'I cannot bend the course of destiny'; then comes the decisive step, when, replacing the word 'kill' which is taboo by the word 'stop', he says: 'For I am chosen, I must stop him now'.[88] The hardest thing in a criminal deed is to know how to refer to it decently, to master the murderer's lexicon. Even speaking to himself Salieri does not want to name names: he refers merely to the innocent action of 'stopping'. And there is another important sophism: Mozart is portrayed as the aggressor, and 'we ministers and acolytes of music' as the defending victims. This is typical of the sophistry of murder: the victim is depicted as a strong and dangerous attacker and the murderer as the defending victim.

Then, finally, come the decisive words: 'What good/If Mozart should live on to reach new heights?/Will music be the better?'[89] Mozart's right to live (and anyone else's) is determined by the 'good' it does to the progress of art. And the 'ministers and acolytes of music' are called upon to be the judges of this case. If they decide that the life of Mozart is no good for the idea of art then they have the right to pass the death sentence on him.

So an abstract dogma, even one whose first premises are noble, if it is valued more than living, pulsating human life and regards that life merely as a means for its own higher aims, grows cold and stony, turning into a kind of inhuman 'idol' and an instrument of murder.

Mozart shares his dinner at the Golden Lion, his last feast, not with a musician friend as he thinks but with a stone guest. On the surface level of the plot, the two who sit at table are, on the one hand, a playful and life-loving person – not a musician but a person (the episode with the blind violinist, the reference to playing on the floor with his child, build up the image not of a priest but of a person) and, on the other hand, one who, though a keen lover and connoisseur of music, says of himself: 'I've little love for life': on the one hand, a man, and on the other, a principle.

But a foreshadowing of the fateful dinner is already glimpsed in the first conversation between Mozart and Salieri when Mozart says:

> Now
> Imagine . . . whom? – Myself, a little younger;
> And I'm in love – not deeply, just a bit;
> I'm with a pretty girl, [with Dona Anna? Yu.L.],
>   or friend – say you, [i.e. Salieri, Yu.L.]
> I'm happy. . . . Then: a vision of the grave,
> Or sudden darkness, something of the kind.[90]

This is a premonition of the appearance of the Comendador. But the nub of the situation is the fact that Mozart's friend is the *Comendador*. Mozart, who believes that genius and evil-doing do not go together, thinks he is feasting with a genius, i.e. with a *person*. Whereas in fact he is sitting at table with a stone, 'a vision of the grave'.

The second reference is when Mozart says that he thinks the man in black who has commissioned the Requiem 'even now/It seems he's sitting here with us'.

The third reference is connected with the name of Beaumarchais which drops from Salieri's lips. Whether slander or truth, the reputation of being a poisoner followed Beaumarchais during his lifetime and stained his name after his death.

So the symbol of the feast and the motif of the struggle between a human being and a stone leads to the fatal moment of the murder.

Two worlds confront one another: Mozart's normal, human world, which affirms that art is tied to humanity, to play, carefreeness, to the simple life and to that creativity which seeks what has not yet been found; and the perverse world of Salieri where murder is called a duty, poison the 'sacred gift of love' and poisoned wine 'the cup of friendship', a world where human life is but a means, truth has been found and formulated, and priests stand guard over it. Factually speaking the second world is the winner, but morally speaking it is the first.

Perversity is the law of Salieri's world, and he treats the contradictory phrase 'I dined in hated company' as something normal and common-place. In 'The Stone Guest' this atmosphere affects all the characters and fills all the space of the drama. Mozart's natural, human, domestic playfulness, the simple good nature of his genius, becomes, in Don Juan, an evil passion which to be fully felt needs the presence of death. Don Juan is also a genius, but he would never say that 'genius and evil-doing don't go together'. Mozart is the personification of naturalness. He proves that being a genius is the norm of human existence. Don Juan is a genius straining to break the norms, to break all bounds just because they are bounds.

If the shift in the authorial point of view shows up something new on the 'human' side (Pushkin analyses the personal principle in a human being: Mozart illustrating the genius in the human, Don Juan the terrible in genius), so also is the world of 'stone' dogmas and principles revealed in a new light: the Comendador, being portrayed as the defender of the ideal of faithfulness, the home and family morals is shown in a different light from the jealous genius, Salieri. The result is that in 'The Stone Guest' both antagonists, each in their own way, are terrible and, each in their own way, are attractive.

The image of Don Juan splits in two: yes, he is the subtle seducer, the calculating cynic, a 'shameless scoundrel' in Don Carlos's words. But he is also the Don Quixote of love, and every false word he utters miraculously becomes true and sincere. Every moment he believes so completely in what he is saying that his words are true. He is the enemy of the women who love him ('How many helpless women have you ruined?'), but he is also their greatest friend. Even as he seduces them he tells them what they secretly long to hear, and for each of them Don Juan's love is both temptation and ruin, triumph and happiness.

Don Juan is 'shameless, depraved and godless' in the monk's words. But his godlessness comes not from a pathological longing for blasphemy but from his boundless audacity which makes him deny the existence of any powers which could instil fear in him. He makes his appearance with the words 'there's no-one I'm afraid of in Madrid' and he triumphs over fear in his last moments:

> *Don Juan*   O God have mercy! Dona Anna!
> *Statue*   Leave her, All is finished. You are trembling, Don Juan.
> *Don Juan*   Not I – I invited you and I'm glad you've come.[91]

He refuses to obey the statue's command and 'leave' Dona Anna and he dies with the name of his earthly love on his lips. (Cunning seduction has turned into the passion described in the Bible: 'For love is strong as Death. . . . Love no flood can quench, no torrents drown' [Song of Songs, 8.6–7].) Don Juan's reckless, boundless audacity gives his image its fascination, while the destructiveness of his passions lays bare the frightening side of the human personality.

The image of the Comendador also splits in two, and this duality distinguishes him from Salieri. He is the Statue, the embodiment of principle, the 'fortunate departed', the 'marble spouse'.[92] But he is also a human being. This duality is expressed in Don Juan's monologue:

> The giant they've portrayed him in this statue!
> Those shoulders! What a Hercules! In life
> The late Comendador was small and frail;
> He'd not have reached his statue's nose on tiptoe.[93]

The contrast between the imposing monumental sign and the physical puniness of the real Don Alvaro has often been commented on. But the words: 'But bold and proud he was, and stern of soul' re-establish the accord between the spiritual essence of Dona Anna's late husband and the external appearance of the Statue. And the real-life Don Alvaro splits in two. On the one hand, he purchased Dona Anna's love ('We were poor, Don Alvaro wealthy', 'My mother gave my hand to Don Alvaro' – the situation is the same as that of Tatyana in *Eugene Onegin*). But on the other hand, he loved Dona Anna ('If you had known Alvaro's love for me') and would have been faithful to her even after her death ('If he had lost a wife: he would have stayed/True to connubial love').[94]

The role of the Statue is also not a simple one. It is both an embodiment of a pitiless and inhuman principle of Duty, denying the right to personal happiness on earth. But it also stands for the moral judgement and supreme retribution on one who has broken ethical norms and brought chaos and destruction into the world.

But there is something else about the Statue.

In 'Mozart and Salieri' there is nothing to represent the third essential component of Pushkin's symbolic order – images of the elements. True, the presence of infernal forces can be felt in the play, but only Mozart senses them – Salieri is deaf to everything except the sophisms of abstract reasoning. In 'The Stone Guest' the intrusion of supernatural powers is one of the basic motifs of the play. Something bursts in on Don Juan's destiny, something that is alien both to human beings and to the abstract principles of culture, duty and even of morality, something incomprehensible and inhuman; and Don Juan, blasphemously laughing at human values, comes in contact with something terrible, something whose existence he did not even believe in. The image of the elements is so capacious that it can encompass such distant meanings as, for example, popular rebellion and the invasion of infernal forces (the snowstorm in *The Captain's Daughter*, and in the poem 'Devils'); and in general terms its capaciousness makes it possible to introduce semantic components that are multi-layered and susceptible to many interpretations. Don Juan invited the 'marble spouse' to 'come to your widow's house', but it was not a dead rival who arrived but something much more frightening. Don

Juan stood up to that encounter too.

The merging in the Statue of the stone 'idol' symbol with that of the inexpressible elemental principle reveals new facets in the symbolism of the idol, which are absent from the image of Salieri; while the Don Juan version of the human being turns out to be in a solitary situation which shows up both his strength of character and the inevitability of his final ruin. In 'The Bronze Horseman' the 'idol' and the elements are in a relationship of hostile opposition. It is the very diversity of the ways these primary semantic groups are combined that enables Pushkin to portray the multi-faceted complexity of historical and social conflicts.

The infernal feast in the presence of death takes place twice in 'The Stone Guest': there is a rehearsal for it at Laura's where Don Alvaro's place is taken by his brother Don Carlos; then at Dona Anna's where the Comendador comes in the guise of the Statue.

The cycle of the 'Little Tragedies' is concluded by a play where the image of the feast is the central semantic organizer.

'The Feast during the Plague' has been less studied than the other plays of the cycle, partly perhaps because it is a translation. Yet the significance of this work is immense. In 'The Stone Guest' the action already takes place in a special, strange and frightening space. Pushkin left out all the minor plots which are part of other versions of Don Juan, such as the seduction of the peasant girl, the scenes in the castle, in the village, etc. What remains is the cemetery and the scenes involving a dead person and supernatural phenomena. The cemetery is both Don Juan's place and the Comendador's. From the cemetery they each in turn come to Don Anna's house. In 'The Feast during the Plague' the cemetery becomes one of the two basic spatial elements.

'The Feast during the Plague' takes us into a world of destroyed and distorted norms. The whole action unfolds as it were in a distorting mirror in unnatural space. An important spatial symbol for the late Pushkin is the House. The House is one's own space, a place that is familiar and at the same time enclosed and protected; it provides space for private life where the ideal of independence can be realized: 'A pot of soup, and you're your own boss' [*Shchei gorshok, i sam bol'shoi*]. But it is also the place where a person lives real life, where national culture is experienced and where (this is an idea that Tolstoy took up) the life of the people is real and internalized, not artificial and for show. This is the world of the human personality, a world that stands up to the elements and to anything which belittles and denigrates the life of the individual. It is both the 'abode' of 'labours and pure pleasures' and the 'little old house' of 'The Bronze Horseman' on whose threshold the corpse of Evgeny was found. But it is also the centre and focus of the world order. The domestic gods, the Penates, are in Pushkin's poem the 'counsellors of Zeus':

Whether you live in the heavenly depths,
Or, mighty gods, to all things
You are the cause, according to the sages,
Or, most mighty gods, to all things
Great Zeus with his white-haired spouse
And the goddess of wisdom, maiden of strength,
Athenian Pallas, – praise to you all.
Accept this hymn, mysterious powers!
[III, 1, 192–3]

It is here in his own House that a person learns 'the first science' – 'to honour himself'. Pushkin underlined the last words.

The House is the natural space for the Feast. But the 'feast during the plague' takes place on the street. The first stage direction reads: 'A street. A table laid.' Already this is a 'joining of the unjoinable'. And when a cart laden with the dead passes by the table and the feasting guests, the effect is almost surrealistic, reminding one of the horses and cart which appear in the drawing room in Buñuel's film *Le Chien Andalou*. These disruptions of the artistic space in 'The Feast during the Plague' are of profound significance: the action takes place in 'a world gone mad'. Houses have been abandoned, no one lives in them and people are afraid to enter them. Domestic life takes place on the street. 'Our homes are dismal places –/And youth loves gaiety' [109]. The Master of the Revels, Walsingham, speaks of the horror 'of the dread emptiness which I find in my home'.[95]

The emptiness of the house is contrasted with the animation of the cemetery. In Mary's song:

Like a burnt-out building
Stands each street of doom; –
All is still and silent,
Save the swelling tomb.
Always dead are carried . . .[96]

The houses of the living are contrasted with the houses of the dead ('cold, underground living-places': the oxymoron of referring to the graves as 'living-places' [*zhilishche*] is typical.[97]

There are three semantic centres in the play: the carousing men and women, whose unnatural space, the street, is turned into a place of feasting; the priest who space is the cemetery ('Amid white faces I pray at the cemetery'); and the Plague itself, which fills the whole world of the play.

The Plague is unique in the series of Pushkin's elemental images. We should note the fundamental difference between the two versions of this image: when the elements are represented by human masses, implacability is tempered with compassion (Arkhip, Pugachev). But when the symbol takes the shape of an elemental disaster, plague or flood, there is no tempering of its implacability and its destructiveness is senseless.

The Plague creates conditions of all-encompassing death and thereby shows up the deeply hidden characteristics of the other protagonists.

The human world which longs for life, happiness and joy responds to the Plague by accepting its challenge. In the original tragedy by Wilson the blasphemous, anti-god strand is much more stressed, especially in the behaviour of the Young Man. Pushkin toned it down although the Priest's remark: 'O godless feast! O godless libertines!' refers to this theme. The merry-making at the feast is a rebellion. But this rebellion is only indirectly aimed at God: its main point is to refuse to acknowledge the power of the Plague; it is a rebellion against Fear. The centre point of this strand is the Master of Revels' song which is an apologia for courage. The merry-making is directed against the fear of death. The feast during the plague is an act equal to 'the savage delight in the thick of the fight', the bravery of the sailor in 'the ocean's dark rage', or of the traveller caught in the hurricane:

> Everything, everything that threatens death.
> Contains for the mortal heart
> Inexplicable delights.[98]

The song to celebrate the Plague has often been compared with Pushkin's poem 'The Hero', which was also written during the autumn of 1830 at Boldino and which takes as its subject the legend that Napoleon visited a plague hospital at Jaffa. In the dialogue between the Poet and his Friend the Emperor's compassion, shown when he 'grasps the cold hand of plague' in order to encourage the sick soldiers, is the height of his glory:

> By the heavens/ I swear: he who risked his life/
> Before the dire disease/ In order to encourage a dying glance/
> I swear, he will be the friend of heaven,/
> Whatever may be the verdict/ Of blind earth . . .
>
> [III, 1, 252]

In their recent study, Pankratova and Khalizev condemn Walsingham, the Master of the Revels, by comparing him with the Napoleon of the poem. They write:

In Napoleon scorn for danger is magnificently accompanied by his compassion for people who have been 'branded by the powerful plague'

. . . . For this noble and compassionate deed, 'he will be the friend of heaven'. Whereas Walsingham, who composed the song to celebrate the Plague, like the Young Man, sees only the pit with its terrible corruption and hears only the resonant thud of the burial cart.[99]

So the authors for some strange reason find a fear of death in the song to celebrate the Plague.

If we do compare Walsingham with the Napoleon of the poem 'The Hero' we must bear in mind that the semantic positions of these two characters are just as different as those of the Bronze Horseman and Evgeny in 'The Bronze Horseman'. Napoleon is a historical figure, one of the 'elect', he is 'on the throne'. He stands for Authority, an embodiment of the idea of the state, and a representative of those forces which, when devoid of humanitarian principle, become the scourge of humanity: 'Let the hero have a heart! What would he be without one? A tyrant . . .' [III, 1, 253]. Walsingham, however, has no authority, he is just a human being. He is himself a victim of the Plague which has robbed him of wife and mother, and tomorrow perhaps will take his life too. He should be compared not with Napoleon but with the soldiers lying in the hospital. Pushkin does not condemn their courage, their bold defiance of the power of the plague.

If Walsingham represents human personality, the Priest represents the moral principle. In the name of moral duty, he condemns individualistic rebellion. However, unlike Don Juan and the Comendador, Walsingham and the Priest have a common enemy – the Plague. And 'The Feast during the Plague' is the only one of the 'Little Tragedies' which does not end with the death of one (or both) of the antagonists, but ends with their actual reconciliation – each recognizes the right of the other to follow his own path in accordance with his nature and his beliefs. The play is steeped in the atmosphere of death, but not one of the characters in it dies. What is more, if we carefully compare Pushkin's text with the English original[100] we find that there is an almost verbatim similarity between parts of Pushkin's drama and John Wilson's dramatic poem 'The City of the Plague'. But this only points up the essential difference between them: Wilson takes a romantic enjoyment in the horrors he describes, the monstrous city of the plague becomes for him a true picture of the world, and the author's desire to shock the reader with his terrible pictures is the central task of his aesthetics.

Behind 'The Feast during the Plague', as behind all Pushkin's 'Little Tragedies' rises the image of the harmony of normal life and human relationships, the image of that Feast of love and brotherhood, freedom and compassion, which for Pushkin is the hidden essence of life.

The study of anomalous conflicts is the way to understand these norms at a deep level, for behind the disharmony rises the hidden image of harmony.

*   *   *

In the examples we have discussed we have seen how the symbol serves as a condensed programme for the creative process. The subsequent development of a plot is merely the unfolding of a symbol's hidden possibilities. A symbol is a profound coding mechanism, a special kind of 'textual gene'. But the fact that one and the same primary symbol can be developed into different plots, and the actual process of this development is irreversible and unpredictable, proves that the creative process is asymmetrical. Using Prigogine's terminology (see p. 231) we can define the moment of creative inspiration as a situation of extreme far-from-equilibrium which precludes any simple predictable development.

7

The symbol in the cultural system

In the semiotic sciences 'symbol' is a word of many meanings. The common phrase 'symbolic meaning' is often used as a simple synomym for signification. Where there is an expression-content relationship, and the conventionality of this relationship is being stressed, the researcher will often talk of symbolic function and of symbols. Yet Saussure contrasted symbols to conventional signs and emphasized their iconic nature. Scales, he suggested, can be the symbol of justice since they iconically involve the idea of balance, whereas a cart could not.

In another classification a symbol is defined as a sign whose meaning is a sign of another order or another language. Against this definition stands the tradition which understands a symbol as a semiotic expression of a higher and absolute non-semiotic reality. According to the former definition symbolic meaning is something rational and the symbol is understood as a means for the adequate translation of expression level into content level. According to the latter definition, the content of a symbol irrationally glimmers through the expression level and the symbol as it were serves as a bridge between the rational world and a mystical one.

Any linguo-semiotic system, whether regarded as a real fact in the history of culture or as a system for describing any signifying object, senses its incompleteness unless it has its own definition of a symbol. Such a definition does not mean a precise and full description of an object that remains identical in all circumstances, but involves rather the presence in each semiotic system of a *structural position*, without which the system is incomplete because certain essential functions cannot be realized. But the mechanisms which carry out these functions are persistently referred to by the word 'symbol' although it is extremely difficult to produce an invariant definition either of these functions or of the mechanisms which realize them. So we conclude that even if we do not know what a symbol is, every system knows what 'its symbol' is and needs one for the working of its semiotic structure.

So here we shall not attempt an all-encompassing definition, but shall take our starting-point in the ideas that our cultural experience intuitively gives us, and then try to generalize.

A symbol, as commonly understood, involves the idea of a content which in its turn serves as expression level for another content, one which is as a rule more highly valued in that culture. We must distinguish a symbol from a reminiscence or quotation since in them the 'outer' level of content-expression is not independent but rather a kind of index-sign pointing to a larger text with which it is in a metonymic relationship. Whereas a symbol both in expression level and in content level is always a text, i.e. it has a single, self-contained meaning value and a clearly demarcated boundary which makes it possible to isolate it from the surrounding semiotic context. We believe that this latter circumstance is especially important for the ability to 'be a symbol'.

A symbol always has something archaic about it. Every culture needs a body of texts which serves the function of archaism. Symbols cluster here thickly and with reason because the core group of symbols are indeed archaic and go back to pre-literate times when certain signs (which are as a rule elementary space-indicators) were the condensed mnemonic programmes for the texts and stories preserved in the community's oral memory. Symbols have preserved this ability to store up extremely long and important texts in condensed form. But even more interesting is another feature, also an archaic one: a symbol, being a finalized text, does not have to be included in a syntagmatic chain, and if it is included in one, it preserves its own semantic and structural independence. It can readily be picked out from its semiotic context and just as readily enter a new textual context. This leads us to another important feature: a symbol never belongs only to one synchronic section of a culture, it always cuts across that section vertically, coming from the past and passing on into the future. A symbol's memory is always more ancient that the memory of its non-symbolic text-context.

Every text of a culture is by definition heterogeneous. Even in a strictly synchronic section the heterogeneity of the languages of culture forms a complex plurality of voices. The common idea that if we say 'period of Classicism' or 'period of Romanticism' we have defined the totality of a cultural period, or at least its dominant tendency, is a mere illusion resulting from the descriptive language we have adopted. The wheels of the various mechanisms of a culture move at different rates. The speed at which natural language develops cannot be compared, for instance, with the speed of fashion; the domain of the sacred is always more conservative than the domain of the profane. Hence the internal diversity which is a fundamental law for a culture's existence. Symbols are among the most stable elements of the cultural continuum.

Since symbols are important mechanisms of cultural memory, they can transfer texts, plot outlines and other semiotic formations from one level of a culture's memory to another. The stable sets of symbols which recur diachronically throughout culture serve very largely as unifying mechanisms: by activating a culture's memory of itself they prevent the culture from disintegrating into isolated chronological layers. The national and area boundaries of cultures are largely determined by a long-standing basic set of dominant symbols in cultural life.

Looked at from this point of view, however, symbols reveal their duality: on the one hand, by recurring throughout a culture's history a symbol shows its invariancy and its repeatability. A symbol stands out as something different from the textual space that surrounds it, like an emissary from other cultural epochs (or from other cultures), a reminder of the ancient (or eternal) foundations of that culture. On the other hand, a symbol actively correlates with its cultural context, transforms it and is transformed by it. Its invariancy is realized in variants. And the changes which the 'eternal' meaning of the symbol undergoes in the given culture highlight the changeability of the context.

This capacity for variancy comes about because the most historically active symbols have a certain degree of indeterminacy in the relationship between text-expression and text-content. The text-content always belongs to a more multi-dimensional semantic space. So expression never entirely covers content, but as it were alludes to it. No matter in this case whether this non-coincidence is caused by the expression being merely a brief mnemonic sign of an eroded text-content, or by the fact that the expression belongs to the profane, open, demonstrative domain of culture, and the content to the sacred, esoteric, secret domain, or whether it is caused by a romantic longing to 'express the inexpressible'. What is important is that the semantic potentials of the symbol are always greater than any realization of them: the links which, with the help of its expression, a symbol establishes with a particular semiotic context, never exhaust all its semantic valency. This is the semantic reserve thanks to which a symbol can enter into unexpected relationships, altering its essence and deforming its textual context in unpredictable ways.

From this point of view we note that symbols with elementary expression levels have greater cultural and semantic capacity than symbols which are more complex. The cross, the circle, the pentagram have many more semantic potentials that Titian's painting 'The flaying of Marsyas' because between expression and content of simple symbols lies a gulf of mutual unprojectability. The 'simple' symbols are the ones that form the symbolic nucleus of a culture, and whether a culture as a whole is of a symbolizing or de-symbolizing tendency can be judged by the number of them.

Now we come to the question of the symbolizing or de-symbolizing reading of texts. A symbolizing reading means reading as symbols texts or fragments of texts, which in their natural context were not intended to be perceived as such. A de-symbolizing reading turns symbols into simple messages. What to the symbolizing consciousness is a symbol is to the de-symbolizing consciousness merely a symptom. The de-symbolizing nineteenth century saw a person or a literary character as a 'representative' (of an idea, a class, or group), whereas the symbolist poet Alexander Blok perceived people and phenomena of everyday life as symbols (see his reaction to Klyuev or Stenich in his article 'The Russian Dandy') and manifestations of the infinite in the finite.

Both tendencies combine in Dostoevsky's artistic thinking. Dostoevsky was an assiduous reader of newspapers and collector of incidents reported in them (especially crimes and court cases) and he saw symptoms of the hidden ills of society in the plethora of journalistic facts. As adherent to the view of the writer as doctor (like Lermontov in the preface to *A Hero of our Times*), as natural scientist (like Baratynsky in 'The Concubine') and as sociologist (like Balzac), he was a decoder of symptoms. Symptomology belongs to the sphere of semiotics (it has long been known as medical semiotics). But in this field of study the relationships between what is 'accessible' (the expression) and what is 'inaccessible' (the content) are constant and one-to-one, and are constructed on the 'black box' principle. Turgenev, for instance, with the sensitivity of a finely tooled instrument, records the symptoms of social processes in his novels; and his approach entailed the idea of a character being 'representative' of something. If Rudin is said to be the *'representative* of "superfluous men" in Russia' this means that he personifies the chief features of that group, and that the group can be judged by his character. But if Stavrogin or Fed'ka in *The Devils* are said to *symbolize* certain phenomena, types or forces this means that these forces are to *some extent* expressed in these characters, but that the essence of these forces stills remains half concealed and mysterious. In Dostoevsky these two approaches, which are constantly at odds with each other, make up the complex texture of his work.

The contrast between symbol and reminiscence is different. We have already remarked on the essential, but there is one more thing to point out: a symbol exists before any given text and independently of it. It surfaces in a writer's memory from the depths of cultural memory and comes to life in a new text like a grain in fresh soil. A reminiscence, a reference, a quotation are organic parts of the new text, functioning only in its synchrony. They pass from the text into the depths of memory, whereas a symbol passes from the depths of memory into the text.

This is why what seems like a symbol in the process of creation (a suggestive memory mechanism) is perceived by the reader as a reminiscence, since the processes of creating and of perceiving move in opposite directions: to the creative process the final text is a summation, to the perceiving process it is a point of departure. The following example will illustrate this point.

Among Dostoevsky's plans for a 'poem' entitled 'The Emperor' (the germ of a novel about Ioann Antonovich[101]) there are somes notes about how Mirovich tries to persuade the young man who had grown up in total isolation and who knew nothing of the temptations of life to agree to a plot: 'He shows him the world, from the loft (the Neva and so on). . . . He shows him God's world. "It's all yours if you want it. Let's go!"'[102] Obviously the story of a temptation by a powerful figure was linked in Dostoevsky's mind with a symbol: the temptation of Jesus in which Jesus is lifted up to high place (a mountain, the roof of the temple; in Dostoevsky it is the loft of the prison tower), and shown the world lying at his feet. For Dostoevsky the Gospel symbolism was unfolded into a plot for a novel, while for the reader the plot of the novel was to be explained by the Gospel reminiscence.

The juxtaposition of symbol and reminiscence is, however, conventional, and in such complex texts as Dostovesky's novels cannot always be analysed.

We have already mentioned that Dostoevsky looked at newspaper items, and facts about criminal trials, both as symptoms and as symbols. This duality is an essential aspect of his artistic and ideological-philosophical thinking. A comparison between Tolstoy's attitude to speech, and Dostoevsky's will illustrate this point.

The principle that was to be typical of Tolstoy throughout his career first appears in the early tale 'The Wood-felling': the officers taking their lunch under enemy fire listen to the cannon shots with feigned indifference and inner anxiety.

'Where did you get the wine?' I asked Bolkhov lazily, while in the depths of my soul two equally distinct voices were speaking: one was saying, 'Lord receive my soul in peace', the other, 'I hope I shan't duck, but keep smiling, as the ball flies past', and at that moment something terribly unpleasant whistled overhead, and a cannon-ball crashed down a couple of paces behind us.

'Now if I had been Napoleon or Frederick,' said Bolkhov, turning to me with complete composure, 'I should certainly have paid you a compliment.'

'You just have done,' I replied, struggling to conceal the fear produced in me by danger.

'Well, and so what? No one will write it down.'

'Yes, they will – I will.'

'Ah, but if you do, it will only be "for criticism", as Mishchenkov says,' he added with a smile.

'Pah, blast you! Nearly grazed my legs!' cursed Antonov from behind us, spitting with vexation.[103]

The first thing to notice about Tolstoy's style in this passage is its total conventionality: the relationship of expression to content is a conventional one. A word may be an expression either of truth as in Antonov's exclamation or of falsehood as in the officers' talk. The fact that we can separate the expression level from a word and join it to any other content makes the word a dangerous instrument, a kind of condenser of social falsehood. So when truth was a question of life and death Tolstoy preferred to do without words. Pierre Bezukhov's verbal declaration of love to Helene is false, and true love is declared without words, 'by looks and smiles', or, as with Kitty and Levin, in cryptograms. Akim's wordless, incomprehensible *tayo* in *The Power of Darkness* has truth as its content, while florid language is always false in Tolstoy. Truth is the natural order of Nature. Life purged of words (and social symbolics), life in its essential nature is truth.

Let us look at some examples of Dostoevsky's style from *The Idiot*. 'There was evidently something else here, some storm of the heart and mind, something in the nature of romantic indignation, goodness only knows why and against whom, a sort of insatiable feeling of contempt that was completely unaccountable – in short, something highly ridiculous and inadmissible in good society'; 'Her eyes looked at him as though they were asking a riddle'; 'He had been horrified by some of the looks she had given him of late, by some of her words. Sometimes he could not help feeling that she was trying to force herself too much, that she was putting too big a restraint on herself, and he remembered how alarmed that had made him'; 'You could not have been in love with him because you're too proud – no, not proud, I'm sorry – but because you are vain – no not that, either – because you're selfish – because your self-love amounts to – to madness'.[104]

These passages which we have chosen almost at random were spoken by different characters and by the narrator himself, yet they are all characterized by one common feature: the words do not name things and ideas but as it were allude to them, at the same time letting it be understood that things cannot be precisely named. 'And there's something else' is a kind of marker for Dostoevsky's entire style, a style which is built up of endless reservations and attempts to be more precise, not one of which make things any more precise, but which merely demonstrate the impossibility of expressing things precisely. Hippolyte's words in *The Idiot* are a case in point:

In every idea of genius or in every new human idea, or, more simply still, in every serious human idea born in anyone's brain, there is something that

cannot possibly be conveyed to others, though you wrote volumes about it
and spent thirty-five years in explaining your idea; something will always be
left that will obstinately refuse to emerge from your head and that will
remain with you for ever; and you will die without having conveyed to
anyone what is perhaps the most vital point of your idea.[105]

In Hippolyte's interpretation, this idea, which was central to Dostoevsky, has a romantic colouring, similar to the idea of the 'inexpressible'.
Dostoevsky had a complex attitude to language. On the one hand, he
uses all sorts of ways to emphasize the inadequacy of language and
meaning, and he constantly has recourse to imprecise, incompetent
language and to witnesses who do not understand what they are witnesses
to and who interpret the outer appearance of facts in a way that is known
to be wrong. But on the other hand, these imprecise and even erroneous
words and evidence are not be treated as if they had no relation to the
truth at all, as if they were just to be struck out, as we are supposed to do
with a whole layer of hypocritical social utterances in Tolstoy. They are
approximations to the truth, allusions to it. The truth glimmers dimly
through them as it glimmers dimly through all words except those of the
Gospels. In this respect there is no difference in principle between
competent and incompetent, perspicacious or dull-witted witnesses since
it lies in the very nature of human language to be both remote from the
truth, inadequate to it, and yet to be the way to the truth.
    We can well understand that in this understanding of it, a word is not
just a conventional sign, but a symbol. Baratynsky's analytical word is
closer to Dostoevsky than Zhukovsky's romantic 'Inexpressible':

> Alien to plain meaning
> For me it is a symbol
> Of feelings for which
> I have not found the expression in languages.[106]

Dostoevsky tended to see a deep symbolic meaning in isolated facts
although this is not his only organizing method.[107]
    The creative process in Dostoevsky provides interesting material: when
thinking up a character, Dostoevsky gives him or her a name or some
identifying mark so that he can associate the character with a particular
symbol in his memory, and then 'play over' various plot situations while
weighing up how this symbolic figure would behave in them. The richness
of the symbol makes it possible to vary the 'debut', '*Mittelspiel*' and
'*Endspiel*' of the plot situations being analysed which Dostoevsky
reworked again and again, picking out particular 'moves'.
    For instance, behind the image of Nastasya Filippovna in *The Idiot*
stands the image of 'La Dame aux Camélias' (which is directly referred to

by Kolya Ivolgin and indirectly by Totsky). Dostoevsky, however, takes this image as a complex symbol linked to European culture and by transferring it into a Russian context, observes, not without a certain polemical intent, how a Russian 'camelia' behaves. But other symbols, preservers of cultural memory, played their part too in the structure of Nastasya Filippovna's image. One of them we can only reconstruct hypothetically. The idea for *The Idiot* and the first work on it dates from the time of Dostoevsky's journey abroad in the late 1860s, when one of the strongest impressions he had was from visiting the Dresden picture gallery. Echoes of this visit (a reference to a Holbein picture) are to be found in the final text of the novel. From the diary of Dostoevsky's wife for 1867 we know that when they visited the gallery she first 'saw all the Rembrandts' on her own, and then coming back again with Dostoevsky: 'Fedya pointed out the best works and talked about art.'[108]

It is hard to imagine that Dostoevsky did not notice Rembrandt's picture 'Susanna and the Elders'. This picture, as well as 'The Rape of Ganymede' which hung in the same room (which Pushkin called Rembrandt's 'strange picture') must have caught Dostoevsky's attention because it deals with a theme which concerned him: child molesting. Rembrandt's picture treats the subject rather differently from the Biblical story: the story of Susanna as told in Daniel 13 concerns a respectable married woman, mistress of her house, while the 'elders' who make an attempt on her virtue are not necessarily 'old men'. But Rembrandt portrays a young girl, thin and pale, unattractive and defenceless. The old men are shown with features of naked lust quite out of keeping with their advanced age (compare the enflamed lust of the eagle and the expression of terror and disgust on Ganymede's face who is shown not as a youth according to the myth, but as a child).

The fact that we find Nastasya Filippovna at the start of the novel at the moment when one 'elder', Totsky, is selling her to another (formally to Ganya, but, it is suggested, in fact to General Yepanchin), and the actual story of her seduction by Totsky when she was hardly more than a child, makes it likely that Nastasya Filippovna was for Dostoevsky not only a 'camelia' but also a 'Susanna'. However, she is also 'the woman taken in adultery' of whom Christ said, 'Let the one who is without sin cast the first stone', while to her he said, 'Neither do I condemn you' (John 8. 7–11). From the intersection of the image-symbols of 'camelia', Susanna and the woman taken in adultery comes that programme which, when it is unfolded into the story space of the novel, develops into (and is transformed into) the image of Nastasya Filippovna. It is likely too that there is a connection between the image of the 'Brigadier's lady' from Fonvizin's play of that name, and General Yepanchin's wife, once again as a symbol recorded in memory and the unfolding of it in a story. Hippolyte is more complicated. This is a character with many levels and probably in the first place various 'symbols of life' (symbolic interpretations of real facts)[109] were woven together in him. One detail, however, is striking and that is Hippolyte's desire before his death to speak to the people, and his belief that he only had to 'speak to the people for quarter of an hour through the window' and the people would immediately 'agree with everything he said' and would 'follow' him.[110] This detail stored in Dostoevsky's memory like a capacious symbol goes back to the time of Belinsky's death which so impressed those who attended it. I. S. Turgenev recalls that before Belinsky died,

> he talked for two hours v:thout stopping, as if addressing the Russian people, and he frequently turned to my wife and asked her to remember all that he was saying and to pass it on to the right people.[111]

Nekrasov recalled this too in his poem 'The Unfortunates':

> And at last the time came . . .
> On the day of his death he lept from his bed,
> And his silent breast
> Found new strength and his voice broke forth!
> . . . Joyfully he shouted 'Forward!' –
> He was proud and lucid and content:
> He imagined the people
> And the tolling of Moscow bells
> His expression was ecstatic,
> On the sqaure, among the people,
> It seemed he stood
> And spoke . . .

This extraordinary episode lodged in Dostoevsky's memory and became a symbol; it began to behave like a symbol in culture: accumulating and organizing new experience around it, turning into a kind of memory condenser, and then unfolding into a variety of stories which subsequently the author selectively combined with other plot constructions. The original similarity with Belinsky was almost lost as the symbol went through numerous transformations.

We should bear in mind that a symbol can be expressed in synchretic verbal-visual form which, on the one hand, can be projected onto various texts and, on the other hand, can be transformed under the reverse influence of the texts themselves. For instance Tatlin's Monument to the Third International (1919–20) is easily recognizable as a recreation of the image of the tower of Babel in the picture by Breughel the Elder. This is no accidental likeness: the interpretation of the revolution as a rebellion against God was persistent and widespread in the literature and culture of the early years of the revolution. In the theomachic tradition of Romanticism the rebellious hero was the Demon who was portrayed with features of extreme individualism, but in the avant-garde literature of the post-revolutionary years it was the anonymity of the rebellious masses that was stressed (see Mayakovsky's *Misteriya-buff*). Marx's saying, which was very popular in those years, that 'the proletariat are storming heaven' referred to the myth of the tower of Babel, but with a double inversion: in the first place the value of earth and heaven were reversed, and in the second place the myth of the separation of the peoples was taken over by the notion of the union of peoples, i.e. the International.

And so there is a chain which runs from the Genesis story[113] through Breughel's picture, Marx's saying, to Tatlin's monument to the Third International. This symbol is a striking example of the mechanism of collective memory.

We can now attempt to define the place of the symbol among other semiotic elements. The symbol is distinguished from a conventional sign by the presence of an iconic element, some likeness between expression level and content level. The difference between iconic signs and symbols could be illustrated by the difference between an icon and a picture. In a picture a three-dimensional reality is represented by the two-dimensional depiction. But the incomplete projection of the expression level onto the content level conceals the illusionary effect: the viewer is encouraged to believe in the complete likeness. In an icon (and a symbol in general) it is in the nature of the communicatory functioning of the sign that the expression level is not projected onto the content level. The content merely glimmers through the expression, and the expression merely hints at the content. In this respect an icon may be likened to an index: the expression indicates the content to the extent that it is depicted. Hence the well-known conventionality of the symbolic sign.

A symbol, then, is a kind of condenser of all the principles of sign-ness and at the same time goes beyond sign-ness. It is a mediator between different spheres of semiosis, and also between semiotic and non-semiotic reality. In equal measure it is a mediator between the synchrony of the text and the culture's memory. Its role is that of a semiotic condenser.

In general terms we can say that the structure of symbols of a particular culture shapes the system which is isomorphic and isofunctional to the genetic memory of an individual.

NOTES TO PART ONE

1. Ferdinand de Saussure, *Course in General Linguistics*, p. 9. Lotman makes the point that the Russian version of this sentence (as indeed the English) omits the word *norme*. Cf. Ferdinand de Saussure, *Cours de linguistique générale*, p. 25.

2. Emile Benveniste, *Problèmes de linguistique générale*, Paris, 1966, pp. 63–4.
3. Roman Jakobson, 'Linguistics and Poetics', in *Style in Language*, 1964, p. 353.
4. A. M. Piatigorsky, 'Nekotorye obshchie zamechaniya otnositel'no rass-motreniya teksta kak raznovidnosti signala' ['Some General Remarks Concerning the Approach to the Text as a Kind of Signal'], in *Strukturno-tipologicheskie issledovaniya*, Moscow, 1962, pp. 149–50.
5. F. Tyutchev, *Stikhotvoreniya* [*Poems*], Moscow, 1976, p. 78.
6. A. S. Pushkin, *Eugene Onegin*, translated by Charles Johnston, Penguin Classics, pp. 225–6.
7. Katsuo Saito and Sadaji Wada, *The Magic of Trees and Stones. Secrets of Japanese Gardening*, New York, Rutland, Tokyo, 1970, pp. 101–4.
8. On the connection between information and fascination, see, Yu.V. Knorozov, 'O fastsinatsii' ['On fascination'], in *Strukturno-tipologicheskie issledovaniya*, Moscow, 1962, p. 285.
9. L. S. Vygotsky, *Myshlenie i rech'. Psikhologicheskie issledovaniya* [*Thought and Language. Psychological researches*], Moscow/Leningrad, 1934, pp. 285–6, 287–92. [Cf. similar passages in L. S. Vygotsky, *Thought and Language*, translated by E. Haufmann and G. Vakar, MIT Press, Cambridge, Mass. 1962.]
10. *Dnevnik V. K. Kyukhelbekera* [*Kyukhelbeker's Diary*], Leningrad, 1929, pp. 61–2. When he wrote these words Kyukhelbeker had been over five years in solitary confinement.
11. *Koran, perevod i commentarii I.Yu. Krachkovskogo* [*The Koran*, translated and annotated by I. Yu. Krachkovsky], Moscow 1963, p. 674.
12. Leo Tolstoy, *Anna Karenin*, translated by Rosemary Edmonds, Penguin Books, 1954, pp. 422–3.
13. *Rukoyu Pushkina. Nesobrannye i neopublikovannye teksty . . .* [*By the Hand of Pushkin. Uncollected and unpublished texts . . .*], ed. M. A. Tsyavlovsky et al., Moscow/Leningrad, 1935, p. 307.
14. Ibid., p. 314.
15. Pushkin, *Eugene Onegin*, translated by Charles Johnston, p. 89.
16. Ibid., p. 101.
17. Ibid., p. 162.
18. *Yunosti chestnoe zertsalo . . . pyatym tisneniem napechatannoe* [*The true mirror of youth . . .*], St Petersburg, 1767, p. 42.
19. Roman Jakobson, 'Two Aspects of Language and Two Types of Aphasic Disturbances', in *Fundamentals of Language*, Mouton, 1971.
20. Ibid., p. 96.
21. See Groupe μ, '*Miroires rhétoriques: sept ans de réflexion*', *Poétique*, 29, 1977.
22. N. Ruwet, 'Synecdoques et métonymies', *Poétique*, 23, 1975.
23. P. Schofer and D. Rice, 'Metaphor, metonymy and synecdoche', *Semiotica*, 21, 1977, nn. 1–2.
24. Quoted in V. V. Bychkov, *Vizantiiskaya estetika* [*Byzantine Aesthetics*], Mosocw, 1977, pp. 30, 61ff.
25. M. Grimaud, 'Sur une métaphore métonymique hugolienne selon Jacques Lacan', *Littérature*, 29, February 1978.

26. Wackenroder, *Herzensergeiessungen eines kunstliebenden Klosterbruders* [translation from the Russian].

27. E. V. Paducheva, 'O strukture abzatsa' ['On the Structure of the Paragraph'], *Trudy po znakovym sistemam*, 2, Tartu, 1965.

28. B. M. Gasparov, 'Printsipy sintagmaticheskogo opisaniya urovnya pred-lozhenii' ['Principles of the Syntagmatic Description of the Sentence Level'], *Trudy po russkoi i slavyanskoi filologii*, XXIII, Tartu, 1975; idem, 'Sovremennye problemy lingvistiki teksta' ['Modern Problems of Text-Linguistics'], *Linguistica*, VII, Tartu, 1976.

29. P. A. Florensky, 'Obratnaya perspektiva' ['Reverse Perspective'], *Trudy po znakovym sistemam*, 3, Tartu, 1967; B. A. Uspensky, 'K issledovaniyu yazyka zhivopisi' ['On the Study of Painting'], in L. F. Zhegin, *Yazyk zhivopisnogo proizvedeniya* [*The Language of the Pictorial Work*], Moscow 1970; I. Danilova, *Ot srednikh vekov k Vozrozhdeniyu. Slozhenie khudo-zhestvennoi sistemi kartiny mira* [*From the Middle Ages to the Renaissance. The Formation of the Artistic System of the World Picture*], Moscow, 1975.

30. M. Foucault, *Les mots et les choses*, Paris, 1966, pp. 318–19.

31. More subtle instances of mutual transcoding within different genres and kinds of pictorial and representational texts also belong to the rhetoric of painting. For instance, Charles Coypel's paintings are often looked at through the prism of theatrical technique and also that of Gobelin tapestries, Daumier's paintings remind one of his graphics. We could compare this with making a film shot fit the structure of a medieval Armenian miniature in the film 'Pomegranate Flower' directed by Paradzhanov.

32. See Lotman's 'The Theater and Theatricality as Components of Early Nineteenth Century Culture' and 'The Stage and Painting as Code Mechanisms for Cultural Behavior in the Early Nineteenth Century', in Yu. M. Lotman and B. A. Uspenskij, *The Semiotics of Russian Culture*, ed. Ann Shukman, Ann Arbor, 1984; G. Francastel, *La Réalité figurative*, ed. Gouthier, 1965 (third part).

33. Karamzin met and corresponded with the Swiss philosoher and physionom-ist, Johann-Caspar Lavater (1741–1801) – *trans*.

34. Danilova., op.cit., pp. 50–1.

35. The unnamed heroine of Lermontov's poem 'Ona poet i zvuki tayut', see M. Yu. Lermontov, *Sobranie sochinenii v 4-kh tomakh* [*Collected Works in Four Volumes*], Moscow, 1964, vol. I, p. 40 – *trans*.

36. P. S. Mochalov (1809–48) and V. A. Karatygin (1802–53) were the leading actors of, respectively, Moscow and St Petersburg in the 1830s and 1840s and were renowned for the difference in their styles – *trans*.

37. From Pushkin's poem of 1828 'Ee glaza', *Polnoe sobranie sochinenii* [*Complete Works*], I, p. 516.

38. The reverse process can be seen when a familiar poem is used as a love letter, album inscription, and so on. Then the readership narrows down to one person and includes intimate details (how and when it was given, what was said at the time, and so on); without such memories the text would lose its full meaning for that addressee.

39. We mean by this not the actual memories of the national collective, but the *ideal* memory of an *ideal* collective as *reconstructed* on the basis of

eighteenth-century theory.

40. Vasilii Maikov, *Izbrannye proizvedeniya* [*Selected Works*], Moscow/Leningrad, 1966, p. 276.

41. This fragment was published in the journal *Moskovsky vestnik* 1827, pt. V, no. 20, pp. 365–7: it was part of an early version of chapter IV of *Eugene Onegin*.

42. Del'vig, *Neizdannye stikhotvoreniya* [*Unpublished Poems*], Petrograd, 1922, p. 50.

43. The name Fanny was mentioned in Pushkin's letter to M. A. Shcherbin of 1819. Fanny, the name of André Chénier's mistress, was used in the circle of Pushkin's friends in the years 1817–20 to refer to an unknown *demi-mondaine*.

44. Leo Tolstoy, 'Happy ever after' [= 'Family Happiness'], in *The Cossacks and Other Stories*, translated by Rosemary Edmonds, Penguin, 1960, p. 97. In Russian usage a person is addressed by name and patronymic only as a sign of respect and this form is only used when addressing adults. To address a child in this way is a semi-ironic game.

45. G. R. Derzhavin, 'Urna' ['The Urn'], in *Stikhotvoreniya*, Leningrad, 1957, p. 253.

46. A. K. Zholkovsky and Yu. K. Shcheglov, 'Strukturnaya poetika – porozh-dayushchata poetika' ['Structural Poetics is Generative Poetics'], *Voprosy literatury*, 1, 1967, pp. 74–89.

47. A. K. Zholkovsky and Yu. K. Shcheglov, *Matematika i iskusstvo (poetika vyrazitel'nosti)* [*Mathematics and Art: Poetics of Expressivity*], Moscow, 1976; *Poetika vyrazitel'nosti. Sbornik statei* [*Poetics of Expressivity. A Collection of Articles*], (*Wiener slawistischer Almanach*, Sonderband 2), Vienna, 1980. This volume contains a bibliography of all works by the authors on this subject. [See also by the same authors, *Poetics of Expressiveness. A Theory and Applications*, Amsterdam 1986, and A. Zholkovsky, *Themes and Texts. Towards a Poetics of Expressiveness*, Cornell, N.J., 1984].

48. *Poetika vyrazitel'nosti*, p. 7. Further page references will be given in the text in square brackets. Emphasis is the authors'.

49. The authors refer to N. Chomsky, *Aspects of the Theory of Syntax*, Cambridge, Mass., 1965.

50. 'F. M. Dostoevsky v rabote nad romanom *Podrostok*. Tvorcheskie rukopisi' ['Dostoevsky at work on the novel *A Raw Youth*. Working manuscripts'], in *Literaturnoe nasledstvo*, vol. 77, Moscow, 1965, p. 64; See also in the same volume, L. M. Rozenblyum, 'Tvorcheskaya laboratoriya Dostoevskogo-romanista' ['The Creative Laboratory of Dostoevsky the Novelist'], pp. 22ff, for an analysis of this remark; and in more detail, see L. M. Rozenblyum, *Tvorcheskie dnevniki Dostoevskogo* [*Dostoevsky's Writing Diaries*], Moscow, 1981, pp. 171–3.

51. Dostoevsky's letters to Maikov.

52. Luke 8. 32–6.

53. On the iconic element in Dostoevsky's manuscripts, see K. Barsht and P. Torop, 'Rukopisi Dostoevskogo: risunok i kalligrafiya' ['Dostoevsky's manuscripts: drawings and calligrpahy'], *Trudy po znakovym sistemam*, 16,

Tartu, 1983, pp. 135–52. In this exceptionally interesting study the authors show that in the period between the germ of the idea and the coherent narrative the elements of iconism reach their apogee and a page turns into a single and indivisible unit of text.

54. Ibid., p. 143.
55. V. M. Alekseev, 'Kitaiskii palindrom v ego nauchno-pedagogicheskom ispol'zovanii' ['A Chinese Palindrome as a Teaching Device'], in *Sbornik pamyati akademika L'va Vladimirovicha Shcherby*, Leningrad, 1951, p. 102.
56. Ibid.
57. Semen Kirsanov, 'Poeziya i palindrom' ['Poetry and palindrome'], *Nauka i zhizn'*, 1966, 6, p. 76.
58. Among such universals we can count the semiotics of 'top and bottom', 'right and left', the idea of the isomorphism of world and body, the dualism of the living and the dead, and so on. The number of primary elements out of which the world-picture is constructed is relatively small and they are universally to be found. The differences arise when they are combined.
59. A. S. Pushkin, *Polnoe sobranie sochinenii [Complete Works]*, vol. III, 1, p. 332. Subsequent references to this edition will be given in the text in square brackets.
60. Nikolai Tarabukin, 'Smyslovoe znachenie diagonal'noi kompozitsii v zhivopisi' ['The Significance of Diagonal Composition in Painting'], *Trudy po znakovym sistemam*, VI, Tartu, 1973, pp. 474, 476.
61. *Russkii arkhiv*, 1905, book III, p. 256.
62. The southern circle of the Decembrists often referred to the image of Vesuvius in eruption as a political symbol. Pestel', in one of his manuscripts of 1820, allegorically represented the uprising in Naples as Vesuvius being toppled (the drawing is reproduced in *Pushkin i ego vremya. Issledovaniya i materialy [Pushkin and his Time. Research work and materials]*, I, Leningrad, 1962, p. 135.
63. The possibility of such a splitting is inherent in Pushkin's view of the statue as something essentially dual in nature. See below, pp. 94–7, on the statue of the Comendador in 'The Stone Guest'. See also Roman Jakobson, *Pushkin and his Sculptural Myth*, translated by John Burbank, The Hague/Paris, 1975, pp. 32–44.
64. Since Pushkin never thought of the Decembrist movement as something elemental, there are no grounds for the interpretation of the flood in 'The Bronze Horseman' as a reference to 14 December 1825.
65. Pushkin, 'The Captain's Daughter', in Alexander Pushkin, *Complete Prose Fiction*, translated by Paul Debreczeny, Stanford, 1983, p. 274.
66. In fact, Pugachev as the peasant tsar, and an alternative head of state to Catherine the Great, is drawn into the second semantic centre of the triad. We must stress that *each* of these structural positions has its own poetry: the poetry of the elemental wildness in the first case, the odic poetry of 'idols' in the second, the poetry of the House and domestic home in the third. But in each particular instance the feature of poeticity may be accentuated or left unmarked. The emphasized elemental quality in the image of Pugachev makes this his predominant position. The image of Catherine, which combines both second and third position, has almost no poetic quality.

Pushkin plays masterfully with the poetic possibilities of all three positions and often constructs a conflict around a confrontation between them. In 'The Feast during the Plague', for instance, the poetry of the elements (the plague, which is compared to battle, hurricane and storm) confronts the position of the home destroyed and the stern poetry of duty. The play of coincidence–noncoincidence of structural positions and the poetic fields attendant on them creates immense semantic possibilities. So the 'domestic' tone of the tsar (Alexander I) in 'The Bronze Horseman' contrasted with the domestic intonations in the description of Evgeny and the odic stylistics of Peter the Great create the impression of 'royal impotence'.

67. Besides the 'natural' combination of 'living–moving–human' we find the unnatural one of 'dead–moving–inhuman'. The second member when it acquires the image of the 'moving corpse' may be marked with irrationality, blind and inhuman progress, while the feature of rationality may fall on the simple 'human' ideals of the third member of the paradigm. Thus one and the same figure (for example, Peter in 'The Bronze Horseman') can in one opposition be seen as the bearer of the rational, but in another opposition of irrationalism. And a real historical movement can be fitted into the first and third positions (see Arkhip in *Dubrovsky* and the words of Pushkin's friend, N. M. Konshin, in his letter to Pushkin [XIV, 216].

Konshin saw in this merely that the people 'had not a spark of common sense' (ibid.). But Pushkin was aware of the profoundly contradictary nature of the real forces of history, which he could 'pin down' only by help of the extremely flexible model which only genuine art is capable of creating.

68. *Rukoyu Pushkina*, op.cit., p. 734. The similarity between Yakovlev's presentation and the germ of 'The Bronze Horseman' is obvious, but not in the sense that Yakovlev gave Pushkin the idea for the poem, rather the other way round: Yakovlev's show made sense to Pushkin in the light of his own ideas.

69. Jakobson, op.cit., p. 1.

70. If we remember the Baron's monologue to his trunks filled with gold then 'The Miserly Knight' can also be included in this series.

71. The idea that the poem 'Bacchic Song' might refer to the Masons is quite unfounded. A toast to love and to 'tender girls' and 'young wives' would be quite impossible in Masonic 'table' poetry. The ritual of throwing the rings into the wine has never been recorded as a Masonic one and is an invention. The point of this action is quite different: when the toast to love is announced, all the young men call out the names of their beloveds. But a shy lover can drink in silence if he puts his 'sacred' ring into the wineglass so that when he drinks down to the bottom his lips will touch it.

72. Vyazemsky remarked about this line [*grozy polunochnykh dozorov*] that 'Probably Pushkin originally had "threats of midnight conspiracies"' [*grozy polnochnykh zagovorov*] (*Russkii arkhiv*, 1887, 12, p. 577); the manuscripts do not support this suggestion though the phrase accords well with the spirit of the verse and should be taken into account. The association between the symbolism of the feast and freedom-loving conspiracy is confirmed in other texts.

73. 'They speed to the fatal feast, seeking prey for their swords' (I, 81); 'the

bloody feast of war' (I, 114); 'the bloody feast calls you' (*Ruslan i Lyudmila*).

74. I. L. Pankratova, V. E. Khalizev, 'Opyt prochteniya 'Pira vo vremeni chumy' A. S. Pushkina' ['A Attempted Reading of Pushkin's "Feast during the Plague"'], in *Tipologicheskii analiz literaturnogo proizvedeniya, sbornik nauchnykh trudov* [*Typological Analysis of the Literary Work. A Collection of Scholarly Works*], Kemerovo, 1982, pp. 53–66. The title of the article shows that the authors were trying not so much to analyse Puskin's work as to describe *their own* reading of it – which, of course, they have every right to do.

75. Ibid., p. 64.

76. Thomas J. Shaw, *Pushkin. A Concordance to the Poetry*, Vol. 2, Columbus, 1984, pp. 764–5.

77. Jakobson suggested that the phrase 'The sleep of the gods amidst the depths of heavens' ('The Miserly Knight', in Alexander Pushkin, *Mozart and Salieri: The Little Tragedies*, translated by Antony Wood, Angel Books, London, 1982, p. 28) on the lips of a medieval knight and Christian was an anachronism. But direct textual parallels show that Pushkin put into the Baron's lips phrases taken from the Epicurean philosophy of the French libertarians though replacing the cult of pleasure by the cult of money. See Lotman, 'Tri zametki k probleme "Pushkin i frantsuzskaya kul'tura"' ['Three Notes on the Problem "Pushkin and French Culture"'], *Problemy Pushkinovedeniya*, Riga, 1983, pp. 75–81.

78. 'The Miserly Knight', translated by Antony Wood [The text of this translation has been followed except in places where a more literal version was required.]

79. Wood, p. 20.

80. Simeon Polotsky, *Izbrannye sochineniya* [*Selected Works*], Moscow/Leningrad, 1953, p. 21.

81 G. A. Gukovsky, *Pushkin i problema realisticheskogo stilya* [*Pushkin and the Problem of Realist Style*], Moscow, 1957, p. 307. It is characteristic of Gukovsky to speak of the system *which creates* Mozart, rather than the one created by him. To Gukovsky the human person is the passive 'product' of milieu and period. The problem of human activity and human effect on the world is overlooked as something 'romantic'. His remark 'if we are not to risk constricting the meaning' is telling: the author obviously understood the risk but could not avoid it. Gukovsky's theory has much to commend it and in its time was new, but it does, in fact, 'constrict' Pushkin.

82. Wood, p. 36.

83. Ibid.

84. Wackenroder, *On Art and Artists. Thoughts of a Hermit, Lover of the Sublime* (Russian translation by V. P. Titov et al., Moscow, 1926, p. 241).

85. Wackenroder [*Praise to our Honourable Ancestor Albrecht Dürer*], in *Literaturnye manifesty zapadnoevropeiskikh romantikov* [*Literary Manifestos of West European Romantics*], Moscow, 1980, p. 74.

86. Wackenroder [*On Art*], p. 233.

87. *Pushkin on Literature*, translated by Tatiana Wolff, London, 1971, p. 100.

88. Wood, p. 39.

89. Ibid.

90. Ibid., pp. 38–9.

91. Ibid., p. 72 (adapted).

92. Ibid., p. 66.

93. Ibid., p. 58.

94. Ibid., p. 66–7 (adapted).

95. Ibid., p. 79 (adapted). [Pushkin's play is a free adaptation of John Wilson's 'The City of the Plague'].

96. Ibid., p. 75 (adapted).

97. Compare the punning remark in Pushkin's tale 'The Coffin-Maker': 'A living person can manage without boots, but a dead one can't live without a coffin.'

98. Wood, p. 78 (adapted).

99. Pankratova and Khalizev, op.cit., p. 57.

100. This was done by N. V. Yakovlev in the commentaries to the first version of the seventh volume of the Academy complete edition of Pushkin's works. Though we have mentioned the lack of literature about 'The Feast during the Plague' we must draw attention to a brief but penetrating comment by L. V. Pumpyansky:

     Pushkin clearly sees the real historical circumstances: the Restoration: the challenge which the aristocrats, the political victors, give to the woes of the people; the priest, a humiliated remnant of the defeated Puritan revolution; the conflict between heightened individualism and social morals. (L. V. Pumpyansky, 'Stikhovaya rech' Lermontova' ['Lermontov's verse speech'], in *Literaturnoe Nasledstvo*, vols 43–4, Moscow 1941, p. 398)

101. Ioann Antonovich (1740–64), i.e. Ivan VI, Russian Emperor, deposed when one year old by the Empress Elizabeth, imprisoned in 1756 until his death. He was killed during Mirovich's attempt, which may have been a put-up job, to put him on the throne.

102. F. M. Dostoevsky, *Polnoe sobranie sochinenii* [*Complete Works*], vol. 9, Leningrad, 1974, pp. 113–14.

103. Leo Tolstoy, 'The Wood-Felling', translated by Angus Roxburgh, in L. Tolstoy, *Father Sergius and Other Stories*, Moscow, 1988, pp. 73–4.

104. Dostoevsky, *The Idiot*, translated by David Magarshak, pp. 66, 67, 568, 571.

105. Ibid., p. 406.

106. Baratynsky, *Polnoe sobranie stikhotvorenii* [*Complete Poetry*], Leningrad, 1936, vol. I, p. 184.

107. Dostoevsky's creative thinking is in principle heterogeneous: along with 'symbolic' meaning-formation he also implies other kinds of reading. Both simple journalism and factual reporting and much else enter his language, finding an ideal model in *The Diary of a Writer*. We have concentrated on the 'symbolic' level because that is our topic in this chapter and not because it is the only level in his artistic world.

108. Cited in, *F. M. Dostoevsky v vospominaniyakh sovremennikov* [*Dostoevsky in the Memories of his Contemporaries*], Moscow, 1964, p. 104.

109. See Dostoevsky's remark in his article 'On the Exhibition' that reality is accessible to a person only as a symbolic signification of an idea and not as

reality 'as it is', because 'there is no such reality, and there never was on earth, because the essence of things is inaccessible to human beings and we perceive nature as it is reflected in our idea of it.'

110. *The Idiot*, pp. 308–9.
111. *V. G. Belinsky v vospominaniyakh sovremennikov* [*Belinsky in the Memories of his Contemporaries*], Leningrad, 1929, p. 256.
112. N. A. Nekrasov, *Polnoe sobranie sochinenii* [*Complete Works*], vol. 4, Leningrad, 1982, p. 49.
113. Genesis, 11. 1–9.

PART TWO

The Semiosphere

8

Semiotic space

Up to this point our argument has followed a generally accepted pattern: we have started by taking the single act of communication by itself, and we have examined the relationships which arise between addresser and addressee. This approach presupposes that the study of this one fact will throw light on all the chief features of semiosis and that these features can then be extrapolated on to the larger semiotic processes. This approach accords with Descartes' third rule in *Discourse on Method*. Descartes wrote:

> The third [rule] was to carry on my reflections in due order, commencing with objects that were the most simple and easy to understand, in order to rise little by little, or by degrees, to knowledge of the most complex.[1]

This approach also accords with the scientific practice which dates from the time of the Enlightenment, namely to work on the 'Robinson Crusoe' principle of isolating an object and then making it into a general model.

However, for this procedure to be a correct one, the isolated fact must be able to model all the qualities of the phenomenon on to which the conclusions are being extrapolated. This is not so in our case. A schema consisting of addresser, addressee and the channel linking them together is not yet a working system. For it to work it has to be 'immersed' in semiotic space. All participants in the communicative act must have some experience of communication, be familiar with semiosis. So, paradoxically, semiotic experience precedes the semiotic act. By analogy with the biosphere (Vernadsky's concept) we could talk of a semiosphere, which we shall define as the semiotic space necessary for the existence and functioning of languages, not the sum total of different languages; in a sense the semiosphere has a prior existence and is in constant interaction with languages. In this respect a language is a function, a cluster of semiotic spaces and their boundaries, which, however clearly defined these are in the language's grammatical self-description, in the reality of semiosis are eroded and full of transitional forms. Outside the semiosphere there can be neither communication, nor language. Of course, the single-channel structure is a reality. A self-contained, single-channel system is a mechanism for transmitting extremely simple signals and for the realization of a single function, but for the task of generating information it certainly will not do. This is why we can imagine that a system like this is an artificially-made construction, but in natural circumstances systems of quite another type are at work. Just the fact that it is a universal of human culture, that there exist both conventional and pictorial signs (or rather that all signs are to some degree both conventional and representational), is enough to show that semiotic dualism is the minimal form of organization of a working semiotic system.

Binarism and *asymmetry* are the laws binding on any real semiotic system. Binarism, however, must be understood as a principle which is realized in plurality since every newly-formed language is in its turn subdivided on a binary principle. Every living culture has a 'built-in' mechanism for multiplying its languages (as we shall see below, the parallel and opposite mechanism for unifying languages is also at work). For instance, we are constantly witnessing a quantitative increase in the languages of art. This is especially so in twentieth-century culture and in other past cultures typologically resembling it. At periods when most creative activity comes from the readership, the slogan that 'art is everything we perceive as art' rings true. In the early years of this century cinema ceased being a fairground amusement and became a serious art-form. It made its appearance not alone but along with a whole procession of traditional and newly invented peep-shows. Back in the nineteenth century no one would have seriously regarded the circus, fairground peep-shows, traditional toys, advertisements or the cries of street traders as art-forms. Once it became an art, cinematography at once split into documentary films and entertainment films, camera films and cartoon ones, each with its own poetics. And nowadays there is another opposition to be added, that between cinema and television. True, art becomes more narrow at the same time as the assortment of art-languages increases: some arts in practice drop out of the picture. So we should not be surprised if, when we look closer, the diversity of semiotic systems within a particular culture is relatively constant. But something else is important: the set of languages in an active cultural field is constantly changing, and the axiological value and hierarchical position of the elements in it are subject to even greater changes.

At the same time, throughout the whole space of semiosis, from social jargon and age-group slang to fashion, there is also a constant renewal of codes. So any one language turns out to be immersed in a semiotic space and it can only function by interaction with that space. The unit of semiosis, the smallest functioning mechanism, is not the separate language but the whole semiotic space of the culture in question. This is the space we term the *semiosphere*. The semiosphere is the result and the condition for the development of culture; we justify our term by analogy with the biosphere, as Vernadsky defined it, namely the totality and the organic whole of living matter and also the condition for the continuation of life.

Vernadsky wrote that

> all life-clusters are intimately bound to each other. One cannot exist without the other. This connection between different living films and clusters, and their invariancy, is an age-old feature of the mechanism of the earth's crust, which has existed all through geological time.[2]

The same idea is expressed more clearly again:

> The biosphere has a quite definite structure which determines everything without exception that happens in it. . . . A human being observed in nature and all living organisms and every living being is a function of the biosphere in its particular space-time.[3]

In his notes dating from 1892 Vernadsky pointed to human intellectual activity as a continuation of the cosmic conflict between life and inert matter:

> the seeming laws of mental activity in people's lives has led many to deny the influence of the personality on history, although, throughout history, we can in fact see a constant struggle of conscious (i.e. not natural) life-formations with the unconscious order of the dead laws of nature, and in this effort of consciousness lies all the beauty of historical manifestations, the originality of their position among the other natural processes. A historical epoch can be judged by this effort of consciousness.[4]

The semiosphere is marked by its *heterogeneity*. The languages which fill up the semiotic space are various, and they relate to each other along the spectrum which runs from complete mutual translatability to just as complete mutual untranslatability. Heterogeneity is defined both by the diversity of elements and by their different functions. So if we make the mental experiment of imagining a model of a semiotic space where all the languages came into being at one and the same moment and under the influence of the same impulses, we still would not have a single coding structure but a set of connected but different systems. For instance, we construct a model of the semiotic structure of European Romanticism and mark out its chronological framework. Even within such a completely artificial space there would be no homogeneity since inevitably where there are different degrees of iconism there can be no mutually complete semantic translatability, but only conventional correspondence. Of course the poet and partisan hero of 1812, Denis Davydov, did compare the tactics of partisan warfare with Romantic poetry, declaring that the leader of a partisan band should not be a 'theorist' with 'a calculating mind and a cold heart': 'This poetic profession needs a romantic imagination, a passion for adventure and it is never content with dry prosaic displays of valour. It is a verse of Byron's!'[5] But we have only to look at his study of tactics, *Attempt at a Theory of Partisan Warfare*, with its plans and maps to realize that this fine metaphor was just a pretext for the contrast-loving mind of a Romantic to juxtapose the incompatible. The fact that the unification of two different languages is achieved by a metaphor is proof of the essential differences between them.

But then we have also to take account of the fact that different languages circulate for different periods: fashion in clothes changes at a speed which cannot be compared with the rate of change of the literary language, and Romanticism in dance is not synchronized with Romanticism in architecture. So, while some parts of the semiosphere are still enjoying the poetics of Romanticism, others may have moved far on into post-Romanticism. So even our artificial model will not give us a homologous picture across a strictly synchronic section. This is why when we try to give a synthetic picture of Romanticism to include all forms of art (and perhaps also other areas of culture), chronology has to be sacrificed. What we have said is true also of the Baroque, of Classicism, and of many other 'isms'.

Yet if we talk not of artificial models but of modelling the actual literary process (or more broadly, the cultural process) then we must admit that – to continue with our example – Romanticism occupies only a part of the semiosphere in which all sorts of other traditional structures continue to exist, some of them going way back into antiquity. Besides, at all stages of development there are contacts with texts coming in from cultures which formerly lay beyond the boundaries of the given semiosphere. These invasions, sometimes by separate texts, and sometimes by whole cultural layers, variously effect the internal structure of the 'world picture' of the culture we are talking about. So across any synchronic section of the semiosphere different languages at different stage of development are in conflict, and some texts are immersed in languages not their own, while the codes to decipher them with may be entirely absent. As an example of a single world looked at synchronically, imagine a museum hall where exhibits from different periods are on display, along with inscriptions in known and unknown languages, and instructions for decoding them; besides there are the explanations composed by the museum staff, plans for tours and rules for the behaviour of the visitors. Imagine also in this hall tour-leaders and the visitors and imagine all this as a single mechanism (which *in a certain sense* it is). This is an image of the semiosphere. Then we have to remember that all elements of the semiosphere are in dynamic, not static, correlations whose terms are constantly changing. We notice this especially at traditional moments which have come down to us from the past. The evolution of culture is quite different from biological evolution, the word 'evolution' can be quite misleading.

Biological evolution involves species dying out and natural selection. The researcher finds only living creatures contemporary with him. Something similar happens in the history of technology: when an instrument is made obsolete by technical progress it finds a resting place in a museum, as a dead exhibit. In the history of art, however, works which come down to us from remote cultural periods continue to play a part in cultural development as living factors. A work of art may 'die' and come alive again; once thought to be out of date, it may become modern and even prophetic for what it tells of the future. What 'works' is not the most recent temporal section, but the whole packed history of cultural texts. The standard evolutionary point of view in literary history comes from the influence of evolutionary ideas in the natural sciences. With this approach the state of literature at any one time is judged by the list of works *written* in that year, instead of by the works *being read* in that year – which would produce a very different picture. And it is hard to say which of the lists is more typical for the state of culture at any one time. Pushkin, for instance, in 1824–5, took Shakespeare as his most topical writer, Bulgakov read Gogol and Cervantes as contemporaries, Dostoevsky is just as relevant at the end of the twentieth century as he was at the end of the nineteenth. In fact, everything contained in the actual memory of culture is directly or indirectly part of that culture's synchrony.

The structure of the semiosphere is asymmetrical. Asymmetry finds expression in the currents of internal translations with which the whole density of the semiosphere is permeated. Translation is a primary mechanism of consciousness. To express something in another language is a way of understanding it. And since in the majority of cases the different languages of the semiosphere are semiotically asymmetrical, i.e. they do not have mutual semantic correspondences, then the whole semiosphere can be regarded as a generator of information.

Asymmetry is apparent in the relationship between the centre of the semiosphere and its periphery. At the centre of the semiosphere are formed the most developed and structurally organized languages, and in first place the natural language of that culture. If no language (including natural language) can function unless it is immersed in the semiosphere, then no semiosphere, as Emile Benveniste pointed out, can exist without natural language as its organizing core. The fact is that the semiosphere, besides the structurally organized language, is crowded with partial languages, languages which can serve only certain cultural functions, as well as language-like, half-formed systems which can be bearers of semiosis if they are included in the semiotic context. Compare the latter with a stone or a strangely twisted tree-stump which can function as work of art if it is treated as one. An object will take on the function ascribed to it.

In order that all this mass of constructions are perceived as bearers of semiotic meaning we must make a 'presumption of semioticity': the semiotic intuition of the collective and its consciousness have to accept the possibility that structures may be significant. These qualities are learnt through natural language. For instance, the structure of the 'families of the gods' and of other basic elements of the world-picture are often clearly dependent on the grammatical structure of the language.

The highest form and final act of a semiotic system's structural organization is when it describes itself. This is the stage when grammars are written, customs and laws codified. When this happens, however, the system gains the advantage of greater structural organization, but loses its inner reserves of indeterminacy which provide it with flexibility, heightened capacity for information and the potential for dynamic development.

The stage of self-description is a necessary response to the threat of too much diversity within the semiosphere: the system might lose its unity and definition, and disintegrate. Whether we have in mind language, politics or culture, the mechanism is the same: one part of the semiosphere (as a rule one which is part of its nuclear structure) in the process of self-description creates its own grammar; this self-description may be real or ideal depending on whether its inner orientation is towards the present or towards the future. Then it strives to extend these norms over the whole semiosphere. A partial grammar of one cultural dialect becomes the metalanguage of description for culture as such. The dialect of Florence, for instance, became during the Renaissance the literary language of Italy, the legal norms of Rome became the laws of the whole Roman Empire, and the etiquette of the Parisian court of Louis XIV became the etiqette of all the courts of Europe. A literature of norms and prescriptions comes into being in which the later historian will tend to see an actual picture of real life of that epoch, its semiotic practice. This illusion is supported by the evidence of contemporaries who are in fact convinced that they indeed do live and behave in the prescribed way. A contemporary will reason something like this: 'I am a person of culture (i.e. a Hellene, a Roman, a Christian, a knight, an *esprit fort*, a philosopher of the age of the Enlightenment, or a genius of the age of

Romanticism). As a person of culture I embody the behaviour prescribed by certain norms. Only what in my behaviour corresponds to these norms is counted as a *deed*. If, through weakness, sickness, inconsistency, etc., I deviate from these norms, then such behaviour has no meaning, is not relevant, simply *does not exist*.' A list of what 'does not exist', according to that cultural system, although such things in fact occur, is always essential for making a typological description of that system. For instance, Andreas Capellanus, author of *De Amore* (c.1184–5), a well-known treatise on the norms of courtly love, carefully codified courtly love and set the standards of faithfulness, silence, devoted service, chastity, courtesy, and so on for the lover; yet he had no compunction in violating a village-girl since according to his world-picture she 'as it were did not exist', and actions involving her as it were did not exist either, since they lay outside the domain of semiotics.

The world-picture created in this way will be perceived by its contemporaries as reality. Indeed, it will be *their* reality to the extent that they have accepted the laws of that semiotics. And later generations (including scholars), who reconstruct life in those days from texts, will imbibe the idea that everyday reality was indeed like that. But the relationship of this metalevel of the semiosphere to the real picture of its semiotic 'map' on the one hand, and to the everyday reality of life on the other, will be complex. First of all, if in that nuclear structure where the self-description originated, the self-description in fact represents an idealization of a real language, then on the periphery of the semiosphere, this ideal norm will be a contradiction of the semiotic reality lying 'underneath', and not a derivation from it. If in the centre of the semiosphere the description of texts generates the norms, then on the periphery the norms, actively invading 'incorrect' practice, will generate 'correct' texts in accord with them. Secondly, whole layers of cultural phenomena, which from the point of view of the given metalanguage are marginal, will have no relation to the idealized portrait of that culture. They will be declared to be 'non-existent'. From the time of the cultural history school, the favourite genre of many scholars has been articles of the type, 'An Unknown Poet of the Twelfth Century', 'Further Remarks about a Forgotten Writer of the Enlightenment Period', and so on. Where does this inexhaustible supply of 'unknown' and 'forgotten' figures come from? They are the writers who in their time were classed as 'non-existent' and who were ignored by scholarship as long as its point of view coincided with a normative view of the period. But points of view change and 'unknowns' suddenly occur. Then people remember that in the year Voltaire died, the 'unknown philosopher', Louis-Claude Saint Martin was already thirty-five, that Restif de la Bretonne had already written over 200 novels which historians of literature still cannot properly place, calling him either 'little Rousseau' or an 'eighteenth-century Balzac'; and that in the Romantic period in Russia there lived a certain Vasily Narezhny who wrote some twenty-five volumes of novels which were 'unnoticed' by his contemporaries until traces of realism were found in them.

So while on the metalevel the picture is one of semiotic unity, on the level of the semiotic reality which is described by the metalevel, all kinds of other tendencies flourish. While the picture of the upper level is painted in a smooth uniform colour, the lower level is bright with colours and many intersecting boundaries. When Charlemagne at the end of the eighth century brought sword and cross to the Saxons, and St Vladimir a hundred years later baptized Kievan Russia, the great barbarian empires of East and West became Christian states. But their Christianity was a self-characterization and as such extended to the political and religious metalevel beneath which flourished pagan traditions and all sorts of real-life compromises with them. It could not have been otherwise considering that the conversions to Christianity were forced on the masses. The terrible bloodshed wrought by Charlemagne on the pagan Saxons at Verdun was hardly likely to foster acceptance of the principles of the Sermon on the Mount among the barbarians.

And yet it would be wrong to suggest that this simple change of nomenclature had no effect on the 'underlying' levels: for Christianization did turn into evangelization, and, even on the level of 'real semiotics', it contributed to the unification of the cultural space of these states. Semantic currents flow not only across the horizontal levels of the semiosphere, but also have their effect in a vertical direction, and promote complex dialogues between the levels.

But the unity of the semiotic space of the semiosphere is brought about not only by metastructural formations: even more crucial is the unifying factor of the boundary, which divides the internal space of the semiosphere from the external, its *inside* from its *outside*.

9

The notion of boundary

Paradoxically, the internal space of a semiosphere is at the same time unequal yet unified, asymmetrical yet uniform. Composed as it is of conflicting structures, it none the less is also marked by individuation. Its self-description implies a first person pronoun. One of the primary mechanisms of semiotic individuation is the boundary, and the boundary can be defined as the outer limit of a first-person form. This space is 'ours', 'my own', it is 'cultured', 'safe', 'harmoniously organized', and so on. By contrast 'their space' is 'other', 'hostile', 'dangerous', 'chaotic'.

Every culture begins by dividing the world into 'its own' internal space and 'their' external space. How this binary division is interpreted depends on the typology of the culture. But the actual division is one of the human cultural universals. The boundary may separate the living from the dead, settled peoples from nomadic ones, the town from the plains; it may be a state frontier, or a social, national, confessional, or any other kind of frontier. There is an amazing similarity, even between civilizations which have no contact with each other, in the expressions they use to describe the world beyond the boundary. The eleventh-century Kievan chronicler-monk, describing the life of other eastern Slav tribes who were still pagan, wrote:

> The Drevlyans lived like animals, like cattle; they killed each other, ate unclean foods, had no marriage, but abducted girls at the waterside. While the Radimichi, Vyatichi and northern tribes shared the same custom: they lived in the forest like wild beasts, ate unclean food and used foul language in front of fathers and female relatives, and they had no marriages, but held games between villages and gathered at these games for dancing and all kinds of devilish songs.[6]

131

And this is how an eighth-century Frankish chronicler, a Christian, described the customs of the pagan Saxons:

> Fierce by nature, worshippers of the devil, enemies of our religion, they respect neither human nor divine rules, and they permit themselves to do what is not permissible.[7]

The last words show the mirror-like relationship between 'our' world and 'their' one: what is not allowed with us is allowed with them.

Whatever exists is subject to the limitations of real space and time. Human history is but a particular instance of this law. Human beings are immersed in real space, the space which nature gives them. Human consciousness forms its model of the world from such constants as the rotation of the earth (the movements of the sun across the horizon), the movements of the stars, and the natural cycle of the seasons. No less important are the physical constants of the human body, which posit certain relationships with the outside world. The measurements of the human body determine the fact that the world of mechanics and its laws seem 'natural', while the world of particles and cosmic space can be conceived of only speculatively and with extraordinary mental effort. The correlation between average human weight, the force of gravity and the vertical position of the body have resulted in what is universal for all human cultures: the opposition of *up* and *down*. There are many ways of interpreting this opposition (religious, social, political, moral, and so on). Would the expression, 'he's reached the top', which can be understood by anyone in any culture, be so clear to a thinking fly or to a person who had grown up in conditions of weightlessness?

'Top', 'summit' do not need explaining. The expression, '*Qui ne vole au sommet tombe au plus bas degré*' ['He who does not fly to the summit falls to the lowest degree'] (Boileau, *Satires*) can be just as universally understood as, '*La lutte elle-même vers les sommets suffit à remplir un coeur d'homme. Il faut imaginer Sisyphe heureux*' ['The very struggle towards the summits is enough to fill the human heart. We must imagine that Sisyphus was happy'] (Camus, *Le Mythe de Sisyphe*).

However great the temporal and spatial distance between Camus and Yan Vyshatich who led a military expedition against the pagans in Russia in the eleventh century, the semantic values of 'top' and 'bottom' are the same for both of them. Before executing the pagan magicians (shamans) Yan asked them where their god was, and received the answer (according to the chronicler-monk) that 'he sits in the abyss'. Upon which Yan gave them the authoritative explanation: 'What kind of god is it who sits in the abyss? It is the devil, for god is in the heavens.' The chronicler liked this phrase and he puts almost the same words into the mouth of the pagan priest from the land of Chud:

The man from Novgorod said: 'What sort of gods are yours, where do they live?' And the sorcerer said: 'In the abyss. They are black of face, winged and have tails; they climb up beneath the heaven to listen to your gods. For your gods are in the heavens.'[8]

The asymmetry of the human body is the anthropological basis for its semioticization: the semiotics of *right* and *left* are found just as universally in all human cultures as the opposition *top* and *bottom*. And the fundamental asymmetries of *male* and *female*, *living* and *dead*, are just as widespread. The *living/dead* opposition involves the opposition of something moving, warm, breathing, to something immobile, cold, not breathing (the belief that cold and death are synonyms is supported by an enormous number of texts from different cultures, and just as common is the identification of death with turning to stone; see the numerous legends about the origins of mountains and rocks).

Vernadsky commented that life on earth is lived in a special space–time continuum, which life itself creates.

It would be logically right to put forward a new scientific hypothesis namely that for living matter on planet Earth we have to do not with a new geometry, nor with one of the geometries of Riemann, but with a special natural phenomenon so far characteristic only of living matter, namely the appearance of space–time, which geometrically speaking does not coincide with space, and in which time appears not as a fourth dimension, but as the succession of generations.[9]

Conscious human life, i.e. the life of culture, also demands a special space–time structure, for culture organizes itself in the form of a special space–time and cannot exist without it. This organization is realized in the form of the semiosphere and at the same time comes into being with the help of the semiosphere.

The outside world, in which a human being is immersed in order to become culturally significant, is subject to semioticization, i.e. it is divided into the domain of objects which signify, symbolize, indicate something (have meaning), and objects which simply are themselves. And the various languages which fill the semiosphere, that many-eyed Argus, make differentiations in this outside reality. The stereoscopic picture which thereby is produced contributes to the unification process with the aid of that metastructural mechanism which claims the right to speak for the whole culture. At the same time, in spite of all the differences between the substructures of the semiosphere, these sub-structures are organized into a general system of coordinates: on the temporal axis into past, present and future, on the spatial axis into internal space, external space and the boundary between them. Non-semiotic reality and its space and time can also be encoded in this system, in order to be made 'semioticizable', i.e. capable of becoming the content of a semiotic text. On this aspect of the question, see below.

As we have already said, the extension of the metastructural self-description from the centre of the culture over all its semiotic space, makes it possible for an historian to look at an entire synchronic section of the semiosphere as something unified, though in fact it only gives an illusion of unification. In the centre the metastructure is 'our' language, but on the periphery it is treated as 'someone else's' language unable adequately to reflect the semiotic reality beneath it: it is like the grammar of a foreign language. As a result, in the centre of the cultural space, sections of the semiosphere aspiring to the level of self-description become rigidly organized and self-regulating. But at the same time they lose dynamism and having once exhausted their reserve of indeterminacy they became inflexible and incapable of further development. On the periphery – and the further one goes from the centre, the more noticeable this becomes – the relationship between semiotic practice and the norms imposed on it becomes ever more strained. Texts generated in accordance with these norms hang in the air, without any real semiotic context; while organic creations, born of the actual semiotic milieu, come into conflict with the artificial norms. This is the area of semiotic dynamism. This is the field of tension where new languages come into being. For instance, as scholars have already remarked,[10] the peripheral genres in art are more revolutionary than those in the centre of culture; they enjoy greater prestige and are perceived by contemporaries to be real art. The second half of the twentieth century has witnessed an aggressive upsurge of marginal forms of culture. The 'career' of cinematography is a case in point: from being a fairground spectacle, free of all theoretical restrictions and regulated only by technical possibilities, it turned into a central art-form, and, what is more, especially in recent decades, into one of the most *written about* of art-forms. The same thing can be said about the art of the European avant-garde as a whole. The avant-garde started life as a 'rebellious fringe', then it became a phenomenon of the centre, dictating its laws to the period and trying to impose its colours on the whole semiosphere, and then, when it in fact had become set in its ways, it became the object of intense theorizing on the metacultural level.

These same processes can be seen even within one single text. It is well known for instance that in early Renaissance painting, everyday, homely details are placed on the periphery of the canvas or in distant landscapes, while the figures in the centre are strictly canonic. A supreme example of this process is to be seen in Piero della Francesca's 'The Flagellation of Christ' in the ducal palace at Urbino. Here the peripheral figures are boldly placed in the foreground, while the flagellation itself is put in the background and painted with muted colours, thus, as it were, forming the semantic background to the colourful trio in the foreground. Analogous processes may take place not in space but in time, in the movement from an outline to the finished text. There are many instances when the preliminary variants, both in painting and in poetry are more boldly relevant to the aesthetics of the future than the 'normalized' final text which has passed the author's self-censorship. It is the same with the footage which a film director rejects during the montage process.

An analogy from another sphere is the activity of semiotic processes during the European Middle Ages in those areas where the Christianization of 'barbarians' did not eradicate popular pagan cults, but merely covered them with its official mantle: we think of such areas as the inaccessible Pyrenees and Alps or the forests and swamps where the Saxons and Thurings lived. This was the soil that later produced 'popular Christianity', heresies, and eventually the Reformation.

The upsurge of semiotic activity, which a situation like this stimulates, leads to an accelerated 'maturing' of the peripheral centres; metalanguages are born which in their turn claim to be universal metalanguages for the whole semiosphere. The history of culture provides many examples of such rivalries. And in fact the attentive historian of culture will find in each synchronic section not one system of canonized norms, but a paradigm of competing systems. A typical example is the coexistence in seventeenth-century Germany, on the one hand, of the 'language societies' (*Sprachgesellschaften*) and 'Fruitful Society' (*Fruchtbringende Gesellschaft*) which had the purist aim of purging the German language of barbarisms, especially Gallicisms and Latinisms, and of normalizing the grammar (see Schottel's grammar); and, on the other hand, the 'Noble Academy of Faithful Ladies' which had exactly the opposite aim of encouraging French and the *précieuse* style of behaviour. We can also point to the coexistence of the French Academy and Madame de Rambouillet's blue salon.

The last example is especially illuminating for both centres actively and consciously worked to create their own 'language of culture'. When the French Academy was founded (the king signed the patent on 2 January 1635) among its first tasks was to 'purify and record the language', while for the *culture galant* of the *Précieuses* of the Hotel Rambouillet the question of language was also pre-eminent. Paul Tallemant wrote:

If the word jargon means nothing more than bad language corrupted by a good one, as is the case perhaps with the lower classes, one could hardly say *jargon des Précieuses* because the *Précieuses* seek what is most beautiful. But the word also signifies affected language and consequently we can say *jargon des Précieuses*. The people we call *Précieuses* do not speak the real language, but use studied phrases which have been deliberately composed.[11]

The last phrase is particulary telling: it shows how artificial and normative the *langage des Précieuses* was. While satires on the *Précieuses* criticized their faulty usage from the position of a higher norm, from their point of view they aimed to raise their usage to the status of a norm, that is to create an abstract image of real usage.[12]

The different attitude to space is just as interesting. Richelieu, who founded the Academy, envisaged the boundaries of a purified and systematized French language as the frontiers of an absolutist ideal France, .the limit of his political dreams. The salon of Madame de Rambouillet created its ideal space too: there is an amazing number of documents of '*précieuse* geography', starting with Mademoiselle de Scudery's *Land of Tenderness* and including *Carte du Royaume des Précieuses* (1659), *Carte de la cours Guéret* (1663) and Tallemant's *Le voyage de l'isle d'amour* (1663). These create an image of space with many levels: real Paris turns into Athens through a series of conventional renamings. But on a higher level there is the ideal space of the 'land of tenderness' which is identified with the 'true' semiosphere. Compare with this the utopian geography of the Renaissance period which had two aims: on the one hand, to create an image of the ideal city, island or state 'above' reality, including geographical and cartographic descriptions of it (such are Thomas More's *Utopia* and Francis Bacon's *New Atlantis*); and on the other hand, to give practical expression to the metastructure by planning and building ideal cities. See, for instance, Luciano Laurano's wonderful picture 'Ideal City' (in the ducal palace at Urbino). Works such as Caspar Stiblin's *Short Description of the State of Eudemonia, Island of the Land of the Blessed* (1553), or Campanello's *City of the Sun* prepared the way for numerous projects of ideal cities. The ideas of Alberti lay behind the Renaissance utopianism. Plans of cities drawn up by Dürer, Leonardo da Vinci, Sforzinda's plan created by Filaret, Francesco di Giorgio Martini's plan for an ideal city were examples of the direct intrusion of the metastructure into reality, for they were all plans intended to be carried out. As Jean Delumeau has pointed out:

> Examples of the successful realization of such plans still standing are Lima (like Panama and Manila in the seventeenth century), Zamostje in Poland, Valetta in Malta, Nancy; they include Livorno, Gattinara in Piedmont, Vallauris, Brouage, and Vitry-le-François.[13]

But the hottest spots for semioticizing processes are the boundaries of the semiosphere. The notion of boundary is an ambivalent one: it both separates and unites. It is always the boundary of something and so belongs to both frontier cultures, to both contiguous semiospheres. The boundary is bilingual and polylingual. The boundary is a mechanism for translating texts of an alien semiotics into 'our' language, it is the place

where what is 'external' is transformed into what is 'internal', it is a
filtering membrane which so transforms foreign texts that they become
part of the semiosphere's internal semiotics while still retaining their own
characteristics. In Kievan Russia there was a term for those nomads who
settled on the borderlands of Russian territory, became agriculturalists,
and in alliance with the Russian princes took part in campaigns against
their own nomadic kin: they were called 'our *pogany*' (*pogany* meant
'pagan' as well as 'foreign', 'incorrect', 'unclean'). The oxymoron 'our
pogany' epitomizes the situation of the boundary.

For Byron to enter Russian culture a cultural double, a 'Russian
Byron', was needed who faced both cultures: as a 'Russian' he was an
organic part of the internal processes of Russian literature and spoke its
language (in the broad semiotic sense). And he could not be excluded
from Russian culture without a gaping void being left behind. But at the
same time he was Byron, an organic part of English literature, and in the
context of Russian literature he would fulfil his function only if he was
experienced as Byron, i.e. as an *English* poet. This is the context in which
we should understand Lermontov's exclamation: 'No, I am not Byron, I
am another.' Not only separate texts or authors, but whole cultures, need
image-equivalents like this in 'our' culture, like two-way dictionaries, for
inter-cultural contacts to be possible.[14] The duality of such images is
manifest in the fact that they are both a means and a hindrance to
communication. The example of Pushkin shows this clearly: Pushkin's
early Romantic poems, the stormy biography of his youth, his exile, all
created a stereotypical image of the Romantic poet in the mind of his
readers, and they read his texts through this prism. Pushkin himself in
these years actively assisted in the build-up of his 'personal mythology',
which was in tune with the general system of 'Romantic behaviour'.
Later, however, this image stood between Pushkin's writing as it evolved
and his readers. Pushkin's stern, true to life writings which rejected
Romanticism were perceived by his readers to be a 'decline' and a
'betrayal' because in their minds the image of the early Pushkin still lived
on.

When the metalingual structure of the semiosphere changes we get
studies of 'unknown' and 'forgotten' writers, and similarly when
stereotype-images change we get works such as 'the unknown Dostoevsky'
or 'Goethe as he really was', which give their readers to understand that
up to now they did not know the real Dostoevsky or Goethe and that the
hour of true understanding has now arrived.

Something similar can be seen when the texts of one genre invade the
space of another genre. Innovation comes about when the principles of
one genre are restructured according to the laws of another, and this
'other' genre organically enters the new structure and at the same time
preserves a memory of its other system of encoding. So when Pushkin

inserted into the text of his novel *Dubrovsky* the actual text of an eighteenth-century court case on slander, and when Dostoevsky included in *The Brothers Karamazov* a carefully composed imitation of actual speeches by procurator and defence counsel, then these texts are organic parts of the narrative and yet, being extraneous documents, they are lapses from the aesthetic key of the literary narrative.

The notion of the boundary separating the internal space of the semiosphere from the external is just a rough primary distinction. In fact, the entire space of the semiosphere is transected by boundaries of different levels, boundaries of different languages and even of texts, and the internal space of each of these sub-semiospheres has its own semiotic 'I' which is realized as the relationship of any language, group of texts, separate text to a metastructural space which describes them, always bearing in mind that languages and texts are hierarchically disposed on different levels. These sectional boundaries which run through the semiosphere create a multi-level system. Certain parts of the semiosphere may at different levels of self-description form either a semiotic unity, a semiotic continuum, demarcated by a single boundary; or a group of enclosed spaces, marked off as discrete areas by the boundaries between them; or, finally, part of a more general space, one side of which is demarcated by a fragment of a boundary, while the other is open. Naturally the hierarchy of codes which activates different levels of signification in the single reality of the semiosphere will correspond to these alternatives.

An important criterion here is the question of who is perceived as the subject in the given system, for example, the subject of the law in legal texts of the given culture, or the 'personality' of a particular system of socio-cultural encoding. The notion of 'personality' is only identified with a physical individual in certain cultural and semiotic conditions. Otherwise it may be a group, it may or may not include property, it may be associated with a certain social, religious or moral position. The boundary of the personality is a semiotic boundary. For instance, a wife, children, slaves, vassals may in some systems be included in the personality of the master, patriarch, husband, patron, suzerain, and not possess any individual status of their own; whereas in other systems they are treated as separate individuals. Disturbances and rebellion arise when two methods of encoding are in conflict: for instance when the socio-semiotic structure describes an individual as a *part*, but that person feels him or herself to be an autonomous unit, a semiotic subject not an object.

When Ivan the Terrible executed those boyars who fell from favour he executed not only the family, but also all the servants; not only the domestic servants but also the peasants from the villages (alternatively the peasants were resettled, the names of the villages changed and the buildings razed to the ground). While making allowances for the tsar's pathological cruelty, we can explain these executions not as a response of fear (as if a serf on a provincial estate could threaten the tsar!), but by the idea that they were all one person, parts of the boyar being punished and so sharing in his responsibility. This attitude is evidently not unlike Stalin's with his psychology of an eastern tyrant.

From the European legal point of view nurtured on the post-Renaissance sense of individual rights, the idea that one person should suffer for the faults of another was incomprehensible. Even in 1732 the wife of the British ambassador in St Petersburg, Lady Rondo, commented on this Russian practice to a European friend (Lady Rondo was not in the least hostile to the Russian court, even being inclined to idealize it: in her letters she praised the 'sensitivity' and 'kindness' of the Empress Anno who was as coarse as a provincial landlady, and the 'nobility' of her cruel favourite, Biron). Writing about the exile of the Dolgoruky family she said:

> You may be surprised at the exile of the women and children; but here when the head of the family falls into disfavour then the whole family is punished with him.[15]

The same notion of collective (in this case, clan) personality, and not individual personality, lies behind the idea of the blood feud, according to which the whole clan of the murderer is perceived to be responsible. The historian S. M. Solov'ev has argued convincingly that the practice of *nestnichestvo*,[16] which to the adherents of the Enlightenment who believed in progress was just a sign of 'ignorance', is closely bound up with a strong sense of the clan as a single personality.

> We can understand that given the strength of the clan, and the responsibility of all members of the clan for each other, the significance of the individual inevitably lost out to the significance of the clan; an individual was unthinkable without the clan. Ivan Petrov was never thought of as just Ivan Petrov, but only as Ivan Petrov with his brothers and nephews. Given this fusion of the person with the clan, when one person was promoted in service, the whole clan was promoted, and when one member was demoted, so was the whole clan.[17]

In the reign of Aleksei Mikhailovich for instance (in the seventeenth century) the courtier Matvei Pushkin who belonged to the thirty-one most distinguished families, refused to go on a diplomatic mission as subordinate to the well-known statesman and favourite of the tsar, A. L. Nardyn-Nashchekin, who was of lower status; he preferred to go to prison and stoically endured the tsar's anger and threats to confiscate all his property, saying with dignity: 'Sire, you may order my execution, but

Nashchokin is younger and less well-bred than I am.'[18]

The space which in one system of coding is a single person, may in another system be the place where several semiotic subjects are in conflict.

Because the semiotic space is transected by numerous boundaries, each message that moves across it must be many times translated and transformed, and the process of generating new information thereby snowballs.

The function of any boundary or filter (from the membrane of the living cell, to the biosphere which according to Vernádsky is like a membrane covering our planet, and to the boundary of the semiosphere) is to control, filter and adapt the external into the internal. This invariant function is realized in different ways on different levels. On the level of the semiosphere it implies a separation of 'one's own' from 'someone else's', the filtering of what comes from outside and is treated as a text in another language, and the translation of this text into one's own language. In this way external space becomes structured.

When the semiosphere involves real territorial features as well, the boundary is spatial in the literal sense. The isomorphism between different kinds of human settlement – from archaic ones to Renaissance and Enlightenment plans for ideal cities – and ideas about the structure of the cosmos has often been remarked on. Hence the appeal of the centre for the most important cultic and administrative buildings. Less valued social groups are settled on the periphery. Those who are below any social value are settled on the frontier of the outskirts (the etymology of the Russian word for outskirts [*predmest'e*] means 'before the place' [*pered mestom*] i.e. before the city, on its boundaries), by the city gate, in the suburbs. If we think of this on a vertical scale then these 'outskirts' will be lofts and cellars, and in the modern city the metro. If the centre for 'normal' life is the flat, then the boundary space between *home* and *non-home* is the staircase and entrance. And these are the spaces which marginalized social groups make 'their own': the homeless, the drug addicts, young people. Other boundary places are public places such as stadia and cemeteries. There is a significant change in the accepted norms of behaviour when moving from boundary to centre.

However some elements are always set *outside*. If the inner world reproduces the cosmos, then what is on the other side represents chaos, the anti-world, unstructured chthonic space, inhabited by monsters, infernal powers or people associated with them. In the countryside the sorcerer, the miller and (sometimes) the smith had to live outside the village, as did the executioner in a medieval town. 'Normal' space has not only geographical but also temporal boundaries. Nocturnal time lies beyond the boundary. People visit the sorcerer if he demands it by night. The robber lives in this anti-space: his home is the forest (the anti-home) his sun is the moon (the 'thieves' sun' in the Russian proverb), he speaks an anti-language, his behaviour is anti-behaviour (he whistles loudly, swears indecently), he sleeps when other people work, and robs when other people are sleeping, and so on.

The 'night-time world' of the city also lies on the boundary of the space of culture or beyond it. This travesty world presupposes anti-behaviour.

We have already discussed the process whereby the periphery of culture moves into the centre, and the centre is pushed out to the periphery. The force of these opposing currents is even stronger between the centre and 'the periphery of the periphery', the frontier zone of culture. After the 1917 October Revolution in Russia this process took place literally in many shapes and forms: poor folk from the outskirts moved in their masses into the 'apartments of the bourgeoisie' who were either turned out or had to squeeze up to accommodate them. There was a symbolic sense too in the moving of the beautiful wrought iron railings which before the Revolution surrounded the royal gardens round the Winter Palace in Petrograd to a working-class area where they were put up round a square, while the tsar's garden was left without a railing, 'open'. In the utopian plans for a socialist city of the future, of which any number were drawn up in the early 1920, a recurrent idea was that the centre of the town should be a giant factory 'in place of the palaces and churches'.

In this sense Peter the Great's transfer of the capital to Petersburg was a typical move to the frontier. The transfer of the politico-administrative centre on to the *geographical* frontier was at the same time the transfer of the frontier to the *ideological* and *political* centre of the state. Later pan-Slavist plans to move the capital to Constantinople involved moving the capital even beyond the actual frontiers.

A similar shift can be observed in the norms of behaviour, of language, of style in dress, and so on, from the frontier area into the centre. Take jeans for example: what were once working clothes intended for people doing physical labour became young people's clothes, since young people rejected the central culture of the twentieth century and saw their ideal in the peripheral culture; subsequently jeans spread over the whole domain of culture, became neutral, that is, 'common to all', which is the most important feature of semiotic systems of the centre. The periphery is brightly coloured and marked, whereas the nucleus is 'normal', i.e. lacking in colour or scent, it 'simply exists'. So the victory of a semiotic system involves it shifting to the centre and an inevitable 'toning down'. We can compare this with the 'usual' cycle of ageing: the rebellious youth with the passage of the years becomes the 'normal' respectable gentleman, passing from provocative 'colourfulness' to sobriety.

In the frontier areas semiotic processes are intensified because here there are constant invasions from outside. The boundary as we have already pointed out is ambivalent and one of its sides is always turned to the outside. Moreover the boundary is the domain of bilingualism, which as a rule finds literal expression in the language practice of the inhabitants of borderlands between two cultural areas. Since the boundary is a necessary part of the semiosphere and there can be no 'us' if there is no 'them', culture creates not only its own type of internal organization but also its own type of external 'disorganization'. In this sense we can say that the 'barbarian' is created by civilization and needs it as much as it needs him. The extreme edge of the semiosphere is a place of incessant dialogue. No matter whether the given culture sees the 'barbarian' as saviour or enemy, as a healthy moral influence or a perverted cannibal, it is dealing with a construct made in its own inverted image. It is entirely to be expected, for instance, that the rational positivistic society of nineteenth-century Europe should create images of the 'pre-logical savage', or of the irrational subconscious as anti-spheres lying beyond the rational space of culture.

Since in reality no semiosphere is immersed in an amorphous, 'wild' space, but is in contact with other semiospheres which have *their own* organization (though from the point of view of the former they may seem unorganized) there is a constant exchange, a search for a common language, a *koine*, and of creolized semiotic systems come into being. Even in order to wage war there has to be a common language. It is a well-known fact that in the last period of Roman history barbarian soldiers ascended the throne of the Roman emperors, while many military leaders of the 'barbarians' served their apprenticeship in the Roman legions.[19] On the frontiers of China, of the Roman Empire, of Byzantium, we see the same thing: the technical achievements of the settled civilization pass into the hands of the nomads who turn them against their inventors. But these conflicts inevitably lead to cultural equalization and to the creation of a new semiosphere of more elevated order in which both parties can be included as equals.

10

Dialogue mechanisms

We have already mentioned that the elementary act of thinking is translation. Now we can go further and say that the elementary mechanism of translating is dialogue. Dialogue presupposes asymmetry, and asymmetry is to be seen first, in the difference between the semiotic structures (languages) which the participants in the dialogue use; and second, in the alternating directions of the message-flow. This last point means that the participants in a dialogue alternately change from a position of 'transmission' to a position of 'reception' and that consequently the dialogue process consists of discrete sections with intervals between them.

However, if dialogue without semiotic difference is pointless, when the difference is absolute and mutually exclusive dialogue becomes impossible. So asymmetry assumes a degree of invariancy.

But there is another condition necessary for dialogue: namely the concern of both participants for the message and their capacity to overcome the semiotic barriers that must inevitably arise. John Newson, for instance, who has studied the dialogic situation between a mother who is breast-feeding and her infant, has noticed that – however strange this may sound in this kind of textbook – a necessary condition for dialogue is love, the mutual attraction of the participants. Incidentally Newson's choice of subject is an exceptionally good one for understanding the general mechanisms of dialogue. Dialogue as a form of semiotic exchange is impossible within an organism where other forms of contact predominate. But it is also impossible between units having no common language. The relationship of mother and child is in this respect ideal experimental material: the participants in this dialogue have *just* ceased to be one being but have *not yet* quite wholly separated. In the purest sense this relationship shows that the need for dialogue, *the dialogic situation*, precedes both real dialogue and even the existence of a language in which

143

to conduct it: the semiotic situation precedes the instruments of semiosis. What is still more interesting is that in the search for a common language each of the participants tries to use the other's language: the mother makes sounds like the baby's burbling; and even more amazingly, the baby's facial expressions, if recorded on film and then played in slow motion, show that he or she is also imitating the mother's expressions, i.e. is trying to adopt her language. Fascinating also is the fact that in this dialogue there is a strict sequence of transmission and reception: when one participant gives a 'message' the other pauses, and vice versa.[20] For instance, and this is something many people will have observed, there is an 'exchange of laughter' between mother and baby, that 'language of smiles' which Rousseau thought was the only conversation guaranteed to be free of falsehood.

Of course we have to bear in mind that discreteness in the change-over from transmission to reception is apparent in practical terms on the level of description when a dialogic situation is being recorded by an external observer. Discreteness, or the ability to issue information in portions, is the law of all dialogic systems. But on the structural level discreteness may be apparent when there are different degrees of intensity in the material realization of a continuity. For instance, if an actual process takes the form of a cyclical alternation of periods of maximal activity and periods of minimal activity, then the recording apparatus, unless it records indices lower than the given threshold, will record the process as a discrete one. The apparatus for the self-description of culture behaves in the same way. The development of culture is cyclical and like most dynamic processes in nature is subject to sinusoidal fluctuations. But in a culture's self-awareness the periods of least activity are usually recorded as intermissions.

These observations are relevant to some aspects of the history of culture. If we isolate one series from the history of world culture, such as 'the history of English literature' or 'the history of the Russian novel' what we get is a continuous line stretched out chronologically in which periods of intensity alternate with relative calms. But if we look at this immanent development as *one partner in a dialogue* then the periods of so-called decline can be regarded as a time of pause in a dialogue, the time when information is being intensively received, after which follow periods of transmission. This is what happens in the relationships between units of all levels – from genres to national cultures. So we propose the following pattern: the relative inertness of a structure is the result of a lull in the flow of texts arriving from structures variously associated with it which are in a state of activity. Next comes the stage of saturation: the language is mastered, the texts are adapted. The generator of the texts is as a rule situated in the nuclear structure of the semiosphere while the receiver is on the periphery. When saturation reaches a certain limit, the receiving structure sets in motion internal mechanisms of text-production. Its passive state changes to a state of alertness and it begins rapidly to produce new texts, bombarding other structures with them, including the structure that 'provoked' it. We can describe this process as a change-over between centre and periphery. What is important is that a vigorous increase takes place: the system which has now come to a state of activity gives out more energy than the system that provoked it and extends its influence over a much larger area. This explains the tendency in cultural systems to universalism.

Let us illustrate this: From the fifth century onwards Italy was shattered by the invasions of the Germans, then the Huns, then the Goths and Ostrogoths, Byzantines, Langobards, Franks, Arabs, Normans, and Magyars; it became just a geographical concept and apparently lost its cultural life. But at the same time new 'hot spots' of civilization came into being in the cultural space which was defined by the boundaries of the ancient Mediterranean civilizations which now attracted the Germans, Slavs and Arabs. Among these 'hot spots' was Provence and the culture which flourished there from the eleventh to twelfth centuries.

For a certain period Italy became a 'text-receiver'. It 'received' the lyric poetry of the Provençal troubadours, together with the fashion for courtly behaviour and the Provençal language. *Chansons* and sonnets in the Provençal language began to be composed in Italy, and – a typical feature of this process – also grammars of Provençal language: 'One of the two oldest Provençal grammars, *Donatz Proensals*, was compiled in Italy about this time and specially for Italians'.[21] Other cultural currents swept in as well: epic poetry from France, Hispano-Arab culture from Sicily and also mediated through Provence. Finally the influence of the classical 'soil' which though it had died down had never ceased altogether was felt once more. Mention should also be made of the cultural influence of the Greco-Byzantine tradition. If, then, cultural production is our criterion, this period can well be regarded, as it often is, as a time of decline. But on the other hand, it was a period of an exceptionally high degree of saturation. Italy, set at the crossroads of many ancient and modern cultures, absorbed all this flood of texts, and within her cultural space these warring and conflicting texts formed themselves into a whole.

The result was at the next stage a burst of cultural activity unheard of in the history of world civilization. Over the next centuries Italy became like a volcano spewing out a great diversity of texts which flooded the cultural *oikumene* of the West.[22] The Renaissance and Baroque periods can rightly be called the 'Italian period' of European culture: Italian became the language of courts and of dandies, of fashion and of diplomacy. It was spoken in the alcoves of ladies and the cabinets of cardinals. Italy supplied Europe with artists and craftsmen, bankers, jewellers, lawyers, cardinals and royal favourites. We can judge the force

of this invasion by the strength of the anti-Italian feeling which broke out
in England, Germany and France, and by the energy with which
Italianized European culture would strive to promote a multitude of 'its
own' national figures in the place of one foreigner.

What the Renaissance did to Italian culture, the Enlightenment did
with French. France had absorbed cultural currents from the whole of
Europe: the ideas of the Reformation from Holland, Germany and
Switzerland, the empiricism of Bacon and Locke and Newtonian
mechanics, the Latinism of the Italian Humanists, and the Mannerism of
the Spanish and Italian Baroque; but in the age of the Enlightenment she
made all Europe speak her language. At the time of the Renaissance each
cultural tendency had had to face a hard choice: either to be a supporter
or an opponent of Humanism and the cult of Antiquity, which amounted
to supporting or opposing the spirit of Italian culture; similarly in the
eighteenth century there was a choice: either to be a follower or an
opponent of the ideas of the Enlightenment, namely, religious toleration
the cult of Nature and Reason, and the eradication of age-old
superstitions in the name of the freedom of Man. Paris became the capital
of European thought, and innumerable texts poured out of France to all
the corners of Europe. Compare this period with the pause which
followed and which was marked by the publication of Madame de Staël'
De l'Allemagne (1810): France 'became a receiver' again and opened
itself to English culture from Shakespeare to Byron, to German culture –
Schiller, Goethe – and to the Romantic writers of northern Europe from
Kant to Walter Scott.

*   *   *

From the point of view of the 'receiving' side the process of reception
falls into the following stages:

1. The texts coming in from the outside keep their 'strangeness'. They
are read in the foreign language (both in the sense of natural language
and in the semiotic sense). They hold a high position in the scale of
values, and are considered to be true, beautiful, of divine origin, etc.
Knowledge of the foreign language is a sign of belonging to 'culture', to
the elite, to the best. Already existing texts in 'one's own' language, and
that language itself, are correspondingly valued lowly, being classed as
untrue, 'coarse', 'uncultured'.

2. Both principles – the 'imported' texts and the 'home' culture
restructure each other. Translations, imitations and adaptations multiply.
At the same time the codes imported along with the texts become part of
the metalingual structure. During the first stage the dominant psychological impulse is to break with the past, to idealize the 'new', i.e. the
imported world-view, and to break with tradition, while the 'new' is
experienced as something salvific. In this second stage, however, there is

a predominant tendency to restore the links with the past, to look for 'roots'; the 'new' is now interpreted as an organic continuation of the old, which is thus rehabilitated. Ideas of organic development come to the fore.

3. During this stage a tendency develops to find within the imported world-view a higher content which can be separated from the actual national culture of the imported texts. The idea takes hold that 'over there' these ideas were realized in an 'untrue', confused or distorted, form and that 'here', in the heart of the receiving culture they will find their true, 'natural' heartland. The culture which first relayed these texts falls out of favour and the national characteristics of the texts will be stressed.

4. During this stage the imported texts are entirely dissolved in the receiving culture; the culture itself changes to a state of activity and begins rapidly to produce new texts; these new texts are based on cultural codes which in the distant past were stimulated by invasions from outside, but which now have been wholly transformed through the many asymmetrical transformations into a new and original structural model.

5. The receiving culture, which now becomes the general centre of the semiosphere, changes into a transmitting culture and issues forth a flood of texts directed to other, peripheral areas of the semiosphere.

In the actual process of cultural contacts this schematically outlined cycle may of course not be fully realized. It anyway demands favourable historical, social and psychological conditions. The process of 'infection' needs certain external conditions to bring it about and needs to be felt to be necessary and desirable. As with any dialogue a situation of mutual attraction must *precede* the actual contact.

*   *   *

In Russian culture these necessary conditions were present and we can follow the main stages of the cycle quite clearly.

Russian culture experienced two periods when it was ready to 'receive' and absorb a flood of texts arriving from outside.

The first of these cycles began in 988 AD with the adoption of Christianity. This event was accompanied by the import of a great number of texts in Greek and in the common Slav literary language (Church Slavonic) which had been artificially created by Kiril and Methodius; these Slavonic texts reached Kievan Russia from the Slav countries which had earlier accepted Christianity (Bulgaria and Serbia). No later than the eleventh century a great number of these works were translated. But parallel with the intake of texts there developed a tendency to separate the Christian faith from Greek influence. This tendency influenced the Kievan Chronicle which includes several legends designed to play down the role of the Greeks in the Christianization of Russia. After the fall of Constantinople to the Turks (in 1456) Russian suspicions about the purity of the Greek faith finally hardened and Christianity was declared to be the 'Russian faith'. Thereafter Christian literature in Russian rapidly developed.

Because of a number of historical causes this cycle did not reach its final stage. This was not so, however, with the gigantic dialogue between Russian and Western cultures which continued throughout the eighteenth and nineteenth centuries and passed fully through all stages of the cycle.

The beginning of this new cycle in the relationship of Russian culture to European coincided with the beginning of the eighteenth century. Without going too deeply into the question of how far the psychological self-evaluation of people of that time coincides with the later opinions of historians, let us note merely that people of that time frequently and firmly called themselves 'new people'. There were two aspects to this appellation: at first the 'new people' thought of themselves as the antithesis to the 'old people' of pre-Petrine Russia. It was a conflict of generations: the new people were the young Russian Europeans, supporters of the Enlightenment and of new customs, while the 'old' were the defenders of the old ways and of deeply ingrained traditions. But later on the accents were shifted: the 'new Europeans' of Russia were contrasted with the 'old Europeans' of the West, and *the young* Russian civilization was contrasted with the *old* West European civilization on the grounds that Russia was capable of achieving what the West had dreamed of but had not been able to accomplish. Interestingly enough, the same reorientation of the word 'new' can be found in Russian texts of the eleventh century. When the Kievan chronicler was describing the baptism of Russia he quotes St Paul: 'The old shall pass away and the new will come', and by 'old' he evidently meant pagan Russia. But when in the eleventh century Metropolitan Ilarion (the first Russian to be appointed Metropolitan by Prince Yaroslav instead of a Greek) compared the Greeks with the Old Testament and the Russian Christians with the New, then evidently novelty was endowed with a special meaning: the pupil is not worse but better than the teacher.

As when Christianity was accepted, so Peter the Great's reforms were accompanied by an abrupt and demonstrative break with tradition. When Peter offended the religious susceptibilities of the Moscovites by ordering a 'sinful' theatre to be built on Red Square (a sacred place) he was doing something similar to St Vladimir who ordered the statue of Perun to be dragged along attached to horses' tails.

If we leave out of account social motivation, we can put the urge to a complete rupture with the past down in part to the exceptionally strong effect of the Enlightenment in general and of Rousseau in particular on Russian culture. The ideas that made Rousseau popular in Russia were:

his emphatic rejection of history, which he contrasted with his theory based on Nature and her unchangeable principles; his rejection of the whole of the previous cultural tradition; and his contrasting of the corrupt culture of the elite with the moral health of the people. The cult of Rousseau which started in Russia in the last third of the eighteenth century continued to flourish even when in France he had been forgotten by all except historians.

Since the French language was universally known among the educated classes,[23] Rousseau's works could be read in the original. Translations when they came were a sign that he had been accepted into the Russian literary situation. But because since the time of Peter the Great Western influence was associated with civilization and now according to Rousseau's ideas civilization was negatively valued, the growth in the influence of Rousseau paradoxically merged with anti-French feelings, the struggle against Gallomania and European influence. Russian feelings towards France were highly complex, especially during the French Revolution and the patriotic upsurge associated with the Napoleonic Wars. These feelings involved the ecstatic acceptance of the ideals of the Revolution, the liberal aim of protecting the men of the Enlightenment from the Jacobins,[24] and the conservative-nationalistic tendency which declared that the French Revolution was the inevitable consequence of *all* French culture (proponents of this view included Shishkov and Rastopchin).

But another tendency stands out against this background. The Rousseauist model was interpreted as follows: French culture, and especially its shadow the French upbringing of the Russian nobility, had led the nobility to forget their own native language, their Orthodox faith, national dress and Russian culture; this French culture was that very civilization which Rousseau objected to. Against it could be contrasted the natural life of the Russian peasantry, their healthy morals and natural kindness. The fundamental opposition for the Enlightenment of 'Nature vs. superstition' 'the natural vs. the unnatural' thus came to be interpreted in a special way. What was natural came to be identified with what is national. In the Russian peasant, the *muzhik*, was to be seen the 'man of Nature', and in the Russian language was an example of a natural language made by Nature herself. France came to be regarded as the source of all superstitions, the kingdom of fashion and 'fashionable ideas'. Russian society, effete and infected with Gallomania, was a society of 'degenerate Slavs' (Ryleev). By contrast the people were regarded as the direct descendant of the heroic and primitive way of life of Homeric and Hellenic culture. Such ideas nourished Gnedich, the translator of *The Iliad*, who was a follower of Rousseau and Schiller; they were shared by Griboedov and that circle of young writers whom Tynyanov dubbed the 'young archaizers'; and finally they had an influence on Gogol.

Of course, Rousseauism is only one of the currents in the general

movement of texts from the West to Russia. In the period between
Pushkin and Chekhov Russian culture became a relaying one (the peak
being the works of Tolstoy and Dostoevsky) and the flow of texts turned
in the other direction.

Of course our picture is highly schematic. In reality the circulation of
texts moves ceaselessly in all directions, large and small currents intersect
and leave their traces. At the same time texts are relayed not by one but
by many centres of the semiosphere, and the actual semiosphere is mobile
within its boundaries. Finally, these same processes occur at different
levels: periods when poetry invades prose alternate with periods when
prose invade poetry; there are times of mutual tension between drama
and the novel, between written and oral culture, and between elite
culture and oral culture. One and the same centre of the semiosphere can
be at one and the same time both active and 'receiving', one and the same
space of the semiosphere can be both in one sense a centre and in another
sense a periphery; attractions provoke rejections, and borrowings
provoke originality. The semiosphere, the space of culture, is not
something that acts according to mapped out and pre-calculated plans. It
seethes like the sun, centres of activity boil up in different places, in the
depths and on the surface, irradiating relatively peaceful areas with its
immense energy. But unlike that of the sun, the energy of the
semiosphere is the energy of information, the energy of Thought.

*   *   *

The semiotics of space has an exceptionally important, perhaps even
overriding significance in a culture's world-picture. And this world-picture
is linked to the specifics of actual space. For a culture to get to grips with
life, it must create a fundamental image of the world, a spatial model of
the universe. The spatial modelling reconstructs the spatial form of the
actual world. But spatial images can be used another way. The
mathematician, A. D. Aleksandrov writes:

> When studying topological qualities we again are faced with the possibility
> of conceptualizing an abstract totality of objects having only those qualities.
> We term this totality abstract topological space.

And further: 'The isolation of these qualities in their pure form leads us
to the idea of an abstract space that corresponds to them.'[25] If by
isolating a certain quality a set of continuously contiguous elements is
formed, then we can speak of an abstract space of that quality. In this
way we can talk of the space of ethics, of colour, of myth. In this sense
spatial modelling becomes a language in which non-spatial ideas can be
expressed.

How the spatial picture of the semiosphere is reflected in the mirror of
literary texts is especially interesting.

11

The semiosphere and the problem
of plot

Semiotic systems are in a state of constant flux. Such is the law too of the semiosphere which is subject to change both in its inner structure and as a whole. In what follows we shall be discussing a particular kind of internal change. Within the framework of each of the substructures which make up the semiosphere there are elements which are fixtures in its space, and elements with relative freedom of movement. The former belong to social, cultural, religious and other structures, while the latter have a higher degree of freedom of choice in their behaviour. A hero of the second type can *act*, that is, can cross the boundaries of prohibitions in a way that others cannot. Like Orpheus or Soslan[26] from the epic of the Narts, he can cross the boundary separating the living from the dead, or like the Benandanti he can wage nocturnal war with witches,[27] or like one berserk he can fling himself into battle, defying all rules – naked or clad in a bearskin, howling like a beast and killing his own people as well as the enemy. He may be a noble robber or a *picaro*, a sorcerer, spy, detective, terrorist or superman – the point is that he is able to do what others cannot, namely to cross the structural boundaries of cultural space. Each such infringement is a deed, and the chain of deeds forms what we call plot.

Plot is a syntagmatic concept and consequently involves the experiencing of time. So we have to do with two typological forms of events, which correspond to two types of time: cyclical and linear. In archaic cultures cyclical time predominates. Texts created according to the laws of cyclical time are not in our sense plot-texts and generally speaking they are hard to describe in our normal categories. The first thing that is striking about them is the absence of the categories of beginning and end: the text is thought of as a constantly repeated system synchronized with the cyclical processes of nature: with the alternation of the seasons of the year, of day and night, with the cycles of the stars. Human life is looked at not as a line running from birth to death, but as an endlessly repeated cycle (See Alexander Blok's line: 'You die – you begin all over again'.) The story, then, can begin at any point, and that point will serve as a beginning for the narrative which itself is a partial manifestation of the Text without beginning or end. This kind of narrative does not aim to inform the listeners of something they did not know, but is a mechanism to ensure the continuity of the flow of cyclical processes in nature itself. So the choice of a particular episode of the Text as the beginning and the content of today's narrative is not the narrator's – for he or she is part of the chronologically fixed and predetermined flow of the natural cycles of the ritual.

Another characteristic associated with cyclicity is the tendency to make certain characters identical with each other. The cyclical world of mythological texts forms a multi-layered system with clearly defined features of topological organization. This means that cycles such as those of the days and nights, of the years, of human or divine deaths and births, are regarded as homeomorphic. For this reason although night/winter/death are in many ways dissimilar, their similarity in this way of thinking is not a metaphor as it might seem to the modern mind; for they are one and the same thing (or rather transformations of one and the same thing). The characters and objects mentioned at different levels of the cyclical mythological system are different proper names of the same thing. A mythological text, because of its exceptional capacity for topological transformation, can boldly make assumptions about the identity and similarity of things which we would be hard pushed to do.

The topological world of myth is not discrete. As we shall attempt to show, when discreteness arises it is the result of an inadequate translation into the discrete metalanguages of a non-mythological type.

The function of myth as a central text-forming mechanism is to create a picture of the world, to establish identity between distant spheres. In fact, it carries out many of the functions of science in pre-scientific cultures. By establishing iso- and homeomorphisms and reducing the diversity of the world to invariant images it has stimulated many cultural achievements of a purely scientific type such as calendars and astronomy. The functional kinship of these systems can be clearly seen from an examination of the sources of Graeco-classical science.

The texts engendered by the central text-forming mechanism classify, stratify and order. They reduce the world of anomalies and surprises which surrounds humanity to norm and orderliness. Even if these texts as we retell them in our language seem to be plot-texts, they are not really such. They tell not of one-off exceptional events, but of events which are out of time, endlessly repeated, and in this sense, unchangeable. Even if the narration is about the death and dismemberment of a god and his subsequent resurrection this is not a plot-narrative in our sense, since these events are thought of as inherent to a particular part of the cycle and thus repeated through the ages. The regularity of the repetition makes them not an anomalous and accidental occurrence, but a law immanent to the world. The central cyclical text-engendering mechanism cannot typologically speaking exist on its own: it must have in opposition to it a text-producing mechanism organized according to linear time and which records not regularities but anomalies. Such were the oral tales about 'surprises', 'news', various happy and unhappy occurrences. If the first type of text records principles, the second records events. If the first mechanism gave rise to law-affirming and normalizing texts both sacred and scientific, the second mechanism gave rise to historical texts, chronicles and records.

The recording of *ad hoc* and chance events, of crimes, disasters, of anything which was thought of as a violation of some established order, was the historical kernel of plot-narration. This is why the foundation element of literary narrative genres is the 'novella', i.e. 'news', which, as has often been pointed out, is based on the anecdote.

We should, incidentally, remark on the different pragmatics of these age-old contrasting types of text. Mythological texts, because of their spatial and topological laws, emphasize the structural laws of homeomorphism: equivalences are drawn between the disposition of the heavenly bodies and parts of the human body, between the seasons of the year and human life-span, and so on. This results in an elementary semiotic situation, namely every message has to be interpreted, or translated, as it is transformed into the signs of another level. Since the microcosm of the internal world of a human being is identified with the macrocosm of the universe, every narrative is perceived as something intimately relevant to each member of the audience. Myth always says something about me. But 'news', or an anecdote, is about someone else. The former organizes the world of the listener, the latter adds something interesting to his or her knowledge of the world.

*   *   *

The modern plot-text is the fruit of the interaction and mutual interference of these two primordial types of texts. But because the process of their interaction was a long drawn-out one over an immense period of time, its history was neither simple nor uniform.

The break-up of the cyclical time mechanism of texts (or at least the restriction of its functioning) stimulated the translation of a vast number of mythological texts into the language of discrete linear systems (among which were the verbal retellings of myths involving rituals and mystery religions) and the creation of those novelistic pseudo-myths which are what first come to mind when we think of mythology.

The first and most obvious result of this translation was loss of the isomorphism between levels of the text. One result was that the characters on different levels ceased to be perceived as different names for one and the same personage and they separated into a number of individual figures. Texts came to have many heroes, something which is in principle impossible in genuine mythological texts. The change-over from cyclic construction to a linear one involved a profound restructuring of the text, in comparison with which any of the variations which took place in the historical evolution of plot-literature seem incidental; so it no longer matters whether we use classical versions of myth or nineteenth-century novels as material for our reconstruction of the mythological origins of the text. Indeed, sometimes later texts provide more fruitful material for this kind of study.

The most obvious result of unwinding cyclical texts into linear ones is the appearance of character doubles. From Menander, the Alexandrian drama, Plautus, and to Cervantes, Shakespeare and – via Dostoevsky – to the novels of the twentieth century (see the system of characters in Gorky's *Klim Samgin*) the hero tends to be supplied with a companion who is his double, and sometimes with a whole paradigm-cluster of companions. In one of Shakespeare's comedies there is a foursome: a pair of heroes who are twins and their servants who are also twins (*The Comedy of Errors*)

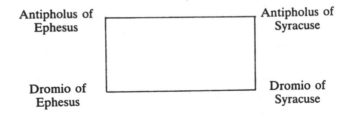

Here, evidently, we have a case when the four characters in the linear text if translated back into the cyclical system would 'wind up' into one character: for there is identity between the twins on the one hand and between the pair of 'nobles' and the pair of 'comics' on the other. Character doubling, which resulted from dividing up a cluster of mutually equivalent names, later turned into a plot-language which lent itself to many different interpretations in all sorts of art-ideologies: doubles could be material for an intrigue,[28] or for pointing up contrasts between characters, or, as in the works of Dostoevsky, for the modelling of the internal complexity of the human personality.

As an example of the use of doubles to create intrigue, let us consider Shakespeare's comedy *As You Like It*.

The characters of this comedy fall into clearly equivalent pairs, which if we attempt a reverse translation into cyclical time would wind up into *one person*. Heading the list are the two Dukes who are brothers, one of whom lives 'in the forest', while the other rules having usurped his brother's land. The characters who live 'at court' and 'in the forest' relate to each other by the principle of complementary distribution: if one moves from the forest to the court another will move in the opposite direction. It is as if they are not able to meet in one and the same circumstances. Since going 'to the forest' and returning again is a common mythological (and folktale) formula for death and rebirth, then obviously these doubles in mythology they would form a single image.

But the contrast between the two brothers is itself doubled on another level by the contrast of Oliver and Orlando, the older and younger sons of Sir Roland de Boys. Like the ruling Duke, Oliver is the usurper of his brother's inheritance and drives Orlando into the forest (the parallel between Duke Frederick and Oliver is pointed out clearly in the text of the comedy). The boundary dividing 'court' from 'forest' is the line beyond which mythological rebirth begins; this is shown by the fact that both wrong-doers when they cross this line instantly change into heroes of virtue.

> Duke Frederick, hearing how that every day
> Men of great worth resorted to this forest,
> Address'd a mighty power; which were on foot,
> In his own conduct, purposely to take
> His brother here, and put him to the sword;
> And to the skirts of this wild wood he came,
> Where meeting with an old religious man,
> After some question with him, was converted
> Both from his enterprise and from the world;
> His crown bequeathing to his banish'd brother.[29]

The same change takes place with Oliver:

> 'Twas I; but 'tis not I. I do not shame
> To tell you what I was, since my conversion
> So sweetly tastes, being the thing I am.[30]

So we arrive at a quadrangle in which the characters on the horizontal could be looked at as one and the same person at different moments of the plot (as if the character had been unwound onto the linear scale of the plot), while on the vertical they are different projections of the same character.

The court   The forest

Duke Frederick ┌────────────────────┐ Duke Senior
               │   │
               │   │
Oliver de Boys └────────────────────┘ Orlando de Boys

But this is not all the parallelisms: the women are obviously hypostases of the main heroes: Rosalind and Celia are daughters of the two Dukes, and, given a reverse transformation of the plot into a cycle, obviously form a single central image. The basic plot division on this level undergoes an essential transformation – both girls go off 'to the forest' (one is exiled, the other goes voluntarily) but there they undergo a transformation: they disguise themselves (Rosalind also changes sex dressing up as a boy) and they change their names – a typical detail of mythological re-embodiment.

Rosalind ┌──────────────────┐ Celia
Ganymede └──────────────────┘ Aliena

A new system of equivalences begins with the start of the love intrigue: a clear system of parallelisms is to be seen, and the dual nature of Ganymede – the boy-girl (which is stressed in the name) – results in new mythological identifications, which on the level of the Shakespearean text are taken as comic confusion:

Orlando   ┌──────────────┐ Rosalind
Oliver   └──────────────┘ Celia

Ganymede ┌──────────────┐ Phebe
Silvius   └──────────────┘ Phebe

Touchstone ┌─────────────┐ Audrey
William   └─────────────┘ Audrey

All these pairs of characters repeat the same situation and the same type of relationship on different levels, mutually doubling each other. Even the fool has a double in the form of an even more lowly character, the village idiot. 'Oliver–Celia' are a more lowly double of 'Orlando–Rosalind' (in the invariant schema the first pair are to be combined with Frederick, and the second with his exiled brother). The quadrangle 'Ganymede–Phebe–Phebe–Silvius' is a more lowly variant of all of them, while the quadrangle 'Touchstone–Audrey–Audrey–William' bears the same relationship to the previous one. In sum, *all* the significant characters of the play could in cyclic space be combined into a single image.

But there is one character who contrasts with *all* the others in the play and that is the melancholy Jaques. He is the only one who plays no part in the intrigue and who does not return from the forest with Duke Senior but stays in the same space with Frederick now a voluntary exile. Jaques has the most sharply delineated character: he is a constant critic of that human world which is situated beyond the forest. Since 'court' and 'forest' form an asymmetrical space of the type 'earthly world–world beyond the grave' (in the mythological sense), and 'real world–ideal/fabulous world' (in Shakespeare's play) then a character like Jaques is needed as an orientation point in the artistic space. Jaques cannot be identified with any character who is mobile in relation to the plot-space, but he represents a personified spatial category, a personified *reference point* of one world to the other. This is why he is the only person who does not cross the boundary between the world of the 'court' and that of the 'forest'.

*   *   *

We are suggesting that doubles are the most elementary and obvious result of a linear reworking of the hero of a cyclical text. And in fact the very appearance of *different* characters is the result of the same process. As we said above, characters can be divided into mobile ones who are free to move about the plot-space, capable of changing their position in the structure of the artistic world, and of crossing the frontier which is the basic topological feature of that space; and immobile ones who are in fact functions of that space.[31]

In the typological sense the primordial situation is when a plot-space is divided by *one* boundary into an internal and an external sphere, and *one* character has the plot-possibility of crossing that boundary. But many and various plots develop from this situation. The mobile character divides into a paradigm-cluster of different characters on the same level, the barrier (the frontier) also multiplies, and a subgroup of personified obstacles emerge who are immobile enemies ('opponents' in Propp's terminology) fixed to certain points of the plot-space. As a result the plot-space 'is inhabited' by all kinds of connected and contrasted characters. One deduction we can make from this is that the more the world of the characters is combined into one (one hero, one obstacle) the closer it is to the primordial mythological type of structural organization. Lyric poetry, because it is bound to an 'I–s/he' or 'I–thou' plot-schema, is obviously in this sense the most 'mythological' of the modern literary genres. Other features confirm this suggestion: for instance lyric poetry shares with the mythological text some of the pragmatic features noted above. A lyric is more likely to be taken by the reader to be a profound and natural model of his or her own personality than is the epic.

Another fundamental result of this same process is that the categories of beginning and end of the text come to have an emphasized modelling function.

Once a text has become detached from ritual and has acquired independent verbal existence in a linear disposition, then automatically the beginning and the end of it become stressed. In this sense eschatological texts may be considered to be the first evidence of the break-up of myth and the start of the narrative plot.

The elementary course of events in myth can be reduced to the sequence: entry into a closed space – exit from it (this sequence is open at either end and can be endlessly multiplied). Since enclosed space can be interpreted as 'cave', 'grave', 'house', 'woman' (and so may be endowed with the features of darkness, warmth or dampness[32]), entry into it can be interpreted on different levels as 'death', 'conception', 'return home', and so on, and all these acts are thought of as identical with each other. The resurrection/birth which follows the death/conception are linked because birth is thought of not as the arrival of a new previously non-existent person, but as the renewal of something that already exists. To the extent that conception is identified with the death of the father, birth is identified with his return. It follows then that diachronic doubles ('father – son'), as well as synchronic ones, are the result of subdividing a single or cyclical text-image.[33] Convincing proof of the persistence of this mythological model is the system of doubling between the Karamazov brothers and their attitude to their father Fedor Karamazov according to the schema: 'degradation – rebirth', complete identification or contrasting opposition with one another.

The mythological origin of doubles in plot is obviously associated with the redistribution of the segmentation boundaries in texts and of the central character's features of identification and difference.

In cyclical myths which derive from this basis one can make out the order of events, but it is not possible to establish time-limits to the narrative: every death is followed by a rebirth and rejuvenation, and they in their turn are followed by ageing and death. The change to eschatological narratives brought about linear plot-development. This at once put the text into the category of our normal narrative. The action, set in linear time, is constructed as a narrative about the gradual decay of the world and the ageing of the god, after which comes his death (dismemberment, torment, eating, burial – the latter are synonyms in the sense that both involve being enclosed in a closed space), and resurrection which marks the end of evil and its final eradication. So the increase of evil is connected with the movement of time, and the disappearance of evil with the end of time, its stopping forever. Other features of the break-up of the age-old mythological structure are the break-up of isomorphic relationships. So, for example, the Eucharist ceased to be an action equivalent to burial (and equivalent also to suffering and dismemberment – which, on the one hand, is associated with the eating and breaking the food, and, on the other hand, was for example identical with the tortures of an initiation ceremony, which also was death in a new guise) and it became a *sign*.

A vestige of myth in the eschatological legend is the fact that the sharply emphasized ending of the text is not coincidental with biological end of the hero's life, his death. Death (or its equivalents: going away and being lost to sight, which is then followed by the hero's 'reappearance'; or a marvellous dream in mysterious place, on a rock, in a cave, which is followed by awakening and return, etc.) comes in the middle of the narrative and not at the end. This prompts another remark: if we agree with the idea that the eschatological legend is the product of rephrasing a myth in linear terms that is typologically closest to myth (and probably historically the earliest) then we have to conclude that the obligatory happy ending such as is found in fairy tales is not only the original form of narrative with a stressed end, but for a certain stage also the only one since there was no alternative form in the shape of tragedy. The eschatological end by definition can only be the final triumph of good and the condemnation and punishment of evil. Our familiar 'good' and 'bad' endings are secondary to it as realizations or not of this primordial scheme.

The category of beginning is not so marked in eschatological legends although it found expression in the form of set openings and set situations; such beginnings can be associated with the idea that there had been some ideal primordial state, which subsequently declined only to be re-established again.

'Beginnings' were much more marked in culturally peripheral texts such as chronicles. In the description of an extraordinary event, to say 'who began it' or 'how it all began', is, even to the modern reader, like giving a causal explanation. The high modelling role of the category of beginning can be clearly seen in *The Tale of Bygone Years* which is in fact a collection of narratives about beginnings, the beginning of the Russian land, of the power of the princes, of the Christian faith in Russia, and so on. The chronicler is also interested in crime but chiefly from this aspect. The point of an event is explained by pointing out who first carried out an act of this kind (so the condemnation of fratricide is explained by reference to Cain). In *The Lay of Igor's Campaign* Igor's independent campaign is explained by reference to Oleg Goreslavich who initiated internecine strife (a fact which is even more significant because Oleg was the blood 'begetter' of Igor's family).

The translation of mythological texts into linear narratives made it possible for these two polar types of texts (those describing the regular course of events, and those concerned with anecdotal deviation from the course) to influence each other mutually. This interaction largely determined the subsequent fate of the narrative genres.

Temporary death as a way of transferring from one state into another, higher one is to be found in an extremely wide circle of texts and rituals. Among such rituals are the whole complex of initiation rites,[34] as well as religious procedures such as tonsuring for monks and the adoption of the *skhima*, and the consecration of shamans. As a rule in these cases death is associated with the body being torn or hacked to pieces, then buried or eaten, and its subsequent resurrection. Vladimir Propp drawing on a large number of sources and especially on N. P. Dyrenkova's study 'Acquisition of the Shamanic Gift in the Beliefs of the Turkic Tribes' remarked:

> The feeling that one's innards are being chopped up, torn apart, picked to pieces is a necessary condition of Shamanism and precedes the moment when a person turns into a Shaman.[35]

Propp also cites many examples of how the manifestation of a prophetic gift is preceded by tongue and ears being perforated, a snake introduced into the body, and so on.

Since these rituals have been noted in a wide range of mythological material (see Propp, Eliade and others), we can easily establish their correlation with the single mythological invariant of 'life – death – resurrection (renewal)', or, on a more abstract level, 'entry into a closed space – emergence from it'. The difficulty lies elsewhere, namely, in how to explain the persistence of this schema when the direct link with the world of myth is known to have been broken. Pushkin in 'The Prophet' gave an amazingly precise, detailed picture of the acquisition of a shamanistic (that is, prophetic) gift down to such details as the insertion into the poet's mouth of 'the little snake which personifies magic powers'.[36] His picture has been widely confirmed, yet he did not know the sources which are now available to the modern ethnographer; and we for our part do not need to remember the parallels with the prophet Isaiah and the Koran which evidently served as Pushkin's immediate sources for the initiatory images of his poem in order to understand it.[37]

To understand Pushkin's text it is no more necessary to know about its link with initiatory rites (or rites for the consecration of a shaman) than it is necessary to know the origins of a language's grammatical forms to be able to speak the language. Such knowledge may be useful, but it is not a minimal condition for understanding the text. The hidden mytho-ritualistic framework becomes the grammatically formal basis for a text that deals with the dying of the 'old' man and his rebirth as a prophet.

An even more obvious example of this dual process is Moravia's novel *Disobedience*. On the one hand, the content of the initiatory complex is forgotten to the extent that the process is entirely formalized and consequently turned into something not consciously felt by the reader (or by the author either perhaps); and on the other hand, the complex which has become unconscious is typically present. The action concerns the growth of a modern teenager into a man. Contemporary issues are raised such as teenage rebellion, the rejection of the world and the painful transition from stormy egocentrism and the cult of self-destruction to open acceptance of life. But the plot movement is constructed according to the ancient scheme: end of childhood (end of *first* life) is marked by an increasing attraction for death and a conscious rupture of the links which hold the hero in the world (rebellion against his parents and against the bourgeois world becomes a rebellion against life as such). Then follows a prolonged illness taking the hero to the brink of death and clearly being a substitute for it (the pages describing the young man's delirium are like the 'descent into death' in mythological texts). His first liaison with a woman (the nurse who looks after him) marks the beginning of his return to life, the change from nihilism and rebellion to acceptance of the world, and new birth. The obviously mythological schema which reproduces the classic outlines of initiation concludes with a striking image of a train, on which the young man, now convalescent, is travelling to a mountain sanatorium, plunging into the dark hole of a tunnel and emerging out of it. The two ends of the tunnel are extremely clear images of that most ancient mythological idea of entry into darkness, into a cave-like space which is like death, and re-emergence from it which is like a new birth.

We have already pointed out that in the modern mind archaic structures of thought have lost their content and so can be compared with the grammatical categories of language; these structures form the foundation of the syntax of large narrative text-sections. But as we know in the literary text, there is a constant process of exchange: what in language has lost independent semantic significance undergoes in literature a secondary semanticization, and vice versa. So there is also a secondary revival of mythological narrative which ceases to be a purely formal organizer of the text-sequences and acquires new meanings which often return us consciously or involuntarily to the myth.[38] An indicative example of this was Moravia's novel described above. The image prompted by modern technology (the train and the tunnel) is a suggestive expression of the most archaic mythological complex (transition to a new state being like death and new birth; the chain: death – sexual intercourse – rebirth; entry into darkness and re-emergence from it as an invariant model of all possible transformations). Here we have a fine example of the mechanism which activates the mythological layer in the structure of modern art.

*   *   *

If we take the central and peripheral spheres of culture to be texts organized in a particular way, then we shall notice that these texts have different types of internal organization.

The central myth-forming mechanism of culture is organized like topological space. When projected along the axis of linear time and from the field of ritual play and performance into the sphere of the verbal text it undergoes substantial changes: in acquiring linearity and discreteness it also gets features of verbal text which is constructed like a sentence. In this sense it becomes comparable with purely verbal texts arising on the periphery of culture. But this comparison will show up the very deep difference between them: the central sphere of culture is constructed on the principle of an integrated structural whole, like a sentence; whereas the peripheral sphere is organized like a cumulative chain organized by the simple joining of structurally independent units. This organization best corresponds to the functions of these texts: of the first to be a structural model of the world and of the second to be a special archive of anomalies.

Each of the groups we have described has its own idea of the universe as a whole.

The law-forming centre of culture, genetically deriving from the primordial mythological nucleus, reconstructs the world as something totally ordered, with a single plot and a supreme meaning. Though it is represented by a text or group of texts, they stand out in the general system of culture as a normalizing mechanism, which in relation to all other groups of texts of that culture stand on a metalevel. All the texts of this group are organically interconnected, which is apparent in the fact that they can readily be wound up into a single sentence. Since the content of this sentence is connected with eschatological ideas, the picture of the world produced by this sentence alternates between the tragic tension of the plot and a final reconciliation.

The system of peripheral texts reconstructs a picture of the world in which chance and disorder predominate. This group of texts also shows itself to be capable of shifting on to the metalevel, but it cannot be reduced to any one single and organized text. Since this group of texts takes anomalies and exceptions as its plot elements, the general picture of the world is one of extreme disorganization. The negative pole in this picture of the world will be realized by narratives about various tragic occurrences, each of which is a violation of order, i.e. what is least probable is, paradoxically, in this world what is most probable. The positive pole is manifest in *miracle*, the solution of tragic conflicts by the least expected and least probable means. However, since these texts lack any overall ordering, the miracle in this group of texts can never be a final solution. So the world-picture is as a rule chaotic and tragic.

In spite of the fact that in each actual culture we can pick out a degree of orientation towards either one of these text-engendering mechanisms and towards one or other group of texts, yet this orientation is a subjective one in the real mechanism of culture we must assume the presence of both centres, of tension between them and their mutual influence. Each of these groups, as it struggles to reach the leading position in the hierarchy of that culture, has its effect on its partner; it strives to define itself as a text of higher rank and to make its opponent into a partial manifestation of itself on a lower level. If examples of the disposition of ordered texts on the highest structural level of culture are trivial, they can be illustrated in philosophy by many systems from Plato to Hegel, and in the theory of science, for instance, in Saussure's ideas, then the opposite construction could be illustrated by Norbert Wiener's picture of the world with its universal advancing entropy, from which point of view information is merely a chance and local episode. When the dying Tyutchev asked to be given 'a little more light' he was but expressing the conviction he had held to all through his life that the world is chaotically disordered and that light, reason and law are merely local, accidental and unstable forms of 'the game of disorder' (the reference to Pascal was typical of him). According to Tyutchev humanity is set on the boundary of these two hostile worlds: by nature we belong to the world of chaos, but by our thinking we belong to the logos which is alien to nature:

> This is why, with nature warring,
> The soul cannot sing what the sea does
> Or what the thinking reed murmurs.

The dispute between the causal-predetermined and the probability theories in theoretical physics of this century is an example of the conflict we have been discussing in the sphere of science.

* * *

The dialogic conflict between the two primordial textual groupings takes on quite another light from the moment when art is born (we mean moment not in a chronological sense, because, though logically we can distinguish the artistic period from the pre-artistic, we cannot do so historically).

In the literary text there is an optimal correlation whereby the conflicting structures are disposed not hierarchically (that is, on different levels) but dialogically on the same level. This is why a literary narrative is the most flexible and effective modelling mechanism for describing extremely complex structures and situations in their entirety.

The conflicting systems do not replace each other but enter into structural relationships, and this gives rise to new kind of orderliness. We shall try to illustrate how this type of narrative structure comes about taking Dostoevsky's novels as an example; they are good material precisely because of their dialogic structure which was analysed with such profundity by Bakhtin. Incidentally, as Bakhtin pointed out, a dialogic structure is not a feature only of Dostoevsky, but is inherent to the novel as a form. We would take it even wider and suggest that it is inherent to literary texts of certain types. But we are not here concerned with the principles of dialogue in all its aspects. We have a much narrower aim, namely to examine how the two opposite plot-forming principles are integrated in the narrative form of the novel.

In Dostoevsky's novels it is easy to detect, as many commentators have already done, two opposing spheres: that of everyday action and that of ideological conflicts.

The first, which is the domain of plot development, can in its turn be divided into the world of everyday events and the sphere of the detective story.

It has often been said that everyday events develop in Dostoevsky with the 'logic of scandals', and the formal expression of the link between the episodes is the little word 'suddenly'.[39] Developing this observation we might say that the events on the everyday order follow each other in Dostoevsky's narratives in accordance with the law of least probability. A reader, relying on his or her life-experience, works out in his or her mind what to expect next, some of these expectations being judged to be very likely, others just possible, and yet others unlikely. The reader coming to an event in the novel naturally applies his or her own scale of expectations (this scale includes of course expectations derived from literary experience: it is quite possible to have a subconscious expectation which divides everyday probability off from literary probability). So the reader can construct the most probable next step in the plot. But in Dostoevsky what is least expected by the reader (both in terms of life and of literature) is the sole one possible for the writer.

Take for instance the chapter 'The Wise Serpent' from *The Devils*. Even the opening situation is a violation of the probable: Stepan Trofimovich Verkhovensky has been invited to Varvara Petrovna Stavrogin's for an important and confidential conversation, but when he arrives no one is there. In the meantime another strange thing has occurred: an unknown woman with odd behaviour has approached Mrs Stavrogin in church (she turns out to be Mary Timofeevna Lebyatkin), and Mrs Stavrogin against all common sense and quite out of keeping with her character has invited her home.[40] Lisa Drozdova, behaving in a quite inexplicable way, also gets involved and has made

Mrs Stavrogin take her home too.

Verkhovensky and the narrator are expecting Varvara Petrovna *alone*, but they hear the noise of many footsteps which 'was really rather odd'. They hear 'someone come in very rapidly', after which remark comes the disclaimer that 'Mrs Stavrogin certainly could not have come in like that'. But it is she who comes in (the younger women following her 'at some distance and at a slower pace'). Then follows the strange and scandalous behaviour of Miss Lebyatkin. As soon as this episode is over, Mrs Drozdov, Lisa's mother, suddenly appears and a scene both scandalous and unexpected breaks out between her and Mrs Stavrogin (meek, oppressed Mrs Drozdov behaving aggressively). The scene finishes with Mrs Stavrogin fainting and a reconciliation. Then a new person appears, Dasha Shatov. But the conversation is not about Verkhovensky's courtship of her, *which was the reason why he had been invited* (most improbably everyone had forgotten about that), instead it is about something quite else – a new complication: Dasha tells them that at the request of Nicholas Stavrogin she had given money to Captain Lebyatkin. This information makes it clear that there are some mysterious relationships going on between people between whom even acquaintanceship was improbable.

Then Captain Lebyatkin himself is announced and in spite of everyone's remark that he was 'not the sort of person who can be admitted into a drawing-room'[41] and so could not be received, he is invited and comes in. At this point Mrs Stavrogin sends Lisa out of the room ('Lisa in particular has no business to be here'), after which Lisa naturally stays put. Then Captain Lebyatkin comes in and his appearance is yet another link in the chain of absurdities for he surprises everyone by *not being* very dishevelled; he is decently and even stylishly dressed and not drunk (Liputin had said of him that 'There are people who look indecent in clean linen'; Lebyatkin's behaviour seems *to him* to be indecent, i.e. not ugly enough). When the bell is rung to show Lebyatkin out the servant who comes in announces that 'Mr Stavrogin has just arrived and is coming here'. After which there appears not Stavrogin but an unknown young man who turns out to be Verkhovensky's son, Peter. Then Stavrogin turns up and is still at the threshold when his mother asks him the most unexpected question of all, 'whether it is true that this unfortunate cripple – there she is – there – look at her! – is it true that she is – your lawful wife?', Stavrogin does not answer but takes his mother's hand and raises it respectfully to his lips, then kisses it and carefully leads Miss Lebyatkin from the room. In his absence Peter Verkhovensky explains Stavrogin's behaviour ('The obtrusive desire of this gentleman who seemed to have dropped from the sky, to relate incidents from another man's private life was rather strange and contrary to the accepted rules of conduct'). Terrorized by Peter Verkhovensky, Captain Lebyatkin is shamefully driven out and there follows a real apotheosis of Nicholas Stavrogin. Then Lisa unexpectedly gets hysterics. Hardly has she been calmed down before Peter Verkhovensky makes an unexpected revelation as a result of which his father is driven out with ignominy. Then unexpectedly, Shatov who all along has been sitting in the corner without saying a word, strikes Nicholas on the face and Lisa falls in a faint.

This list of episodes is devoid of any internal connection between them. The sequence of separate atom-like clusters of actions is quite unmotivated and this is emphasized by the fact that in most of the cases there is indeed some degree of predictability, but a reverse one: episodes follows each other in the order not of most but of least probability.

Between unexpectedness on the level of everyday life and unexpectedness in the detective story there is a significant difference. The disconnected sequence of events in a detective story is only seemingly accidental. It seems so to the reader who does not know the *secret* of the plot and who is inclined to see significance in what is unimportant and vice versa. Since the reader has to be kept in ignorance for as long as possible the mistakes of his or her assumptions are not exposed until later. The wrong answer is the one that seems the most logical and seemingly convincing. Only occasionally is the lack of connection between the different episodes shown up in order to hint at the error in the reader's assumptions.

There is some such logic of the detective story in *The Devils* and it can be seen in the episode described. Part of the events just seem like an accumulation of absurd happenings, though the revelation of secret crimes will show how logical and deliberate they are. But this cannot be said of the whole chain of episodes in this chapter: for the most part the absurdity and the coincidences are purely accidental. In a detective story the absurdity (mistake) of false connections drawn by someone who does not know the hidden springs of the action is concealed until a certain point in the narrative; but in the section we have been discussing (as in others like it), Dostoevsky takes care to warn us in case his readers do not notice the principle according to which the text is constructed ('a day of surprises', 'everything turned out in a way that no one expected', etc.).

Each level has its own syntagmatic organization characteristic of it alone and this ensures the complexity of the interaction.

Many years ago Boris Engelgardt made the point that the ideological nucleus of Dostoevsky's novels directly organize the movement of the plot. Bakhtin went further and said that monologic construction is the natural result of the linear unfolding of myth into a normalizing text whereas in Dostoevsky this has been replaced by making dialogue the nuclear structure of his novels. 'The ideas of Dostoevsky the thinker, upon entering his polyphonic novel, change the very form of their existence . . . they are liberated from their monologic isolation and finalization, they become thoroughly dialogized and enter the great dialogue of the novel.'[42]

'Thus the ideological centre absorbs the structural features of peripheral texts. And an opposite process takes place at the same time making the everyday layer into a chain of scandals and shocks. Does this mean that the everyday level in Dostoevsky with all its chance happenings and the frustration of all legimate expectations is a portrayal of the insanity and 'sinfulness' of the material world? Yes and no, because unpredictability and even absurdity in Dostoevsky are a sign not only of scandal but also of miracle. Scandal and miracle are the poles which mark, on the one hand, final ruin and, on the other, final salvation and they are both unmotivated and abnormal. So the eschatological moment of instant and final solution to all the tragic contradictions in life is not brought into life from outside, from the domain of ideas, but is found in life itself.

A model of this fusion of 'scandal' and 'miracle' which illustrates how akin they are is the card game or roulette.

On the one hand, gambling embodies the outrageousness of outrageous life: 'Today has been funny, outrageous and absurd'.[43] On the other hand, it embodies the eschatological miracle of a solution of all conflicts. At the centre of *The Gambler* is a hunger for miracle. A win is 'something miraculous. . . . Although it is completely capable of mathematical proof, nevertheless to this day it remains for me a miraculous happening.'[44] And the novel frequently emphasizes that the love of gambling is not a matter of money but of a hunger for instant and final salvation. A win is associated with the purely mythological idea of resurrection, an end to the old sinful life and the beginning of a completely new existence: 'What am I now. Zero. What may I be tomorrow? Tomorrow I may rise from the dead and begin to live again.'[45]

In this respect Astley's remark that 'roulette is a mostly Russian game' is significant as is the initial antithesis between German caution and the Russian longing for instant ruin ('[the Russian] squanders it outrageously and for nothing') or for instant salvation, miracle ('getting rich quickly, in a couple of hours, without working').[46] In a sense Raskolnikov is already to be found in *The Gambler* for he shared this longing for instant destruction or instant salvation for all. But it is Sonya who in fact brings Raskolnikov the miracle of instant salvation for his soul.

So if dialogism is the penetration of the diversity of life into the ordered sphere of theory, at the same time mythologism penetrates into the sphere of the extraordinary.

Dostoevsky's novels are a clear illustration of what can be thought of as a feature common to all narrative literary texts.

*   *   *

We have seen how as a result of the linear unwinding of a mythological text the primordial single hero is divided into pairs and into groups. But the opposite process also happens. When, as a result of translation into a linear system, the categories of beginning and end are stressed, this does not necessarily mean that these categories are identified with the biological limits of a human life-span; indeed, this is a fairly late phenomenon. In the eschatological legend and texts similar to it the segmentation of the human life-span into continuous sections may be brought about in a way that is quite unexpected to the modern mind. So, for instance, the isomorphism between burial (being eaten) and conception, between birth and rebirth may result in a narrative about a hero beginning with his death, while the birth/rebirth occurs in the middle of the narrative. The full eschatological cycle: the hero in existence (as a rule the narrative does not begin with his birth), his ageing, decline (sin of incorrect behaviour), or congenital defect (the hero is misshapen, a fool, sick), then death, rebirth and a new, now ideal, existence (which ends as a rule not with his death but with his apotheosis) all this is perceived as a narrative about one *single* person. If a death occurs in the middle of the story and the death entails a change of name, a complete change of character, and a diametrical change of behaviour (a great sinner becomes a great saint) this does not make us treat the story as one about *two* people as we might expect in a modern narrative text.

An example is the story of the conversion of Saul from The Acts of the Apostles. The story of Saul/Paul begins not with his birth but with a reference to him as present at the death of the first martyr Stephen. He is described as 'breathing murderous threats against the Lord's disciples' (Acts 9.1) and a persecutor of Christians. On the road to Damascus, 'suddenly a light from heaven shone all round him' (Acts 9.3). He heard a voice, lost his sight, and then when his sight had been miraculously restored, became 'the chosen instrument' of the Lord (Acts 9.15) and changed his name to Paul.

This story is an almost ideal realization of the schema: death and birth do not frame the hero's story but are placed in the middle, for the events on the road to Damascus are a kind of death leading to rebirth. The name change is significant. There is no beginning and no end to the story: it does not begin with birth and does not end with death. And another thing is striking: from the point of view of classical 'unity of action' or realist 'logic of character' there are no grounds for identifying Saul with Paul as *one* person. Yet in this text there are not two sequentially existing characters, but just one.

This schema of character delineation is influenced by mytho-legendary traditions and in later literary works it is used as the language of texts about 'new vision' or a sudden change in the hero's character. Such for instance are fairy tales about the fool who turns into a tsar (the journey into the forest, to Baba-yaga, expressions such as: 'he climbed into one ear, he climbed into the other, and turned into a fine young man', and other such transformations, which of course basically mean death and rebirth). In later texts we can find this same schema again in stories about great sinners who became saints (St Andrew of Crete, Pope Gregory)[47] and Nekrasov's poem *Vlas*.

At the start of the poem the hero is a great sinner:

> People say that formerly he was
> a great sinner. In this peasant
> God was absent; with beatings
> he drove his wife to the grave;
> He harboured horse-thieves who
> lived by robbery.

Then comes his illness. A vivid picture of hell which in this poem is functionally equivalent to death:

> People say that in his delirium
> he had a vision
> He saw the light fading
> He saw sinners in hell:
> Nimble devils tormenting them,
> Fidget-witch stings them,
> Ethiopians – all black
> with eyes like coals . . .

His return to life entails his complete transformation:

> Vlas gave away his farm
> Himself barefoot and in rags
> . . . . Full of inconsolable grief
> Dark of face, tall and upright,
> With measured step he walks
> through villages and towns.[48]

The critical moment of rebirth is often stressed by the hero being given a double (we have already discussed this above). This double is not reborn (or does not get younger) but perishes. We can find such episodes in many texts from the myth of Medea (the magical restoration to youth of the boar which had been dismembered and cooked, and the death of King Peleus in the same procedure) to the ending of Yershov's *Little Hunchback Horse*.

The pattern 'decline – rebirth' can also be found widely in modern literature. It lies behind many of Pushkin's lyrics including the poem

'Resurrection'. Remember Mikhalevich's lines in Turgenev's *A Nest of Gentlefolk*:

> I gave myself to new feelings with all my heart,
> And my soul became as a child's!
> And I have burnt all that I adored,
> And now adore all that I burnt.[49]

Here we find a character consisting of two diametrically opposed parts and the change-over from the one to the other is thought of as a renewal. Childhood comes not at the beginning, but in the middle of the temporal development of the image. Tolstoy's novel *Resurrection* is constructed along the same lines. In spite of all the difference in the actual historical ideas which are relayed through this plot-mechanism, the similarity of titles cannot be mere chance.

On to the schema of the eschatological legend there is added the identification between a literary character in everyday life and humanity in general; this has made it possible to treat the internal world of a character as a model of the macrocosm and to interpret one individual like a conflict-ridden collective.

*   *   *

Plot is a powerful means for making sense of life. Only when narrative forms came into being could people learn to distinguish the plot aspect of reality, that is, to divide the non-discrete flow of events into several discrete units, linking these units together by semantic interpretations, and organizing them into ordered chains by syntagmatic interpretations. The essence of plot lies in selecting the events, which are the discrete units of plot, then giving them meaning and a temporal or causal or some other ordering.

The more people acquire freedom from the automatism of genetic planning, the more important it is for them to construct plots of events and behaviour. But in order to make such schemata and models they have to know the language. The original language of literary plot had such a role; later it became more complicated, and moved away from the elementary schemata which we have been discussing in this chapter. Like any language, the language of plot, in order to be able to transmit and model a content, must be separate from that content. The models which arose in archaic times are separate from actual messages, but can serve as material for the textual construction of messages. Then we must remember that in art, language and text constantly change their places and their functions.

By creating plot-texts humanity learnt to distinguish plots in life and in this way to make sense of life.

12

Symbolic spaces

1. GEOGRAPHICAL SPACE IN RUSSIAN MEDIEVAL TEXTS

Our understanding of geographical space is one of the ways the human mind models space. Geography came into being in particular historical circumstances and took on different forms according to the nature of the general models of the world, of which it was a part. We do not intend here to describe the medieval sense of geographical space in its totality, but briefly to point out some of differences between it and our modern one.

In the medieval thought-system earthly life itself was a value category in opposition to heavenly life. So the earth as a geographical concept was also perceived as the place of earthly life (i.e. it was one member of the opposition 'earth/heaven') and consequently acquired a religious and moral significance which is unknown to modern geography. These ideas were applied to all geography: some lands were righteous and others were sinful. Movement in geographical space meant moving in the vertical scale of religious and moral values, the top of the scale being heaven, and the bottom hell.

But we must remember that to the Russian medieval mind the very oppositions 'earth/heaven', 'earthly life/life hereafter' implied a spatial location for the second members of the oppositions. The idea that earthly life could be opposed to heavenly existence as space is to non-space, though this was the belief of the medieval mystical tradition, was firmly rejected by the more 'realistic' thinking of Orthodoxy. Bishop Vasily of Novgorod condemned Bishop Feodor of Tver for affirming that the afterlife was outside of space, purely ideal. He wrote: 'And now brother, when Christ in the Gospel spoke of his Second Coming, was he speaking figuratively?' Moreover, since earthly life is transitory and subject to corruption, while heaven is incorruptible and eternal, then the 'materiality'

171

of heaven is much more 'real': the holy beings who dwell there are not
subject to decay, corruption or death for·they are not non-material, but
eternally material:

> All the things of God are incorruptible. I myself, brother, am a witness,
> when Christ went into Jerusalem freely to His Passion, and with His own
> hands closed the gates of the city, and to this day they are still closed. . . .
> Christ planted a hundred fig trees and they have not moved, they have not
> died or rotted.[50]

So earthly life can be opposed to heavenly life as temporal to eternal, but
there is no opposition in the spatial sense. Moreover notions of moral
value and of locality fuse together: places have a moral significance and
morals have a localized significance. Geography becomes a kind of
ethics.[51]

So any movement in geographical space is significant in the religious
and moral sense. In medieval literature, a person's journey to hell or to
heaven is always thought of in geographical terms. This explains the
composition of *La Divina Commedia* (see below) and of *Journey of the
Mother of God through Torments*; in the latter work the Archangel
Michael who is guiding the Mother of God asks her: 'Where would you
go, Blessed One . . . to the East or to the West, to Paradise on the right,
or to the left where there are great torments?'[52] These ideas are
especially clear in Bishop Vasily's letter to Bishop Feodor: 'Paradise is in
the East in Eden', and from Eden flow four rivers, the Tigris, the Nile,
the Euphrates and the Fison, while hell is in the West 'over the roaring
seas' (the Arctic Sea) 'and many of my Novgorodian children will see it'.
Paradise can be reached by geographical movement, as happened with a
Novgorod sailor:

> And that place of holy paradise was discovered by Moislav of Novgorod
> and his son Jacob and in all there were three boats, and one of them got
> lost and perished, and two of them were then borne by the wind and sea for
> a long time, and brought to high mountains . . . and on the mountains they
> heard much merrymaking and many voices rejoicing.[53]

In accordance with these ideas medieval man regarded a geographical
journey as a movement in a religious and moral sense: countries were
classified as heretical, pagan or holy. Social ideals and all social systems
which the medieval mind could imagine were thought of as really
existing in some geographical place. Geography and geographical
literature were utopian in essence and every journey was like a
pilgrimage.

Typically for the Middle Ages, geography was not yet treated as a scientific discipline but rather as a branch of religious utopianism. This view found expression in the special attitude towards travelling and the traveller: a long journey makes a person more holy, and at the same time the path to holiness implies necessarily leaving the settled life and setting off on a journey. Unburdening oneself of sin meant going away, a spatial shift. So going away to a monastery was a movement from a sinful place to a holy place and in this sense was like a pilgrimage and death, for death was also thought of as a movement in space.

Mystics, such as the trans-Volga *startsy*, who held to a non-material view of paradise, denied the need to travel. Profound prayer and the ecstatic expectation of the 'light' had nothing to do with travelling. In Masonic literature of the eighteenth century the geographical semantic field was wholly replaced by a moral one and a story of a journey through space was treated as an allegory of moral regeneration. But this leads us beyond our present topic. The birth of the new scientific approach to geography put paid to these medieval concepts.

In this respect it is interesting to compare Afanasy Nikitin's *Journey beyond Three Seas* with the *Tale of the Indian Kingdom*. These two works show India in quite different lights. In the latter India is a Utopia which is antithetically contrasted with Russia within a single system of social, moral and religious attitudes. And this ideal, utopian India enjoys happier social relations than Russia, it has a special climate, animals and plants. The spatial journey there brought the traveller to another degree of goodness. And the unusual degree of goodness assumes an unusual geography. John who is king and priest of the Indian kingdom says this about his land:

> In my country there are people who are half birds and half people, and others who have dogs' heads, and elephants, dromedaries, crocodiles and camels breed in my country. The crocodile is a fierce beast. If he gets angry and wets a tree or anything else, it at once burns up. . . . I have a land covered with grass where the wild beasts run and in my land there is neither enemy nor robber nor envious person and my land is full of riches. And in my land there are no snakes or toads or serpents and if one comes here it dies.[54]

In medieval literature we find a close association between the degree of goodness and the climate: paradise is especially fertile and its climate well-suited for mankind, while hell is the opposite. In paradise the soil is rich and everything grows in abundance, while in hell the climate makes life impossible, it is a land of ice and fire.

In the Russian medieval translation of Josephus' *History of the Jewish War* the after-life where dwell the souls of the blessed is a place 'beyond the ocean, a place where there is neither rain nor snow nor the burning of

174   *Symbolic Spaces*

the sun but the wind that blows over it from the sea is gentle and the south is scented'. Whereas hell has a different climate: 'If there is a sinner he is taken to a dark and wintry place.'[55]

The India described by Afanasy Nikitin is quite different from the India of King-Priest John. It has a peculiar climate and customs but no special rank on the scale of sin and goodness. But then Russia is not on the scale either, for there is no such scale. In fact the medieval concept of space has disappeared and in its place has come the idea of space in the modern sense. Afanasy Nikitin's understanding of space is closer to that of the Enlightenment than to that of the Middle Ages.

The medieval understanding of geographical space also involved the notion of the elect since the world was held to be divided into righteous and sinners. This idea, which came about from the tendency of medieval societies at certain stages to close in on themselves, had its influence on spatial notions. The 'own/other' opposition came to be seen as a variant of the 'righteous/sinful', 'good/bad' oppositions. According to this system of thought, own's one land was no longer to be compared with a blessed Utopia in a foreign land, because everything that was not 'ours' was sinful. In Ostrovsky's play *The Thunderstorm* Feklusha expresses this idea very clearly:

> People say, my darling, that there are countries where there are no Orthodox tsars, but Sultans rule the land. . . . And they judge all the people unjustly. Nothing they do, darling, is right. . . . We have a righteous law, but theirs, darling, is unjust. . . . And then there is another land where all the people have dogs' heads because they do not believe.[56]

Contrast the remark about the people with dogs' heads with the *Tale of the Indian Kingdom* where the people, half dog and half human, live in a righteous land, although it is a foreign and exotic one.

Archpriest Avvakum's writings reflect the idea that the Russian land was especially chosen. For him foreign lands are 'sinful'. 'The folk of Palestine, Serbia, Albania, the Wallachians, they of Rome and Poland, all these do cross themselves with three fingers.'[57] But since Orthodoxy has left Russia ('Satan asked God for holy Russia') his own country has become 'abroad': 'For he that will be crowned [with the crown of martyrdom, Yu.L.] for that he had not need to go to Persia. We have our Babylon at home.'[58] The use of the term 'Babylon' as a synonym for something that is not at all geographical shows something of the medieval understanding of locality.

The diagram below demonstrates how a change in moral status meant a change in space, a transfer from one situation to another:

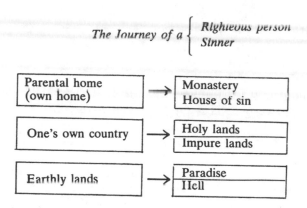

There are many interesting consequences of this fusion of geographical and ethical space. First of all the motivation for leaving home is often not a personal whim but the need to seek reward for virtue or punishment for vice. In the *Life of St Agapy*, Agapy is told to leave the monastery, and the fratricide Svyatopolk fled to the wilderness to escape God's wrath. The end of the journey, the arrival point, is determined not by geographical circumstances, in our modern sense, and not by the intentions of the traveller, but by his or her moral worth. This journey is a special one: not only is the first stage (taking vows) regularly compared with the last one (dying), but it is firmly believed that the traveller can reach paradise or hell in bodily form. Another popular idea in the Middle Ages follows from this, namely that a righteous person could be taken in life into paradise, and a sinner sent alive to hell.

An apocrypha, *The Life of St Agapy*, is interesting in this connection. This righteous person completes the full cycle of the journey: he leaves home and goes to a monastery, then obedient to the voice he hears, he leaves the monastery for a journey. His journey ends when he meets a saint who leads him into heaven. And this heaven is quite material for St Elijah gives him some bread which he eats himself. This bread is like earthly bread since it is for eating and people eat it. It differs from earthly bread only in that a small piece of it can feed many people for a long time.[59]

Our diagram shows another interesting thing: the left-hand box from which the journey starts is a single box, whereas the right-hand ones are divided into two according to whether the journey is a righteous or a sinful one. But the left-hand box too divides on closer inspection: for it may be either a place of abundant and pleasant living, or a place of guilt from which the traveller seeks to 'liberate' him or herself.

The medieval idea of space conflicted with certain ideas of Orthodox

Christianity. For instance, the antithesis between earthly and heavenly life implied sorrow for the righteous on earth and rejoicing in heaven. But the idea that heaven and hell had geographical positions overlaid this sharp antithesis and substituted for it the idea of a gradual increase of righteousness and of rejoicing at the same time. The intrusion of 'localized' ethics distorted some basic Christian ideas. In the link 'house – monastery' the geographical factor is still hardly felt and the normal Christian scale of values operates: sorrow is positively marked and rejoicing negatively. This is why the norm of monastic life is a hard one and the monastery is situated in a wilderness. The concept of desert-living excludes images of soil fertility, abundant fruits or a beneficent climate. But in the second link the geographical element is more stressed: the 'holy lands' have a good climate and consequently enjoyment is the norm of life, and not a violation of it; whereas the sinful lands are sorrowful, though life there does not add to a person's moral worth. The most distant point of all, paradise, is contrasted with all other lands in that it is a place of rejoicing, joy and ease of life in the earthly sense.

Taking account of the special meaning of geographical distance we can explain why the medieval utopia had to be set a long way away. The land of blessings is a land to which the journey was a long one.

The medieval understanding of geographical space was something which Gogol understood intuitively. In his story 'A Terrible Vengeance', which is full of folk fantasy, there is an episode when the terrible sinner, the wizard, escaping punishment decides to escape from Kiev to the Crimea: 'Leaping on his horse he rode straight to Kanev thinking to go from there straight through the Cherkassy straight to the Tatars in the Crimea.' The wizard drives his horse southwards but his sins mysteriously pull him to the West:

> He rode for one day, for another, but still there was no Kanev. It was the same road, Kanev should be appearing, but it was nowhere to be seen. In the distance the church roofs glistened. But it was not Kanev but Shumsk. The wizard was astonished to find that he had ridden in quite the opposite direction. He spurred his horse back towards Kiev and the next day a city appeared; but it was not Kiev but Galich, a town even further from Kiev than Shumsk, and not far from the Hungarians. Not knowing what to do, he again turned his horse round, but again felt that though he was moving forwards he was travelling in the opposite direction.[60]

Scientific thinking of the modern age has changed our experience of geographical space. But the asymmetry of geographical space and its close link with our general picture of the world have resulted in the fact that even to our modern way of thinking geographical space is a domain of semiotic modelling. How easily we metaphorize concepts such as East and West, how significant the renaming of geographical places seems to us, and so on. It is so easy to make geography symbolic, as we see when a geographical point becomes subject to persistent wars or national and religious conflicts, or when it acquires different value to different national traditions.

The history of geographical maps is the notebook of historical semiotics.

2. THE JOURNEY OF ULYSSES IN DANTE'S *DIVINE COMEDY*

Dante compared himself with a 'geometer' (*Paradise*, XXXIII, 133–4).[61] We might rather say cosmologist or astronomer when we think how even in *La Vita Nuova* there were very complex and specially calculated laws of cosmic movement. But best of all would be to call him an architect, for the whole of the *Divine Comedy* is a vast architectural complex, a construction of the universe. This approach involves transferring the psychology of individual creation onto the cosmic universe: the world as someone's creation must have purpose and meaning; and of each detail we can then ask, 'What does it mean?' If this question, which is a natural one to ask of a work of architecture, is applied to Nature and the Universe, it assumes that we are treating them as semiotic texts whose meaning is to be deciphered. And as with architecture, the first thing is the semiotics of space.

If the world is like a vast missive from the Creator then there is a mysterious message encoded in the language of its spatial structure. Dante deciphers this message by re-creating this world for a second time in his text; he thereby adopts the position of a transmitter of the message rather than its receiver, and the poetics of the *La Divina Commedia* is thus oriented towards enciphering. But what is special about Dante's position as author is that though he adopts the point of view of the Creator, he does not forsake the point of view of humanity. This is the point we shall be illustrating in what follows. We shall be dwelling on the meaning of the spatial axis 'top/bottom' in Dante's created world. This axis, however, has two distinct senses in the *Comedy*: in the one sense it is relative and operates only in Earth. In this sense the 'bottom' is identified with the centre of gravity of the globe, and the 'top' with any radius directed away from the centre.

> When we were where the thigh turns, just on the swelling of the haunch, the Leader with labour and strain brought round his head where his legs had been and grappled on the hair like one climbing, so that I thought we were returning into Hell again. . . .
> And he said to me: 'Thou imaginest thou art still on the other side of the centre, where I took hold of the hair of the guilty worm that pierces the

world. Thou wast on that side so long as I descended; when I turned myself
thou didst pass the point to which weights are drawn from every part.'
(*Inferno*, XXXIV, 76–81, 106–11)

But Dante's cosmic edifice also has an absolute top and bottom. While
people at different poles of the globe 'face each other with the soles of
their feet' (*Convivio*, III, v, 12), the absolute vertical is the axis of which
Dante wrote in the *Convivio*: 'If a stone could fall from the Pole Star it
would fall in the Ocean and if a person were on that stone, the Pole Star
would always be over his head' (ibid., 9). This axis penetrates Earth, its
lower end being turned to Jerusalem, it passes through Hell, the centre of
the Earth, Purgatory and ends in the shining centre of the Empyrean.
This is the axis down which Lucifer was cast from heaven.

Commentators have often remarked on the contradiction between
Dante's relative and absolute top and bottom. Pavel Florensky, the
philosopher and mathematician, tried to explain it away by using concepts
of non-Euclidean geometry and relativistic physics.[62] Florensky illustrated
his idea from the *Divine Comedy*. Commenting on the verses from the
Inferno quoted above, Florensky wrote:

After this boundary the poet ascends the mountain of Purgatory and is
carried up through the heavenly spheres. Now, the question is, in which
direction? The underground way by which they came up was formed by the
fall of Lucifer flung headlong from heaven. So the place where he was
thrown down from is *somewhere* in heaven in the space that surrounds the
earth, and on the side of that hemisphere which the poets reached. The
mountain of Purgatory and Sion which are diametrically opposite each
other rose up as a result of Lucifer's fall, but have a reverse meaning. So
Dante is always moving in a straight line and in heaven stands with his feet
towards the place of his descent; looking around from that spot from the
Empyrean at God's Glory, he finds himself *without* turning back, in
Florence. . . . So moving forward always in a straight line and turning over
once on the way the poet comes back to the same place in the same position
as he left it in. So, if he had not turned over on the way, he would have
come back in a straight line to the place he set out from but upside down.
So the surface which Dante journeyed over was such that a straight line on
it, with one turn-over of direction, brings one back to the previous spot in
an upright position, and a straight movement without turning over brings
the body back to the same place upside down. This surface then is obviously
1) a Riemannian plane since it contains enclosed straight lines, and 2) a
single-sided surface since it turns over when moving along it perpendicu-
larly. These two circumstances are sufficient to describe Dante's space as
constructed according to the type of elliptical geometry . . . In 1871 C. F.
Klein showed that a spherical surface is like a two-sided surface, while an

elliptical surface is one-sided. Dante's space is extremely like elliptical space. This throws an unexpected light on the medieval notion of the finiteness of the world. But these general geometrical ideas have recently received unexpected concrete rethinking in the principle of relativity.[63]

Florensky in his eagerness to show how much closer to the twentieth century is the medieval mind than the mechanistic ideology of the Renaissance gets somewhat carried away (for instance the return of Dante to earth [*Paradiso*, I, 5–6] is only hinted at and there are no grounds for assuming that he travelled in a straight line); but the problem of the contradiction in the *Commedia* between real-everyday space and cosmic-transcendental space, which he highlights, is a crucial one, although the solution to this contradiction has to be sought in another direction.

According to Aristotle's ideas, the northern hemisphere, being less perfect, occupies the lower position and the southern hemisphere the upper position of the globe. So when Dante and Virgil move down the relative scale of the earthly 'top/bottom' axis, that is when they go deeper from the surface of the Earth towards its centre they are at the same time in relation to the absolute axis rising up. The solution to this paradox is to be found in Dante's semiotics. In Dante's belief-system space has meaning, and each spatial category has its own meaning.[64] But the relationship of expression and content is not an arbitrary one, unlike semiotic systems based on social conventions. In Saussure's terminology, we are dealing here not with signs but symbols. For Pseudo-Dionysius the Areopagite, one of the functions of the symbol is to 'manifest the transcendent world on the level of being. . . . However, the function of signification is limited by the constraints of isomorphism, although this isomorphism is in principle different from classical mimesis'.[65] The content, the meaning of the symbol is not bound to its expression by convention (as happens with allegory) but shines through it. The closer the text is placed in the hierarchy to the heavenly light which is the true content of all medieval symbolics the brighter the meaning shines through it and the more direct and less conventionalized is its expression. The further the text is from the source of truth, then the more dimly will it be reflected and the more arbitrary will be the relationship of content to expression. Thus on the highest step truth is accessible to direct contemplation through the eye of the spirit, while on the lowest step truth is glimpsed through conventional signs. Because sinners and demons of different degrees use purely conventional signs they can lie, commit perfidy, treachery and deceit – all ways to separate content from expression. The righteous also converse with each other in signs but they do not put convention to ill use, and with recourse to the highest sources of truth they can penetrate into the conventionless symbolic world of meanings.

Thus between one step on the hierarchy and the next the relationship of content to expression alters. The higher one goes the greater the symbolism and the less conventionality. But semantically speaking each new hierarchical level will be isomorphic to all the others and so a relationship of equivalence will be established between elements of different levels having a similar meaning.

All this has direct relevance to our task of understanding Dante's notions of 'top' and 'bottom' in the *Comedy*. The 'top/bottom' axis organizes the entire semantic architectonics of the text: all parts and cantos of the *Comedy* are marked by their position on this basic coordinate. Consequently, movement in Dante's text is always a descent or an ascent, and these concepts have a symbolic meaning: behind the actual descent or ascent can be glimpsed the spiritual ascent or descent. All sins, which Dante arranges in a strict hierarchy, have spatial attachment so that the weight of the sin corresponds to the depth of the sinner's position.

Dante and Virgil's descent into Hell *has the meaning* of a descent downwards. The paradox whereby as they descend they go upwards is emphasized in the verse about the Moon which, passing into the southern hemisphere, floats at the feet of the poets as they journey on: 'And already the moon is beneath our feet' (*Inferno*, XXIX, 10). Consequently in a higher sense this descent is an ascent (by going down into hell and seeing the abyss of sin Dante in an absolute sense is morally uplifted, so his descent is equivalent to an ascent), but at the same time, by earthly criteria, this really is a descent and has all the features of a real descent, including the physical exhaustion of the travellers. This downward journey brings the poets to the *'woeful city'* (*Inferno*, III, 1) where they see the torments of hell.

The complex dialectics of conventionality and unconventionality which we are confronted with as soon as we begin to think about the fundamental semiotic axis of Dante's space, leads us into the centre of the moral hierarchy of the *Comedy*. Commentators have often pointed out that the positioning of the sins in the circles of hell is significant: Dante departs from the Church norms and from generally accepted ideas. If the fourteenth-century reader could not help being amazed that hypocrites were put in the sixth fissure of the eighth circle and heretics only in the sixth, then the modern reader will be amazed that murder (first round of the seventh circle) is punished less than robbery (seventh ditch of the eighth circle) or counterfeiting (tenth ditch of the eighth circle). But there is a strict logic to this.

We have already mentioned that the further away from the heights of Divine Truth and Love the greater the degree of arbitrariness in the link between expression and content. In earthly life people are guided by divine symbols in questions of Faith and by conventional signs in relations with each other. The conventionality of these signs contains the potentiallty for double interpretation: they can be used as a means of truth (when the conventions are observed) or of falsehood (when the conventions are violated or distorted). The Devil is the father of lies, the one who inspires people to violate conventions and any other agreements. When the true association of expression and content is tampered with, this is a sin worse than murder because Truth is harmed and Falsehood, in all its infernal implications, is let loose.[66] So there is a profound logic in the fact that Dante judges evil deeds to be less grave than sins involving the falsification of signs, whether the signs are words (and the sins are slander, flattery, false advice, etc.), or valuables (involving the sins of counterfeiters, alchemists, and so on), or documents (forgers), or trust (robbers), or ideas and marks of respect (hypocrites and simoniacs). But worst of all are the traitors, those who break agreements and obligations. A sinful act is a single evil, whereas the violation of preordained semiotic links destroys the very basis of human society and turns the Earth into the kingdom of Satan, into Hell.

In hell falsehood naturally reigns for the links between sign and content are torn apart, and falsehood is not a deviation from the norm but the rule. The devils lie when they tell Virgil in canto XXI that only the sixth bridge over the ditch has been destroyed, when in fact all bridges have been destroyed. But even Dante in canto XXXIII swears to Alberigo that he will take the ice from his eyes and thereupon breaks his oath: 'And it was courtesy to be a churl to him' (*Inferno*, XXXIII, 150). The worst crime, treachery, is valour in the place where rudeness is courtesy.

The opposition of Truth to Falsehood in the spatial model is realized in the opposition of the straight line directed upwards and the circular movement on a horizontal plane. It was a common idea that circular movement was a feature of sorcery and magic, and from the medieval Christian point of view, concerned the Devil. Compare St Augustine who denied the circular movement of time and the cyclical repetition of events, contrasting them with the idea of the linear movement of time 'for Christ died once for our sins'.[67]

The ethical model of space Dante relates with his cosmic model. Dante's cosmic model was influenced by the ideas of Aristotle, Ptolomey, Al Fergani and Albert the Great, and especially by those of Pythagorus. In the light of Pythagorean ideas about the perfection of the circle and the sphere among geometrical figures and bodies, we can explain the circular construction of Hell as follows: the circle is the image of perfection; a circle set at the top is the perfection of good, but the circle at the bottom is the ultimate evil. So the architecture of hell is ultimate evil. The Pythagorean system of binary oppositions had its influence on Dante, and in particular the opposition of the straight line taken as equivalent to good, to the curve which is the equivalent of evil. The movement of the sinners in Hell is round closed curves, while that of Dante is along an ascending spiral which eventually becomes a straight vertical. But of course Dante's individuality stands out against the Pythagorean background, for it is not the centre of the sphere but the top of the Axis that is his point of spatial and ethico-religious orientation. The Pythagoreans selected a number of basic binary oppositions such as 'odd/even', 'left/right', 'finite/infinite' 'male/female' 'single/multiple' and 'light/dark', but for Dante the basic opposition was that of 'top/bottom' which was not important to the Pythagoreans.[68]

So the spatial model of Dante's world forms a continuum onto which are inscribed trajectories of individual paths and fates. After death a soul makes its journey through this continuum of the World Construction and arrives at the spot corresponding to its moral value. The souls of the blessed are in eternal peace, while sinners are in constant cyclical motion: sometimes this takes the form of movement through space (endless flights and circling), and sometimes the form of repeated transformations – those who are cut in pieces are made whole only to be cut up again; those who are burnt are reconstituted out of the ash only to be burnt again; those who are flayed grow new skin and are flayed again, and so on.[69]

The figure of Dante stands out against all of this: he is free to move in all directions since his upward path includes the *knowledge* of all the ways of falsehood as well. But besides Dante another person in the *Commedia* has the right to move freely, and that is Ulysses. The Ulysses episode is unique as many scholars have pointed out.[70]

The image of Ulysses in the *Comedy* is a dual one. Ulysses finds himself in the 'ditches of the evil ones' because he has given false counsel. In view of what we discussed above, this fact should not surprise us. Our interest is rather Ulysses' story of his journey and his death. Ulysses and Dante both are granted individual paths, and their journeys share a common feature – they are heroes of the straight line.[71] The similarity is apparent also in the fact that their journeys are open-ended, they both plunge into infinity; starting from precisely named places they move in a preordained direction though without a previously indicated destination. But there is an essential difference between them: the point of Dante's journey is summed up in his striving upwards, each step he takes is judged on that scale either as a step down or as a step up. Ulysses' journey is the only one in the *Comedy* for which the top/bottom axis is not relevant: his whole journey is along the horizontal. While Dante is placed within the crystal cosmic globe whose three-dimensional space is transsected by the vertical axis (the fact that Dante points out and even measures its decline does not detract from its metaphysical meaning [*Purgatory* IV, 15–16, 67–9, 137–8]), Ulysses journeys as it were on a map. So when Dante from Gemini looks down on Earth he sees 'beyond Cadiz the mad track of Ulysses' (*Paradise*, XXVII, 82–3).

Ulysses in two respects is like Dante's double. First, both of them are 'heroes of the road', unlike the other characters, whose sins or virtues pin them to certain places in the Dantean universe. Dante and Ulysses are constantly in movement and, what is more important, they cross the boundaries of forbidden spaces. The crowd of other characters either stay in one place or hasten to some appointed place, the boundaries of which define their place in the Universe. Only Dante and Ulysses are voluntary or forced exiles, driven by passion, crossing the boundaries which separate one area of the cosmos from another. Second, both of them cover the same route in the same direction as they make their way to Purgatory – Dante through Hell and through the caves formed by Lucifer's body when he fell, Ulysses over the sea past Spain, Gibraltar, Morocco. Although Dante's journey takes place in the infernal world and Ulysses' in real geographical space, they have the same goal. This is confirmed by the fact that Dante in his journey through Purgatory and Paradise as it were takes over the dead Ulysses' baton. Twice the poet recalls the drowned hero and both reminiscences are full of significance.

During the second night in Purgatory the Siren appears to him and says: 'I turned Ulysses, eager on his way, to my song' (*Purgatory* XIX, 22–3). The image of the Siren brings to mind Ulysses' bravery during his sea adventures of the *Odyssey*, but the Siren's duplicity, her ability to separate outward form from inner essence and to conceal what is repugnant under her beauty (the capacity to transform is for Dante a sign of falsehood: this is why liars and deceivers are punished in hell) is a reference to the world of deceit and the ditches of evil in which Dante set Ulysses.

The second time Ulysses is referred to is when the poet approaches the constellation of Gemini. Finding himself at the spot which is the antipode to the place where Ulysses perished, Dante flies to the meridian of the Pillars of Hercules and on and up into the infinite, repeating Ulysses' journey until he comes to the place where he died on the meridian of Sion-purgatory. Here on the axis of the fall of Lucifer which passes through the place where Ulysses' ship was wrecked, he rises to the Empyrean. So Dante's journey as it were carries on Ulysses' journey from the moment of his shipwreck. But up to that moment they have been doubling each other.

But the point of any reduplication is to show up the differences on the base of the similarity. And this is our intention here.

Like Dante, Ulysses combines a longing to know humanity with a desire to understand the secrets of the world: 'this so brief vigil of the senses that remains to us, choose not to deny experience, in the sun's track, of the unpeopled world' (*Inferno*, XXVI, 115–18). Dante is obviously inspired by this noble hunger for knowledge. In the *Comedy* there is a frequently made comparison between genuine people and beast-like beings in human form (see in the XIV canto of *Purgatory* the enumeration of the people living along the Arno, the swine-like inhabitants of Porciano, the dog-like Aretinians, the wolf-like Florentines, and fox-like Pisans). Many of the torments of hell are realized metaphors of bestiality. So Ulysses' words reminding his companions that they are people and not beasts and are called to noble knowledge and not for animal-like existence have significance for the poet: 'Take thought of the seed from which you spring. You were not born to live as brutes, but to follow virtue and knowledge' (*Inferno*, XXVI, 118–20).

But Dante and Ulysses have different paths to knowledge. For Dante knowledge is always linked with a constant ascent along the axis of moral values, it is knowledge which comes through the moral perfection of the seeker. Knowledge elevates and the higher morality enlightens the mind. But Ulysses' thirst for knowledge is indifferent to morals, it is not linked either to morality or immorality, it lies in another plane and has no concern with ethical problems. Even Purgatory for him is just a white patch on the map, and the aim of reaching it just a journey for the sake of geographical discovery. Dante is a pilgrim, while Ulysses is a traveller. This is why Dante in his pilgrimage through the infernal and cosmic regions always has a Guide, while Ulysses is led only by his boldness and valour. With the mind and character of the seeker after adventures he joins the rebelliousness of Farinata. The rogue of the epic, the deceitful hero of the folktale who in Homer became the wily king of Ithaca, becomes in Dante the man of the Renaissance, the first discoverer and the traveller. This image appeals to Dante by its integrity and its strength, but repels him by its moral indifference. But in this image of the heroic adventurer of his time, of the seeker, of the one who is inquisitive in all areas except that of morals, Dante discerned something else, not just the features of the immediate future, the scientific mind and cultural attitudes of the modern age; he saw the coming separation of knowledge from morality, of discovery from its results, of science from the human personality.

So the differences between Dante and Ulysses are not merely a conflict which is now past history between the psychology of the Middle Ages and that of the Renaissance.

In the history of world culture we often find that thinkers who stand at the threshold of a new epoch see its sense and results more clearly than succeeding generations who are already involved in it. Standing on the threshold of the modern age, Dante saw one of the greatest dangers of the future. Integrity was essential to his ideal: his encyclopedic knowledge which included virtually the entire arsenal of science of his time, was not kept in his mind as a collection of isolated bits of information, but formed a single integrated edifice which in its turn merged with the ideal of the world empire and the harmonious construction of the cosmos. At the centre of this vast construction was humanity, powerful, like the giants of the Renaissance, but integrated into the surrounding world and therefore steeped in moral feeling. Dante had a presentiment of our modern tendency to exclude the individual person, to over-specialization, which has led to the separation of mind from conscience and of science from morality, and this tendency was deeply alien to him.

It would of course be naive to identify Dante, the hero of the *Comedy*, with Dante its author. Dante the hero is the antipode of Ulysses for he reminds us that none of those in hell should be pitied; whereas Dante the author cannot help feeling sorry for Ulysses and emotionally involved with him. Dante's thinking derives from the complex dialogic relationship between these images.

3. THE HOME IN BULGAKOV'S *THE MASTER AND MARGARITA*

Among the universal themes of world folklore an important opposition is that of 'home' to 'forest' ('home' being the place which is one's own, a place of safety, culture and divine protection, while 'forest' is somewhere alien, where the Devil dwells, a place of temporary death and to go there is the equivalent to a journey to the afterlife).[72] Archaic models of this opposition have persisted and been productive even in the modern period. In Pushkin's poetry of the late 1820s and 1830s, the theme of the home is a focus for his ideas about cultural traditions, history, individual kindness and independence. In Gogol this theme is developed to become, on the one hand, the opposition of home and anti-home (the latter belonging to the Devil, or the brothel, or the offices of the bureaucracy in the *Petersburg Tales*), and, on the other hand, the opposition of home as a place of introverted egoism, and homelessness and the open road, which are ascribed a higher value. In Dostoevsky the mythological archetype merges with Gogol's tradition: the hero who lives in the 'underground', in coffin-like rooms which are themselves places of death, has to pass through the 'house of the dead' and, 'trampling down death with death', be reborn and resurrected.

This tradition is especially significant for Bulgakov, and the symbolism of the opposition 'home/anti-home' is one of the organizing ideas of all his writings. What follows is an examination of this motif in his novel *The Master and Margarita*.[73]

The first thing we notice is the value accorded to homelessness: the only character who is found all through the novel from the first page to the last and who at the end will be addressed as 'disciple' [444] is 'the poet Ivan Nikolayich Ponyryov who wrote under the pseudonym of Bezdomny [Homeless]' [13]. Yeshua is similarly first introduced as someone homeless:

'Where is your fixed abode?'

'I have no home,' said the prisoner shamefacedly, 'I move from town to town.'

'There is a shorter way of saying that – in a word you are a vagrant,' said the Procurator.[30]

Note that shortly after this Yeshua is accused of intending 'to destroy the temple building'; while Ivan's address will subsequently be 'the poet Homeless' from the mental hospital.

Alongside the theme of homelessness is the theme of the false home, of which there are many variants, the chief one being the communal flat. To Vanya's words, 'you might have been dining at home', Ambrose answers, 'Just imagine your wife trying to cook *filets de perche au naturel* in a saucepan in a kitchen you share with half a dozen other people' [71]. The idea of 'home' and of 'communal kitchen' are quite incompatible for Bulgakov and their coincidence is an ingredient of his fantasmagoric world.

The communal flat is the centre of an abnormal world. The escapades of the infernal forces, the mystifications of the bureaucrats and everyday rows all take place here. Just as all cursing in the devil's name in the novel can be taken in two ways – as an emotional interjection and as direct designation, so too all talk about living accommodation has a double meaning with an absurd or infernal subtext: behind the jargon of the housing authorities (it is not permitted to enter the rooms formerly occupied by the late Berlioz) lies the nightmare image of Korovyov occupying the dead man's rooms (the horror of the image is supported by the stories of the seizure of Berlioz' head and the decapitation of Bengalsky).[74]

The flat symbolizes not a place of life, but something quite the opposite, and in fact there is a firm link between the themes of flat and of death. The first time the word 'flat' is used in the novel it is in a very ominous context. Berlioz asks, 'but where are you going to live?' to which Woland answers, 'In your flat' [56]. This theme is developed in Korovyov's words to the chairman of the tenants' association, Nikanor Ivanovich, 'You must admit the flat's no use to him now, is it?' [115]. Berlioz' uncle, Maximilian Andreyevich Poplavsky, comes to Moscow in order to take over the dead man's three rooms, as if the death of his nephew was but an episode in the problem of where to live: 'The telegram came as a shock to Maximilian Andreyevich. It was a chance that would be sinful to miss. Practical people know that opportunities of that sort never come twice' [224]. So the death of his relative was a moment he could not let slip.

'Flat No. 50' is the scene of infernal happenings, but they started there long before Woland and his suite settled in: the flat was always 'spooky'.

The amazing disappearances that take place there are however a feature shared by all the anti-homes of the novel: people do not live in them but they disappear from them (they run away, fly away, walk away or disappear without trace). The theme of the flat as a place where rationality is abandoned is pointed up by the parallel story of how to 'anyone who knows how to handle the fifth dimension it's no problem to expand any place to whatever size you please' [286], and how one man 'without using the fifth dimension or anything like that' had turned a three-roomed flat into a four-roomed one and then 'exchanged it for two sepaate flats in different parts of Moscow, one with three rooms and the other with two. . . . He exchanged the three-roomed one for two separate two-roomers and . . . you talk of the fifth dimension!' [287].

The universal pursuit of 'living space' is also full of irrationality (Poplavsky's attempts to exchange 'a flat on University street in Kiev for a smaller flat in Moscow' [224] shows up the falsity of bureaucratic jargon, and the irreality of the actual action – living in 'living space' being the same as living in a dead person's flat) because this hunt is incompatible with life. (Bengalsky's cry, 'Give me back my head, my head . . . . You can have my flat, you can have alll my pictures, only give me back my head!' [148]).

The flats in Bulgakov's novel do not look lived in. At house no.13 (!) where Ivan Homeless runs to in pursuit of Woland,

> he did not have to wait long. The door was opened by a little girl of about five, who silently disappeared inside again. The hall was a vast, incredibly neglected room feebly lit by a tiny electric light which dangled in one corner from a ceiling black with dirt. On the wall hung a bicycle without any tyres, beneath it a huge iron-banded trunk. On the shelf over the coat-rack was a winter furcap, its long earflaps untied and hanging down. From behind one of the doors a man's voice could be heard booming from the radio, angrily declaiming poetry. [64–5]

And in this flat Ivan finds a 'naked woman', 'hellish light' and 'coals smouldering in the geyser' [65].

But what distinguishes a home from an anti-home is not just delapidation, neglect and lack of cosiness. 'Margarita knew nothing of the horrors of living in a shared flat' [249], but she felt that she could not live in her private house, she would die there. In the same way Pontius Pilate hates Herod's palace and he lives, eats and sleeps under the columns of the arcade, without the strength to go in even during the storm ('I can't bear sleeping in it' [345]). Only once in the novel does Pilate go into the palace: 'inside his darkened, shuttered room the Procurator spoke to a man whose face . . . remained half covered by a hood' [48–9]. The rooms are used not for living but for meetings with the head of the secret service. Arthanius and Niza go indoors in order to agree a price for the murder of Judas ('to kill a man with a woman as decoy or accomplice needs a very great deal of money' [364]). In the stories of the poisoners and murderers, who turn up at Satan's rout, there is mention of the walls of rooms which always imply something gloomy. When the news of Berlioz' death spread through the apartment house. Nikanor Ivanovich received thirty-two statements of need for housing. 'they contained entreaties, threats, intrigue, denunciations' [112]. The flat is a synonym for something sinister and above all for denunciation. Desire for a flat was the reason why Aloysius Mogarych denounced the master:

> 'Is your name Mogarych?' Azazello asked him.
>
> 'Aloysius Mogarych,' said the new arrival, trembling.
>
> 'Are you the man who lodged a complaint against this man' – pointing to the master – 'after you had read an article about him by Latunsky, and denounced him for harbouring illegal literature?' asked Azazello.
>
> The man turned blue and burst into tears of penitence.
>
> 'You did it because you wanted to get his flat, didn't you?' said Azazello in a confiding, nasal whine. [328]

The 'housing problem' is like a vast symbol. Woland sums up his opinion of Muscovites: 'They're ordinary people, in fact they remind me very much of their predecessors, except that the housing shortage has soured them' [147].

But the flat is not the only anti-home in the novel. The heroes pass through many 'houses' of which the main ones are: the Griboedov House, the madhouse, and the camp where the master was kept in Margarita's dream ('a log cabin that looked like a kind of outhouse. the surroundings looked so lifeless and miserable that one might easily have been tempted to hang oneself on that aspen by the little bridge. . . . In short, hell' [251]). The Griboedov House, which houses the Writers' Union, is especially important because of the traditional semantic connotation of such a place with culture; but this House is a travesty. Everything in it is false, from the notice 'Apply to M. V. Podlozhnaya [counterfeit]' to the 'brief and completely incomprehensible legend: "Perelygino"' [69]. And buildings which have special symbolic value are punished in the novel: Margarita wreaks havoc with the flats (but saves Latunsky from Woland's suite), while Korovyov and Behemoth set the Griboedov House on fire.

These pseudo-homes have something infernal about them, as does the whole city. At the beginning and end of the novel we see the houses of the city in the evening light. Woland's 'gaze halted on the upper storeys, whose panes threw back a blinding, fragmented reflection of the sun which was setting on Berlioz for ever' [17]. And towards the end of the novel Woland and Azazello 'stood watching the setting sun reflected in all the westward-facing windows. Woland's eyes shone with the same fire, even though he sat with his back to the sunset' [405]. The comparison with Woland's eyes makes clear the ominous symbolism of these flaming windows whose light resembles that of the burning coals which are so often referred to in the novel. The shining windows are a sign of the anti-world.

Bulgakov builds up this opposition between the 'home' of the living and the anti-home of the pseudo-living with the help of a whole gamut of repeated images of light and sound. For instance, the sounds of a gramophone can be heard coming from the anti-home (the master describes hearing it when on a cold January night wearing an overcoat without buttons he returns to his flat now occupied by Aloysius Mogarych [171–2]), or in all the flats the sound of the same radio programme is to be heard. A proper home is characterized by the sound of a piano being played. Flat No. 50 is ambivalent because the sounds of a piano and a gramophone are to be heard in it.

Bulgakov uses spatial language to express non-spatial concepts. He makes the 'home' the centre of spiritual values, which are expressed in the riches of private life, creativity and love. These values are set by Bulgakov in a complex hierarchy: on the lowest step is inert materiality, and on the highest absolute spirituality. The former needs living space and not a home, while the latter does not need a home: Yeshua does not need a home for his earthly life is the eternal way. Pontius Pilate in his good dreams sees himself endlessly walking along a moonbeam.

But life in all its diversity is set between these poles. On the lower steps are the devils inventing cruel tricks which plague and agitate the inert world of materiality, bring irony to it, mock it and shake it up. These malicious tricks rouse those who can be roused and in the final count help the victory of a higher spirituality than their own. This is the sense of the epigraph from Goethe with its Manichean flavour, which Bulgakov put at the opening of his novel: '"Say at last – who art thou?" "That Power I serve which wills forever evil yet does forever good".'

Art is on a higher plane. Art is something entirely human and it cannot reach the absolute (the master does not deserve light). But it is higher in the hierarchy than either the physically stronger servants of Woland, or activists such as Athranius who is endowed with some creativity. Art as a great spiritual element is represented spatially. Woland's suite when they come to Moscow stay in a flat, Athranius and Pilate meet in the palace, but the master needs a home. The master's destiny can be described in terms of the search for a home.

His destiny is a pilgrimage.

The story of the master is marked by clear passages from one space to another. His story begins when he wins 100,000 roubles in a lottery; he then ceases to be an employee of the museum and a translator and becomes a writer and master. He buys books (books are a special feature of the real home, signifying both spiritual values and also a special atmosphere of intellectual cosiness[75] and gives up his 'filthy hole' of a room on Myasnitskaya street [160]. The master rents two rooms in the basement of a small house with a garden near the Arbat ('"Ah, that was a golden age! . . . A completely self-contained little flat with a hall with a sink and running water. . . . And there was always a blaze in my little stove! . . . The main room was huge – fourteen square metres! – books, more books and a stove"' [160–1]). This is his 'marvellous little place' made into a home not by the basin in the hall but by its cultured and intimate atmosphere. For Bulgakov, as for Pushkin in the 1830s, culture was inseparable from private life. Work on his novel turns the 'marvellous little place' in to a poetic home in contrast to the Griboedov House with its false hothouse atmosphere. But when the master denies his creativity the home turns back into a miserable basement: 'I have no more dreams . . . I'm finished. My only wish is to return to that basement' [331]; and Woland says: '"So the creator of Pontius Pilate proposes to go and starve in a basement?"' [332].

But the master does get his home in the end:

> 'Listen to the silence,' said Margarita to the master, the sand rustling under her bare feet. 'Listen to the silence and enjoy it. Here is the peace you never knew in your lifetime. Look, there is your home for eternity, which is your reward. I can already see a Venetian window and a climbing vine which grows right up to the roof. It's your home, your home for ever.' [431]

After all his experiences of pseudo-homes, the camp, the madhouse, and after being purged by the flight (flight is the way to leave the world of flats) the master is rewarded with a world of tender domesticity, of life steeped in culture which is the fruit of the labours of past generations; he is rewarded by an atmosphere of love, a world without cruelty.

> 'In the evenings people will come to see you – people who interest you, people who will never upset you. They will play to you and sing to you and you will see how beautiful the room is by candlelight. You shall go to sleep with your dirty old cap on, you shall go to sleep with a smile on your lips.' [431]

The theme of the home in *The Master and Margarita* which we have been discussing sheds light on Bulgakov's other works. *The White Guard* is a novel about the destruction of the domestic world. It begins with the death of the mother, a poetic description of the 'domestic nest', and at the same time with the ominous words: 'The walls will fall down, the startled falcon will fly away from the white gauntlet, the light in the bronze lamp will die out. ... Mother said to her children: "Live." But they had to suffer and die.'[77]

And at the other end of Bulgakov's career is his *Theatrical Novel* in which the homeless writer (who lives in a poor room which is not a room when he is writing his novel but a cabin in an airship) resurrects the home of the Turbins: he sees it looking like a little box with the familiar figures in it, he hears the piano being played. And then the little box grows to full-size and the heroes recover their lost home.[78]

At the lowest point of this creative curve lies 'Zoya's Flat' in which the flat takes on the symbolic meaning which it has in *The Master and Margarita*, the novel which sums up all of Bulgakov's evolution and which has a place in the great literary and mythological tradition.

In Bulgakov the home is an internal, closed space, the source of security, harmony and creativity. Beyond its walls lie chaos, destruction and death. A flat, and especially a communal flat, is chaos masquerading as home and making a real home impossible. The home and the communal flat are antipodes: this means that the common feature they share – being a dwelling place, living quarters – loses its significance, and all that remains are the semiotic qualities. The home becomes a semiotic element of the cultural space.

Here we have an example of an important principle in human cultural thinking: real space is an iconic image of the semiosphere, a language in which various non-spatial meanings can be expressed, while the semiosphere in its turn transforms the real world of space in which we live into its image and likeness.

4. THE SYMBOLISM OF ST PETERSBURG

In the system of a culture's symbols, the city has an important place. City symbolism can be divided into two main areas: the city as symbolic space and the city as symbolic name. The latter aspect has already been discussed by the present author with B. A. Uspensky[79] and will not be touched on here.

There are two ways in which a city as a demarcated space may relate to the earth which surrounds it: the city may be isomorphous with the state, and indeed personify it, *be it* in some ideal sense (Rome the city is also Rome the world); but the city can also be an antithesis to the surrounding world. *Urbs et orbis terrarum* can be perceived as antagonistic to each other.

In its relation to the surrounding world a city may be like a church in relation to the city at whose centre it is situated, i.e. the idealized model of the universe is situated at the centre of the earth. Or rather, no matter where it is situated, the city is *considered* to be the centre. Jerusalem, Rome, Moscow have all been treated as centres of their worlds. As an ideal embodiment of its country, the city is at the same time an image of the heavenly city and a sacred place.

But a city can also be placed eccentrically to its earth, beyond its boundaries. So for instance, Svyatoslav transferred his capital to Pereyaslavets on the Danube, and Charlemagne his to Aix-la-Chapelle.[80] In both cases the action had a direct political import and was proof of the ruler's aggressive intentions to acquire new lands of which the new capital would be the centre.[81] But there is also a semiotic aspect to such actions. The existentialist code is activated: what already exists is declared to be non-existent, and what has yet to appear is declared to be the only thing to exist. For when Svyatoslav announced that Peryaslavets on the Danube was at the centre of his lands he was thinking of a state which he still had to create, while Kiev which actually existed was declared to be non-existent. There was a sharp increase in value-marking: what exists and has present existence and is 'our own' is negatively valued, while what is yet to come into existence in the future and is 'someone else's' is highly valued. We may also in general observe that 'concentric' structures tend towards enclosure, separation from their surroundings which are classed as hostile, while eccentric structures tend towards openness and contacts with other cultures.

The concentric situation of the city in semiotic space is as a rule associated with the image of the city on the hill (or hills). This city is the mediator between earth and heaven, it is the focus for myths of origins (the gods invariably have played a part in its foundation), it has a beginning but no end – it is the eternal city, *Roma aeterna.*

The eccentric city is situated 'at the edge' of the cultural space: on the seashore, at the mouth of a river. The antithesis that is activated in this case is not earth/heaven but natural/artificial. This city is founded as a challenge to Nature and struggles with it, with the result that the city is interpreted either as the victory of reason over the elements, or as a perversion of the natural order. Eschatological myths will concentrate on this city, and predictions of ruin, of doom and the victory of the elements will be part of this city's mythology. There will be a flood or the city will be drowned at the bottom of the sea. Methodius of Patara predicted that this fate would befall Constantinople (the 'non-eternal Rome').[82]

This variant of the eschatological legend persisted in Petersburg mythology: the flood theme was confirmed by periodic inundations and gave rise to numerous literary works; and the detail – the tip of the Alexander column or of the spire of the Peter-Paul fortress projecting above the waves and serving as a moorage for ships – leads one to assume that the legend about Constantinople was directly transferred on to Petersburg. In his memoirs V. A. Sollogub wrote:

Lermontov . . . loved doing pen or brush sketches of a furious sea out of which showed the tip of the Alexander column with the angel on top. These pictures reflected his gloomy imagination and his thirst for disasters.[83]

The idea of the doomed city includes an eternal struggle between elements and culture, and in the Petersburg myth this struggle is realized as the antithesis between water and stone. The stone of Petersburg is not 'natural' or 'wild' (unhewn), not primordial rocks set in their places, but stone specially quarried, worked, 'humanized', acculturized. Petersburg stone is an artefact, not a natural phenomenon. So stone, rock, cliff in the Petersburg myth are not endowed with the usual features of immobility, fixity, capacity to withstand winds and water, but the unnatural feature of movability.[84] But the motif of moving what is unmovable is only part of the picture of the perverse world in which stone floats on water.

The natural semantics of stone and rock is evident for instance in Tyutchev's poem, 'The Sea and the Cliff':

> But calm and proud
> Not gripped by the frenzy of the waves,
> Immobile, unchangeable,
> *As old as the universe*, (my emphasis, Yu.L.)
> You stand, our giant![85]

Petersburg stone, however, is stone laid on water, on a marsh, stone without support, not 'as old as the universe', but placed there by mankind. In the 'Petersburg picture' water and stone change places: water is eternal, existing before stone and conquering it, while stone is temporal and transitory. Water can destroy it. In Odoevsky's *Russian Nights* (where he pictures the ruin of Petersburg):

> Now the walls are rocking, a window bursts and another, water pours
> through them filling the room. . . . Suddenly with a crash the walls collapse,
> the ceiling shatters, and the waves carry the coffin and everything else that
> was in the room out to the boundless sea.[86]

The theme of 'the world turned upside down', which includes the ruined city and which is to be found very widely in European culture of the sixteenth and early seventeenth centuries and is associated with the Baroque,[87] lends itself to two interpretations. The upside-down world in the tradition of the Baroque, which was akin to the folklore carnival tradition (see Bakhtin's profound ideas which have been too broadly interpreted by his followers), was either a Utopia, a land of Cockaigne,[88] or inverse world in Sumarokov's chorus. Or it had the frightening features of Breughel or Bosch.

Petersburg was also, however, identified with Rome[89] and by the beginning of the nineteenth century this idea was widespread. As Pavel L'vov wrote in 1804: 'One cannot but admire the magnificence and might of this new Rome!'[90] But this view of Petersburg contained two archetypes: the 'eternal Rome' and the 'non-eternal, doomed, Rome' (Constantinople) and these combined in the image of Petersburg as both doomed and eternal.

Because Petersburg was subject to this dual understanding it could also be treated both as 'paradise', a utopian ideal city of the future, the embodiment of Reason, and as the terrible masquerade of Antichrist. Both ideas were extreme idealizations but from opposite poles. The double reading of the Petersburg myth can be illustrated by the following example: in the Baroque tradition the symbolism of the snake under the hooves of the horseman in Falconet's statue of Peter the Great is an allegory of envy, hostility, and the obstacles placed in Peter's way by his enemies and the internal opponents of his reforms. But in the context of Methodius of Patara's prophecies which would have been well known to a Russian readership, the snake meant the Antichrist.[91] In this interpretation the horse, the rider and the snake are not opponents of each other but combine to form a sign of the end of the world, with the snake no longer being a secondary symbol but the chief figure in the group. This is the reason why the snake of Falconet's monument has been given an interpretation which the sculptor had not foreseen.

The ideal artificial city, the realized rationalist utopia must by definition have no history since the rationalism of the 'regular state' involved denying historically formed structures. So the city was built on a new place and everything 'old' was destroyed – if any such things were to be found in that place. So in Catherine the Great's reign the idea of founding an ideal city on the place of the historical Tver was mooted after the old city had in fact been destroyed by fire in 1763. The fire was a fortunate accident from the point of view of the plans. But history is a necessary condition for a working semiotic system, and a city created 'suddenly' by the wave of a demiurge's hand, without any history and subject to a single plan, is in principle unrealizable.

The city is a complex semiotic mechanism, a culture-generator, but it carries out this function only because it is a melting-pot of texts and codes, belonging to all kinds of languages and levels. The essential semiotic polyglottism of every city is what makes it so productive of semiotic encounters. The city, being the place where different national, social and stylistic codes and texts confront each other, is the place of hybridization, recodings, semiotic translations, all of which makes it into a powerful generator of new information. These confrontations work diachronically as well as synchronically: architectural ensembles, city rituals and ceremonies, the very plan of the city, the street names and thousands of other left-overs from past ages act as code programmes constantly renewing the texts of the past. The city is a mechanism, forever recreating its past, which then can be synchronically juxtaposed with the present. In this sense the city, like culture, is a mechanism which withstands time.[92]

The rationalist utopian city[93] had none of these semiotic reserves. But the lack of history gave rise to a great wave of myth-making, which would no doubt have appalled the rationalist Enlighteners of the eighteenth century. Myth filled the semiotic void and the artificial city turned out to be extremely mythogenic.

St Petersburg is very typical: the history of the city is inseparable from its mythology, and we are not using the word 'mythology' in a metaphorical sense. Long before the great writers of nineteenth-century Russian literature, from Pushkin and Gogol to Dostoevsky, made Petersburg mythology into a fact of the nation's culture, the actual history of Petersburg absorbed many mythological elements. If we look beyond the official bureaucratic history, reflected in official statistics, to the life of the mass of the population, then we cannot help being immediately struck by the enormous number of rumours, oral tales about unusual occurrences, a special kind of urban folklore which played so great a part in the life of the 'Palmyra of the North' since its very foundation. The Privy Chancellory were the first to collect this folklore. In 1833–5 Pushkin evidently intended to make his diary into a kind of archive of city rumours; Delvig was an assiduous collector of 'scary stories', and Dobrolyubov produced a theoretical explanation of popular oral creation in the manuscript student newspaper, *Rumours*.

A special feature of this 'Petersburg mythology' is that it is aware of its own oddness, it, as it were, presupposes an external, non-Petersburg observer. Sometimes this was a 'view from Europe' or a 'view from Russia' (i.e. 'view from Moscow'). The constant feature was that it posited someone looking at it from outside. There are, however, also examples of the opposite point of view, of Europe or of Russia (i.e. Moscow) 'from Petersburg'. Petersburg could be regarded as 'Asia in Europe' or 'Europe in Russia'. Both approaches emphasized how artificial and unorganic was Petersburg culture.

Awareness of 'artificiality' is part of Petersburg's own *self-evaluation* of its culture though this awareness later spread and became a feature of other different ideas. Hence the supernatural and theatricality which are constantly emphasized in the Petersburg 'picture of the world'. One might have expected that the medieval tradition of visions and prophecies would be more a part of the Moscow tradition than of 'rationalist' and 'European' Petersburg. But it was Petersburg where such things flourished. The idea of the supernatural is clearly put in the stylized legend about the foundation of the city which Odoevsky put into the mouth of the old Finn:

They began to build the city, but whenever they laid a stone the marsh sucked it in; they piled stone on stone, rock on rock, timber on timber, but the marsh swallowed it all and on the surface there was only mud. Meanwhile the tsar was building a ship and looked round: he saw that there was still no city. 'You don't know how to do anything' he said to his people and thereupon began to lift rock after rock and to shape them in the air. In this way he built the whole city and let it down on to the ground.[94]

This story is not, of course, a piece of Finnish folklore but the fantasy about Petersburg that was current among those Petersburg writers of the 1830s who were close to Pushkin and who included Odoevsky. The city hewn in the air and without foundations – this is Petersburg the supernatural and phantasmagoric space. From a close study of contemporary material it appears that in the first third of the nineteenth century an oral genre flourished in the salons of Petersburg, a genre which undoubtedly had a major influence on literature though it has not yet been properly studied or even taken into account. This was the genre of the scary or fantastic story with a 'Petersburg local colour'. The roots of this genre must be sought in the eighteenth century. The story told by Grand Duke Pavel Petrovich on 10 June 1782 in Brussels, for instance, which was noted down by Baroness Oberkirch undoubtedly belongs to this genre.[95] Here already are the obligatory features of the genre: insistence that the event is true, an appearance of the ghost of Peter the Great, predictions of tragedy and finally the Bronze Horseman as the marker of Petersburg space (the actual monument had not yet been put up but the ghost of Peter leads the future emperor Paul I to the Senate Square and disappears having promised to meet him on that spot).

Another typical story in this genre is E. G. Levasheva's story of Delvig's ghost. Ekaterina Gavrilovna Levasheva was a cousin of the Decembrist Yakushin, a friend of Pushkin and of M. Orlov, patron of Herzen in exile. Chaadaev lived in her house on New Basmannaya Street. She was especially close to Delvig, whose nephew later married her daughter Emiliya. She recounts how her husband, N. V. Levashev, had an agreement with Delvig, which he describes as follows:

[Delvig] loved to talk about the after-life, of its links with this life, of promises made in life and carried out after death, and once in order to throw light on this topic and check the tales which he had heard and read, he made me promise, and he promised too, to appear after death to which ever one of us was left. When we made this promise there were no oaths, no signings in blood, no ceremonies, nothing. . . . It was a simple, ordinary conversation, *causerie de salon*.[96]

The conversation was forgotten. Seven years later Delvig died and according to Levashev exactly one year after his death, at midnight, he silently appeared in Levashev's study, sat down in an armchair and then without having said a word, disappeared.

This story is of interest as an example of Petersburg 'salon folklore' and its connection with Delvig is not accidental. Delvig cultivated the oral 'Petersburg' ghost story. Pushkin's (and Titov's) *An isolated house on Vasilevsky Island* shares the atmosphere of Delvig's circle. Titov says it was published in *Northern Flowers* 'at the insistence of Delvig'.[97]

Gogol and Dostoevsky based their 'Petersburg mythology' on the oral traditions of Petersburg, they canonized it and raised it, along with the tradition of the oral anecdote, to the level of literature.

All this mass of 'oral literature' from the 1820s and 1830s made Petersburg into a place where the mysterious and fantastic was the norm. The Petersburg tale is like the yuletide ghost story, except that the temporal fantasy is replaced by spatial one.

Another feature of Petersburg space is its theatricality. The architecture of the city, unique in the consistency of the huge ensembles which cannot be divided up into buildings of different periods, as is the case in cities with long histories, gives the feeling of a stage set. This feature strikes both foreigners and Muscovites. But while the latter think of it as 'European', Europeans who are used to the juxtaposition of the Romanesque and the Baroque, the Gothic and Classicism in an architectural mixture are amazed at the original and strange beauty of the vast ensembles. The marquis de Custine remarked on it: 'At each step I was amazed seeing the endless mixture of two such different arts: architecture and stage decoration: Peter the Great and his successors looked on their capital as a theatre.'[98]

The theatricality of Petersburg is shown too in the clear demarcation between 'stage' and 'behind the scenes', a constant awareness of the spectator and, crucially, the replacement of existence by an 'as if existence': the spectator is always there, but, for the participants in the stage action, the spectator 'as it were exists' (to acknowledge his presence would be to break the rules of the game). Similarly behind-the-scenes space does not exist from the point of view of the stage. From the point of view of stage space the only thing that is real is stage existence, while from the point of view of the behind-the-scenes space, stage existence is just play and convention.

The feeling that there was a viewer, an observer who must not be noticed, accompanied all the ritual ceremonies which filled the daily routine of the 'military capital'. The soldier, like an actor, was constantly in the view of those who watched the parade, changing of the guard or other ceremony, but at the same time he was separated from them by a wall transparent only from one side: the soldier could be seen and existed for the observers but for him they could not be seen and did not exist.

The emperor was no exception. The marquis de Custine wrote:

> We were presented to the emperor and empress. It is obvious that the
> emperor cannot for a moment forget who he is nor the attention that is
> constantly paid to him. He is *endlessly posing* [de Custine's emphasis]. It
> follows that he is never natural even when he is sincere. His face has three
> expressions, not one of which is simple kindness. His normal expression is
> one of sternness; the second, which is less frequent but better fits his
> handsome face, is an expression of majesty, and the third one is
> courtesy. . . . One could talk of the masks which he puts on and takes off at
> will. . . . I would say that the emperor is forever playing his part and
> playing it like a great artist. . . . The lack of freedom is felt in everything,
> even in the autocrat's face: he has many masks but no face. Are you
> seeking the man? You will only find the emperor.[99]

The need for an audience has a semiotic parallel in eccentric
positioning in geography. Petersburg does not have its own point of view
on itself – it has always to posit a spectator. In this sense both Westerners
and Slavophiles are equally the creation of Petersburg culture. It was
typical in Russia to find a Westerner who had never been to the West,
knew no Western languages and was not even interested in the real West.
Turgenev walking through Paris with Belinsky was struck by his
indifference to the French life on all sides of them:

> I remember how he saw the Place de la Concorde for the first time and said
> to me, 'Is it true that it's one of the most beautiful squares in the world?'
> And when I answered in the affirmative he exclaimed, 'Well, that's
> splendid; so now I know', and aside he said 'basta!' and started to talk
> about Gogol. I told him that on this very spot during the revolution the
> guillotine had stood and that this was where Louis XVI had his head
> chopped off. He looked around, said, 'ah!' and started to talk about the
> execution scene in *Taras Bulba*.[100]

The West for the Westerner was just an ideal point of view and not a
cultural geographical reality. But this artificially constructed 'point of
view' had a higher reality with regard to the real life it observed from its
position. Saltykov-Shchedrin, recalling that in the 1840s he had been
'reared on Belinsky's articles' and so was 'naturally drawn to the
Westerners', wrote: 'In Russia, incidentally, not so much in Russia as in
Petersburg, we existed just factually, or, as we said in those days, we had
an "image of life" . . . but spiritually we lived in France.'[101] The
Slavophiles, on the other hand, like the Kireevsky brothers, studied
abroad and heard Schelling and Hegel lecture, or, like Yu. Samarin who
did not know any Russian until he was seven years old, employed

university professors to teach them Russian; but they created a similarly conventionalized idea of ancient Russia as the point of view they needed from which to observe the real world of post-Petrine, Europeanized civilization.

This constant fluctuation between the reality of the spectator and the reality of the stage, when each of these realities was, from the point of view of the other, illusory, was what produced the Petersburg effect of theatricality. The other aspect of it was the relationship between the stage-space and behind-the-scenes space. The spatial antithesis between the Nevsky Prospekt (and all the parade-ground 'palace' quarter of Petersburg), and Kolomna, Vasilievsky island and the outskirts, was interpreted in literature as a mutual relationship of non-existence. Each of the two Petersburg 'scenes' had its own myth relayed in tales, anecdotes and associated with particular spots. There was the Petersburg of Peter the Great who served as protecting divinity for 'his' Petersburg, or who like a *deus implicitus* was an unseen presence in his creation; and there was Petersburg of the clerks, of the poor, the 'person without citizenship in the capital' (Gogol). Each of these personages had their own streets, districts, their own space. A natural consequence was that plots were born in which these two personages came into contact with each other through some unusual circumstances. One story went like this: in 1844 E. P. Lachnikova (who wrote under the pseudonym of E. Khamar-Dobanov) published a satirical novel *Escapades in the Caucasus*. It met with uproar. A. V. Nikitenko noted in his diary for 22 June 1844: 'The War Minister read it and was appalled. He pointed it out to Dubelt and said, "This book is all the more dangerous in that every word of it is true."'[102] Krylov, the censor who had passed the book, was attacked. Subsequently he had this to say about the episode. To understand his story we have to remember that there were widespread rumours that in the study of the head of the gendarmerie in the Third Section there was an armchair which dropped its occupant halfway down a hatch whereupon hidden executioners not knowing who their victim was despatched him. Talk about this secret place of execution which circulated even in the eighteenth century in connection with Sheshkovsky (see A. M. Turgenev's memoirs) was renewed in the reign of Nicholas I and it seems through Countess Rastopchina reached the 'Russian' novels of Alexandre Dumas. Pirogov tells the story:

> Krylov was the censor and that year he had passed a novel which created a great uproar. The novel was forbidden by the Head of the censorship and Krylov was summoned to the chief of the Petersburg gendarmerie, Orlov. . . . Krylov came to Petersburg as might be expected in the gloomiest frame of mind and went first to Dubelt and then together they went to Orlov. It was damp, cold and overcast. Driving across St Isaac's

Square past the monument to Peter the Great, Dubelt who was wrapped in his greatcoat and squeezed against the corner of the cab said as if to himself, so Krylov reports, 'If there is anyone who should be whipped it is Peter the Great for his stupid idea of building Petersburg on a marsh.' Krylov heard him and thought to himself, 'I understand your game, my friend, you're trying to catch me out. I won't answer.' Dubelt tried once more on the way to start a conversation but Krylov stayed silent. . . . Eventually they arrived at Orlov's. They were well received. Dubelt, turning aside, left Krylov face to face with Orlov. 'Forgive me, Mr Krylov,' said the head of the gendarmerie, 'for having troubled you almost in vain. Be so good as to sit down and we will have a talk.'

In Krylov's account he stood there more dead than alive and wondered what to do: he couldn't not sit down since he had been invited, yet if he sat down in the presence of the head of the gendarmerie he would be beaten. Finally there was nothing to be done, Orlov invited him to sit a second time and pointed to the armchair standing by him. 'So then', says Krylov, 'I sat down very carefully and gently on the edge of the armchair. My heart fell to my boots. Any minute now and the seat will give way underneath me and you know what . . . Orlov evidently noticed, smiled at me and assured me that there was nothing to worry about.'[103]

There are many interesting things about Krylov's story. In the first place since it is told by someone who took part in the incident it is already compositionally organized and is halfway to turning into a city anecdote. The *pointe* of the story is that a civil servant and Peter the Great come together as equals, and the Third Department has to choose which one to flog (Dubelt's remark, 'that's the one to whip' shows he is at a moment of choice, and the choice is not at all in favour of the 'mighty founder'). It is significant that the question is posed on the Senate Square, a traditional place for such thoughts. Besides, a ritual flogging of the statue is not simply a form of condemning Peter but a typical pagan magic action against a divinity who is behaving 'incorrectly'. In this respect Petersburg anecdotes about blasphemous attacks on the monument to Peter the Great is, like any blasphemy, a form of worship (there is the well-known story about Countess Tolstoy who, after the flood of 1824, drove specially to the Senate Square to put her tongue out at the emperor).[104]

'Petersburg mythology' developed out of other deeper levels of the city's semiotics. Petersburg was thought of as Russia's seaport, the Russian Amsterdam (and the parallel with Venice was common too). But it was also the 'military capital' and the imperial residence, the state centre of the country, even, as we have shown elsewhere, the New Rome with all that implied for imperial ambitions.[105] But these layers of practical and symbolic functions contradicted each other and were often incompatible. Petersburg had to be built both to replace Novgorod, which

Ivan IV had destroyed, and in order to restore the cultural balance that was traditional for early Russia, namely the existence of two historic centres and the links with Western Europe. This city had to be both an economic centre and the place where different cultural languages came together; and semiotic polyglottism is the law for this type of city. At the same time, the ideal of the 'military capital' demanded uniformity and strict conformity to a single semiotic system. Any deviation from it was, from this point of view, a dangerous breakdown of order. Note that the first type of city always tends to 'incorrectness' and to the contradictions such as we find in a literary text, while the second type of city tends towards the normative 'correctness' of a metalanguage. It is not accidental that the philosophical ideal of the City, which was one of the Petersburg codes of the eighteenth century, fitted in perfectly with 'military' and 'bureaucratic' Petersburg but not at all with cultural, literary and merchant Petersburg.

The struggle between Petersburg the literary text and Petersburg the metalanguage fills the entire semiotic history of the city. An ideal model struggled with its embodiment in reality. No wonder de Custine saw Petersburg as a military camp where palaces took the place of tents. But there was a strong and persistent resistance to this tendency; life itself filled the city: the nobility in their town houses where independent private cultured life went on, and the *declassé* intelligentsia with their original cultural tradition whose roots went back to the life of the clergy. The transfer of the seat of government to Petersburg, a move which was not at all necessary for the role of the Russian Amsterdam, heightened the contradictions. As the capital, the symbolic centre of Russia, the new Rome, Petersburg was to be an emblem of the country, an expression of it, but as the seat of government which was a kind of anti-Moscow, it became the antithesis of Russia. The complex interweaving of 'our own' and 'other people's' in the semiotics of Petersburg laid its mark on the self-assessment of the whole culture of this period. 'By what black magic have we become strangers to each other!' wrote Griboedov, voicing one of the most important questions of the age.

As Petersburg developed historically it became more and more distanced from the conscious ideal of the rationalist capital of the 'regular state', from the city organized by precepts and deprived of history. It grew its own history, acquired a complex topo-cultural structure supported by the multitude of castes and nationalities who lived there. Life rapidly became more complex. Already Paul I was frightened by its diversity. The city ceased to be an island in the empire, and Paul had to create an island in Petersburg. In the same way Mariya Fedorovna tried to bring to Pavlovsk a little of the intimacy of Montbellard. By the 1830s Petersburg had become a city of cultural and semiotic contrasts which served as soil for an exceptionally intense intellectual life. By the sheer number of texts, codes, connections, associations, by the size of its cultural memory build up over the historically tiny period of its existence, Petersburg can rightly be considered to be unique, a place where semiotic models were embodied in architectural and geographical reality.

13

Some conclusions

Humanity, immersed in its cultural space, always creates around itself an organized spatial sphere. This sphere includes both ideas and semiotic models and people's recreative activity, since the world which people artificially create (agricultural, architectural and technological) correlates with their semiotic models. There is a two-way connection: on the one hand, architectural buildings copy the spatial image of the universe and, on the other hand, this image of the universe is constructed on an analogy with the world of cultural constructs which mankind creates.

The importance of spatial models created by culture lies in the fact that, unlike other basic forms of semiotic modelling, spatial models are constructed not on a verbal, discrete basis but on an iconic continuum. Their foundation are visually visible iconic texts and verbalization of them is secondary. This image of the universe can better be danced than told, better drawn, sculpted or built than logically explicated. The work of the right hemisphere of the brain here is primary. But the first attempts at self-description of this structure inevitably involve the verbal level with the attendant semantic tension between the continual and the discrete semiotic pictures of the world.

The spatial picture of the world is many-layered: it includes both the mythological universum and scientific modelling and everyday 'common sense'. Every normal person has these (and many other) layers which form a heterogeneous mixture which functions as a whole. In the mind of modern man there mingles Newtonian, Einsteinian (and even post-Einsteinian) ideas with deeply mythological images as well as persistent habits of seeing the world in its everyday sense. Against this substratum can be seen images created by art or deeper scientific ideas and also the constant transcoding of spatial images into the language of other models. The result is the complex semiotic mechanism which is in constant motion.

The spatial image of the world created by culture is situated as it were between humanity and the outer reality of Nature and is constantly drawn to these two poles. It turns to humanity in the name of the outside world whose image it is, while the historical experience of man subjects this image to constant reworking, striving for accuracy in its representation of the world. But this image is always universal while the world is given to human beings through experience only partially. The contradiction between these two mutually associated aspects is inevitable and ineradicable; together they form the universal plan of content and expression, and the reflection of content in expression is inevitably not wholly accurate.

No less complex are the relationships between human beings and the spatial image of the world. On the one hand, the image is created by man, and on the other, it actively forms the person immersed in it. Here it is possible to draw a parallel with natural language. We could say that the activity generated by human beings towards the spatial model has its origin in the collective, whereas the reverse tendency affects the individual. But there is also a parallel in poetic language, which creates a personality which then has a reverse effect on the collective. As in the process of language-formation so in the process of spatial modelling both tendencies are active.

NOTES TO PART TWO

1. René Descartes, 'Discourse on Method', in *The Essential Descartes*, ed. Margaret D. Wilson, New York, 1969, p. 118.
2. V. I. Vernadsky, *Izbrannye sochineniya* [*Selected Works*], vol. 5, Moscow, 1960, p. 102.
3. V. I. Vernadsky, *Razmyshleniya naturalista. Nauchnaya mysl' kak planetarnoe yavlenie* [*Thoughts of a Naturalist. Scientific Thinking as a Planetary Phenomenon*], book 2, Moscow, 1977, p. 32.
4. V. I. Vernadsky, 'Filosofskie zametki raznykh let' ['Philosophical Notes from Various Years'], *Prometei*, 15, Moscow, 1988, p. 292.
5. Denis Davydov, *Opyt teorii partizanskogo deistviya* [*An Outline Theory of Partisan Action*], 2nd edition, Moscow, 1822, p. 83.
6. *Pamyatniki literatury drevnei Rusi. Nachalo russkoi literatury* [*Literary Memorials of Early Russia. The Beginning of Russian Literature*], Moscow, 1978, p. 31.
7. Franco Cardini, *Alle radici della cavalleria medievale*, ed. La nuova Italia, 1982.
8. *Pamyatniki*, pp. 191, 193.
9. V. I. Vernadsky, *Khimicheskoe stroenie biosfery Zemli i ee okruzheniya* [*The Chemical Structure of the Biosphere of the Earth and its Surroundings*], Moscow, 1965, p. 201.

10. B. A. Uspensky, *A Poetics of Composition*, Berkeley, 1973, pp.156–8, citing M. Schapiro, 'Style', in *Anthropology Today. An Encyclopedic Inventory*, Chicago, 1953, p. 293.

11. P. Tallemant, *Rémarques et décisions de l'Académie française*, 1698; cf. *Le Dictionnaire des précieuses par le Sieur de Somaize*. Nouvelle ed. par M. Ch.-L. Livet, Paris, 1856.

12. In more detail, see Roger Lathuillère, *La préciosité, étude historique et linguistique*, vol. 1, Geneva, 1966; B. A. Uspensky, *Iz istorii russkogo literaturnogo yazyka XVIII–nachala XIX veka. Yazykovaya programma Karamzina i ee istoricheskie korni* [*From the History of the Russian Literary Language of the 18th to early 19th centuries. Karamzin's Language Programme and its Historical Roots*], Moscow, 1965, pp. 60–6.

13. Jean Delumeau, *La civilisation de la Renaissance*, ed. Arthaud, Paris, 1984, pp. 264–5.

14. Out of the many works on this topic I should like to pick out for the clarity of its methodological approach Roman Jakobson's 'Le mythe de la France en Russie', in Roman Jakobson, *Russie, folie, poésie, textes choisies et présentés par Tzvetan Todorov*, Paris, 1986, pp. 157–68.

15. *Pis'ma ledi Rondo, zheny angliiskogo rezidenta pri russkom dvore v tsarstvovanie imp. Anny Ivanovny* [*The Letters of Lady Rondo, Wife of the English Resident to the Russian Court in the Reign of Empress Anna Ivanovna*], ed. S. N. Shubinsky St Petersburg, 1874, p. 46.

16. *Mestnichestvo* in Muscovite Russia of the fifteenth to seventeenth centuries was a system whereby boyars were appointed to state duties depending on their rank and the importance of the duties fulfilled by their ancestors. A special department dealt with these appointments, from the seating at the Tsar's banquets, to position in a campaign, an embassy or military command. The system was the cause of innumerable disputes since family honour was at stake.

17. S. M. Solov'ev, *Istoriya Rossii s drevneishikh vremen*, book 3, St Petersburg [n.d.], col. 679.

18. Ibid., cols 681–2.

19. Owen Latimore, *Studies in Frontier History*, London, 1962; Stanislaw Piekarczyk, *Barbaryncy i chrzescijanstwo*, Warsaw, 1968; Cardini, op.cit., 'Rome and the Barbarians' and 'The Barbarians and Christianity'.

20. John Newson, *Dialogue and Development: Action, Gesture and Symbol. The Emergence of Language*, ed. A. Lock, Lancaster, 1978, pp. 31–42.

21. Adolf Gaspari, *Istoriya ital'yanskoi literatury* [*A History of Italian Literature*], vol. I, Moscow 1895, p. 67. The work of Ramon Menedes Pidal has done much to confirm the 'Andalusian' theory for the origins of Provençal poetry; and it has become obvious that the role of Provence as catalyst of the Renaissance poetry of Italy is symmetrical in relation to the role of Andalusia as 'provoker' of the lyrics of the Aquitaine troubadours. Without exaggerating the role of the Arab-Andalusian impulse and pointing out the significance of the local folklore and the Roman classical traditions as well as that of medieval Latin poetry, Pidal concludes:

> In its conception of courtly love, Arab-Andalusian poetry was the forerunner of Provence and of other Romance countries and served them

as model with regard to strophic form. This explains the similarity between all seven kinds of stanza with unison refrain in Arab-Andalusian and Romance poetry. . . .

The Provençal lyric even at its origins in the period of the greatest Hispano-Aquitaine rapprochement was influenced by Andalusia; the result was the conception of the cult of love which was different from the cult of chivalry since the latter demanded reciprocity from the lord in relation to his vassal. The cult of love required the lover to yield to the despotic power of his mistress and to praise her cruelty to him: Thanks to the Andalusian influence the troubadours perceived love in a new way as an unquenchable longing and sweet torment. The same influence led them to use the stanza with unison refrain. So the Provençal song could only have been born at the courts of southern France; but it could not have been born without the important influence of the Arab-Andalusian lyric. (R. M. Pidal, 'Arab Poetry and European Poetry', in R. M. Pidal, *Izbrannye proizvedeniya* [*Selected Works*], Moscow, 1961, pp. 503–4)

Subsequently Provençal lyric poetry took on more and more national features and independence and matured to a point when it could become a cultural 'transmitter'.

22. We are not concerned here with the social and historical causes of the Renaissance. Semiotic processes are never entirely self-contained and are always bound to extra-semiotic reality. We are concerned not with the causes of the Renaissance but with the semiotic mechanism of cultural dynamics which has its own internal logic, just as a language while dependent on non-linguistic phenomenon for its content has its own immanent mechanisms for its internal structure.

23. In the reign of Catherine the Great, a young officer, G. Vinsky, was exiled to the southern Urals for an indiscretion. In order to earn his keep he taught French. His pupil, the fifteen-year-old daughter of an official, 'could translate Helvetius, Mercier, Rousseau and Mably without a dictionary' (G. Vinsky, *Moe vremya* [*My Time*], St Petersburg, 1914, p. 139). So the books of all these authors could be obtained at that time on the very borders of Asia!

24. Vinsky wrote: 'No matter how many old believers and young believers and all their crew shout "Crucify the French!" still Voltaire is not Marat, Jean-Jacques Rousseau is not Couton, Buffon is not Robespierre. If ever a time of truth prevails then the great minds of the eighteenth century, these benefactors of the human race, will receive the honour and recognition due to them.'

25. A. D. Aleksandrov, 'Abstraktnye prostranstva' ['Abstract Spaces'], in *Matematika, ee soderzhanie, metody i znachenie* [*Mathematics, its Content, Methods and Meaning*], vol. III, Moscow 1956, pp. 130–1.

26. Soslan (Sosyryko) 'comes back on his horse from the land of the dead where he had gone to take counsel with his first wife who had died', G. Dumesil, *Osetinsky epos i mifologiya* [*The Ossetian Epic and Mythology*], Moscow, 1976, p. 103.

27. Carlo Ginzburg, *Les batailles nocturnes. Sorcellerie et rituels agraires aux XVI et XVII siècles*, Paris, 1984.

28. O. M. Freidenberg, 'Proiskhozhdenie literaturnoi intrigi' ['The Origin of the Literary Intrigue'], *Trudy po znakovym sistemam*, 6, Tartu, 1973.
29. William Shakespeare, *As You Like It*, V. iv.
30. Ibid., IV. iii.
31. S.Yu. Neklyudov, 'K voprosu o svyazi prostranstvenno-vremennykh otnoshenii s syuzhetnoi strukturoi byliny' ['On the Question of the Connection between the Spatial-Temporal Relationships with the Plot-Structure in the Folk Epic'], *Tezisy dokladov vo vtoroi letnei shkole po vtorichnym modeliruyushchim sistemam*, Tartu, 1966; Yu. Lotman, *The Structure of the Artistic Text*, trans. R. Vroon, Ann Arbor, 1977.
32. Vyach. Vs. Ivanov, V. N. Toporov, *Slavyanskie yazykovye modeliruyushchie sistemy (Drevnii period)* [*Slavonic Linguistic Modelling Systems (The Ancient Period)*], Moscow, 1965.
33. The birth of Tristan after the death of his father is just such a consecutive duplication, as is the synchronic dupliction of Isolde the Golden and Isolde the blonde.
34. V. Ya. Propp, *Istoricheskie korni volshebnoi skazki* [*Historical Roots of the Magic Tale*], Leningrad, 1946.
35. Ibid., p. 80.
36. Ibid., p. 79.
37. Isaiah 6; K. S. Kashtaleva, '*Podrazhanie Koranu* Pushkina i ikh istochnik' ['Pushkin's *Imitation of the Koran* and its Sources'], *Zapiski kollegii vostokovedov*, V; N. I. Chernyaev, '"Prorok" Pushkina v svyazi s ego zhe "Podrazhanie Koranu"' ['Pushkin's "Prophet" in relation to his "Imitation of the Koran"'], 1898.
38. Proof of Moravia's conscious orientation on myth in his novel is the method of death chosen by the young man intent on self-destruction: he does not think of suicide but of being torn to pieces and eaten by wild animals. In the novel this idea is psychologically based on the stories he heard as a child about a young man who he thinks is buried near the zoo, and about the Christian martyrs, and so on; it is not hard to sense here one of the universal motifs of death in myth (dismemberment and being eaten). See Propp, op.cit., p. 80: 'the dismemberment of the human body has an enormous part in very many religions and myths, and it is also important in the folktale.' There is any amount of ethnographical material showing that dismemberment is followed by burial in the ground (burial and sowing coincide as in Robert Burns' ballad, 'John Barleycorn' where torture, burial in the ground and being boiled in the pot are just precursors of rebirth, and in which a three-fold plot structure is created: an archaic mythological level, a folktale level (the war of the three kings against John), and the third level which incorporates the poetry of agricultural labour – sowing or swallowing). Both dismemberment and burial are isomorphic to conception, for they are following by sprouting or throwing up, which are new kinds of birth. Eliade, for instance, cites an African myth about the giant Ngakola who used to eat people and regurgitate them. Among certain tribes this myth is the basis of the initiation rite. Interesting too that in Moravia's novel the hero's passage from the life and world of childhood, of his parents and property takes the form of tearing up money and burying the pieces in the ground (this is

prompted by his discovery that in his parents' room behind the picture of the Madonna to whom he had been forced to pray was a safe full of banknotes). So the extremely archaic plot of the overthrow of the old divinity, his dismemberment and sowing the pieces of his body in the ground, after which comes renewal both of god and man and the start of a 'new life' has become a language in which the writer treats burning contemporary issues.

39. A. Slonimsky, '"Vdrug" u Dostoevskogo" ['"Suddenly" in Dostoevsky'], *Kniga i revolyutsiya*, 8, 1922.
40. Dostoevsky's heroes tend systematically to commit actions which are inconsistent with their characters and which seem 'strange' and unmotivated.
41. Fyodor Dostoevsky, *The Devils*, Penguin Classics, p. 177. Further quotations from the same chapter 'The Wise Serpent'.
42. Mikhail Bakhtin, *Problems of Dostoevsky's Poetics*, edited and translated by Caryl Emerson, Manchester 1984, p. 92.
43. Fyodor Dostoevsky, 'The Gambler', in *The Gambler/Bobok/A Nasty Story*, Penguin Classics, p. 38. Cf. also 'And what a lot of clamour and uproar and talk and noise!' (p. 51).
44. Ibid., pp. 128.
45. Ibid., pp. 153. The remark is an obvious paraphrase of the Abbé Sieyes: 'What is the *tiers état*? Nothing. What could it become? Everything', which gives the hunger for miracle a political connotation, as with Raskolnikov in *Crime and Punishment*. Cf. also 'To be restored to life, to rise again' (p.161).
46. 'The Gambler', p. 40.
47. N. K. Gudzy, 'K istorii legendy o pape Grigorii' ['On the History of the Legend of Pope Gregory'], *Izvestiya ORYaS za 1914 g.*, XIX, book 1, Petrograd, 1915, pp. 247–56; Gudzy, 'K legendam o Iude-predatele i Andree Kritskom' ['On the Legends about Judas the Betrayer and Andrew of Crete'], *Russkii filolog, Vestnik*, 1915, No. 1, pp. 11, 18.
48. N. A. Nekrasov, 'Vlas', *Izbrannye proizvedeniya*, I, Moscow, 1966, pp. 100–3.
49. Ivan Turgenev, *A House of Gentlefolk*, translated by Constance Garnett, London, 1922, p. 144.
50. *Polnoe sobranie russkikh letopisei [Complete Collection of Russian Chronicles]*, vol. VI, St Petersburg, 1853, p. 88.
51. See the very clear expression of this idea in the 'apocrypha', 'The Conversation of the Three Holy Men': 'What is the height of heavens, the breadth of the earth and the depth of the sea? Ioann said, Father, Son and Holy Spirit' (*Pamyatniki starinnoi russkoi literatury*, III, St Petersburg, 1862, p. 169).
52. *Pamyatniki*, pp. 119, 122. See also in 'The Lay of the Three Monks, how they found Saint Mokary' where heaven is described as a special country: you have to pass through the cities 'one of iron, one of brass and beyond the cities is God's paradise' (ibid., p. 139).
53. *Polnoe sobranie*, vol. VI, pp. 87–8.
54. A. N. Veselovsky, *Yuzhnorusskie byliny [Southern Russian Folk Epics]*, St Petersburg, 1881, p. 345.
55. N. A. Meshchersky, *Istoriya Iudeiskoi voiny Iosifa Flaviya v dreverusskom*

perevode [*The History of the Jewish War by Josephus Flavius in an Early Russian Translation*], Moscow/Leningrad, 1958, p. 256.

56. A. N. Ostrovsky, *Groza* [*The Storm*], in *Izbrannye proizvedeniya*, Moscow, 1965, p. 111.
57. *The Life of the Archpriest Avvakum*, translated by Jane Harrison and Hope Mirlees, London, 1963, p. 120.
58. Ibid., p. 131.
59. *Pamyatniki*, p. 134.
60. Nikolai Gogol, 'Strashnaya mest'' ['A Terrible Vengeance'], *Sobranie sochinenii v semi tomakh* [*Collected works in seven volumes*], I, pp. 199–200.
61. All references are to *The Divine Comedy of Dante Alighieri*, with translation and comment by John D. Sinclair, Oxford, 1961.
62. Pavel Florensky, *Mnimosti v geometrii. Rasshirenie oblast' dvukhmernykh obrazov (opyt novogo istolkovaniya mnimostei)* [*Illusions in Geometry. The Extension of the Domain of Two-Dimensional Images (An Attempt at a New Interpretation of Illusions)*], Moscow, 1922, pp. 43–44. 'The turnover of a normal is determined by whether we are staying on the same side (i.e. on a single-sided surface) or whether we go on to the other side, one coordinate of which is actual, and the other illusory (a two-sided surface). . . . And now with regard to *this very* one and the same transformation, the one-sided surface and the two-sided surface behave *in opposite ways*. If it turns over the normal on one surface it will not turn it over on the other, and vice versa' (Florensky's emphasis).
63. Ibid., pp. 46–8.
64. On the semiotic saturation of the *Comedy*, see D'Arco Silvio Avalle, *Modelli semiologici nella Commedia di Dante*, Milan, 1975, especially the section 'Ulysses' last journey'; for further literature on the theme 'Dante and semiotics' see the bibliography prepared by Simonetta Salvestroni in Ju. M. Lotman and S. Salvestroni, 'Il viaggio di Ulisse nella *Divina Commedia* di Dante', in Yury M. Lotman, *Testo e contesto. Semiotica dell'arte e della cultura*, Rome/Bari, 1980. The present chapter is a shortened version of the latter.
65. V. V. Bychkov, *Vizantiiskaya estetika. Teoreticheskie problemy* [*Byzantine Aesthetics. Theoretical Problems*], Moscow, 1977, p. 129.
66. 'But because fraud is a sin peculiar to man it is more offensive to God, and for that reason the fraudulent have their place lower and more pain assails them' (*Inferno*, XI, 25–8).
67. [St Augustine] *Tvoreniya blazhennogo Avgustina, episkop Ipponiiskogo* [*The Works of the Blessed Augustine, Bishop of Hippo*], 2nd edition, Kiev, 1905, p. 258.
68. P. Vinassa de Regny, *Dante e Pitagora* [*Dante and Pythagorus*], Milan, 1955. None the less it is indicative that in Purgatory movement upwards is allowed only during sunlight, during the hours of darkness it is allowed only to go down or to go in a circle around the mountain (*Purgatory*, VII, 52–9). The association of circular movement with darkness and direct movement and ascent with the light is an indication of the sinfulness of the former and the righteousness of tthe latter. In Purgatory circular movements are made to the right (*Purgatory*, XIII, 13–16) while in Hell, with two exceptions they

are to the left.

69. The sinfulness of circular movement is felt only in Hell since it is associated with ever-increasing spatial confinement, as against the ever-widening spaciousness of the heavenly spheres and the infinity of the shining Empyrean.

    The space of Hell is not only confined but coarsely material. It is to be contrasted with the ideal space which is both infinitely reduced to a single Point (*Paradise*, XXVIII, 16, 22–5; XXIX, 16–18) and infinitely expanded. This opposition is supplemented by those of light/darkness, fragrance/stench, warmth/extreme heat or cold, which all add up to the semiotic structure of Dante's universe.

70. A. Hartmann, *Untersuchungen über die Sagen vom Tod des Odysseus*, Munich, 1917; W. Standford, 'Dante's Conception of Ulysses', *The Cambridge Journal*, 4, 1953; idem, *The Ulysses Theme. A Study in the Adaptability of a Traditional Hero*, 2nd edition, Oxford, 1966 (bibliography); see also, M. Grabar-Passek, *Antichnye syuzhety i formy v zapadnoevropeiskoi literature* [*Classical Plots and Forms in West European Literature*], Moscow, 1966; D'Arco Silvio Avalle, op.cit., pp. 33–64; E. Forti, *Magnanimitade*, Bologna, 1977, pp. 162–206.

71. The actual line of Dante's movement through the circles of Hell is a spiral, i.e. it goes in two directions: around and down, and the line of his movement in the heavenly spheres is a complex one, but the *semantics* of his movements in the code structure of Dantean space is an ascent. Ulysses' path is slightly distorted by the surface of the earth and the inclination of his ship to left ('always gaining on the left' *Inferno*, XXVI, 126). But in the code sense he also travels in a straight line.

72. S. Ya. Lur'e, 'Dom v lesu' ['The House in the Forest'], *Yazyk i literatura*, VIII, Leningrad, 1932; V. Ya. Propp, *Istoricheskie korni volshebnoi skazki* [*The Historical Roots of the Folktale*], Leningrad, 1946, pp. 42–53, 97–103; on the symbolism of the Home, see G. Bachelard, *La poétique de l'espace*, Paris; Vyach. Vs. Ivanov, V. N. Toporov, *Slavyanskie yazykovye model-iruyushchie semioticheskie systemy* [*Slavonic Linguistic Modelling Semiotic Systems*], Moscow, 1965, pp. 168–75.

73. Mikhail Bulgakov, *The Master and Margarita*, trans. by Michael Glenny, London 1988. (Page references to this edition are given in the text in square brackets.)

74. ' "Completely!" cried Koroviev . . . "I saw it happen. Can you believe it? Bang – his head was off, scrunch – away went his right leg, scrunch – off came his left leg!" ' [226].

75. In the Turbins' home, in Bulgakov's novel, *The White Guard*, there was 'a bronze lamp with a shade, the most wonderful bookcases smelling of mysterious old-fashioned chocolate with Natasha Rostov and the Captain's Daughter in them.' The end of the home was signalled by the burning of 'the Captain's Daughter in the stove'.

76. Cf. in *The White Guard*, 'For many years before [mother's] death the tiled stove in the dining room warmed and nurtured little Elena, Aleksei who was older, and tiny Nikolka.' The stove is the symbol of the home, its penates its protecting divinity. Contrasting with it is the infernal glow of the coals in

the flat; compare the contrast between candlelight in the windows of the Home and electric light in the anti-home

77. *The White Guard.*

78. The force of the theatre for rebirth is a symmetrical mirror-image of Woland's miraculous destructive globe: 'A house the size of a pea grew until it was as large as a matchbox. Suddenly and noiselessly its roof flew upwards' [296]. Here a real house shrinks to the size of a matchbox and loses reality while in *Theatrical Novel* the box grows to the size of a house and becomes a real one.

79. Yu. M. Lotman, and B. A. Uspenskij, 'Echoes of the Notion "Moscow as the Third Rome" in Peter the Great's Ideology', *The Semiotics of Russian Culture*, ed. Ann Shukman, Ann Arbor, 1984, pp. 53–67.

80. On the comparison of this with the transfer of the capital to Petersburg, see [Wackerbart], *Sravnenie Petra Velikogo s Karlom Velikim [A Comparison of Peter the Great with Charlemagne]*, translated from the German by Yakov Lizogub, St Petersburg, 1809, p. 70; cf. E. F. Shmurlo, *Petr Velikii v russkoi literature [Peter the Great in Russian Literature]*, St Petersburg, 1889, p. 41.

81. So Svyatoslav transferring his capital to Bulgaria paradoxically declared: 'Since it is the centre of my lands, all good things will come to it.' *Polnoe sobranie russkikh letopisei [Complete Collection of Russian Chronicles]* vol. I, Moscow, 1962, col. 67.

82. 'And the Lord God is angry with it and will send his archangel Michael and will cleave that city with his sickle, smite it with his sceptre, roll it like a millstone and will drown it with the people in the depths of the sea and that city will perish; only a steeple will remain. . . . And the merchants arriving in their ships will moor their vessels to the steeple and will begin to cry saying: "O great and proud Tsar-City! How many years have we come to you to trade and to grow rich; and now in a trice the mighty sea has covered you and all your precious buildings and you have vanished without trace".' *Pamyatniki otrechennoi russkoi literatury, sobrany i izdany Nikolaem Tikhnravovym [Memorials of Unacknowledged Russian Literature Collected and Published by Nikolai Tikhonravov]*, vol. II, Moscow, 1863, p. 262; cf. 'the great city will be drowned by God's wrath under the waters of the river Edes' (A. Popov, *Obzor khronografov russkoi redaktsii [Survey of Chronographers of Russian Redaction]*, Moscow, 1869, p. 62); also, ibid., 'about the drowning of the city of Lakris'; cf. V. Peretts, 'Neskol'ko dannykh k ob'yasneniyu skazanii o provalivshikhsya gorodakh' ['Some Data to Explain the Tales about Ruined Cities'], *Sbornik istoriko-filologicheskogo obshchestva pri Khar'kovskom universitete*, 1894 (off-print, Kharkov, 1896).

83. V. Sollogub, *Vospominaniya [Memoirs]*, Moscow/Leningrad, 1931, pp. 183–4. Cf. M. Dmitriev's poem 'The Drowned City', Odoevsky's story 'The Deadman's Mockery' from *Russian Nights*, and many others. N. Pakhomov, who made a study of Lermontov's paintings, described these sketches, which have, unfortunately, been lost, as 'views of the flood in Petersburg' (*Literaturnoe nasledstvo*, vols 45–6, Moscow, 1948, p. 211). But of course the sketches were eschatological views of the end of the city and not views of a flood. See Dmitriev's poem 'The Drowned City' when the old fisherman

says to the boy: 'Do you see the spire? Just a year ago/We were rocked a year gone by/Do you remember how we tied/ Our boat to it?/This was a city, free for everyone/master of all;/Now from the belltower we can see only the spire above the sea!' (M. A. Dmitriev, *Stikhotvoreniya* [*Poems*], part 1, Moscow, 1865, p. 176).

84. See A. P. Sumarokov's lines: 'The mountain moved, and changing its place/And seeing an end to its upright position/Crossed the Baltic waves/And fell at the feet of Peter's horse here' (*Izbrannye proizvedeniya* [*Selected Works*], Leningrad, 1957, p. 110). This is the motif of unnatural movement: something immobile (a mountain) is given features of movement ('moved', 'changing its place', 'crossed', 'fell'). Cf. the self-parody: 'This mountain is not bread – it's made of stone not dough/And it's difficult to move it from its place/But it moved and changing its place/Fell at the tail of the bronze horse here' (ibid., p. 111).

85. F. I. Tyutchev, *Lirika* [*Lyrics*], Leningrad/Moscow, 1966, p. 103. In the symbolic structure of this poem the rock is Russia, which for Tyutchev was an antonym, rather than a synonym, for Petersburg. Cf. the typically 'Petersburgian' oxymoron of the marsh turned to stone: 'In defiance of all the elements/With creative force, in a moment/the marsh turned to stone/The city rose up' (V. Romanovsky, 'Peterburg s admiralteiskoi bashni' ['Petersburg from the Admiralty Tower'], *Sovremennik*, 5, 1837, p. 292.

86. V. F. Odoevsky, *Russkie nochi [Russian Nights]*, Leningrad, 1957, pp. 51–2.

87. *L'image du monde renversé et ses répresentations littéraires et paralittéraires de la fin du XVI-e siècle au milieu du XVII-e. Colloque international.* Tours, 17–19 novembre 1977. Paris, 1979.

88. See F. Delpech, *Aspects des pays de Cocagne*, pp. 35–48; *La mort des pays de Cocagne. Comportements collectif de la Renaissance a l'âge classique*, Paris, 1976 (sous la direction de Jean Delumeau).

89. Lotman and Uspenskij, op.cit.

90. Pavel L'vov, 'Puteshestvie ot Peterburga do Belozerska' ['A Journey from Petersburg to Belozersk'], *Severny vestnik*, part IV, no. 11, 1804, p. 187.

91. *Pamyatniki otrechennoi literatury* II, p. 263. With this reading it is the serpent which commands the mountains to change place. He then is the cooperator and not the opponent of Peter who commands the elements. The persistent identification of the horse with Russia ('he has made Russia rear up'), which is supported also by Methodius of Patara's prophecy puts the horseman and the serpent on the same side.

92. In this respect culture and technology are opposed: in culture all of its past is operative in the present, whereas with technology only the latest temporal period. This is why the technologization of the city which happened so rapidly in the twentieth century has inevitably led to the destruction of the city as an *historical* organism.

93. On Petersburg as a utopian attempt to create the Russia of the future, see D. Greyer, 'Peter und St Petersburg', *Jahrbucher für Geschichte Osteuropas*, Wiesbaden, 1962, vol. 10, no. 2, pp. 181–200. Cf. the comparison between Petersburg which was momentarily created and 'historical' Moscow by Dmitriev (op.cit., p. 18): '[Petersburg] obedient to the Great One,/Was created by a powerful hand!/Our city [Moscow] is not made with hands/It

formed itself.'

94. V. F. Oduevsky, *Sochineniya v dvukh tomakh* [*Works in two volumes*], vol. 2, Moscow, 1981. The story 'The Sylphide' from which this quotation comes was published in Pushkin's journal *The Contemporary* [*Sovremennik*], vol. V, 1837, after Pushkin's death in January 1837, but Pushkin undoubtedly knew it because it was passed by the censor on 11 November 1836.

95. Oberkirch, *Mémoires*, vol. 1, Paris, 1853, p. 357; *Russkii arkhiv*, 3, 1869, p. 517.

96. [I. V. Selivanov] *Vospominaniya proshedshego. Byli, rasskazy, portrety, ocherki i proch, avtora provintsial'nykh vospominanii* [*Memories of the Past. Events, stories, portraits, sketches and other things of an author of provincial memories*], no. 2, Moscow, 1868, pp. 19–20.

97. A. I. Del'vig, *Moi vospominaniya* [*My Memories*], vol. 1, Moscow, 1912, p. 158. Anna Petrovna Kern was mistaken about the almanac in which the story was published, but that the publisher was Delvig she remembered clearly. After the publication, Delvig recommended Titov to Zhukovsky as a promising writer.

Delvig's death set off a whole cycle of mystery stories. His mother and sister told how on the day of his death on their estate in Tula which was many hundreds of miles from Petersburg, the village priest prayed 'not for the health, but for the repose of the soul of Baron Anton'. Delvig's nephew, an extremely rational person, when he told this story, remarked, 'I would not have mentioned this easily explained mistake were it not that in Delvig's lifetime many seemingly miraculous things kept happening' (A. I. Delvig, *Zapiski. Polveka russkoi zhizni* [*Notes. Half a century of Russian Life*], vol. I, Moscow/Leningrad, 1930, p. 168. The poet Kozlov also cultivated mystery stories as did other literary salons of the 1830s.

98. *La Russie en 1839 par Marquis de Custine*, 2nd edition, vol. I, Paris, 1843, p. 262.

99. Ibid., pp. 352–3.

100. Quoted from *Vissarion Grigor'evich Belinsky v vospominaniyakh sovremennikov* [*V. G. Belinsky in the memories of his contemporaries*], Leningrad, 1929, pp. 250–1.

101. N. Shchedrin (M. E. Saltykov), *Polnoe sobranie sochinenii* [*Complete collected of Works*], vol. XIV, Leningrad, 1936, p. 161. The expression 'they lived spiritually in France' did not exclude but rather presumed that the confrontation with the actual life of the West often ended in tragedy and converted the 'Westerner' into a critic of the West.

102. A. V. Nikitenko, *Dnevnik v trekh tomakh* [*Diary in three volumes*], vol. I, Leningrad, 1955, p. 283.

103. N. I. Pirogov, *Sochineniya* [*Works*], vol. I, St Petersburg, 1887, pp. 496–7. The last words find an echo in Aleksei Tolstoy's verses 'Councillor Popov's dream': 'He asked Popov maliciously/To be calm/Courteously showed him the chair.' This is evidence of the connection of Krylov's story with city gossip.

Important too is the pun which gives the story a literary completeness. From the time of Feofan Prokopovich there was a recurrent image in apologetic literature: Peter the Great, the sculptor, hewing [*vysekayushchii*] a beautiful statue, Russia, out of native rock. In a court sermon from the time of the Empress Elizabeth, Peter is described as transforming Russia 'with his own hands into a beautiful statue' (Shmurlo, 13). Karamzin began his outline for a panegyric to Peter with the image of Phidias sculpting [*vysekayushchii*] Jupiter out of a 'formless piece of marble' (N. M. Karamzin, *Neizdannye sochineniya i perepiska* [*Unpublished Works and Correspondence*], part I, 1862, p. 201). In Krylov's story the function of 'whipping [*vysech'*] Russia' is given to the Third Department which thus becomes the heir to Peter and turns its creative energy onto him.

Talk of 'secutions' (i.e. punishments) was the obligatory second pole of the Petersburg folklore. Eschatological expectations and the mythology of the Bronze Horseman were organically complemented by 'anecdotes' about the innocent clerk who is flogged [*vysechennom*]. The rich eccentric, S. V. Saltykov, whose stories Pushkin loved, made a remark to his wife which became a saying: 'Today I saw *le grand bourgeois* [the tsar, Yu. L.] . . . I assure you, *ma chère*, he *can* flog [*vyporot'*] you with birches if he *wants*; I repeat: he *can*' ('Dnevnik A. S. Pushkina' ['Pushkin's Diary'], *Trudy gos. Rumyantsovskogo muzeya*, I, Moscow, 1923, p. 143. We should add to this the rumours that Pushkin was whipped at the police station. With Gogol the theme of 'secution' grew out of the city anecdote.

104. P. Vyazemsky, *Staraya zapisnaya knizhka* [*Old Notebook*], Leningrad, 1929, p. 103. The somewhat obscure idea behind Pushkin's poem 'The tsar scowling' ['Brovi tsar' nakhmurya'] seems to be connected with city anecdotes of this kind since it provides all the main motifs of this plot.

105. Lotman and Uspenskij, op.cit., p. 57.

PART THREE

Cultural Memory, History and Semiotics

14

The problem of the historical fact

What are the aims of historical science? Is history a science? These questions have often been raised and the answers to them have been numerous. The historian not given to theorizing who concentrates on research into the primary material is usually content with Ranke's formula of re-establishing the past *'wie es eigentlich gewesen'* – as it actually was. The idea of re-establishing the past involves elucidating the facts and making connections between them. The facts are established by collecting and comparing documents and adopting a critical approach to them. From Scaliger to Francis Bradley and his followers, the critical approach to documents has meant testing which documents are genuine, analysing which interpolations are unreliable and which versions are tendentious. An important part of the preliminary work of an historian is to be able to read a document and, by textological procedures as well as intuition, to arrive at an understanding of its historical meaning.

But even granted that the reader of the document has broad erudition, experience and shrewdness, his or her position is in principle different from that of colleagues in any other field of science. The point is that by the word 'fact' the historian means something very unusual. Unlike the deductive sciences which construe their premises logically, or the experimental sciences which can observe them, the historian is condemned to *deal with texts*. In the experimental sciences a fact can be regarded at least in the initial stages as something primary, a datum which precedes the interpretation of it. A fact can be observed in laboratory conditions, can be repeated, can be subjected to statistical study.

The historian is condemned to deal with *texts*. The text stands between the event 'as it happened' and the historian, so that the scientific situation is radically altered. A text is always created by someone and for some purpose and events are presented in the text in an encoded form. The historian then has to act as decoder, and the fact is not a point of departure but the end-result of many labours. The historian creates facts by extracting non-textual reality from the text, and an event from a story about it.

Positivistic 'text criticism', which was popular in the nineteenth century, turned historians' attention to what seemed like conscious distortions of the truth, or the fruits of superstitions and ignorance; in the former case the sources of the 'untruth' were most frequently held to be the political prejudices of the text's author, and in making this judgement the historian often ascribed to the epoch being studied the psychology and political passions of his own time; in the latter case the judgement was made from the point of view of nineteenth-century science. Whatever did not accord with the scientific ideas of the day was declared to be the fruit of ignorance and fantasy. It was enough, so it was thought, to translate the text into the language of today (for instance, to subject mythological texts to psychoanalytic interpretation) and to remove or 'scientifically' explain away elements of the miraculous for the 'event' to emerge from the text.

For the researcher with experience of the semiotic interpretation of sources the question must obviously be looked at in another way: the code (or set of codes) which the creator of the text used has to be reconstructed and then correlated with the codes used by the researcher. The creator of the text recorded events which from his or her point of view seemed significant (i.e. correlated with elements of his or her code), and left out everything that was 'insignificant'. If the Russian chronicler entered the year into the chronicle but wrote nothing under the date – either leaving a blank or writing 'it was peaceful' (as we find in the Laurentian Chronicle for 1029)[1] this does not, of course, mean that from the point of view of the modern researcher nothing happened in those years.

A decoding is always a reconstruction. In fact, the researcher uses the same method whether reconstructing a lost part of a document or reading the part that has been preserved. In both cases the researcher proceeds from the fact that the document is *written in another language* whose grammar has to be learnt.

So before establishing the facts 'in themselves', the researcher establishes what were the facts for the person who composed the document being analysed. The researcher has be aware of the extent to which every document is incomplete in its reflection of life, of what huge layers of reality were not considered to be facts or worth recording. This domain of the 'excluded' is both vast and variable. The 'non-facts' of different periods would make interesting lists.

But it is not enough to know something of the general 'world outlook of the time'. Within any one period there exist various genres of texts, and each of them as a rule has its code specifics: what is permitted in one genre is forbidden in another. The researchers who contrast the 'realism' of classical comedy to the conventionality of tragedy assume that in the comedies we find 'genuine' life, not encoded by the rules of genre and other code systems. This is of course a naïve view. 'Realism' in this sense usually means that the text-code is similar to the historian's general views on life. The cinema-goer is subject to the same aberration when watching a film about another national or cultural tradition, and naively thinking that the film is 'simply' reproducing the life and customs of a distant country with ethnographic precision. The fact which the historian has to deal with is always a construct, conscious or unconscious, of the text-creator. For instance, in ancient Egyptian frescoes of the birth of Queen Hatshepsut she is shown as a boy in accordance with the rules of the genre, and if there had been no inscription or if it had not been preserved we would have had 'realistic' proof of her maleness. The 'facts of an epoch' form a complex and heterogeneous picture. Each genre, each culturally significant kind of text, makes *its own* selection of facts. A fact for a myth is not one for a chronicle, a fact on the fifteenth page of a newspaper is not a fact for the front page. So from the point of view of the addresser, a fact is always the result of selecting out of the mass of surrounding events an event which *according to his or her ideas is significant*.

But a fact is not a concept, not an idea, it is a text, i.e. it always has an actual material embodiment; it is an event which is considered meaningful, and not, like a parable, a meaning which is given the form of an event. As a result, a fact selected by the addresser is wider than the meaning ascribed to it in the code; it is consequently unambiguous for the addresser, while for the addressee (which includes the historian) it *has to be interpreted*. The historian reconstructs the sender's code in order to explain the sender's attitude towards the facts being communicated, but also has to re-establish the entire spectrum of possible interpretations which the contemporary receivers of the text gave to what they thought were facts and the significance they gave them. Finally, because the fact, being a text, invariably includes extra-systematic elements which, from the point of view of the codes of the epoch which created it, are insignificant, the historian can select the elements which *from his or her point of view* seem significant.

In 1945 in Upper Egypt near the village of Nag Hammadi (the ancient Henoboskion) a cache was found of several codices of Gnostic writings in the Coptic language. Among them was the so-called 'Gospel of Thomas'.[2] In logion 76 (according to Doresse's division which is accepted by Trofimova) we read: '[A man said] to Him: Tell my brethren to divide my father's possessions with me. He said to him: O man, who made Me [a] divider? He turned to His disciples, he said to them: I am not a divider, am I?'

The reader can choose whether to interpret this saying literally or symbolically. According to a literal interpretation, Jesus is refusing to take part in the division of earthly possessions because this is a matter of 'this world'. According to a symbolic interpretation the meaning lies in the ever-deepening image of evil which is associated with division, and of good which is characterized by union and the fusion of opposites. The symbolic reading leads eventually to the Gnostic idea that division is a characteristic of the material and illusory world and that unification is a characteristic of the spiritual essence of the All. But in either event both the transmitter and the receiver of the text took the meaning from Jesus' words which are open to deep interpretation. The rest of the text, since it contains no teaching, is 'outside the system'. But for the modern researcher the 'fact' may also be the whole scenario described in the logion as well as Jesus' words: first, there are the words with a direct bearing on everyday life: Christ speaks addressing 'a man' and evidently standing with his back to the disciples who are in the background. Then turning to the disciples he translates the whole situation into the language of hidden mysteries with the words: 'I am not a divider, am I?'

From a certain point of view, even the gestures of a scenario can be a 'fact' for the researcher. But whether these details are seen as an element in the poetics of the given text or as evidence of a visual memory of a scene which actually took place, is a question for further interpretation.

So historical science has from the very beginning been in a strange position: in other sciences a fact is the point of departure, the primary foundation from which science proceeds to discover connections and laws. But in the sphere of culture a fact is the result of a preparatory analysis. It is created by the scholar in the research process and is never something absolute. A fact is relative in relation to the universum of culture. It floats up from the semiotic space and is dissolved in it as the cultural codes alter. Yet because it is a text this semiotic space does not wholly determine it: with its non-systematic elements it revolutionizes the system, prompting the system to become restructured.

15

Historical laws and the structure of the text

(Many of the ideas in this section were discussed with B. A. Uspensky and it is through our long-standing friendship and our many conversations that my own ideas have taken shape. Uspensky's views on the problems of the historical process can be found in his articles published in Trudy po znakovym sistemam, *vols. 22–4. Yu. L.)*

The historian has to deal with texts; this circumstance has a crucial effect on the structure of the historical fact and the interpretation of it, as we mentioned in the last chapter, but it also affects our ideas about historical laws. The historian cannot observe events, but acquires narratives of them from the written sources. And even when the historian is an observer of the events described (examples of this rare occurrence are Herodotus and Julius Caesar) the observations still have to be mentally transformed into a verbal text, since the historian writes not of what was seen but a digest of what was seen in narrative form. In the past historians sometimes drew a distinction between information derived from written sources, which was felt to be ambivalent and in need of interpretation, and the irrefutable evidence of material culture, archaeological data and iconic depictions. But from the point of view of semiotics these are all texts and all share the consequences of using a text as medium, so the question of the influence of the text on historical knowledge cannot be avoided.

The transformation of an event into a text involves, first, narrating it in the system of a particular language, i.e. subjecting it to a previously given structural organization. The event itself may seem to the viewer (or participant) to be disorganized (chaotic) or to have an organization which is beyond the field of interpretation, or indeed to be an accumulation of

221

several discrete structures. But when an event is retold by means of a language then it inevitably acquires a structural unity. This unity, which in fact belongs only to the expression level, inevitably becomes transferred to the level of content too. So the very fact of transforming an event into a text raises the degree of its organization. Besides, the interpreter invariably applies to the real-life associations of the event the system of associations in the language. Roman Jakobson in this connection made a perspicacious remark that,

> When considering the grammatical universals or near-universals detected by J. H. Greenberg, I noted that the order of meaningful elements by virtue of its palpably iconic character displays a particularly clear-cut universalistic propensity (see my paper in *The Universals of Language*, ed. J. Greenberg, 1963). Precisely therefore, the precedence of the conditional clause, with regard to the conclusion, is the only admitted or primary, neutral, non-marked order in the conditional sentences of all languages. If almost everywhere, again according to Greenberg's data, the only, or at least the predominant, basic order in declarative sentences with nominal subject and object is one in which the former precedes the latter, this grammatical process obviously reflects the hierarchy of the grammatical concepts. The subject on which the action is predicated is, in Edward Sapir's terms, 'conceived of as the starting point, the "doer" of the action' in contradistinction to 'the end point, the "object" of the action.' The subject, the only independent term in the clause, singles out what the message is about. Whatever the actual rank of the agent, he is necessarily promoted to hero of the message as soon as he assumes the role of the subject. 'The subordinate obeys the principal'. Notwithstanding the tables of ranks, attention is first of all focused on the subordinate as agent, turns thereupon to the undergoer, the 'goal' of his action, the principal obeyed.[3]

We should bear in mind that Jakobson is in fact here speaking of two different things. In the first part of his argument he is stressing his polemics with Saussure that there is an element of iconism in linguistic structures and as a result of which in grammar too, as in non-linguistic reality, causes and conditions precede consequences and results. But in the latter part of the quotation he is arguing that the grammatical structure of a text predetermines the disposition of roles in the non-textual sphere. In the first part reality imposes its structure on language, while in the second language is imposing its organization on reality.

A speech utterance inevitably organizes material in temporal and causal coordinates since these are inherent to the structure of language. However, in a sentence we clearly perceive the compulsion of grammatical organization of the material, but in the higher levels of syntagmatic organization what we notice are the principles of narrative organization. Narration presupposes that the text is coherent. Text-coherence is achieved by the repetition of certain structual elements in sequentially disposed sentences. E. V. Paducheva, in her study of the problems of text-coherence, gives an example of what happens when this postulate is violated; her examples comes from the speech of one of the characters in Evgeny Shvarts's play *The Dragon* who is pretending to be a schizophrenic:

> *Mayor*: Millers have just got in a new delivery of cheese. Nothing goes better on a girl than modesty and a dress you can see through. At sunset wild ducks flew over the cradle. They're waiting for you at the council meeting, Sir Lancelot.[4]

Paducheva concludes:

> A description of how the combination of units in the text is restricted requires as a rule an analysis of the structure of these units. Very often the laws governing the combination of units can be reduced to the need to repeat some component parts of these units. So the formal structure of verse is based (in part) on the repetition of phonetic syllables; the agreement of noun and adjective on the similarity of gender, number and case; the combination of phonemes can often be reduced to the rule that in contiguous phonemes a differential feature of the same significance must be repeated. The coherence of a text in a paragraph is largely based on the repetition of the same semantic elements in contiguous sentences.[5]

The semantic coherence of narrative segments is what forms plot, and plot is as much the law of a narrative text as syntagmatic ordering is the law for correct speech. But if a narrative about reality requires a plot (or plots) this in no way means that plots are immanent to reality. Events of real life which occupy a particular space–time continuum, are drawn out into a linear plot by a narrative text.

Consequently the very necessity that compels the historian to rely on texts, and compels the texts to narrate the events according to the laws of linguistic, logical, rhetorical and narrative constructions, means that historical reality reaches the historian in a form which he knows is distorted. On top of this is the ideological encoding which is hierarchically the highest stage in the construction of the narrative text: it includes the genre code as well as political, social, religious and philosophical ones.

In an attempt to overcome the difficulties which we have been listing there arose a new trend in French historiography, one which has lasted now over fifty years and which is known as the school of *l'histoire nouvelle*, or *l'histoire de la longue durée*.

The immediate impulse for this new direction was the apparent crisis in political history of a positivistic approach; since the second half of the nineteenth century this school had been reduced to fact-gathering and theoretical poverty. The new school aimed to rid history of lists of the doings of rulers and biographies of great men and instead to study the life of the masses and the anonymous processes of history. Jacques Le Goff counted among his predecessors in this approach Voltaire, Chateaubriand, Guizot and Michelet.[6] We could add the name of Leo Tolstoy, who was uncompromising in his belief that real history happens in private life and in the unconscious movements of the masses, and who never tired of ridiculing apologias for 'great men'.[7]

But the *histoire nouvelle* movement had a more serious aim than just distinguishing itself from long-discredited scholarly eclecticism. One of its chief impulses was to escape from the charmed circle we have been describing. This impulse led them to criticize the very notion of 'historical fact' and to try to rid history of 'historical personalities'. Hence the well-known saying of Lucien Febvre and Marc Bloch: *'l'histoire des hommes, non de l'Homme'*. The school has studied the impersonal, collective historical processes which determine the movement of the masses who are not aware of the forces acting on them; this innovatory approach has led them to subjects far beyond the normal, routine topics for research. We refer to the works of Le Goff, J. Delumeau, M. Vovelle, Ph. Ariès and among Italian historians, Carlo Ginzburg.

No less remarkable is their aim of escaping from the narrativity normal in historical writings. In fact this aim is a reflection of their idea of history 'over a long period' or, as Fernand Braudel put it more boldly, *'l'histoire prèsqu'immobile'*, or Le Roy Ladurie still more trenchantly, *'l'histoire immobile'*. True though, there has not been much support for such extreme views. But their attempt make history resemble anthropology and to focus attention on the slowest-moving processes is indicative of their desire to avoid the danger of narrative history. In its place they put descriptions of historical continua. In the final analysis history is regarded as a kind of geological process which has its effect on people without any assistance from them.

This trend brought a breath of fresh air into historical science and enriched it with many works which are already classics.

Yet not all the principles of this school can be totally accepted. History is not *only* a conscious process, and it is not *only* an unconscious process. It is a mutual tension between the two.

The *nouvelle histoire* school stood for a broad synthesis of all the sciences. Hence the title of the journal *Revue de synthèse historique* and the title of H. Berr's book published as far back as 1921, *L'Histoire traditionelle et la synthèse historique*. Marc Bloch also emphasized this,[8] but it is glaringly obvious that this synthesis, which is made basically with economics and sociology, takes no account of linguistics although this was just the period when linguistics was making its revolutionary changes. The French historical school hardly noticed one of the most significant events in the science of this half-century: the historic meeting between Roman Jakobson and Claude Lévi-Strauss which led to linguistics being put as the foundation of both anthropology and ethnology, at least in the works of Lévi-Strauss. At about the same time French structuralism was developing and advocating synchronic analysis, though it made no incursions into the 'alien' territory of the historians.

Yet a parallel between history and the history of language seems entirely appropriate. The history of language, or at least of languages with written cultures, develops in the tension between two poles: living, oral speech and the written literary tradition. In his study of the history of the Russian language, Boris Uspensky has written:

> The literary language tends towards stability, living speech towards change. Hence there is always a gap between the literary language and living speech, and this gap creates as it were a constant tension between these poles, rather like a magnetic field. The degree of difference between the literary language and living speech is determined by the *type* of literary language . . .
>
> We might say that the different nature of evolution in the system [i.e. of the living language, Yu. L.] and in the norm [i.e. of the literary language, Yu. L.] comes down to the difference between discrete and continuous development.

Uspensky explains that 'unlike the evolution of a system, the evolution of a norm – including also . . . the norm of the literary language – is not continuous, but discrete (goes in stages).' And further:

> So if the history of the language can be understood as an objective process which in principle is not dependent on the attitude of the speakers to it, then the development of the literary language is directly dependent on the changing attitudes of the language-users.[9]

The history of a language is a typical mass and anonymous phenomenon, a process of *longue durée*. But the history of a literary language is a history of creativity, a process which is bound up with individual activity and which is highly unpredictable. If 'political history' overlooked one aspect of the dual historical process, then the 'new history' has overlooked the other. Like the history of language, any dynamic process involving human beings, fluctuates between the pole of continuous slow change, typical of processes on which the consciousness and will of humanity has no influence and which are often simply ignored because their periodicity is longer than that of one generation; and the pole of conscious human activity resulting from individual efforts of mind and will. The one pole can no more be detached from the other than north from south. The opposition between them is a condition for their existence. What is more, these tendencies are realized on all levels. In the individual genius of Byron there are large elements of anonymous mass processes, and in any representative of the early nineteenth century 'mass culture' of European Byronism there are elements of creative individuality. Whatever people do or participate in must to some extent involve the anonymous processes of history, but also involves the personal principle. The very essence of the human relationship to culture ensures this: the personality is both isomorphic to the universum, and at the same time a part of it. Moreover whether an element of history belongs to either of the two possible hypostases in any given case depends not on that element's immanent essence, but on the position adopted by the historian describing it. Is dandyism a fact of mass culture as we are inclined to think on account of our normal disparagement of such phenomena as fashion, or is it individuality laying its imprint on the anonymous 'slow' history of its time? The simple act of shifting a fact from one line of associations to another can turn what is a matter of tradition into something individual.

The different degree to which conscious human efforts are involved in different levels of the single historical process affects our evaluation of chance and of individual creative potential. The aim of 'freeing history from the great men' may turn out to be history without creativity and history without thought or freedom: without either freedom of thought or freedom of will, i.e. without the possibility of *choice*. In this respect there is an unexpected similarity between Hegel and the historians of the 'new school', who are complete opposites in all other ways. Hegel's historiosophy is based on the idea of movement towards freedom as the aim of the historical process. But this primordially determined aim itself surely negates the question of freedom, as is quite clear from Hegel's own argument. Hegel's conviction that 'the world of reason and self-conscious will is not given over to chance' follows quite logically. There is a direct connection between the denial of the role of chance in history and Hegel's idea that 'the world of reason' as it comes to be realized is the last act of world history which, having acquired self-knowledge, reaches its conclusion. In the introduction to his *Philosophy of History* Hegel wrote:

> The principle of *Development* involves also the existence of a latent germ of being – a capacity or potentiality striving to realize itself. This formal conception finds actual existence in Spirit; which has the History of the World for its theatre, its possession, and the sphere of its realization. It is not of such a nature to be tossed to and fro amid the superficial play of

accidents but is rather the absolute arbiter of things; entirely unmoved by contingencies, which, indeed, it applies and manages for its own purposes.[10]

This trend of thought leads logically to a picture of the unconditional and predetermined fusion of the particular with the general:

> The principles of the successive phases of Spirit that animate the Nations in a necessitated gradation, are themselves only steps in the development of the one universal Spirit, which through them elevates and completes itself to a self-comprehending *totality*.[11]

So in Hegel's argument the freedom for the individual is not the freedom to choose between alternatives but the freedom to merge the self with the necessity of the historical process.

For Hegel the Spirit is realized through great men, while for the historians of the new school the anonymous forces which direct historical development are realized through the unconscious manifestations of the masses. In both cases the movement of history is a movement which allows no choice.

Is this really so?

Let us leave aside what these approaches do to human intellectual capacity and moral responsibility and let us look at the question from another point of view. Indeterminacy is the measure of information. Minimal information is contained in the choice between two equally probable possibilities. As the reserve of indeterminacy becomes exhausted the degree of information drops, falling to zero at the moment when it becomes entirely redundant, i.e. totally predictable. Let us imagine a stone thrown along a certain trajectory. If we could calculate all the forces acting on it before it was thrown and if we could wholly exclude any new factors affecting its flight, then we will know where it will fall before it began its trajectory. Consequently, in order to find out at what time the stone will be at any given point in the trajectory, it is not necessary to throw it. But let us change the circumstances. Suppose we cannot calculate *all* the factors which will appear as the stone moves along its trajectory. Then the accuracy of our prediction will increase as the flight proceeds and at the same time the redundancy of the rest of the text will increase as well (by text we mean the trajectory of the stone which a tracking mechanism synchronically outlines on its screen). Redundancy is in reverse proportion to information, and information will proportionally decrease the greater the distance the stone has travelled and the fewer possible alternatives present themselves in its further course. Of course, if the stone were able to choose its path from moment to moment of its flight the information-potential would be high.

The documented history of mankind has lasted some thousands of years. If the historical process had not had mechanisms of unpredictability, i.e. if it had not involved chance, – chance, not merely 'the embroidery on the surface of the canvas of the constant factors' (Febvre's expression in his review of Braudel's *La Meditéranée et le Monde meditérranéen à l'époque de Philippe II*) but chance as an important functioning mechanism – history would long since have been redundant, and we would have been able to predict its course. But we know that this is not so. Even when the role of the individual is negligible and when the preceding state of the system is sufficiently well known (for instance, in the history of economics over the last three centuries, in the history of certain languages, in the history of technical inventions and living customs) prognosis is famed not for its successes but for its brilliant mistakes. And this is still more true of the history of human creativity which *l'histoire nouvelle* lost along with the cult of great men.

Let the reader understand me clearly. The new history school has been like a breath of fresh air in contemporary historiography and the works of Braudel, Le Goff, Delumeau, Vovelle and others have given the specialist professional pleasure and aesthetic pleasure as well, for there is a beauty to be found in precision of thought. Our criticism of some aspects of the methodology of these scholars is intended to point out the need for further development and not to deny their achievements.

Lying behind the methodology of this school we glimpse that age-old scientific conviction that science comes to an end at the point where determinacy ends. From Laplace's famous demon to Einstein's remark that 'God does not play dice', scientists have striven to exclude chance from the world or at least to put it outside the boundaries of science. Henri Poincaré was especially concerned with the nature of chance in his book *Science et Méthode* (Paris, 1908):

> We have become complete determinists, and even those who wish to reserve the right of human free will at least allow determinism to reign undisputed in the inorganic world. Every phenomenon, however trifling it be, has a cause, and a mind infinitely powerful and infinitely well informed concerning the laws of nature could have foreseen it from the beginning of the ages. If a being with such a mind existed, we could play no game of chance with him; we should always lose.[12]

And although later Poincaré qualified his belief that it is in reality impossible to account for many factors other than by probability, the spirit of Laplace's demon still haunted him: 'If we knew exactly the laws of nature and the situation of the universe at the initial moment, we could predict exactly the situation of that same universe at a succeeding moment.'[13]

As far as historical science is concerned, its special circumstances force the historian to choose between replacing history by non-scientific biographies of 'great men', or adopting strict determinism. We have already discussed the deformation which non-textual reality undergoes when it is turned into the text which is the historian's primary material. We have also seen how historians attempt to avoid this danger. But there is another source of deformation of reality, not this time originating with the text-creator but resulting from the actions of the interpreting historian.

History develops along a time-vector: its course is defined by the movement from past to present; but a historian looks at the texts from the present to the past. For the majority of authors who have studied the epistemology of historical science, the identity of the forward-looking and the retrospective points of view has been a self-evident truth and the question has not even been taken into account. They believed that the essence of the chain of events did not alter whether we look at them in the direction of the time vector or from the opposite point of view. Indeed, for those who regard history as a movement towards a certain goal, this view seemed a natural one, while for their opponents (see, for instance, Arnold Toynbee's criticism of the *nouvelle histoire* school) it was a methodologically convenient one.

Two chapters of Marc Bloch's *Apology for History* are symmetrically entitled 'Understanding the Present by the Past' and 'Understanding the Past by the Present', as if the historian were emphasizing the symmetry of the time-flows. Bloch indeed believed that the retrospective view allows the historian to distinguish the essential from the accidental:

> Even though [historians] restore its true direction afterwards, they have only benefited at the outset by reading history, as Maitland said, 'backwards'. . . . We must add that, in proceeding mechanically from early to late, there is always the risk of wasting time in tracking down the beginning or causes of phenomena which, in the event, may turn out to be somewhat imaginary.[14]

Comparing the past which the historian re-establishes to a film, Bloch makes use of a metaphor:

> In the film which he is examining, only the last picture remains quite clear. In order to reconstruct the faded features of the others it behooves him first to unwind the spool in the opposite direction from that in which the pictures were taken.[15]

Our reaction to Bloch's ideas is to say that in this film all the shots except for the first one are entirely predictable and consequently entirely redundant. But this is not the main point. More important is to notice that the very essence of the historical process is distorted. History is an asymmetrical, irreversible process. To use Marc Bloch's image history is a strange film because if we play it backwards we will not get back to the first shot. This is the nub of our disagreement. According to Bloch, and this is a natural consequence of adopting the retrospective view, the historian has to treat the events of the past as if they were *the only ones possible*:

> To evaluate the probability of an event is to weigh its chances of taking place. That granted, is it legitimate to speak of the possibility of a past event? Obviously not, in the absolute sense. Only the future has contingency. The past is something already given which leaves no room for possibility.[16]

Bloch's argument is strictly logical: his retrospective view inevitably leads to the conclusion that what actually happened is not only the most probable but also the only scenario possible. If, however, we start from the premise that an historical event is always the result of one of many possible alternatives and that the same conditions do not always produce the same results, then we must adopt other approaches to our material. Our methods will have to be different: we shall see that the events which actually took place are surrounded by clusters of unrealized possibilities. Let us imagine a film of someone's life from birth to death. If we view it backwards we shall say: this person was always presented with only one possibility and iron determinism governed his/her life until its end. The error of this approach will be obvious if we run the film in forward motion: then we shall see the film as a tale of missed opportunities and if we are to understand that person's life in depth we need a series of alternative shots. And it may be that in one version the hero dies at the age of sixteen on the barricades, while in another at the age of sixty he is denouncing his neighbours to the state security organs.

We have already made the point that history is an irreversible (unbalanced) process.

*   *   *

In order to grasp the essence of such processes and to understand what the implications are for history let us turn to the work of Ilya Prigogine and Isabella Stengers who have analysed these phenomena in their study of dynamic processes in chemistry, physics and biology. Their work has revolutionary significance for scientific thinking as a whole because they have tackled the problem of chance in the sciences and have moreover demonstrated the function of random phenomena in the general dynamics of the world.

Prigogine and Stengers in observing irreversible processes have identified various different forms of dynamism. Distinguishing between balanced and unbalanced structures, they point out that dynamic processes behave differently in different areas: 'The laws of equilibrium are universal. Matter near equilibrium behaves in a "repetitive" way.'[17] Dynamic processes occurring in conditions of equilibrium follow pre-determined curves. But the further they move from the entropic points of equilibrium the closer the movement comes to those critical points at which the predictable course of the processes breaks off. (Prigogine and Stengers call them bifurcation points.[18]) At these points the process reaches a point when clear predictability of the future is no longer possible. The next stage comes by the realization of one of several equally probable alternatives.

For our argument the important point is this: at the beginning of their book the authors refer to Isaiah Berlin for whom the difference between the natural and the humanitarian sciences lies in the difference between interest in the repeatable and interest in the unique. Then the authors remark that 'When we move from equilibrium to far-from-equilibrium conditions we move away from the repetitive and the universal to the specific and the unique.'[19]

In extreme conditions of disequilibrium the processes flow not in a smooth predetermined course, but they fluctuate.[20] At the moment of bifurcation the system is in a state when it is impossible to predict what new state it will move into. The most we can do it to indicate which of the states is possible. At this moment chance plays a decisive role (understanding chance not as the absence of causality, but as a phenomenon from another causal series). We should remember Ross Ashby's definition of some years' standing:

> By saying a factor is *random*, I do not refer to what the factor is in itself, but to the relation it has with the main system. Thus the successive digits of π are as determinate as any numbers can be, yet a block of a thousand of them might serve well as random numbers for agricultural experiments, not because they *are* random but because they are probably *uncorrelated* with the pecularities of a particualr set of plots. Supplementation by 'chance' thus means (apart from minor, special requirements) supplementation by taking effects (or variety) *from a system whose behaviour is uncorrelated with that of the main system.*[21]

The trajectory of movement in space with unequal distribution of equilibrium and disequilibrium relationships is outlined by Prigogine and Stengers as follows: '[a] fluctuation occurring at the "right moment" resulted in favouring one reaction path over a number of other equally possible paths'. Furthermore:

> Self-organization processes in far-from-equilibrium conditions correspond
> to a delicate interplay between chance and necessity, between fluctuations
> and deterministic laws. We expect that near a bifurcation, fluctuations or
> random elements would play an important role, while between bifurcations
> the deterministic aspects would become dominant.[22]

Chance and determinacy, therefore, cease to be incompatible concepts
and can now be seen as two possible states of one and the same object.
When it moves in a predetermined field it is like a point in a linear
development, but in the fluctuating field it is like a continuum of potential
possibilities with chance serving as the starter mechanism.

Prigogine and Stengers' ideas shed light on the general theory of
dynamic processes and can fruitfully be applied to the study of history.
The study of world history with its complex facts and the interweaving of
spontaneous and unconscious processes with personal and conscious ones
lends itself to this approach. We can explain the phenomenon we have
already remarked on that redundancy is maintained at a relatively
constant level by pointing to the alternation of predetermined epochs (or
rather epochs when predetermined processes predominate) and periods
when the role of bifurcation points increases. It would, though, be an
oversimplification to envisage the anonymous processes as totally
predetermined, and individual activity as subject to chance. First of all, in
history elements are neither wholly anonymous nor entirely the result of
personal efforts; it is always easy to see both principles at work. It is a
question of what proportion. Secondly, both these tendencies have their
periods of peaceful, predictable development and sudden break points
when determination and clear predictability recede to the background.
Something else is important which is specific to historical development
whose elements are individuals endowed with intelligence and freedom of
will. Back in 1929 Leo Szilard had published a work under the declarative
title 'On the decrease in entropy in the thermodynamic system under
interference from the thinking being'.[23] History is a process which takes
place 'with interference from a thinking being'. This means that at the
bifurcation points what comes into action is not only the mechanism of
chance but also the mechanism of *conscious choice* and this becomes the
most important *objective* factor in the historical process.

The task facing historical semiotics is to understand this factor in a new
light, to analyse how that human individual who has to make a choice
looks at the world. This approach is not too different from what the
nouvelle histoire calls *mentalité*. However the results of researches in this
field and a comparison of what Soviet scholars have achieved, (including
V. N. Toporov, B. A. Uspensky, Vyach. Vs. Ivanov, A. A. Zaliznyak,
and A. M. Piatigorsky, now living in England, as well as many others), in
the reconstruction of different ethno-cultural types of consciousness leads

us to the conclusion that historical semiotics is the most promising way forward.

If we look at the historical process as a time trajectory the bifurcation points are those historical moments when the tension between the opposing structural poles reaches a point of highest tension and the whole system leaves the state of equilibrium. At these moments the behaviour of individuals and of the masses ceases to be automatically predictable and determinacy recedes to the background. At these moments the movement of history should be pictured not as a trajectory but as a continuum that is potentially capable of resolving itself into any number of variants. These nodal points with diminished predictability are times of revolution or other dramatic historical shifts. The choice which will be realized depends on a complex of chance circumstances, but even more on the self-awareness of the people involved. This is why at such times speech, discourse, propaganda have especially great *historical* significance. And if *before* the choice was made the situation was unpredictable, *after* the choice has been made the situation is one that in principle is a new one, a situation for which that choice was essential, and which in the future course of history will seem to have been inevitable. The choice which was open to chance *before* seems predetermined *afterwards*. A retrospective view intensifies determinacy and for the future course of history that choice will seem like the first link in a new law of history.

Prigogine remarks that at moments of bifurcation the process acquires individuality taking on the characteristics of a human being. We could chart the degrees of intensity of unpredictability: the interference of chance – the interference of a thinking being – the interference of a creative consciousness. If at one pole of the historical process there is iron determinacy, at the other there is creative (artistic) activity. Neither pole is to be found in pure form in the actual process. But we can demonstrate the isomorphism of these processes at different levels by pointing to a work of art which *before* its creation is unpredictable and *afterwards* seems like the predetermined beginning of a predestined tradition.

Take the behaviour of an individual. As a rule it accords with several stereotypes which define the 'normal', predictable course of that person's actions. But the number of stereotypes within any particular society is much larger than what one individual can enact. Some possible stereotypes are rejected on principle, others are held to be less preferable, and others again are regarded as permissible. At a moment when the historical, social and psychological tension reaches the point where a person's world picture dramatically alters (as a rule under intense emotional pressure) a person can dramatically change his or her stereotype, as it were leap into a new mode of behaviour, quite unpredictable in 'normal' circumstances.[24] Of course, if we consider the behaviour of the crowd at such a moment, we shall see a degree of repeatability in that many individuals are altering their behaviour and under the new circumstances are choosing unpredictable modes. But what is predictable in average for the 'crowd' is unpredictable for the individual. As Kant remarked:

> Marriages, and the births and deaths conditioned by them, over which human free will has so large an influence, would seem not to be subject to any law which would forecast the number of them. Yet the annual statistics of large countries show that they too are subject to the constant laws of nature.[25]

From Kant's observation we might conclude that individual phenomena are characterized by a decrease in predictability and this is what distinguishes them from mass phenomena. But such a conclusion seems premature. The historian knows purely empirically how often the behaviour of a crowd is less predictable than the reaction of an individual. And theoretically as we have already argued the actual notion of 'individuality' is not primary or self-evident but depends on the means of encoding. More to the point is Prigogine and Stengers' idea that near the bifurcation points the system has the tendency to change to a regime of individual behaviour. To take Kant's example we can say that a marriage between individuals is as a rule carried out in circumstance of heightened emotion; it is the result of a choice of alternatives, of a free act of the will. But if we think in terms of 'population' then marriage is a norm. And the closer to the norm the more predictable will be the behaviour of the system.

But there is another aspect to this question: when we can predict the next link in the chain of events then it follows that there was no act of choice between equal alternatives. But consciousness is always a choice. So it follows that if we exclude choice (unpredictability which the outside observer sees as chance) then we exclude consciousness from the historical process. And historical laws are different from all others in that they cannot be understood without taking account of people's conscious activity, including semiotic activity.

*   *   *

Creative intelligence is especially indicative in this respect. As we have already argued, creative intelligence is operative when a text comes into being which could not have been predicted by automatic algorithms. Certain aspects of the text will, however, always be predictable (e.g. 'tradition') and if we only take account of them, then the historical process will seem to be smooth and continuous; other aspects of the text are predictable with some degree of probability, while others again are completely unexpected. However, even the degree to which it is unexpected will differ depending on whether we place the text in a temporal sequence of texts, or a reverse one. An unexpected text is not impossible, but merely less probable (or somewhat less probable). For instance, the situation *before* 'Byronic Romanticism' before Byron appeared was such that there was a low degree of probability that such a phenomenon would arise. But in the sphere of culture the more unexpected something is, the stronger will be its influence on the cultural situation *after* it has come into being. An event that is quite unexpected (the appearance of an unpredicted text) radically alters the situation of the next one. The improbable text becomes a reality and subsequent development makes the fact of its existence a starting point. The unexpectedness is forgotten, and the originality of the genius becomes the routine of the imitators: Byronists followed after Byron and the fops of the whole of Europe after Beau Brummel.

When a text is looked at from a retrospective point of view the dramatic discreteness of the process is forgotten: Byron is seen as the 'first Byronist', the follower of his followers or, to use a hackneyed term from cultural history, a 'precursor'.

Friedrich Shlegel in his *Fragments* coined the aphorism: 'The historian is a prophet, turned to the past.'[26] His witticism leads us to the distinction between a fortune-teller predicting the future and an historian who 'predicts' the past. No fortune-teller or predicter ever says the future is inevitable and the only outcome possible: the prediction is either made on the principle of a two-step condition (such as 'if you do such and such, then such and such will follow'), or it is deliberately formulated in vague terms which need further interpretation. In either case the prediction always has a store of indeterminacy and leaves open the choice between several alternatives. Hence the frequently found motif in folklore and archaic texts of the misunderstood prediction. Thucydides for example tells the following story:

> Cylon went to Delphi to consult the god, and the reply he received was that he was to seize the Acropolis of Athens during the great festival of Zeus. Theagenes gave him some troops and, summoning his own friends to join him, when the time came for the Olympic festival in the Peloponnese, he seized the Acropolis with the intention of making himself dictator, believing that the Olympic festival must be 'the great festival of Zeus' and also that there was something appropriate in it to his own case, since he had won a victory at the Olympic Games. Whether perhaps the festival referred to was meant to be in Attica or somewhere else he never even considered, nor did the oracle offer any enlightenment.[27]

The result was disastrous for Cylon. In Rome a special college of Decemvirs was chosen to interpret the predictions of the Sybilline books. Cicero in his treatise 'On Divination' remarks:

Men capable of correctly interpreting all these signs of the future seem to approach very near to the divine spirit of the gods whose will they interpret, just as scholars do when they interpret the poets.[28]

Summing up, Cicero wrote:

Chrysippus filled a whole volume with your oracles; of these some, as I think, were false; some came true by chance, as happens very often even in ordinary speech; some were so intricate and obscure that their interpreter needs an interpreter and the oracles themselves must be referred back to the oracle; and some so equivocal that they require a dialectician to construe them. For example, when the following oracular response was made to Asia's richest king: 'When Croesus o'er the river Halys goes/He will a mighty kingdom overthrow', Croesus thought that he would overthrow his enemy's kingdom, whereas he overthrew his own.

Then Cicero quotes the prediction made to Pyrrhus: '*Aio, te, Aeacida, Romanos posse*' ['O son of Aeaus, my prediction is that you the Roman army will defeat'], which is so formulated that either interpretation is possible, that the Roman army might defeat him, or that he might defeat the Roman army.[29]

The historian who 'predicts backwards' is different from the fortune-teller in that indeterminacy is eliminated: what in fact did not take place could not, in the eyes of the historian, have taken place. The historical process loses its indeterminacy, i.e. ceases to be informative.

Indeterminacy presupposes an interpreter. Here too a parallel comes to mind: the artistic text, unlike a scientific one, also has a high degree of indeterminacy and needs an interpreter (a critic, literary scholar, an enthusiast). But a scientific text does not need any mediator. The difference evidently lies in the fact that the scientific text looks at the world as something already made, constructed, and consequently in a sense looks at it retrospectively (though not as much as the historian does). The literary text creates a world in which are embedded mechanisms of unpredictable self-development. This brings us to another point, namely, that the very notion of unpredictability is relative and depends on the degree of probability for a particular event. The nearer the trajectory of events comes to the points of bifurcation, the more individual it will be. Besides at one and the same historical moment there will be a different degree of predictability/unpredictability in different types of texts. In science for instance the most unexpected ideas often arise at the same time: Newton and Leibniz both worked on integral and differential calculus at the same time; Darwin and Wallace independently of each other arrived at the idea of evolution; Poincaré came to the ideas of the theory of relativity at the same time as Einstein; Lobachevsky,

Boiani, Gauss, Schweikart and Taurinus all came to the problem of non-Euclidean geometry at the same time. In the history of art such things do not occur. Hence another thing: if we suppose that a great inventor died before he had made his discovery, we need have no doubt that sooner or later (and as a rule within a short period) that discovery will have been made. In this sense the unexpected death of a scholar will not radically change the course of the historical process. But if Dante or Dostoevsky had died in childhood their works would not have been written and the development of literature and of the general history of mankind would have been different. We can say this without altering our opinion that Einstein was as much a genius as Dante was. The principal difference betwen them is that the ideas of a scientist can be extracted from the text they are expressed in and consequently can be translated; whereas the ideas of an artist *are a text*, and a text is created once only.

So we conclude that the necessity of relying on texts makes the historian face an inevitable double distortion. On the one hand, the syntagmatic linear drive of the text transforms the event into a narrative; and on the other hand, the historian reconstructs the events in the opposite direction. In order to understand the historian's special position let us imagine the following experiment: in one of his arguments, Flammarion invented a little man (he named him Lumen) who left the earth at a speed greater than that of light. For an observer like him, time would flow in a reverse direction and, as Poincaré remarked, 'history would be reversed, and Waterloo would come before Austerlitz'.[30] Now let us imagine that Flammarion's Lumen came back to earth, entered a history department, became subject to earthly time and the linear laws of human speech and had to write a history on the basis of his impressions. The historical events in his essay would be doubly transformed: first, on account of his experience of the reverse flow of time, and second, because of the turnabout which returned time to its 'normal' earthly sequence. In these circumstances our Lumen would be a strict determinist.

* * *

There is, however, still one more kind of deformation which the narrative structure imposes on the historical text. A narrative especially in its most ancient form as myth always cuts across the continuum of non-textual reality with powerful delimitations: namely, beginnings and endings. By definition every text has limits. But not all of these limits have a similar modelling weight. Some cultures and texts are oriented towards the beginning and give it semiotic significance, others are oriented towards the end. Myths of origins and eschatological myths immediately come to mind. But the significance of these orientations is wider than this.

Not only archaic myths of 'origins' see in the basis of culture modelling in the sources and beginnings. Let us take some examples from medieval texts.

In *The Lay of Igor's Campaign* there is the following passage:

> Nor do I see any longer/the sway of my strong/and wealthy/
> and multi-militant/brother Yaroslav/with his Chernigov boyars/
> with his commanders/and his Tatrans/and Shelbirs and Topchaks/
> and Revugs and Olbers./For they without shields/
> with knives in the legs of their boots/
> vanquish armies with war cries/
> to the ringing of ancestral glory.[31]

Though scholars have ofen commented on the seemingly mysterious 'Chernigov boyars' and the commanders, Tatrans and so on, the meaning of the phrase 'to the ringing of ancestral glory' ['zvonyachi v pradednyu slavu'] has seemed clear and has not called for special explanations.[32] Yet it is not at all clear why the exploits of Yaroslav's warriors resound to the glory of the ancestors and not to their own, or why the grandsons carry out the exploits and the glory that resounds is not theirs but that of their grandparents who performed other deeds in other times.

In order to understand this passage in the text we need to refer to D. S. Likhachev's profound observation about the nature of the feeling of time in early Russian literature:

> The past was somewhere ahead, at the beginning of the events the course of which did not correlate with the subject perceiving it. Events 'at the back' were events of the present or the future. 'The back' was the inheritance left by the deceased, it was that 'last thing' which bound him with us. 'Glory in front' was the glory of the distant past, of the 'first' times, while 'glory at the back' was glory of the last actions.[33]

Likhachev has pointed to something extremely important. The linear time of contemporary cultural consciousness is closely bound up with the idea that each event is replaced by the next one and that what recedes into the past ceases to exist. Reality is something only in the present time. The past exists as a memory and a cause, the present as reality, and the future as a consequence. Bound up with this is the idea that while only the present has genuine reality, its meaning will only be discovered in the future. Hence the urge to order events into a single moving chain of causes and results.

Early Russian thinking started from other premises. The 'first' events which are the foundation of the world order do not pass into the shadowy domain of memory – they eternally exist in their reality. Each new event of this kind is not something distinct from its 'first' proto-image, it is merely a renewal and growth of this eternal 'signpost' event. Each murder of brother by brother is not a separate, new action but a re-enactment of the sin of Cain, which in itself is eternal.

New and previously unheard of crimes are especially heinous: they exist from the first moment they are committed and each repetition of the same crime falls on the head not so much of the criminal who perpetrates it as on the soul of the first sinner.

In exactly the same way great and glorious deeds merely reactivate the 'first glory' which has existed through all eternity and which is the only real one; such deeds resound in it as it were in a bell which even when silent really exists and whose chimes do not exist in themselves but prove the bell's existence. In the cyclic time of myth events continually repeat the primordial order of the eternal Cycle, but in order that each event, uniquely preordained in the Order, should come about, magic intervention of a ritual action is required. So in the same way the heroic deeds of the descendants are required in order that the eternal bell of the ancestors' glory should resound.

This type of consciousness focuses its thinking not on the end or result, but on the beginning or origin.

It will be easier for us with our modern minds to imagine this way of thinking if we illustrate it with some examples which are closer to us in time.

Both intellectually and intuitively Gogol had an acute sense of the archaic world outlook. His story 'A Terrible Vengeance' reflects this system of categories particularly clearly. In murdering his sworn brother, the evil-doer Petro committed an unheard of crime which combined in one the sins of Cain and of Judas, and new and unheard of evil ensued. His crime was not a thing of the past but engendered a chain of new crimes and the evil continued to exist into the present and to increase relentlessly. The image of the corpse which grew in size under the ground with each new crime is an expression of this idea.

A text exists on the page of a book outside time, but in the process of reading it is activated: it will be read, it is being read and it has been read. So a text of world history to the medieval mind has a deep existence outside time and only acquires temporal sequence when it is activated through people's actions. This metaphor has a profound influence on the medieval idea of history. We should also bear in mind that the very notion of reading was different from ours: it presupposed not only a repeated and constant return to certain texts but also the ordering of these returns. By analogy human deeds could be perceived as the repetition of actions that have already happened, or rather a second realization of their deep proto-images.

So this way of thinking involves two activities: on the one hand, there is the action of the originator. It is he who creates the constant constructive features of the world. Being once and for all created these basic constructions exist outside time, are not part of human history, but lie at deeper levels of existence. Hence the questions which were so typical for early Russian literature of 'who began it?' 'where did it come from?'[34] *The Tale of Bygone Years* is steeped in the idea of origins from its very opening lines.[35] The one who does the 'first' deed bears responsibility before God since that deed does not disappear but exists eternally and is renewed in subsequent actions.

But on the other hand, a 'renewer' is needed, someone who through his deeds, good or evil, will as it were shake the dust from the ancient deeds of the originator. The renewer is of immense importance. But a parallel type also sometimes occurs who by some means or other weakens the importance of the first deeds, whether they are good or ill.

The medieval story-teller was interested above all in such deeds and actions, while stories of 'first deeds' are more typical of the mytho-epic stage. These stories are not yet historical narratives because they are oriented not towards the results of an action, but towards its origins. The structural weight is given to the categories of 'beginning' and 'end' in the text is an indicator of the text's orientation.

Historical narrative[36] and novels which are associated with it are subject to temporal and causal sequence and as such are oriented towards the end. The main structural meaning is concentrated at the end of the text. The question 'how did it end?' is typical of our perception both of the historical episode and of the the the novel. Mythological texts which tell of the act of creation and of legendary originators are oriented towards the beginning. We see this not only in the persistent question 'where did it come from?' but also in the markedness of the beginning of the text and the subdued role of the ending. Secular medieval narratives, including *gestes* and to some extent chronicles are a medium type. The hero is an 'historical person' yet the meaning of the events is focused on the origins.[37]

The Tale of Woe and Misfortune is interesting as an example of a unique compromise between these two principles: the entry of the hero, the Young Man, into a monastery concludes the story and brings the course of events to a halt; yet the narrative is oriented to the beginnings in that it tells of the creation of Adam and Eve and of the Fall. So the whole plot of the story is a 'renewal' of the original sin of mankind.[38]

The Lay of Igor's Campaign is a typical *geste*. Although the main characters are historical figures, the meaning of the events is interpreted by reference to the origins. Hence the basic idea of the *Lay*: that Igor's campaign is a 'renewal' of the campaigns of Oleg Goreslavich who was the 'originator' of the internecine struggles in Russia. And yet the author also contrasts the political wars of the 'present' with the ideal times of the 'first princes'. The beginning of the text is much more strongly marked than its rather subdued ending.

The notion of glory in the *Lay* is indicative in this respect for it is thought of as something pre-existing from the time of the ancestral originators (glory is always 'ancestral'). It can be dimmed if not renewed by fresh heroic deeds, but it will never disappear since it exists outside time. There are numerous references to the tarnishing of ancestral glory, though it can also be renewed.[39]

The author of the *Lay* portrays Igor and Vsevolod as full of boundless ambition (since they are vassals of the great Prince of Kiev, this ambition casts a negative light on their deeds, though as heroes and knights they personally are endowed with special beauty and worth). They are not satisfied with honour but have decided to win glory for themselves and by their glorious deeds to create a new standard of glory which would put all past deeds in the shade and resound through all generations ('Let us grasp the past glory for ourselves and share the future glory' [lines 481–2]).

Glory as well as other fundaments of the world order may lie dormant and inactive until a time of renewal ('For those two brave sons of Svyatoslav, Igor and Vsevolod, roused the perfidy which their father, dread Svyatoslav, Great Prince of Kiev, had kept all but curbed' [lines 350–6]. 'Perfidy' here is something more primordial than the actual Khans of the Polovtsians whose names were well known to the Russians: it is Evil which after Svyatoslav's successful campaigns had been dormant but which was reactivated by the actions of Igor and Vsevolod.

In these medieval tales and lays faith in the preordained structures of the world unites with the idea of individual activity which is capable both of reactivating ancestral glory and of awakening ancient Perfidy. This combination creates that balance between the preordained order and personal freedom and responsibility which are typical of Russian medieval literature of the pre-Muscovite period.

*　　*　　*

Some culture types are oriented towards eschatology. Examples are the mythology of the Aztecs or the Ragnarok of Scandinavian mythology, the apocalyptic beliefs of many religious sects, Wagner's *Götterdämmerung* and the ensuing eschatology of late nineteenth- and early twentieth-century modernism, as well as the burgeoning of such moods in the nuclear age and with the threat of ecological catastrophe.

What concerns us here, however, is not the content of eschatological ideas and myths, but the modelling significance of the end in certain types of texts. The beginning of a text, its set beginning as we find in folklore, serves as a semiotic indicator: from it the readership learns what semiotic key the ensuing text is in. It is rather like the mechanism of an organ which has several keyboards and registers. Before playing a piece the organist has to switch to the appropriate register. If we imagine the entire set of codes in a particular culture as a hierarchy of registers, then the opening of a text is like a switch that activates the register in which the rest of the text is to be heard. When the ensuing text does not accord with the opening, the effect is a strange one; it is a device much used in modern cinema to create 'false expectations', and is also found in parodies, in comic heroic (travesty) poems of the eighteenth century, and so on. When Chernyshevsky on hunger strike in his cell in the Peter-Paul fortress was writing his social utopian novel *What is to be Done?*, he deceived his jailers and the censorship by giving the novel the beginning of a detective story.

More important than the opening is the ending of the narrative structure on which great demands are placed. A 'happy ending' or a 'tragic ending' are features on which readers place great importance. When the hero marries or achieves his aims the readers are left with a feeling that the outcome has been fortunate, while the death of the hero, even if the action is set in ancient history and in reality the people concerned are long since dead, leaves a feeling of tragedy. But the point is that a discrete, articulated text always has its own time which begins at the beginning of the text and ends with its last word. So if the hero is happy and young at the last sentence of the text, then for the reader he is always happy and young. And what is more the actual text becomes a space in which people are happy and young. Hence the hypnotic effect of happy endings in films about modern Cinderellas and in other genres of mass literature. Every verbal text is articulated into discrete units but the plot-text, thanks to the distinctive categories of beginning and end, can be a final model of an infinite world.

When this quality of narrative is transferred on to the material of history it has a profoundly disturbing effect, and this disturbance has two aspects to it: on the level of the source-text the chronicler, memoirist or other creator of the document or source-material is compelled to subject the text to a plot-narrative structure, so that each 'story' is given a moralizing, philosophical or literary resonance. The director of *A Man for All Seasons* (Columbia, 1966) ends the film not with the final shot of Thomas More's execution, but with a voice which tells how fate took vengeance on both Henry VIII and Cardinal Wolsey, so that the audience feel relieved and reassured that there is justice in the course of history. The same intention guided those who created the historical sources for the life of Thomas More. Thomas Stapleton's biography of More[40] shows the influence of a certain literary tradition for he includes More's life in a trilogy about three Saint Thomases, the Apostle Thomas, Thomas Becket and Thomas More. The anonymous author, who wrote as 'Ro:Ba' (c.1599, published in 1950) also constructed his biography of More in accord with literary and hagiographic canons. So it may be extremely difficult to distinguish a historical source, even a legal document, from a literary text.

The other aspect is more important: this is the disturbance produced by narrative models on the mind of the historian. The historian's aim to periodize is bound up with the necessity of retelling the material of reality, which is continuous, in the discrete metalanguage of science. In this repect the historian is no different from any other scholar, when, for instance, he or she starts to see *his/her own* classification as an immanent quality of the non-textual material and transfers the eschatological experience of 'beginnings' and 'endings' from the level of descriptions onto the level of what is being described. For example, the eschatology of *fin-de-siècle*, of Wagner's *Götterdämmerung*, of Nietzsche and their followers gave shape to Oswald Spengler's ideas of impending catastrophe. The literary tradition provided the language, and the reality of the philosopher's own times was convincing enough material. But Spengler made language, the *instrument* of description, into the *object* of description – which was world history. The first action required is to cut up the historical material into pieces, and provide them with absolute beginnings and absolute ends. Historical material is of course divided into periods and its boundaries are marked by the bifurcation points which serve as the stimuli for irreversible and unpredictable changes. But the point is that even at moments of greatest change which involve large clusters of the historical strands, these changes never involve *the whole* of life (except perhaps when it is a matter of the physical destruction of a whole people or culture). On some levels life is intermittent, on others continuous, and if we talk of a boundary we must know from whose point of view it is meant. Spengler, however, speaks of absolute ruptures brought about by the death of one spirit of culture and the birth of another. If we make these cultural divisions absolute then we can look at each of the sections as a separate organism and apply the categories of youth, maturity and old age and inevitable death to them. But this way of thinking requires that all aspects of culture are born and die at the same time and that all are consequently procreated from a single centre. This centre, and here Spengler falls under the influence of Hegel, can only be the spirit of culture.

The narrativity of the researcher's thought processes then obviously has its effect on the construction of history which he or she creates. Arnold Toynbee's great project shows the results of treating the whole of world history as a series of closed cultures with 'beginnings and endings' though his approach is much more subtle than Spengler's.

The search for the 'beginnings of history', the beginnings of civilization and following from this the paradoxical term 'prehistoric civilization', can be put down to the effect of mythological narrative models.

In recent decades archaeologists have made several discoveries which have radically extended the limits of our knowledge about the most ancient period of human cultural development. What in the past seemed to be a beginning is now seen as the summation of a long period of development, and what once was thought to be primitive now is shown to have profundity and complexity. Defending the idea of the continuity of human cultures, N. I. Konrad, the Orientalist, made the following remarks in a letter to Arnold Toynbee:

> Yes of course entire civilizations perish. Of the ancient Achaean culture all that remains are some ruins, the Lion gates, the palace at Knossos and not much else. But surely it left behind something far more important – the *Iliad*. The *Iliad* is in no way the beginning of a new literature; it is the summation of the whole preceding culture; but a summation made by the new people who inherited that culture. The true beginnings of Greek literature lie in the primitive poetry and prose which we find in the 'post-Homeric epoch'. . . .
>
> I think that we could tackle another mysterious literary work, the Indian *Ramayana* in the same way. Until we learnt of the existence in India of culture more ancient than that which we know; until the finds were made at Harappa and Mohenjodaro, we had to assume that there was an unbelievably developed mythopoeic fantasy which was expressed with amazing artistic skill. But perhaps it can be explained more simply? And purely historically? Perhaps here too we have one of history's mysteries, like that which surrounds the *Iliad*. In any case the *Ramayana* is not primitive. Not a beginning. It is a great cultural world far back in the past but brought to life again in new form by those who destroyed it. In a word, it is an analogy with the Greek *Iliad*.[41]

In the light of the findings of modern archaeology it is extremely risky to talk of an absolute beginning, and the idea which someone once mooted that if we have a developed civilization then you can be certain that there was another developed civilization before it no longer seems a paradox. There seems to be a parallel with an autocatalytic reaction when the presence of some quantity of the substance at the beginning of the reaction which is *the final* result hastens the process of its formation. Being near a culture hastens the process of new culture-generation.

We may move back the time boundaries of culture, or we may rather dismiss this question because it smacks of mythology or because we have no truly scientific approach to it and anyway there will never be enough data, but we shall still have to accustom ourselves to the idea that the forms of culture which we know are certainly not the only ones possible. Can we for instance suppose that powerful civilizations may have existed which had no literacy and which therefore *as far as we are concerned* have disappeared?

16

An alternative: Culture without literacy or culture before culture?

A temptation for many who are concerned with history and the typology of cultures and civilizations is to say, 'That didn't happen, so it can't happen', or, in other words, 'I don't know anything about that, so it must be impossible'. This in fact means that the chronological section, so tiny in comparison with the total written and oral history of mankind, which we can study thanks to the written documents which have been preserved, is taken as the norm for the historical process, and the culture of this tiny period as the standard for human culture.

To take an example: all culture known to European scholars is based on writing. We find it hard to imagine a developed non-literate culture or indeed any developed non-literate civilization (and if we do then only by conjuring up the familiar images of the cultures and civilizations we know). Not long ago two well-known mathematicians[42] put forward the idea that since the global development of writing became possible only with the invention of paper, the whole 'pre-paper' period of the history of culture is a complete late fabrication. There is no point disputing this paradoxical idea but to note it as a clear example of extrapolating blinkered views into unexplored regions: what is familiar is declared to be the only thing possible.

Developed civilizations, with their class societies, divisions of labour and high levels of public works and of construction and irrigational technology, are so obviously linked with the ability to write that alternative possibilities have been rejected *a priori*. Arguing from the vast data at our disposal we might well say that the link between writing and civilization is a universal law, were it not for the mysterious phenomenon of the South American pre-Inca civilizations.

The evidence that archaeologists have accumulated about these civilizations builds up a truly amazing picture. Here is a series of successive civilizations stretching over thousands of years which created

245

great buildings and irrigation systems, built towns and great stone idols, civilizations with developed skills in pottery, weaving, metallurgy, and a complex system of symbols . . . and yet they have left no traces whatever of writing. This paradox is still unexplained. The idea sometimes advanced that their writing was destroyed by the invaders, first the Incas and then the Spanish, is not convincing. Their stone monuments, those of their burial grounds which have not been looted and are still in perfect condition, their pottery and other wares would surely have yielded some trace of writing if there had been any. We know from historical experience that destruction on a scale to leave no trace at all is beyond the might of any invader. So we have to assume that they had no writing.

Without restricting ourselves *a priori* to any notions of what is possible and what is not, let us try to imagine (since this is the way open to us) what this civilization would have been like, if indeed it existed.

Writing is a form of memorizing. Just as the individual mind has its own memorizing mechanisms, so the collective mind, which has to record what is held in common, creates its own mechanisms. One of these mechanisms is writing. But is writing the first, or more importantly, is it the only possible form of collective memorizing? The way to answer this question is to suppose that forms of memorizing are derivative from what people think has to be remembered, and what that is depends on the structure and orientation of that civilization.

We normally suppose that memory is for remembering exceptional events (i.e. that these are what mechanisms of collective memory record); by exceptional events we mean unique events, or events that occur for the first time, or events which should not have happened, or events that were unexpected. These are the kinds of events recorded in chronicles and nowadays in newspapers. For the kind of memory which is geared to memorizing anomalous and unusual occurrences writing is essential. The culture with this kind of memory constantly multiplies the number of texts: its laws are amplified with precedents, its legal acts record particular events – sales, wills, settlements – and a judge has in each case to deal with one separate incident. Literature is subject to this tendency as well. This kind of culture fosters the development of private correspondence, memoirs and diaries, which also serve to record 'events' and 'incidents'. The literate mind will pay attention to relationships of cause and effect and to resultant actions: what is recorded is not the time of year to do the sowing but what in one particular year the harvest was like. All this leads to a heightened concern with time and the beginnings of the idea of history. We could even say that history is one of the by-products of the emergence of writing.

But let us imagine another possible type of memory which aims to preserve information about the established order and not about its violations, about laws and not about anomalies. Suppose for example that when watching a sports competition we are not concerned with who won or what unforeseen circumstances attended this event, but that we concentrate on something else, namely, on recording for posterity information about how and at what season the competition took place. Then what we need is not a chronicle or a newspaper report, but a calendar or a custom, which records the established order, and a ritual which allows all this to be stored in the collective memory.

A culture that is oriented not towards an increase in the quantity of texts but on the repeated reproduction of texts once and forever established requires a collective memory with a different make-up. Writing is not needed. Mnemonic symbols will take its place, natural symbols (such as especially prominent trees and rocks, the stars and all the heavenly bodies), and symbols made by man: idols, tumuli, buildings and rituals in which these landmarks and holy places are included. The ritualization and sacralization of memory which is typical of such cultures makes observers brought up on European traditions identify these landmarks with centres of religious cults in the sense in which we use the term. But by concentrating attention on the sacred function of these places, which indeed exists, the observer will tend to overlook their other functions, namely of regulating and controlling: for it is at these places that the mnemonic (sacred) symbol of the rite takes place. Yet the activities associated with these centres preserve the memory for the collective of those deeds, ideas and emotions which correspond to that place. So without knowing the rituals and without taking account of the vast number of calendaric and other signs (for instance, the length and angle of the shadow cast by the tree or building, the abundance or lack of · leaves or fruit in a particular year on the sacred tree, etc.) we cannot work out what the functions of the buildings that have been preserved were. We must, moreover, bear in mind that written culture is oriented towards the past, while oral culture is oriented towards the future. Predictions, fortune-telling and prophecy play an enormous part in it. The landmarks and sacred places are not only sites where the rituals which preserve the memory of laws and customs are performed, but also the sites of fortune-telling and prediction. Sacrificial offerings can be looked at as a kind of futurological experiment since they always involve appealing to the divinity for assistance in making a choice.

We would be wrong to suppose that civilization of this type suffers from an 'information famine' on the grounds that their rituals and customs seem to make all actions preordained by fate. A society like that simply could not exist. Members of an 'un-lettered collective' are constantly faced with the necessity of making a choice but their choices are made without reference to history or to expectations of cause and effect but, as many illiterate peoples do, by consulting the fortune-tellers and sorcerers. Perhaps our need for consultations (with a doctor, a lawyer, one's elders) is a vestige of this tradition. This kind of tradition is the opposite to Kant's ideal of the person who is capable of making decisions about their own opinions and actions. Kant wrote:

> Enlightenment is humanity's emergence from a state of immaturity in which it is kept by its own fault. Immaturity is the inability to use one's reason without guidance from another person. . . . It's so easy to be immature! If I had a book which did my thinking for me, if I had a spiritual guide who acts as my conscience, and a doctor who prescribes me a particular regime, then I have nothing to worry about.[43]

Culture without writing with its orientation towards omens, fortune-telling and oracles makes the choice of behaviour something impersonal. So the ideal person will be the one who is able to understand and correctly interpret predictions, does not waver in fulfilling them, and who acts openly without concealing his or her intentions. In contrast a culture oriented towards a person's capability to choose his or her own behaviour strategy requires rationality, caution, circumspection and discretion, since each event is regarded as 'happening for the first time'. Turner cites an interesting example of this in his work on divination among central African people and in particular among the Ndembu. The prediction is made by shaking a basket containing special ritual figurines and the result is read from their positions. Each figurine has a certain symbolic meaning and whichever one of them is on the top is particularly significant. Turner writes:

> The second figurine we shall consider is called *Chamutang'a*. It represents a man sitting huddled up with chin on hands and elbows on knees. *Chamutang'a* means an irresolute, changeable person. . . . *Chamutang'a* also means 'the man whom no one knows how to take'. His reactions are unnatural. Capriciously, informants say, he will at one time give presents to people, at another time he will act meanly. Sometimes he will laugh immoderately with others, sometimes he will keep silent for no apparent reason. No one can guess when he will be angry, or when he will fail to show anger. Ndembu like a man whose behaviour is predictable. They praise both openness and consistency, and a man whom they feel is not genuine may very likely be a sorcerer. The theme that what is hidden is probably dangerous and malevolent is once again exemplified.[44]

All the main gestures of the *Chamutang'a* figure resemble those of Rodin's 'The Thinker'. The symbolism of the gesture of holding one's chin is so well known that Rodin's statue needs no elucidation. This is all the more remarkable in that the sculptor's intention was to depict the 'first' thinker: neither the forehead nor the proportions of the figure have the features of a stereotype intellectual – the entire significance lies in the pose. It is interesting to recall that these same gestural stereotypes were used by Garrick to create the 'Hamlet type' (with the difference only that he stood which made the gesture all the more telling):

> In profound reverie he comes on to the stage, chin held by his right hand, elbow supported by his left hand, his eyes are cast down and to the side. Then taking his right hand from his chin, but still if I remember rightly continuing to support it with the left he utters the words: 'To be or not to be?'[45]

Garrick's acting standardized the gestures of the Hamlet type for over a hundred years on the stages of Europe.

What do the Ndembu's *Chamutang'a*, Hamlet and Rodin's 'thinker' have in common? They are all people on the point of making a choice. But for the Ndembu the state of choosing means rejecting customs and a role established for centuries. The idea of choice has semantic associations with the violation of the established order, i.e. with sorcery (since the Ndembu ascribe everything abnormal to sorcery), or with such negative human features as duplicity and indecision.

But omens and predictions which give prognoses of the future bind the function of choice to the collective experience, leaving to the individual the possibility of open and decisive action. Baratynsky wrote:

> A wolf ran from the forest onto his path,
> Circling round with hackles raised,
> It prophesied victory, and boldly
> He flung his troops against the enemy.[46]

Society founded on custom and collective experience must inevitably have developed powerful means of prognostication. But this inevitably serves to stimulate the observance of nature especially the stars, and hence serves to stimulate theoretical knowledge. Some forms of descriptive geometry are in no way excluded from non-literate cultures as such, and may serve to complement the oral poetry of calendars and astronomy.

The world of oral memory is full of symbols. It may seem paradoxical that the emergence of writing, far from complicating the semiotic structure of culture, in fact simplified it. The material objects which represented the mnemonic sacred symbols are found not in verbal texts but in ritual ones. And in relation to that text they preserve a certain freedom: their material existence continues outside the ritual, or they may be included in many different rituals, which gives them multiple significance. The very existence of them presupposes an enveloping mass of oral tales, legends and songs associated with them. The result is that the syntactic bonds between these symbols can be loosened in different contexts. The verbal text (and in particular the written one) is based on syntactic bonds. Oral culture weakens them extremely. This is why oral culture can include a large number of symbolic signs of a lower order which are as it were on the verge of writing, such as amulets, signs of ownership, calculating objects, signs of a mnemonic 'letter', but extremely reduces the possibility of fitting them into syntactic-grammatical chains. Objects capable of carrying out quite complex arithmetical calculations are not excluded from such cultures. In cultures of this type there are often rapid developments of magic signs which are used in rituals and which use simplest geometrical figures: the circle, the cross, parallel lines, the triangle, etc., and the primary colours. These signs should not be confused with hieroglyphs or alphabetic letters: since the latter tend towards a certain semantic value and acquire their meaning only the the syntagmatic chain where they form chains of signs; whereas the former have an unspecific meaning, often internally contradictory, and acquire specific meaning in relation to ritual and oral texts whose mnemonic signs they are. We can see the difference between them if we compare a sentence (a chain of linguistic symbols) with an ornament (a chain of magic-mnemonic and ritual symbols).

The development of ornamentation and the absence of inscriptions on sculptural and architectural monuments are also characteristic of oral cultures. A hieroglyph or written word or letter are phenomena at the opposite pole to an idol, tumulus, or landmark, and the two groups are in a sense mutually exclusive. The former signify meaning, while the latter *remind* one of it. The former are a text or part of a text, and a text which has a purely semiotic nature; whereas the latter are included in the syncretic text of ritual or are mnemonically connected with oral texts which are bound up with the particular place and time.

The antithesis between writing and sculpture is vividly shown in the Biblical episode of the confrontation between Moses and Aaron, between Moses' tablets which were to give the people a new mechanism of cultural memory ('a testament'), and the syncretic unity of Aaron's idol and ritual dancing which were the old way of preserving information:

> Moses turned and came down the mountain with the two tablets of the Testimony in his hands, tablets inscribed on both sides, inscribed on the front and on the back. The tablets were the work of God, and the writing on them was God's writing, engraved on the tablets.
>
> When Joshua heard the noise of the people shouting, he said to Moses, 'There is the sound of battle in the camp!' But he replied: 'No song of victory is this sound, no lament for defeat this sound; but answering choruses I hear!'

And there, as he approached the camp, he saw the calf and the groups dancing, Moses blazed with anger. He threw down the tablets he was holding, shattering them at the foot of the mountain. He seized the calf they had made and burned it. (Exodus 32. 15–20)

On this topic there is some extremely interesting material in Plato's dialogue *Phaedrus*. This work which is devoted to questions of the art of rhetoric is also concerned with problems of mnemonics. At the very beginning of the dialogue Plato leads Socrates and Phaedrus outside the city walls of Athens in order to show his readers the connection between landmarks, groves, hills and springs with the collective memory which is enshrined in myths:

Phaedrus: Tell me, Socrates, isn't there a story that Boreas abducted Oreithyia from somewhere here on the banks of the Ilissus?
Socrates: So they say.
Phaedrus: Was it here, do you think? The water is delightfully fresh and clear, just the place for girls to play.
Socrates: No, it was some quarter of a mile downstream, where one crosses to the temple of Agra; an altar to Boreas marks the spot, I believe.[47]

Further on Socrates suddenly suggests to his companion a paradoxical idea about the harm that writing can do to memory. A society based on literacy seems to Socrates to be one without memory and anomalous, while a society without literacy which is the normal one has a well-established collective memory. Socrates tells the story of the divine inventor Theuth who gave science to the king of Egypt:

But when it came to writing, Theuth declared: 'Here is an accomplishment, my lord the king, which will improve both the wisdom and the memory of the Egyptians. I have discovered a sure receipt for memory and wisdom.' 'Theuth, my paragon of inventors,' replied the king, 'the discoverer of an art is not the best judge of the good or harm which will accrue to those who practise it. So it is in this case; you, who are the father of writing, have out of fondness for your offspring attributed to it quite the opposite of its real function. Those who acquire it will cease to exercise their memory and become forgetful; they will rely on writing to bring things to their remembrance by external signs instead of on their own internal resources. What you have discovered is a receipt for recollection, not for memory. And as for wisdom, your pupils will have the reputation for it without the reality: they will receive a quantity of information without proper instruction, and in consequence be thought very knowledgeable when they are for the most part quite ignorant. And because they are filled with the conceit of wisdom instead of real wisdom, they will be a burden to society.'[48]

The point to notice is that Plato's Socrates associates writing not with cultural progress but with the loss of the high level achieved in non-literate society.

Oral texts revolving round idols and landmarks are associated with a particular place and time: an idol functions – as it were 'comes to life' in a cultural sense – at a certain time which in ritual and by calendar is 'its time', and local legends become attached to it. Consequently, the local landscape is experienced quite differently in literate and non-literate cultures. A literate culture tends to regard the world created by God or Nature as a text, and strives to read the message contained in it. Meaning then which is to be found in the written text, whether sacred or scientific, is extrapolated from the text onto the landscape. From this point of view the meaning of Nature is revealed only to a 'literate' person: that person seeks for laws, not omens, in Nature; belief in omens is treated as a superstition; and the future is to be determined from the past and not from fortune-telling and predictions.

Non-literate cultures have a different relationship to the landscape. Since a landmark, holy place or idol is 'included' in the cultural round of ritual, sacrifice, fortune-telling, songs and dances, and since all these activities are fixed to certain times of the year, the landmarks, holy places and idols are associated with particular positions of the stars or sun and moon, recurrent winds or rains, periodic changes in water levels in rivers, etc. These natural phenomena are taken signs which remind or predict. The change-over between these two types of memory are symbolized on the one hand by the rainbow which God gave to Noah as pledge, and on the other by the inscribed tablets which he gave to Moses.

'Folk' medicine and scientific medicine derive from these two different types of consciousness, the non-literate and the literate. At the dawn of the age of positivism it needed Baratynsky's penetrating mind and capacity for independent thought to see in superstition and in omens not falsehood and barbarism but the relics of another truth which had come down from another type of culture:

> Superstition! It is a relic
> Of ancient truth – the temple has fallen
> And the descendant cannot make out
> the language of its ruins.[49]

Interesting that the poet associates superstition with a temple, an architectural building, and not with a 'tombstone inscribed in an unknown tongue' as Pushkin did when referring to an incomprehensible word. Baratynsky's image comes to mind when thinking about the lost meaning of the pre-Inca architectural buildings of ancient Peru.

The passages from the Bible which we have cited present a familiar picture: non-literate and literate cultures are like two successive stages, one higher, one lower.

But from the fact that historical development took this path on the Eurasian continent which we are familiar with have we the right to conclude that this was the only possible path? The existence over many millenia of non-literate cultures in pre-Columbian America is convincing proof that such civilizations are viable, the high cultural levels achieved show that their cultural potential. For writing to become necessary, historical conditions had to be destabilized, circumstances had to become unpredictable and dynamic, and there had to be frequent and prolonged contacts with other ethnic groups in order for the need for semiotic translations to be felt. There is a polar difference between, on the one hand, the historical area comprising the Balkans and northern Africa, the Near and Middle East, the Black and Mediterranean Seas, and, on the other, the Peruvian altiplano, the Andes region and the narrow strip of the Peruvian coast. The former has been a melting-pot of ethnic groups, the scene of frequent migrations and semiotic and cultural conflicts; while the latter has been an area of age-old isolation, without many trade and military contacts with other cultures; it has in fact provided ideal conditions for an uninterrupted cultural tradition (and when the isolation was breached this as a rule meant the total disappearance of one of the ancient Peruvian civilization). So it seems natural that literate civilization was victorious in the first area and the non-literate in the other.

17

The role of typological symbols in the history of culture (contract and self-surrender as cultural archetypes)

Among the most archaic socio-cultural models we can identify two which are of particular interest because of their subsequent transformations in the history of culture. We shall term them the magical model and the religious one, always bearing in mind that these terms are approximate conventions and that we are not talking of real cultures but of typological principles. Most of the historical religions of the world combine both elements, and in some, the magic principle predominates.

The magical system of relationships is characterized: 1. by reciprocity: both the agents involved in these relationships are active (for instance, the magician performs certain actions, *in response to which* the power invoked performs others). In magic there are no one-sided actions, because if a magician through ignorance performs actions that are incorrect and therefore incapable of invoking the power concerned and making it active, then his words and gestures do not count as actions in the system of magic; 2. by compulsion: this means that certain actions by the one party entail obligatory and precisely predictable actions by the other. There are numerous texts bearing witness to the fact that the magician forces the supernatural power to appear and to act against its will, although the magician has less power at his disposal. The performance of certain actions by the one party *requires* specific actions in response from the other. Power is as it were equally divided: the supernatural forces have power over the sorcerer and he has power over them; 3. by equivalence: the relationship between the parties is like an exchange of equivalent values and can be likened to an exchange of conventional signs; 4. by contract: the two parties involved enter into a kind of contract which may be given external expression (the conclusion of an agreement, oath-taking, the observance of conditions, etc.), or may be implicit. But a contract implies also the possibility that it may be broken, just as in a conventional semiotic exchange there is the potential for deceit and disinformation.[50] Hence the possibility that the contract can be interpreted in various ways, each party endeavouring to put into the express formulations of the agreement a content to suit their own purposes.

A religious act, on the other hand, is based on an unconditional act of *self-surrender*, rather than on an exchange. The one party surrenders itself to the other without making any conditions at all, except that the receiving party is acknowledged to be the supreme power.[51] Relationships of this type are characterized by: 1. onesidedness: they are unidirectional in that the subject surrendering him or herself looks for protection though there is no guarantee that his or her action will be responded to, and the absence of reward cannot be grounds for breaking off relationships; 2. from this follows the absence of compulsion in the relationship: the one party surrenders everything, but the other party may respond or not, may refuse a worthy donor and reward someone unworthy (even someone who has no place in the system or whose has violated it); 3. there is no principle of equivalence: the relationship precludes the psychology of exchange and does not admit of any conditionality or conventionality in the basic values. So the means of communication are not signs but symbols whose very nature precludes the possibility of expression being alienated from content and hence precludes also the possibility of deceit or interpretation; 4. consequently relationships of this type are not like a contract but like an unconditional gift.

We must emphasize that we are dealing with a model of the cultural psychology of these types of relationship. Actual world religions have never been without some degree of magical psychology: as an example, though rejecting the idea of equivalent exchange in the relations between man and God on earth, many of the religions of the world contain the idea of recompense in the afterlife brought about by a set system of compulsory relationships (i.e. relationships that are unambiguously conditioned and therefore just) between our earthly life and the hereafter.

St Augustine's held to a different view: he believed that ultimate salvation or condemnation did not depend on human righteousness but wholly on the will of God.

The official religion of pagan Rome during the last centuries of its existence was a magical one; though behind the public façade there were many secret religious cults. Sacrifice was the basis of the contractual relationships with the gods, and the official cult of the emperor was like a legal agreement with the state. Because of these magical features, as listed above, the 'religion' of the Romans in no way contradicted either their sophisticated and deeply-held sense of legality, or the whole structure of the legally-based state. From the point of view of the

Romans, Christianity was a profoundly anti-state movement, since it was a religion in the precise meaning of the word and consequently took no account of feelings of formal legality or of legal contractual rights. And the abandonment of this form of consciousness was for someone of Roman culture a denial of the very notion of statehood.

The pagan cults of early Russia were evidently shamanistic, i.e. magical. The fact that the introduction of Christianity coincided with the rise of the Kievan state had a number of important consequences in the area we are discussing. The ensuing coexistence of two faiths [*dvoeverie*] gave rise to two opposite models of social relationships. The relationships between the prince and his personal troops, which needed to be formally clarified, tended towards the contractual principle. This model most adequately reflected the emergent system of feudalism which was founded on patronage and vassaldom, and the whole system of mutual rights and obligations, and of etiquette, on which the ideological framework of chivalric society rested. The tradition of Russian magical paganism became an organic part of the new order which emerged from the European synthesis between the tribal institutions of the barbarian peoples and the Roman legal tradition; for the Roman tradition had remained firmly rooted in the old cities of the empire where the communes maintained their own rights, a complex system of legal relationships held sway and there was an abundance of lawyers.

However, in the West contractual consciousness, in the distant past originating in magic, was cloaked in the authority of the Roman imperial tradition and took an equal place alongside the authority of religion; but in early Russia it was felt to be pagan in character. This attitude affected the way society evaluated it. In the Western tradition a contract as such was axiologically neutral: it could be made with the devil (see the life of St Theophilus who sold his soul to the devil and later redeemed it through repentance), but it could also be made with the powers of holiness and goodness. In *The Little Flowers of St Francis* there is the well-known story of the agreement between St Francis and the savage wolf of Gubbio. Having accused the wolf of behaving 'like a villain and the worst of murderers' devouring not only animals but also attacking people who are made in the image of God, St Francis concluded: 'Brother wolf, I want to make peace between you and them [the people of Gubbio, Yu. L.].' St Francis offered the wolf a fair exchange: he the wolf would give up his evil ways and the inhabitants of Gubbio would stop hunting him and would supply him with food. '"Do you promise?" And the wolf nodding his head made a clear sign that he did.'[52] The contract was concluded and both parties observed it until the death of the wolf.

No such texts are to be found either in Russian folklore or in the medieval literary tradition of early Russia: a contract is only possible with the Devil or with his pagan equivalents (the contract between the peasant and the bear). This idea first of all lends an emotional hue to contract as such – it lacks the aura of cultural value. In the Western chivalric way of life where relationships with God and the saints could be modelled on the pattern 'suzerain–vassal' and subjected to a conventional ritual similar to initiation to knighthood and the service of the lady, the contract and the ritual that seals it, the gesture, parchment and seal are cloaked in an aura of holiness and acquire authorization from above. In early Russia a contract was regarded as a purely human affair ('human' in the opposite sense to 'divine'). The introduction of the practice of kissing the cross when a contract had to be ratified is evidence that without this unconditional, non-contractual, divine authorization, it was not sufficiently guaranteed. Secondly, whenever an agreement was made with a satanic power, it was considered sinful to keep it, while to violate it meant saving one's soul. The conventionality of verbal semiotic communication is an important factor in dealings with such forces and both parties can use words for deception. The fact that it is possible to interpret a word in different ways (casuistry) was taken as the desire to deceive rather than the desire to arrive at a true meaning (see in Dostoevsky, 'A lawyer has a corrupt conscience' [*Ablakat – prodazhnaya sovest'*]). Another example is the eposide from the folk tale 'The Dragon and the Gipsy'[53] when the dragon and the gipsy agree to a whistling competition:

> The dragon whistled so loudly that the leaves fell off all the trees. 'You whistle well, my friend,' said the gipsy, 'but I whistle better. Bind up your eyes or else when I whistle they'll pop out of your head!' The dragon believed him and tied a cloth round his eyes and said 'Now you whistle!' The gipsy took a cudgel and how it whistled against the dragon's head.

The play on words which exposes the conventionality of the sign and turns the agreement into a deception was permissible when dealing with the Devil, a dragon, a bear, but unthinkable when dealing with God or any of the saints. Daniel the Prisoner said: 'Lies are for the the world, not for God; you cannot lie to Him, nor play with the sublime' (note that lying [*solgati*] and playing [*igrati*] are equated).

This is why the system of relationships established in medieval society, a system of mutual obligations between the supreme power and the feudal lords, came very early on to be viewed negatively. Daniel the Prisoner assured his prince that his councillors were deceitful servants and would bring sorrow to their lord. He contrasts them with the ideal of loyalty: he himself would not be ashamed to be compared with a dog. Service based on contract is bad service. And even Peter the Great wrote an angry letter to Prince Boris Sheremetev whom he suspected of secret sympathy for the ancient rights of the nobles in which he said: 'This is like a servant who seeing his master drowning does not want to save him without first checking whether it is written in his contract that he should pull him out of the water.'[54] Compare what Kurbatov wrote to Peter: 'I wish to serve you truly, my sovereign, and unfeignedly, as I serve God.'[55] The comparison between the sovereign and God is not accidental, but has deep roots. In Russia, the centralized power structure was much more based on the religious model than it was in the West. The isomorphic model is expressed in the *Householder's Manual [Domostroi]*: God is in the universe, the tsar in his kingdom and the father in his family: here are three degrees of unconditional of self-surrender which on their different levels matched the religious system of relationships. The idea of 'service to the sovereign' then took for granted *the absence of conditions* between the parties: from the one party total and unconditional self-surrender was expected, and from the other, favour. This concept of 'service' derived from the psychology of the bondsmen on the prince's lands. As the role of the bureaucracy which was personally dependent on the prince increased and turned into the state bureaucracy, and as at the same time the role of the prince's hired soldiery expanded, what had been the mentality of the prince's court became the state mentality of the service class. Religious feelings were transferred on to the sovereign, and state service became a form of religious service. Merit was determined by favour: 'If it were not for your favour, where would I be?' Vasily Gryaznoi, who was a noble and member of the *oprichnina*, wrote to Ivan the Terrible.

The clash between these two types of psychology can be traced over the whole period of the Russian Middle Ages. While the psychology of exchange and contract cultivates the sign, ritual and etiquette, the state-religious mentality is paradoxically oriented towards both symbolism and praxis. But this should not surprise us.

Chivalric culture was oriented towards the sign. In order to acquire cultural value in this system, a thing had to become a sign, i.e. it had to be maximally purified of its practical and non-semiotic function. Hence for a feudal lord in early Russia, 'honour' was bound up with the acquisition of a rich portion of the booty of war, or a large handout, from his sovereign. However, once obtained, the law of honour required that it should be used in a way that maximally belittled its material value, and thereby emphasized its semiotic value: 'They started making bridge across the marshes and miry places using their coats, their mantles, their sheepskin jackets and all their embroidered Polovtsian clothes.'[56] A model of chivalric behaviour is to be found in the Russian redaction of the epic poem *The Exploit of Devgeny* (translated from the Greek in the eleventh to twelfth centuries): the warrior Devgeny decided to win as his wife 'the beautiful daughter of Stratigos' whose suitors her father and brothers always killed. When he reached Stratigos' court he found the girl alone, her father and brothers being away. Devgeny could easily have carried her off, but he ordered her to stay at home and to inform her father of the impending abduction. Stratigos refused to believe her. Then Devgeny burst through the gates into the courtyard and 'began shouting loudly for Stratigos and his strong sons *to come out and see their sister being abducted*' [my emphasis, Yu. L.]. But still Stratigos refused to believe that a warrior had appeared brave enough to challenge him to battle. Devgeny having waited three hours in vain carried off his bride. But his success brought Devgeny not joy but sorrow, for 'great shame have I suffered'.[57] Eventually he got his battle, defeated the father and brothers and took them prisoner, then released them and sent his wife home; then again he came to court her and this time won his bride 'with great honour'. Everything, the bride, the battle, the wedding, are converted into signs of chivalric honour and have no value in themselves but only in terms of the significance ascribed them. The bride is valued not in herself but because of the difficulty of obtaining her and she has no value without the difficulty. The battle is valued not for the victory as such but because first it was won according to certain rules, and second the circumstances were particularly difficult. Death and defeat while attempting the impossible are more highly valued than victory and its ensuing practical gains especially if these have been won by calculation, practicality or humdrum military efforts. Effect was valued more highly than effectiveness. Igor's hopeless venture with his small band seeking the city of Tmutarakan inspires the author of *The Lay of Igor's Campaign* more than the modest but highly effective actions of the united troops of the Russian princes in 1183–4. The singer of *The Song of Roland* shares the same attitudes.

The semiotic aspect of behaviour stresses the play element: the aim of an action lies less in its practical result than in the correct use of the language of behaviour. In West European chivalry the tournament became the equivalent of battle, while in Russia hunting had the function of a tournament in the life of a feudal lord: as a special form of play it epitomized the semiotic values of chivalric military behaviour. This is why Vladimir Monomakh listed his hunting expeditions alongside his military exploits as matters of equal pride.

The opposite kind of behaviour excludes conventionality: it tends to reject play and the relativity of semiotic methods and it identifies truth with an absence of conventionality. Unconventionalized social behaviour may be either of two types: for those at the top of society there is a tendency towards symbolism in behaviour and throughout the semiotic system, but for those at the bottom of society there is a tendency towards zero-degree of semioticity, behaviour being transposed into the purely practical sphere.

Saussure noted the difference between the conventional sign and the non-conventional symbol in semiotic thinking:

> For it is characteristic of symbols that they are never entirely arbitrary. They are not empty configurations. They show at least a vestige of natural connexion between the signal and its signification. For instance, our symbol of justice, the scales, could hardly be replaced by a chariot.[58]

Power from the point of view of the symbolic consciousness of medieval Russia is endowed with the traits of holiness and truth. Its value is an absolute one for it is the image of heavenly power and embodies eternal truth. The rituals which surround it are like those of heaven. In face of it the individual is not a party to a contract, but a drop of water flowing to the sea. In surrendering to it the individual demands nothing in return except the right to self-surrender. After the battle of Poltava Peter Shafirov wrote to Peter the Great from Istanbul advocating a military raid to abduct Charles XII from Turkish territory: 'And even if they do find out that the Russians are behind it, nothing will happen except that I will suffer here.'[59] Many other analogous instances can be cited. The point is that the person of 'conventional' mentality, when faced with the obligation to forfeit his life, regarded death as a kind of exchange of his life for glory: 'If a man is killed on the field of battle,' said Daniel Galitsky to his troops, 'what is amazing about that? Others have died *ingloriously* at home, whereas these die *gloriously*.'[60] From the opposite point of view, there is no thought of exchanging anything, instead the poetry of *anonymous death*. the reward is the merging of the self in the absolute from which nothing can be expected in return. Dracula does not promise his soldiers glory, nor does he link death in battle with the idea of just recompense;[61] he simply expects them to die at his orders without any conditions: 'whoever wishes to give thought to death, let him not come to battle at my side.'[62]

Because this type of social consciousness extended the religious sense to the state, society had in effect to hand over all semiosis to the tsar who became a symbolic figure, a sort of living icon.[63] Other members of society were apportioned behaviour with a zero semiotic value: all that was required of them was practical activity (and such activity continued to be very lowly valued. This is why Ivan the Terrible referred to his colleagues as labourers [*stradniki*] thereby demoting them to the level of serfs in early feudal society who had no place at all in the semiotics of society.) The tsar's subjects were expected to perform practical service which had real results. If they worried about the socio-semiotic side of their life and activities this was regarded as 'laziness', 'deceitfulness' or even 'treason'. There was an indicative change in attitude towards hunting: from being a matter of honour hunting came to be regarded as a shameful pastime, a distraction from the matters of state (the sovereign still had the right to hunt for his pleasure). Already in the *Tale of the Battle on the Pyana* the negligent army commanders' passion for hunting is contrasted with military service for the state. Later Ivan wrote in similar terms to Vasily Gryaznoi, accusing him of hunting instead of fighting. Gryaznoi had no objection to being described as a labourer (he had written to the tsar: 'You, my lord, are like God: you make great things out of small ones'), but he took offence at this last reprimand and wrote to Ivan that he had been wounded in battle in his sovereign's service and not out hunting.

The eighteenth century brought far-reaching changes in the whole system of Russian culture. But this new stage in social consciousness and the semiotics of culture was a transformation of what had gone before, not a total break with it. The most striking change on the surface of culture and the way of life was the change in official ideology. The state-religious model did not disappear but was transformed in various interesting ways: in the system of values the top and the bottom changed places. Practical activity was elevated from the bottom to the very highest place in the hierarchy of values. Life was de-symbolized and the symbols of the past were trampled under foot and held up for public laughter. Practical work was held in higher esteem. The poetry of craftsmanship, of useful knowledge, of actions which are neither signs nor symbols but valued in themselves, largely contributed to the spirit of the Petrine reforms and Lomonosov's scientific activities. Osip Mandelshtam saw this spirit as the very essence of the eighteenth century:

> I am constantly drawn to citations from the naive and wise eighteenth century; here I am reminded of the lines from Lomonosov's famous 'Epistle on Glass':
>> 'They think improperly about things, Shuvalov,
>> Who value Glass less than Minerals.'
> Whence this pathos, the elevated pathos of utilitarianism, whence this inner warmth which stimulates poetic meditation on the fate of the industrial crafts? What a striking contrast to the brilliant, cold indifference of nineteenth-century scientific thought![64]

Lomonosov, writing of Peter the Great, stressed that though he was 'born for the sceptre, [he] stretched forth his hands to work.'

The ideal of the worker-tsar was to be oft-repeated, from Simeon Polotsky (see his poem 'Doing' [*Delati*] in *The Many-Flowered Garden*) to Pushkin's 'Stanzas'. But this inverted system though differing from the previous form, also resembled it. Petrine statehood was not the embodiment of a symbol, since in itself it represented the final truth and, having no higher authority than itself, was neither the representative nor the image of anything else. But like the pre-Petrine centralized state, it did demand of its subjects their *faith* in it and their total merging with it. Subjects *surrendered themselves* to it. A secular religion of statehood came into being and 'practical activities' now ceased to be part of extra-semiotic empirical experience.

There was a radical change in the relative importance of the semiotics of contract in the general structure of the culture of the period. Having been almost totally destroyed along with the whole cultural heritage of the early Russian Middle Ages, the notion of contract found powerful support in the cultural influence of the West. In Feofan Prokopovich's speeches and those of other propagandists of Peter's camp, the political ideas of Puffendorf and Hugo Grotius were elaborated though curiously refracted through the Russian tradition. The tsar's power is seen as a divine gift and justified by reference to St Paul (Epistle to the Ephesians, 6.5). Yet in assuming power the tsar enters into an implicit contract which obliges him to rule for the good of his subjects. Ceasing to be a symbol, the tsar is just as bound to serve his subjects *practically* as they are to serve him:

> If all rank is derived from God . . . that same is most necessary to us and pleasing to God, his own high rank demands that I should have mine, you yours and likewise for everyone. If you are tsar you should rule, making sure that there is no unhappiness among the people, that the government is just and that the fatherland is secure from enemies. if you are a senator, attend to your duties likewise. Moreover, you should speak in a simple way, weigh everything up carefully, that your calling requires of you, and do your duty vigorously.[65]

The system of national honours and ranks which was introduced in the eighteenth century and which contended with the principle of unconditional and innate nobility based on blood, was also founded on the notion of exchange of merit for signs. In theory the principle of equivalence was to have been strictly observed in this exchange, but in practice it was infringed. The elaborate statutes and the system of promotion through the ranks was based on a strict succession according to length of service. Someone who had been passed over for reward might, in accordance with the customs and laws of the time, draw attention to himself and demand his due by listing his rights: this proves that in the consciousness of the time reward was not an extra-legal favour but an exchange of obligations between the government and its public servants, which was regulated and established by rule.

The contractual spirit which permeated eighteenth-century culture entailed a reassessment (or at least a rewording) of attitudes to traditional institutions. Although everyone knew that Russia was an autocracy and that it was part of official ideology and practical government to acknowledge this fact (as in the official use of titles), it was considered poor form to acknowledge it. In her 'Instruction' [*Nakaz*], Catherine the Great argued that Russia was a monarchy, not an autocracy, i.e. governed by laws and not arbitrarily. Alexander I would repeatedly stress that autocracy was an unfortunate necessity which he personally did not favour. For him, as for Karamzin, autocracy was a fact, not an ideal. The reassessment was especially marked in the question of the rights of the nobility. As early as 1730 Kantemir in his second satire looked on the privileges of the nobility as advance payment granted them for the merits of their fathers which had to be worked off by personal service to the state. In writers such as Sumarokov, this idea turned into a theory of exchange of personal services in return for honours obtained for the merits of the ancestors. The nobleman who failed to perform these services was no better than a cheat, who takes and gives nothing in return:

> The title to nobility flows in our blood from generation to generation.
> But let us ask why nobility is thus bestowed.
> If my grandfather's life was to the benefit of society,
> For himself he earned payment, for me an advance:
> And I receiving this advance through another's merit,
> Should not let his noble deeds end with him. . . .
> For encouragement I have taken a decent advance,
> Is it right that I should have plenty without myself doing work?[66]

An opposite process was at work against this background. Alongside the tendencies to rationalize semiotic exchange, to focus on its content, there was a counterflow, an irrational urge to stress the sign system as such. Conventions, rituals and the arbitrariness of the sign all were emphasized. And the rapidly developing closed culture of the nobility cultivated etiquette and the theatricalization of life. A semiotics of personal honour became established and duels became frequent as a ritual for the satisfying of offended honour.

The emergent cult of the dandy had play on the *conventional* association of the content and expression of signs at its basis. People came to demand dictionaries to explain the meanings of conventional forms of expression, in particular the language of courtly love. Drieux du Radier's *Lexicon of Love* which was adapted to Russian usage by A. V. Khrapovitsky, was constructed on the lines of a normal dictionary (the word, then an example in a phrase, then the dictionary entry):

> *Disquiet   I am suffering mortal disquiet.* This means: 'I am obeying the accepted rules and am presenting a seemly aspect to my ardour.'

> *To Talk*   If a beautiful woman should say pleasantly: *You are talking*
> *nonsense*, this means: 'Although I do want a lover, I am
> afraid of your tendency to be indiscreet . . . .Remember*
> *whom you are talking to*, or, *I do not understand this*, and
> other such expressions have the same meaning.
>
> *Torment*   *I am enduring intolerable torment* usually means: 'I am
> pretending to be in love, and as you often go to the theatre
> you think that people are not in love unless they suffer
> torment. To please you I have to use these passionate
> words.'[67]

The language of beauty spots needed the same such metatexts to be
understood:

> A velvet beauty spot . . . on the temple indicates *ill-health*, a taffeta one on
> the left side of the forehead stands for *pride*, below one of the lower eye-
> lashes it denotes *tears*, on the upper lip a *kiss*, on the lower one, *inclination*,
> and so on. . . . The key to this code, like that of a minister [i.e. ambassador
> or diplomat, Yu. L.] is not fixed; words are arbitrarily selected and changed
> for security reasons.[68]

There were languages of fans. Masquerades were popular bringing an
element of relativity even into what would seem a natural opposition: the
men dressed as women and the women as men.[69] At the same time to the
popular mind the unmotivated sign was identified with the Devil. In
moralistic literature the relativism of dandy culture was popularly
associated with atheism and moral relativism.

It would be a mistake, though, to regard eighteenth-century dandy
culture with the eyes of its critics and to see in it only an ugly social
anomaly. For awareness of the autonomy of the sign emerged from the
depths of that culture, which was to be an important stimulus in the
shaping of the personal culture of the age of Romanticism. Trediakovsky
in his *Voyage to the Island of Love* (1730) marks the start of this culture
and Karamzin in his *Letters of a Russian Traveller* (1791–2) brings down
the curtain on it. There was more to this culture than a chain of
caricatures ranging from Korsakov in Pushkin's *The Negro of Peter the*
Great to Slyunyai in Krylov's *Trumf*.

The tense social conflicts at the end of the eighteenth century brought
about further shifts in the structure of the languages of culture. The close
bond between the world of signs and the social structure of society
discredited the sign as such in the eyes of the Enlighteners. Following
Voltaire they subjected what Pushkin called the 'age-old prejudices' to
thorough criticism, which in practice meant a review of the entire store of
semiotic ideas accumulated over the centuries. Rousseau exposing the

falsity of the world of civilization found that it derived from the conventionality of the content-expression bond in language. The opposition he proposed between word on the one hand, and intonation, gesture and facial expression on the other, was in fact an antithesis between unmotivated and motivated sign. But while striving for liberation from signs, Rousseau based his social ideal on the social contract, that is on the idea of the equivalent exchange of values between people; but this is impossible without conventional signs. While rejecting social semiotics, Rousseau wanted to keep its results.

Masonic ideology evolved at the opposite pole. The Masons were opponents of the contractual theory of society; against it they advocated the idea of self-surrender to some absolute principle (their order, or ideal humanity, or God) and the merging of the self with the absolute without thought of recompense. But though subjectively oriented towards the Middle Ages, they remained men of the eighteenth century. Their emblems were not medieval symbols but a conventional secret language for their initiates, which lay closer on the semiotic scale to the language of beauty-spots than to medieval symbolism.

Both these attempts to escape from linguistic conventionality ended in failure: the eighteenth century ended with two extravagant masquerades, a 'Roman' one in revolutionary Paris and a chivalric one at the court of Paul I.

*　　*　　*

The fate of Rousseau's ideas in Russia shows up the interaction of the contractual and non-contractual principles in Russian culture. His ideas held sway in Russia more profoundly and for much longer than they did in France. The very paradoxes inherent to the ideas of the 'citizen of Geneva' made it possible to interpret them widely in accordance with the inner dynamic of Russian culture. In the eighteenth century Rousseau meant for the Russian reader the *Discourse on the Sciences and the Arts* (1750), *La Nouvelle Héloïse* (1761), *Emile* (1762), but above all *On the Social Contract* (1762). The influence of the latter was enormous, and ideas of the contractual origins of society lay behind all political thinking of the last third of the eighteenth century. Radishchev, who was a follower of Helvetius, when he turns to questions of sociology and rights, immediately becomes a Rousseauist. Someone quite the opposite to Radishchev, the aristocratic rationalist, Prince M. Shcherbatov, also refers to the *Social Contract*. Arguing against Catherine the Great's Instruction,[70] he wrote:

> Rousseau says that since great rulers were originally chosen by the peoples to ensure their well-being, then in creating the contract with the chosen rulers, the people, while giving up their rights, could not give up their natural liberty, since that is a thing without which there can be no well-

being; and if, that writer continues, there were a people reckless enough to give up their natural freedom, one would have to think them mad, and so the contract would not be valid.[71]

This translation in Shcherbatov's customary heavy style is from the well-known passage in the fourth chapter ('On Slavery') of Rousseau's *Social Contract*:

> To say that a man gives himself freely, is to say what is absurd and inconceivable; such an act is null and illegitimate, from the mere fact that he who does it is out of his mind. To say the same of a whole people is to suppose a people of madmen; and madness creates no right.[72]

Shcherbatov was so certain that contract was the only form to justify civil society that he completely omitted the contrast which was important for Rousseau between the idea of the exchange of rights between individual and society, and the idea of self-surrender without recompense, which from Rousseau's point of view was mad.

For the generation of the Decembrists Rousseau was still associated with the idea of the social contract, but by the middle of the nineteenth century there was a interesting change. Tolstoy, for instance, whose views were immensely influenced by Rousseau and who in his youth carried a portrait of Rousseau on his chest beside his cross, recalled in old age that he knew all of Rousseau's works, including his musical works, almost by heart. Yet the ideas of the *Social Contract* hardly left a trace in his mind. For Tolstoy, Rousseau was a protester at civilization and inequality, the author of pedagogic ideas, the enemy of falsehood in all its manifestations, the unflinching author of the *Confessions*. From another point of view, Dostoevsky was just as passionate about Rousseau, attacking and denouncing him with passion and a kind of jealous concern, and what he had in mind was always the *Confessions*. The idea of contract was profoundly alien to Dostoevsky's very mode of thinking and for him 'self-surrender without recompense' was not madness but the norm for religious behaviour.

Interesting that the generation of the Nihilists of 1860–70 who proclaimed materialism and atheism and who rejected the idea of self-surrender to the Truth which came from God, soon found another object to which to surrender themselves: this was the deified idea of the People. Not surprising that Maxim Gorky referred to the writings of the *Narodniks* as 'holy scripture about the peasant'.

On the other hand, in the popular thinking about rights, ideas of contract and exchange were closely bound together with deception, since one of the contracting parties was thought to be the devil or his substitutes: the master, a 'German', with whom an oath was never binding. This explains why the merchant in folklore was always cast in the role of the villain. But one can add to this perception the numerous complaints by foreigners against the dishonesty of Russian merchants. One such example is from Joseph de Maistre's letter to Prince Peter Kozlovsky:

> Some strange spirit of dishonesty and deceitfulness circulates through all the veins of the State. Theft by armed robbery is more rare with you because you are no less gentle than brave; but theft by deception is continuous. Buy a diamond and it will have a flaw; buy a match and it will have no sulphur. This spirit which is to be found in all channels of the administration does immense harm.[73]

Foreigners visiting Russia were inclined to accuse Russian merchants of dishonesty and cheating. Yet paradoxically the cause lay in the merchants' attitude towards *contract as such*: the opportunity to cheat a 'foreigner' (and contracts were thought of as a way of relating to foreigners) was as it were assumed. Cheating in this case was like the folklore tricks of the trickster. The popular attitude towards dealings among themselves was quite different: cheating was a grave sin, but then a contract was not needed, in its place was *trust*. Fascinating light is shed on this by the memoirs of a serf who lived in the first half of the nineteenth century, N. Shipov. This extraordinary life-story tells of a serf who became a millionaire, who paid his master, the landowner Saltykov, quit-rent amounting to over 5000 roubles a year.[74] Shipov was a man of untiring energy and many gifts. His story takes us into the world of serfs who were wealthier than their landowner, who carried on trade, set up factories. But their property is the property of people who have no right to property and who have no legal guarantees whatsoever. So all these very considerable financial operations were founded on trust and not on the safeguards of the law. Since at any moment the landowner could take *everything* away ('Who knows? Anything could happen to a serf,' was Shipov's melancholy remark) all his dealings, sometimes involving thousands of roubles, were carried out on the basis of personal trust and on the quiet. There were of course instances of cheating and the violation of trust, but they were sternly condemned as immoral.

*   *   *

To conclude we can observe how this typological opposition which varies according to conditions of milieu and period yet remains underneath an invariant. As a result in order to understand the actual content of this historico-semiotic category (in this case the notion of contract), it must be studied both from the typological and historical point of view.

Very recently doubt was cast on the opposition we are proposing between contract and self-surrender in the culture of early Russia by the medievalist Ya. S. Lur'e. He writes:

> If this observation has any basis then only in as far as it relates to the Russia of Vladimir-Suzdal from the second half of the thirteenth century. From the twelfth century the political organization of Novgorod, one of the most important states in early Russia, was characterized precisely by the principle of contract: the ritually sealed contract between the *veche* [popular assembly] and the town administration on the one hand, and princes who were invited to Novgorod, on the other.[75]

This objection seems to me to be the best vindication of my ideas. Of course the trading republic, member of the Hanseatic League, where even the feudal upper class was the city's trading aristocracy, had a different attitude towards contract than the rest of Russia, and especially Vladimir-Suzdal out of which grew the kingdom of Moscow. Of course we are dealing with typological tendencies which always, to use Hegel's expression, 'are realized through non-realization' and point to one tendency and not to a hundred per cent of the facts. Without some elements of contract no society can exist. But our concern is something else: how does a society value the one category or the other? What place in the hierarchy of values does it allot it?

18

Can there be a science of history and what are its functions in the cultural system?

We have looked at the difficulties facing historical science as it strives towards the age-old aim of re-establishing the past 'as it really was'. The question naturally arises whether history as a science is possible at all, or whether history is some other kind of knowledge. This is not a new question: Benedetto Croce was tormented with doubts about it.

The difficulties facing historical science are peculiar to it, but not unique. They are peculiar because they are difficulties that affect only historical science; they are not unique because they are versions of some general problems of scientific methodology today. The same problem confronts many different areas of science, and that is the problem of *language*, the interaction between the metalanguage of description and the language being described. Science has moved away from the naive view according to which the normal methods of perceiving and generalizing data were held to be valid, and the problem of the position of the describer in relation to the world being described was barely accounted for; it has moved away from the view according to which the scientist looked at reality 'from the position of truth', into the world of relativity. Questions of language affect all the sciences. The crux of the matter goes as follows: science as it was shaped after the Renaissance, based on the ideas of Descartes and Newton, assumed that the scientist was an external observer looking at his object from outside and therefore enjoying absolute 'objective' knowledge. Modern science from nuclear physics to linguistics sees the scientist as inside the world being described and as a part of that world. But the object and the observer are as a rule described in different languages, and consequently the *problem of translation* is a universal scientific task. When Plato defined thought as the 'dialogue of the soul with itself' he made the assumption that the conversation would be carried on in one language. This is how Heisenberg formulates the problem with regard to physics:

269

Quantum mechanics have placed even more serious demands on us. We have had altogether to renounce the objective description of nature – in the Newtonian sense, according to which definite meanings were ascribed to such basic features of system as place, velocity, energy; and in its stead we have had to put the description of observation points, and for them the only certainty are the probabilities of some of the results. The very *words* applied to the description of the atomic level then turn out to be problematic. We may talk of waves and particles, while remembering that we are not dealing with a dualistic, but with a fully unified description of the phenomena. *The meaning of old words has lost precision.*[76] (My emphasis, Yu. L.)

Historical science is also undergoing this experience. The times we live in are inducing shock-waves in history and in other domains of science. As always at turning-points between one age and the next the age-old question raises its head again: 'What is truth?' As we move away from naive faith in an 'absolute point of view' to historical semiotics we are faced with the problem of translating the language of the source into the language of the researcher. The crux of this problem will be apparent if we compare it with one of the most complete summations of previous historical methodology. We refer to R. G. Collingwood's *The Idea of History*. Analysing the difficulties involved in making a historical interpretation of facts, the author suggests that the historian should identify totally with the historical personage:

So the historian of politics or warfare, presented with an account of certain actions done by Julius Caesar, tries to understand these actions, that is, to discover what thoughts in Caesar's mind determined him to do them. This implies envisaging for himself the situation in which Caesar stood, and thinking for himself what Caesar thought about the situation and the possible ways of dealing with it.[77]

Collingwood insists on this idea and returns to it again:

Suppose, for example, he is reading the Theodosian Code, and has before him a certain edict of an emperor. Merely reading the words and being able to translate them does not amount to knowing their historical significance. In order to do that he must envisage the situation with which the emperor was trying to deal, and he must envisage it as that emperor envisaged it. Then he must see for himself, just as if the emperor's situation were his own, how such a situation might be dealt with; he must see the possible alternatives, and the reasons for choosing one rather than another; and thus he must go through the process which the emperor went through in deciding on this particular course. Thus he is re-enacting in his own mind the experience of the emperor; and only in so far as he does this has he any historical knowledge, as distinct from a merely philological knowledge, of the meaning of the edict.[78]

Behind these arguments lies an assumption that the semiotic (and consequently also the psychological) world of the twentieth-century Englishman is identical with that of Caesar or Theodosius, and that all one needs in order to become Caesar or Theodosius is to use one's imagination and intuition, informed by study of the sources. Of course these qualities can help the historian but they should not disguise the fact that historian and hero may understand the 'situation' and its 'solution' very differently; and that what would be a natural solution for a person of one epoch, even as an abstract possibility, may not enter the head of someone from another age. Furthermore the notion of 'alternative methods' can arise only as a *result* of describing 'the world of Theodosius' and not from the researcher's 'natural' psychological experience, for this is not a premise but an outcome of scholarly study. Collingwood's ideas are an extreme example of common sense, this very demiurge of the post-Cartesian world, in the centre of which is 'truth bright as the sun'. Descartes expressed this faith in common sense in the second part of his *Discourse on the Method*:

> The sciences found in books – in those at least whose reasonings are only probable and which have no demonstrations, composed as they are of the gradually accumulated opinions of many different individuals – do not approach so near to the truth as the simple reasoning which a man of common sense can quite naturally carry out.[79]

Collingwood proposes to bridge the gap between the 'world of Theodosius' and the 'world of the historian' by making them completely identical. Semiotics takes the opposite way, which entails completely exposing the differences between the structures of these worlds, describing the differences and treating understanding as a *translation* from one language to another. This does not mean completely abstracting the researcher from the work (which is in practice impossible) but rather recognizing the researcher's presence and being maximally aware of how this presence affects the description. So just as the instrument of semiotic research is translation, the instrument for historico-cultural study is typology, always allowing for the historian and for the type of culture he or she belongs to.[80]

The historian and history both are part of human culture but in principle they speak different languages and their relationship is an asymmetrical one. Another function of history in culture follows from this: history has often been referred to as humanity's memory, though this expression has rarely been thought through. If the function of history is still the same aim of 'thinking of the past as it really was' (the formulation is an old one but it is surely true of every historian), then memory is an instrument for thinking in the present although the content of the thought is the past. Or in other words, the content of memory is the past, but without memory we cannot think 'here' and 'now': memory is the deep-seated ground of the actual process of consciousness. And if history is culture's memory then this means that it is not only a relic of the past, but also an active mechanism of the present.

If we have to use a metaphor in order to imagine the capacity for memory, then, the least appropriate one is the image of the library with books on its shelves, or a computer with data of whatever quantity stored in its memory. Memory is more like a generator, reproducing the past again; it is the ability, given certain impulses, to switch on the process of generating a conceptualized reality which the mind transfers into the past. This capacity is part of the general process of thinking and is inseparable from it.

The interrelationship between cultural memory and its self-reflection is like a constant dialogue: texts from chronologically earlier periods are brought into culture, and, interacting with contemporary mechanisms, generate an *image* of the historical past, which culture transfers into the past and which like an equal partner in a dialogue, affects the present. But as it transforms the present, the past too changes its shape. This process does not take place in a vacuum: both partners in the dialogue are partners too in other confrontations, both are open to the intrusion of new texts from outside, and the texts, as we have already had cause to stress, always contain in themselves the potentiality for new interpretations. This image of the historical past is not anti-scientific, although it is not scientific either. It exists alongside the scientific image of the past like another reality and interacts with it also on the basis of dialogue.

Just as different prognoses of the future make up an inevitable part of the universum of culture, so culture cannot do without 'prognoses of the past'.

19

Conclusion

The individual human intellect does not have a monopoly in the work of thinking. Semiotic systems, both separately and together as the integrated unity of the semiosphere, both synchronically and in all the depths of historical memory, carry out intellectual operations, preserve, rework and increase the store of information. Thought is within us, but we are within thought, just as language is something engendered by our minds and directly dependent on the mechanisms of the brain, and we are with language. And unless we were immersed in language, our brain could not engender it (and vice versa: if our brain were not capable of generating language, we would not be immersed in it). The same with thought: it is both something engendered by the human brain and something surrounding us without which intellectual generation would be impossible. And finally the spatial image of the world is both within us and without us.

We are both a part and a likeness of a vast intellectual mechanism. Hence the difficulties but also the importance of the kind of research we are doing. The emergent synthesis becomes ever clearer: whether we are studying the structure of the literary text, the functional asymmetry of the hemispheres of the brain, the problems of oral speech or of deaf and dumb language, the advertisements of our modern age or the religious ideas of archaic cultures – we find the different mechanisms of the single intellectual life of humanity. We are within it, but it – all of it – is within us. We are at the same time like *matryoshkas*, and participants in an endless number of dialogues, and the likeness of *everything*, and 'the other' both for other people and for ourselves; we are both a planet in the intellectual galaxy, and the image of its universum.

This book is an attempt to raise these questions and the answer to them lies in the creation of a general and historical semiotics of culture.

NOTES TO PART THREE

1. The Laurentian Chronicle is a chronicle copied by the monk Lavrenty in 1377 in north east Russia, which includes the ancient Kievan chronicle, *The Tale of Bygone Years*. Compare what has been said about the Scandinavian chronicles: 'If there were no conflicts then it was thought that nothing had happened and there was nothing to describe. "Everything was peaceful" is what the sagas of the Icelanders say in such cases' (M. I. Steblin-Kamensky, 'Sagi ob islandakh i Saga o Grettire' ['Sagas about the Icelanders and the Saga of Grettir'], in *Saga o Grettire*, Novosibirsk, 1976, p. 152).

2. M. K. Trofimova, *Istoriko-filosofskie voprosy gnostitsizma* [*Historico-philo-sophical Questions of Gnosticism*], Moscow, 1979. See pp. 160–70 for the Russian translation of this text. We have made use of Trofimova's translation and the French one by J. Doresse, *L'Evangile selon Thomas ou les Paroles secrètes de Jesus*, Paris, 1959. [English from *The Gospel according to Thomas*, Coptic text established and translated by A. Guillaumont, H. Ch. Puech, G. Quispel, W. Till and Yassah Abd Al Masih, Leiden, 1976, p. 41 (logion 72)].

3. Roman Jakobson, 'The Quest for the Essence of Language', in *Selected Writings*, vol. II, pp. 350–1.

4. Yevgeny Schwartz, 'The Dragon', translated by Max Hayward and Harry Shukman, in *Three Soviet Plays*, Penguin Books, 1966, p. 166.

5. E. V. Paducheva, 'O strukture aabzatsa' ['On the structure of the para-graph'], *Trudy po znakovym sistemam*, II, Tartu, 1965, p. 285.

6. *La Nouvelle Histoire, sous la direction de Jacques Le Goff et Roger Chartier*, Jacques Revel, Paris, 1978, pp. 222–6.

7. See Tolstoy's story 'From Prince Dmitri Nekhlyudov's Notebooks. Lucerne':
   On the 7 July 1857 an itinerant beggar sang and played on the guitar for half an hour outside the Schweizerhof Hotel in Lucerne where the very wealthiest people stay. Some hundred people heard him play. Three times the singer asked them to give him money. No one gave him anything and many of them laughed at him.

   Tolstoy continues:
   Here is an event which the historians of our age should note down in indelible letters of flame. This event is more significant, more serious and has deeper meaning than the facts recorded in newspapers and history books. . . . It is not a fact for the history of great deeds but for the history of progress and civilization. . . . Do people spend their entire lives in the domain of the law? Only one thousandth part of it belongs to the law, the rest is not concerned with it but passes in the domain of morals and public opinion.

   Any of the 'new historians' could have put their name to these words.

8. The title of their publications are indicative; *Annales d'histoire économique et sociale*, which in 1946 became *Annales, Economie, Sociétiés, Civilization; Revue de synthèse*, Marc Bloch wrote: 'We recognized that in society, whatever kind, everything is connected and mutually influencing; the political and social structure, the economy, beliefs, the most elementary manifesta-tions of mentality as well as the most subtle ones.'

9. B. A. Uspensky, *Istoriya russkogo literaturnogo yazyka (XI–XVII vv.)* [*The

History of the Russian Literary Language (11th to 17th centuries)], Tan-konyvkiado, Budapest, 1988, pp. 12–13.

10. G. W. F. Hegel, *Lectures on the Philosophy of History*, translated by J. Sibree, London, 1900, p. 57.

11. Ibid., p. 82.

12. Henri Poincaré, *Science and Method*, translated by Francis Maitland, London [1914], pp. 64–5.

13. Ibid., p. 68.

14. Marc Bloch, *The Historian's Craft*, translated by Peter Putnam, Manchester, 1954, p. 45.

15. Ibid., p. 46.

16. Ibid., p. 124. Condorcet, a few weeks before his suicide when he was in hiding from the Jacobin tribunal, was working on a book about historical progress which was inspired with all the optimism of the Enlightenment. Marc Bloch, a hero of the Resistance, a fighter in the anti-Fascist underground who was shot before he could finish the work we are quoting, totally ignores the question of personal action and responsibility as historical categories. These two heroic biographies are one more proof that ideas are tenacious and tend to follow their own course. They are more conservative than personal behaviour and change more slowly under the pressure of circumstances.

17. Ilya Prigogine, Isabelle Stengers, *Order out of Chaos. Man's new Dialogue with Nature*, London, 1984, p. 13.

18. Ibid., pp. 160ff.

19. Ibid., p. 13.

20. Ibid. pp. 140ff.

21. W. Ross Ashby, *An Introduction to Cybernetics*, London, 1956, p. 259.

22. Prigogine and Stengers, p. 176.

23. Leo Szilard, 'Uber die Entropirverminderung in einem thermodinamischen System bei Engriffen intelligenter Wesen', in *Zeitschrift für Physik*, vol 53, 1929, p. 840.

24. From historians who held to the belief that a person like a character in a classical tragedy always preserved 'unity of character' it was natural to see the *sansculottes* as Dickens depicted them in *A Tale of Two Cities*: 'In the hunted air of the people there was yet some wild-beast thought of the possibility of turning at bay' (Charles Dickens, *A Tale of Two Cities*, Oxford, The World's Classics, 1989, p. 35). All the more surprising it was to find out that both the people who stormed the Bastille and the participants in the September murders were in the main decent bourgeois of the middle class and fathers of families (see Michel Vovelle, *La Chute de la monarchie 1787–1792*, Paris, 1972, pp. 207–9, etc.). But the point is that at moments of acute disequilibrium in the historical situation a person may unpredictably change the behavioural stereotype. Of course it is 'unpredictable' for that person, but may be quite predictable in another connection. For instance, he may adopt the behavioural norms of a stage hero, a 'Roman figure' or an 'historical personage'.

25. Immanuel Kant, 'The Idea of World History on the Universal-Civil Level', translated from the Russian in *Sochineniya v shesti tomakh*, vol. VI, Moscow, 1966, p. 7.

26. Quoted from *Literaturnaya teoriya nemetskogo romantizma. Dokumenty* [*Literary Theory of German Romanticism. Documents*], ed. N. Ya. Berkovsky, Leningrad (1934), p. 470. Boris Pasternak liked this saying though when he quoted it he ascribed it wrongly to Hegel.

27. Thucydides, *The Peloponnesian War*, translated by Rex Warner, Penguin Classics, pp. 110–11.

28. Cicero, 'Divination', in *Cicero in Twenty-Eight Volumes*, XX, *De Senectute, De Amicitia, De Divinatione*, with an English translation by W. A. Falconer, London, 1979 (Loeb Classical Library), I, xviii, 34 (p. 265).

29. Ibid., II, 1vi, 116 (p. 501).

30. Poincaré, op.cit., p. 71.

31. *The Song of Igor's Campaign*, translated by V. Nabokov, New York, 1960, pp. 52–3.

32. Even the first publishers of the *Lay* translated this phrase as 'resounding with' the glory of the ancestors' and this is the reading that has remained. See Roman Jakobson, 'Perevod *Slova o polku Igoreve* na sovremennom russkii yazyk (prilozhenie k stat'e "Izuchenie *Slova o polku Igoreve* v SShA")' ['The Translation of *The Lay of Igor's Campaign* into modern Russian (appendix to the article "The Study of *The Lay of Igor's Campaign* in the USA")'], *TODRL*, XIV, Moscow/Leningrad, 1958, p. 119; *Slovar'-spravochnik Slova o polku Igoreve*, 2, Leningrad, 1967, pp. 119–20; I. I. Sreznevsky, *Materialy dlya slovarya drevnerusskogo yazyka*, vol. I, [Moscow, 1958], col. 964.

33. D. S. Likhachev, *Poetika drevnerusskoi literatury* [*The Poetics of Early Russian Literature*], Leningrad, 1967, p. 262.

34. On the special characteristics of the thinking oriented towards 'beginnings', see Mircea Eliade, *Aspects du mythe*, Paris, 1963, pp. 33–54; Likhachev, op.cit., pp. 263ff.; Yu. M. Lotman, 'The Modelling Significance of the Concepts "End" and "Beginning" in Artistic Texts', translated by Wendy Rosslyn, *Russian Poetics in Translation*, 3, 1976, pp. 7–11.

35. *Polnoe sobranie russkikh letopisei*, I, Moscow, 1962, col. 92.

36. See, V. N. Toporov, 'On the Cosmological Origins of Early Historical Descriptions', translated by Christopher English, *Russian Poetics in Translation*, 3, 1976, pp. 38–81.

37. In a letter to Kurbsky, Ivan the Terrible says that Kurbsky by betraying him has not only destroyed his soul 'but also the souls of his ancestors' (John Fennell, *The Correspondence between Prince A. M. Kurbsky and Tsar Ivan IV of Russia, 1564–1579*, Cambridge, 1963, p. 23). The result of the action has its effect in the opposite direction to that of historical and pragmatic thought.

38. *Demokraticheskaya poeziya XVII veka* [*Democratic Poetry of the Seventeenth Century*], Moscow/Leningrad, 1962, p. 34.

39. There are many other references to 'ancestral glory' in the *Lay*.

40. *Tres Thomae, Thoma Stapletono Anglo S.Theolog. Dotore, Dvaci.*

41. N. I. Konrad, 'Pis'mo A. Toinbi' ['Letter to A. Toynbee'], in, N. I. Konrad, *Izbrannye trudy*, Moscow, 1974, p. 278.

42. M. M. Postnikov, A. T. Fomenko, *Novye metodiki statisticheskogo analiza narrativno-tsifrovogo materiala drevnei istorii (Predvaritel'naya publikatsiya)* [*New Methods for the Statistical Analysis of the Narrative-Numerical Material of Ancient History (Preliminary Publication)*], Moscow, 1980.

43. I. Kant, 'Answers to the Question: What is Enlightenment?' (translated from the Russian in *Sochineniya v shesti tomakh* [*Works in Six Volumes*], vol. 6, Moscow, 1966, p. 27.

44. Turner adds the footnote: 'A high value is therefore attached to the man who observes custom'. See V. W. Turner, *The Drums of Affliction: A Study of Religious Processes among the Ndembu of Zambia*, Oxford, 1968, pp. 36–7.

45. From a letter by G. Ch. Lichtenberg in *Khrestomatiya po istorii zapadno-evropeiskogo teatra* [*A Reader on the History of West European Theatre*], ed. S. Mokul'sky, Moscow, 1955, vol. 2, p. 157.

46. E. A. Baratynsky, *Polnoe sobranie stikhotvorenii* [*Complete Collection of Poetry*], Leningrad, 1936, vol. 1, p. 206.

47. Plato, *Phaedrus*, translated by Walter Hamilton, Penguin Classics, p. 24.

48. Ibid., p. 96.

49. Baratynsky, op.cit., p. 201.

50. Claude Reichler, *La Diabolie, la Seduction, la Renardie, l'Ecriture*, Paris, 1979.

51. We do mean power and not goodness because it is possible to worship in a religious sense the powers of evil.

52. *I Fioretti del glorioso messere Santo Francesco e de suoi Frati*, ed. G. L. Passerini, Florence, 1903, pp. 58–62.

53. No. 149 in *Narodnye russkie skazki A. N. Afanas'eva* [*Russian Folk Tales collected by A. N. Afanas'ev*], ed. M. K. Azadovsky et al., Moscow, 1936–9; in the editions prepared by A. E. Gruzinsky (1897 and 1913–14) it is no. 86. If a contract has been made with an evil power the usual way of getting out of it is by repentance (see *The Tale of Savva Grudtsyn*). A more complex example is to be found in the *apocrypha* of Adam: in one text (according to A. N. Pypin it comes from an Old Believers' manuscript though he gives no details) Adam makes a contract with the devil in return for the healing of Eve and Cain ('And the devil said: "Give me a written undertaking saying 'Living I belong to God, but dead to you'"' (N. Tikhonravov, *Pamyati otrechennoi russkoi literatury* [*Monuments of Non-Canonical Russian Literature*], vol. I, St Petersburg, 1863, p. 16;. But a better known version of the story, more typically, has Adam concluding a contract with the Devil but consciously cheating him. After the expulsion from Paradise, Adam harnesses an ox and begins to plough:

> And the Devil came and said: 'I will not let you work the land since it is mine, whereas the heavens and paradise belong to God. . . . Write down a declaration that you are mine, then you can work my land. Adam said: 'Whoever the land belongs to, I and my children belong to them too.'

Then the author explains that Adam outwitted the Devil for he knew that the land belonged to the devil only temporarily and that in the future Christ would be incarnate ('the Lord would come down to earth and be born of a virgin') and redeem the earth and its inhabitants from the Devil by his blood (Tikhonravov, p. 4).

In the West European tradition a contract is neutral: it may be either a good or a bad one, while in its specifically chivalric variant with the cult of the sign, keeping one's word is a point of honour. There are numerous stories of knights who keep their word to Satan (the Don Juan legend is an inversion of this legend: although breaking all moral and religious precepts he keeps his word given to the statue of the Comendador). In the Russian tradition a contract takes its 'force' from a holy object which guarantees that it will be kept to. A contract without such authority from the non-conventional power of faith, has no 'force'. So a pledge given to Satan *must* be broken.

54. *Pis'ma i bumagi Petra Velikogo* [*Letters and Papers of Peter the Great*], vol. III, p. 265.

55. S. M. Solov'ev, *Istoriya Rossii s drevneishikh vremen* [*The History of Russia from the Most Ancient Times*], book IV, St Petersburg, col. 5.

56. *The Song of Igor's Campaign*, transated by Vladimir Nabokov, p. 37.

57. V. D. Kuz'mina, *Devgenievo deyanie* [*The Exploit of Devgeny*], Moscow, 1962, p. 149.

58. Ferdinand de Saussure, *Course in General Linguistics*, translated by Roy Harris, p. 68. In the Russian translation this remark sounds less categorical [lit. 'are never entirely conventional' – *uslovnyi*]. The distinction between sign and symbol is argued by Tzvetan Todorov in his *Théories du symbole*, Paris, 1977, pp. 9–11 et seq.

59. Solov'ev, op.cit., col. 42.

60. *Polnoe sobranie russkikh letopisei*, vol. II, 2nd edition, p. 822 (my emphasis, Yu. L.).

61. 'Death on the battlefield is usually called "judgement"' (N. A. Meshchersky, *Istoriya iudeiskoi voiny Iosifa Flaviya v drevnerusskom perevode* [*The History of the Jewish War by Josephus in an Early Russian Translation*], Moscow/Leningrad, 1958, p. 85.

62. *Povest' o Drakule* [*The Tale of Dracula*], Moscow/Leningrad, 1964, p. 127.

63. Because the tsar's authority was symbolic and not semiotic, play was not excluded from his behaviour. In this respect the play element in Ivan the Terrible's behaviour was perceived both subjectively and objectively as satanic.

64. Osip Mandel'shtam, 'The Nineteenth Century', in *The Complete Critical Prose and Letters*, ed. Jane Gary Harris, Ann Arbor, 1979, p. 139.

65. Feofan Prokopovich, *Sochineniya* [*Works*], Moscow/Leningrad, 1961, p. 98.

66. Sumarokov, *Stikhotvoreniya* [*Poetry*], [Leningrad], 1935, p. 203.

67. Dreux du Radier, *Lyubovnyi leksikon* [*Lexicon of Love*], translated into Russian from the French [*Dictionnaire d'amour*, The Hague. 1741] by A. V. Khrapovitsky, 2nd edition, 1779, pp. 9, 18, 42.

68. *Lyubov. Knizhka zolotaya* [*Love. The Golden Book*], by Gl[eb] Gr[omov], St Petersburg, 1798, pp. 134–5.

69. See Catherine the Great's note [original in French]:

I have had a very amusing idea. We must have a ball at the Hermitage. . . . We must tell the ladies to come *en deshabillé* and without panniers and without great wigs. . . . In the room we will have four boutiques of clothes and masks on one side and four boutiques of clothes and masks on the other side, one side for the men and the other for the ladies. . . . On the boutiques with the men's clothes we must put a notice saying 'Dressing room for ladies', and on the boutiques with the ladies' clothes one saying 'Dressing room for gentlemen'.

(*Sochineniya imp. Ekateriny II* [*Works of the Empress Catherine III*], vol. XII,

St Petersburg, 1907, p. 659)

70. The 'Instruction' was formally the Empress' instruction to the deputies of the Commission on the new constitution (1767) but in fact was a widely publicized declaration of the Enlightenment ideas about monarchy. Catherine, in composing the Instruction, drew widely (her own expression was that she 'stole' them) on the ideas of the Enlighteners, in particular Montesquieu and Beccaria.

71. M. M. Shcherbatov, *Neizdannye sochineniya* [Unpublished Works], [Moscow], 1935, p. 23.

72. J. J. Rousseau, *The Social Contract and Discourses*, translated by G. D. H. Cole, revised and augmented by J. H. Brumfitt and John C. Hall, Everyman classics, 1988, p. 186.

73. Joseph de Maistre, *Lettres et opuscules inédits*, vol. I, Paris, 1851, p. 335.

74. 'Istoriya moei zhizni i moikh stranstvovanii. Rasskaz byvshego krepostnogo krestyanina Nikolaya Shipova (1802–1862)' ['The Story of my Life and Wanderings. Told by the former Serf Nikolai Shipov (1801–1862)'], in V. N. Karpov, *Vospominaniya Nikolay Shipova. Istorya moei zhizni* [*The Memoirs of Nikolai Shipov. The Story of my Life*], 1933, p. 391. For a comparison, on the estates of A. P. Vorontsov which were in a similar geographical position during the same years the peasants on average paid 25–30 roubles each a year (E. I. Indova, *Krepostnoe khozyaistvo v nachale XIX veka. Po materialam votchinnogo arkhiva Vorontsovykh* [*Serf Economy at the Beginning of the Nineteenth Century. From Materials in the Estate Archives of the Vorontsovs*], Moscow, 1955, p.88).

75. Ya. S. Lur'ye, *Russkie sovremenniki Vozrozhdeniya* [*Russian Contemporaries of the Renaissance*], Leningrad, 1988, p. 27.

76. See also Heisenberg's remark: 'To make a broad generalization we might say that the change in the structure of thought is outwardly manifest in the fact that words have acquired other meanings than the ones they had before and that other questions are being raised than previously' (W. Heisenberg, *Schritte über Grenzen*, Munich, 1973, pp. 275–87. (Translated from the Russian edition, V. Geizenberg, *Shagi z gorizont*, Moscow, 1987, pp. 191, 193).

77. R. G. Collingwood, *The Idea of History*, Oxford, 1986, pp. 205.

78. Ibid., p. 283.

79. René Descartes, *'Discourse on Method'* p. 114. In the first part of the treatise Descartes remarks that by following experience and common sense we can 'meet with much more truth in the reasonings that each man makes on the matters that specially concern him . . . than in the case of those made by a man of letters in his study touching speculations which lead to no result, and which bring about no other consequences to himself excepting that he will be all the more vain the more they are removed from common sense' (p. 112).

80. An example of a mistake of this kind is the following: Levi Bruhl tells the story of a Kaffir whose son a missionary wanted to send to the mission school. Not wanting to refuse him outright the Kaffir answered, 'I'll have a dream about it.' Levi Bruhl remarks that here is a situation in which any European would have said, 'I'll think about it', and concludes that dreaming for a Kaffir has the same function as thinking 'for us'. In fact, the Kaffir's words should be

translated as 'I'll take advice about it' since he is talking about getting a prediction from the dream, about divination which is the natural consequence of wanting to get the most authoritative information and which in no way differs from a European's remark, 'I'll consult my lawyer, my doctor or my computer'. If we leave out of account the tinge of European condescension, we find that desire which is fairly widespread and not a monopoly of 'pre-logical thinking', which Kant referred to when he contrasted 'enlightenment' and 'immaturity' (see above note 43), namely the desire to hand over responsibility to someone else: nowadays it may be to one's psychoanalyst, to 'public opinion', Party directives, and so on.

Index

allegory 179
Aleksandrov, A.D. 150
Alekseev, V.M. 78
allusion 67, 107–8
analogy 45, 47
anti-behaviour 141
Anitchrist 194
anti-home 140, 187
anti-language 141
antinomy 41
anti-romanticism 46
anti-space 140
archaism 103
architectural code 32
Ariès, P. 224
Aristotle 40, 179, 181
art 16, 32, 43, 54, 124, 189
   evolutionary process 52
   Renaissance 55
artificial language 13, 15, 16
artificial norms 134
Aseev, N.N. 16, 17
a-semantic text 28
Ashby, W. Ross 231
asymmetry 3, 79, 143
   of body 133
   and dialogue 143
   semiotic 127
autocatalytic reaction 3, 244
autocommunication 22, 26, 29, 33
   and human culture 33
   mnemonic function 27
auto-psychotherapy 29

Bacon, F. 136
Bakhtim, M. 5, 164, 166, 193
Balanov, L. Ya. 3
Balzac, H. de 105

Baratynsky, E.A. 105, 108, 249, 252
Baroque 43, 46, 56, 126, 145, 193, 197
beginnings 159, 240, 243
   of history 243
Belinsky, V.G. 110
Bely, A. 1
Benveniste, E. 12, 128
Berlin, I. 231
Berr, H. 224
bifurcation points 231, 232, 233, 236, 243
bilingualism 142
binarism 124
binarity, asymmetrical 74
binary opposition 182
birth 168; *see also* rebirth; resurrection
Bloch, M. 224, 229, 230
Blok, A. 105, 152
Boileau, N. 83, 132
boundary 51, 131, 136–7
brain, asymmetrical 3
Braudel, F. 224, 228
'Bronze Horseman' 83, 84–5, 97, 100
Brothers Karamazov, The 138
Bryullov, K. 82, 83
Bugaev, N.V. 1
Bulgakov, M. 127, 185–91
   Master and Margarita, The 185–91
Byron, Lord 51, 137, 146, 226, 235

Campanello 136
Camus, A. 132
Cantor's theory 45
Capellanus, A. 129
Captain's Daughter, The 85, 96
causality 40
centre/periphery 140, 145
Cervantes 127
character delineation 168

281